THE SOVIET PROBLEM IN AMERICAN-GERMAN RELATIONS

THE SOVIET PROBLEM IN AMERICAN-GERMAN RELATIONS

Edited by UWE NERLICH
and JAMES A.THOMSON

CRANE RUSSAK • NEW YORK

**The Soviet Problem
in American-German Relations**

Published in the United States by

Crane, Russak & Company, Inc.
3 East 44th Street
New York, NY 10017

Copyright © 1985 The Rand Corporation

Library of Congress Cataloging in Publication Data

The Soviet problem in American-German relations.

86-10382   Includes index.
1. United States—Foreign relations—Soviet Union—
Addresses, essays, lectures.   2. Soviet Union—Foreign
relations—United States—Addresses, essays, lectures.
3. Germany (West)—Foreign relations—Soviet Union—
Addresses, essays, lectures.   4. Soviet Union—Foreign
relations—Germany (West)—Addresses, essays, lectures.
I. Nerlich, Uwe.   II. Thomson, James A., 1945–   .
     E183.8.S65S59   1985   327.73043   85-7914
                              ISBN 0-8448-1488-1

Printed in the United States of America

Contents

Authors' Biographies

Editors

Uwe Nerlich is director of research at Stiftung Wissenschaft und Politik, vice-president of the European-American Institute for Security Research in Los Angeles, and a council member of the International Institute for Strategic Studies (London). He has been a Fellow at the Center for Advanced Study in the Behavioral Sciences at Stanford University and Visiting Distinguished Professor at the Naval Postgraduate School in Monterey, California. He has published widely on international relations, strategy, and arms control, including *Beyond Nuclear Deterrence,* co-edited with Johan J. Holst.

James A. Thomson is vice-president for The Rand Corporation's Project AIR FORCE research division. In addition, he directs two research programs at Rand—the National Security Strategy program for Rand's Project AIR FORCE and the International Security and Defense Policy program for Rand's other national security clients. In these roles he oversees Rand's research agenda in national strategy, foreign policy, defense policy, and arms control. Before joining Rand in 1981 he served on the National Security Council staff and in the Office of the Secretary of Defense.

Other Authors

Hannes Adomeit is a senior staff member at the Stiftung Wissenschaft und Politik. He was awarded postgraduate degrees from Freie Universitat Berlin and Columbia University, New York, and has held teaching or research posts at the International Institute for Strategic Studies (London), Institute of Soviet and East European Studies (Glasgow), and Queen's University (Kingston, Ontario). He is the author of *Soviet Risk Taking and Crisis Behavior* (1982) and co-editor of *Foreign Policy Making in Communist Countries* (1979).

Abraham S. Becker joined The Rand Corporation in 1957, where he is now a senior economist. He received MA and Ph.D. degrees in economics, as well as the Certificate of the Russian Institute, from Columbia University. He has been a professorial lecturer at the University of California, Los Angeles, and Visiting Professor of Economics and Russian Studies at the Hebrew University of Jerusalem and consultant on Soviet studies to its president. He was the U.S. member of the United Nations Expert Groups on Reduction of Military Budgets in 1974 and 1976, and has been a consultant to several U.S. government agencies. In addition, Dr. Becker is the author of numerous books, papers, and monographs on various issues of the Soviet economy and Soviet foreign policy.

Arnold L. Horelick is a senior political analyst with The Rand Corporation. In addition, he is director of the newly formed Rand/University of California, Los Angeles, Center for the Study of Soviet International Behavior. A Soviet affairs specialist, he has written and lectured widely on Soviet foreign policy and military strategy. He has been a visiting professor of political science at the City University of New York, Columbia University, University of California, Los Angeles, the California Institute of Technology, and Cornell University. From 1977 to 1980 he served in Washington, D.C., as the National Intelligence Officer for the Soviet Union and eastern Europe.

Alan A. Platt is a senior policy analyst with The Rand Corporation, specializing in European security studies. He received his Ph.D. degree in political science from Columbia University. From 1977 to 1981 he held several senior positions with the U.S. Arms Control and Disarmament Agency and was a National Fellow at the Hoover Institute. Before joining the U.S. government Dr. Platt taught at Stanford University and worked as a Senate legislative assistant for foreign affairs. In addition, he has lectured and written widely on arms control and European security issues.

Christoph Royen is a senior researcher at the Stiftung Wissenschaft und Politik, specializing in Soviet and eastern European politics at the Osteuropa-Institut of the Freie Universitat Berlin and at the Russian Institute of Columbia University. He has written widely on questions of Soviet foreign policy and East-West relations. Most recently he authored publications on developments in Poland and their external implications.

Reinhardt Rummel is a member of the Stiftung Wissenschaft und Politik Western European Affairs Research Group. He has been a visiting scholar at Harvard University and a temporary officer to the European Community in Brussels. In addition, he has written on European Community integration and European foreign policy, including *European Political Cooperation* (1982).

Gebhard Schweigler is a senior research associate at the SWP, in charge of North America studies. He holds a BA from Harvard, an MA from the University of California, Berkeley, and a Ph.D. from Harvard. Before coming to the SWP in 1979, he worked as a research associate at the Research Institute of the German Society for Foreign Affairs (Bonn); from 1976 until 1979 he was also a European representative of the German Marshall Fund of the United States (Washington, D.C.). He has published extensively on German and American politics, his latest major publication being a study of American foreign policy in the years from Kissinger to Carter.

K.-Peter Stratmann is a research associate at the Research Institute of Stiftung Wissenschaft und Politik. He was educated in Hamburg and Munich universities in political science, sociology, and modern history. He is the author of numerous articles on NATO military strategy and arms control.

John Van Oudenaren is a research associate with The Rand Corporation. He received his Ph.D. in political science from the Massachusetts Institute of Technology. Formerly, he was a research associate at the International Institute for Strategic Studies (London). In addition, he has published and lectured on subjects related to West German politics, European security, and East-West relations.

Foreword

The problem of how to fashion a strategy toward the Soviet Union has dominated German-American relations almost since the end of World War II. It played a determining role when the Federal Republic of Germany was established and the German Reich divided; it formed the background for Adenauer's "policy of strength" that tied West Germany firmly to the West, and it reappeared when Willy Brandt finally turned to the East with his new Ostpolitik. It seemed to wane in importance during the years of détente and then made its presence known with unanticipated vigor—and potentially serious consequences—in the early 1980s, when German and American differences on how to deal with a newly assertive Soviet Union began to widen

It stands to reason that two major national security research institutes in the two countries—The Rand Corporation of Santa Monica, California, and the Stiftung Wissenschaft und Politik of Ebenhausen, Bavaria—would become involved in efforts to find common conceptual grounds for handling the Soviet problem and thus to ease the strains imposed on German-American relations. Both institutes have been active in designing conceptual approaches to dealing with the Soviets. Because informal contacts between the two institutes had always existed (indeed, when the Stiftung Wissenschaft und Politik was established in 1965, one of the models was The Rand Corporation, which was then nearly twenty years old), the decision to engage in a more formal cooperative effort came almost naturally. Precisely because German-American relations had come under strain, both institutes had previously decided to enlarge their research programs in German-American affairs. A more formalized cooperative effort promised to help both sides to improve their research work and, over the long run, to institutionalize German-

American research cooperation. The goal of such cooperation was—and remains—to help dispel misperceptions and to contribute to a better understanding of the other country's underlying political processes and motivations.

We are satisfied that the result of our first formal cooperative venture—this publication on *The Soviet Problem in German-American Relations*—has brought us a step closer to achieving our goal. We asked members of our research staffs to compile papers on some important aspects of the complex triangular relationship among the United States, the Federal Republic, and the Soviet Union. These papers were then subjected to several rounds of intensive discussions, first within each institute, then between the two institutes, and finally with a group of outside experts. The papers, as they are being published now, reflect the results of these discussions; we hasten to add that each author bears final responsibility for his contribution. We are confident, however, that we succeeded in our goal of learning to understand one another better. This achievement is surely reflected in all the papers we are now publishing.

We are grateful to all who made this achievement possible: the two project managers (who are also the editors of this volume), Nanette Brown (who assisted in the preparation of this volume), the authors of the chapters, the participants of the discussion rounds, and our critical outside readers. Our special thanks belong to four institutions that provided the financial support without which our cooperative venture would not have been possible: the Ford Foundation, the NATO Information Service, the German Marshall Fund of the United States, and the Fritz Thyssen Stiftung.

Donald B. Rice, President, The Rand Corporation
Klaus Ritter, Director, Stiftung Wissenschaft und Politik

Introduction

> As long as the American-German relationship was essentially
> without conflict, . . . there existed a sympathology which was based
> on or at least made a claim on parallelism, complementarity or simi-
> larity of interests, institutions, trends and sentiments. One recog-
> nized each other in a series of similarities and commonalities. . . . It
> was when conflict began that the emphasis shifted to dissimilarities.[1]

"Sympathology" and "conflict" were used to describe the state
of U.S.-German affairs a hundred years ago, but they also fit
the current political situation. Although the structure of U.S.-
German relations has changed profoundly, the relationship is
still characterized by elements of both antagonism and mutual
dependence. The permanence of the Soviet challenge, the division of Europe, and the direct military confrontation of the
Soviet Union and the United States in the heart of Europe en-
dowed the American-German relationship with a crucial but
problematic importance.

Although this relationship is recognized as pivotal to both the
viability of the U.S. presence in Europe and the continued existence of West Germany and western Europe at large, growing
strains in U.S.-German relations have become apparent in recent
years. Among the many roots to the current and enduring problems between the United States and the Federal Republic, two
factors emerge: the strains that stem mainly from different views
of the appropriate policy toward the Soviet Union and the apparent exacerbation of these strains by the lack of understanding of
different approaches to security problems by the Federal Republic and the United States.

Policy Toward the Soviet Union

The potential for conflict between the United States and the
Federal Republic originates in part from the same structural rea-

son that requires continued and steady cooperation between the two countries. The Soviet Union has been a central problem for U.S.-West German relations since the 1940s. Because of the Soviet threat in Europe, the United States needs West Germany's commitment to NATO. However, the Federal Republic's national security depends on the U.S. defense commitment. The two states thus play a vital role in the continued existence of the Western alliance because they are the only states that can unilaterally change its structure and basic policies.[2] Both also have unique responsibilities that require special bilateral relationships with the Soviet Union—the United States with regard to the management of nuclear force relations and the Federal Republic in view of the German division. In the past it has been in defining these responsibilities that conflicting policies have arisen.

The unique nature of the U.S.-West German relationship is based on three considerations:

1. *The development of the relationship.* These are intrinsic reasons, such as how American global power became defined in the context of the German issue and how the political fabric of the Federal Republic was shaped by American political culture.
2. *The structure of the Atlantic alliance,* which is crucially dependent on the state of this relationship
3. *The nature of the perennial Soviet challenge,* which produces both common and divergent U.S. and West German interests

Although this complex relationship has displayed a remarkable stability over the decades, a recurrence of frictions, policy gaps, and, to a degree, conflict of interest was predictable. There was never a Golden Age in this relationship or for the alliance at large. Managing the built-in tensions has become routine since the early 1950s. Perceptions of growing cleavages have been part of the process and are derived from choosing between policies toward the partner (and the alliance at large) and policies toward the Soviet Union.

In the late 1970s emphasis shifted unprecedentedly to "dissimilarities." American and West German policies were out of step with one another, and the political capacity to cope with the common policy agenda seemed to diminish rapidly owing to the following factors:

- *Conditions* had changed. Above all, because the Soviet Union had achieved nuclear parity with the United States, strategic conditions no longer provided the painless extended nuclear deterrence on which the alliance had been based in the past. Economic conditions had also deteriorated. Concurrently with both, geopolitical conditions changed: The United States increasingly had turned its attention to areas outside Europe. At the same time, West Germany had developed strong ties with eastern Europe that it did not want to break. As a result, policy orientations tended to diverge.
- *Policies* were running out of options or needed reorientation. Defense and economic policies within the alliance, as well as arms control and trade policies toward the Soviet Union and eastern Europe, had become stale. Instead of reorienting these policies, however, the United States and West Germany spent their efforts defending the rationale of their divergent policies. The NATO double-track decision, linking deployment of the Ground Launched Cruise Missile (GLCM) and Pershing II nuclear forces to arms control negotiations, exemplifies this because it put the future of the alliance at stake but left the relationship of the defense and arms control issues unresolved.
- Similarly, the *domestic politics of foreign policy* displayed countervailing trends on either side. The 1970s saw foreign-policy setting come to an end in both countries. With the passing of the Vietnam era and the Tehran debacle, the United States became increasingly assertive about coping with external, particularly Soviet, challenges and did so with broad domestic support. Conversely, in West Germany governmental survival became increasingly dependent on maintaining the Eastern-oriented policies developed during the most active phase of German foreign policy in the early 1970s. Consequently, these countervailing trends—a more

outward-looking American foreign policy and a West German foreign policy more driven by domestic approval—diminished both governments' maneuverability in foreign affairs. Domestic processes, for the first time, limited the range of policy options available for the governments.

In the early 1980s these changes appeared to be nearing a point of no return.[3] Two critical events coincided: The unfolding controversy over the NATO double-track decision put pressure on the Reagan administration to trim its assertive anti-Soviet policy. (Because the Reagan administration had not participated in the formulation of the double-track decision, it was at first dubious about its execution.) By the same token, the American sanctions imposed on the Soviet/European gas pipeline deal turned the heat on Bonn, even though the Reagan administration's style obviously served Soviet interest in Europe better than any Soviet initiative could have at the time (although drawing a line for the Soviet Union had been Reagan's overriding objective).

Public irritations notwithstanding, earlier crises in the Atlantic alliance, particularly in U.S.-West German relations, could confidently be left to the network of bureaucratic structures that had been instituted to manage U.S.-German relations. By the early 1980s this confidence no longer existed, nor could even the will to rebuild consensus be taken for granted on either side. Thus U.S. and West German policymakers were faced with a dilemma that could not be solved through quick fixes or sloganism. On the one hand the interaction of principal allies no longer seemed to be guided by common concepts, oriented toward a similar policy agenda, and channeled through institutions with a capacity for expanding consensus and developing new concepts. On the other hand the commonality of the Soviet challenge to the United States and western Europe as well as mutual interests mandated continued cooperation.

Approaches to Security Problems

Besides the growing strains in German-American relations caused by different views of appropriate strategy toward the

Soviets, many of the current and enduring problems between the two nations are linked to each one's lack of understanding about how the other approaches its security problems. The United States and the Federal Republic possess uniquely different security approaches that stem from different geostrategic positions, historical experiences, governmental structures, educational systems, and cultural patterns.

In the United States the analysis of security issues is often approached in a wide open, freewheeling way. Americans are wont to consider numerous options (or a range of alternative hypotheses)—often a far wider range of options than is realistically available for choice, from a political standpoint, if only for the purpose of analysis. This reflects the U.S. historical context as well as existing perceived constraints. This approach conflicts with the German approach of constructing a line of argument in support of a single proposition or recommendation. This difference has many roots. As a superpower and the leader of the Western alliance, the United States inherently has a far greater freedom of policy choice than the Federal Republic, which is constrained by its geographic position, its relative power standing to the superpowers, and its reliance on American guarantees for its security. To Americans, everything seems possible, and naturally, they want to examine every option.

In addition, the U.S. national security decision-making process has been strongly influenced by the techniques of systems analysis (or operations research), which was first applied in a comprehensive way to problems of defense policy by The Rand Corporation, among others, in the late 1940s and 1950s. By the end of the 1960s the systems analysis approach to decision making had spread throughout the U.S. national security apparatus. This reinforced the American tendency toward options analysis and gave American analysis a decidedly technical and quantitative cast. Even though policy decisions are inevitably influenced chiefly by political factors, the systems analytic approach is often the venue for political decisions. In Germany, operations research remains confined to specific military issues. It has not been elevated to national decision making, which remains more explicitly political and less technical or analytic than in the United States.

A related phenomenon is the differing educational background of national security policymakers and analysts in the United States and the Federal Republic. In the United States the mixed political, technical, and analytic nature of the decision-making process has brought into the field individuals with a variety of educational training—the hard sciences, engineering, economics, and social sciences, to name a few. It is not unusual to find people with technical backgrounds in high policy positions in the U.S. government; national security studies are a true interdisciplinary field. In the Federal Republic, by contrast, the governmental separation between policy decisions and technical matters influences the educational background of national security policymakers and analysts. To a far greater extent than in the United States, policymakers come from the social sciences, often political science, or even the legal profession (many German diplomats are lawyers).

Further, in the United States, military and defense matters are handled by a mixture of civilian and military people. In government the chiefly civilian staff of the Office of the Secretary of Defense wields considerable power and, depending on the administration of the day, can often influence defense policy, strategy, and programs more strongly than the combined weight of the military services. The community of civilian analysts of military and defense affairs is not only large (some would argue too large), but also often as knowledgeable about military details— tactics, logistics, force structure—as American military officers are. The contrast to the situation in the Federal Republic could not be more striking. There is no counterpart to the Office of the Secretary of Defense in the German Ministry of Defense (MOD): The few civilian decision-making positions at the MOD are staffed principally by the armed forces *(Fühungsstab)* of the Bundeswehr. Consequently, there are few civilian analysts of defense affairs in the Federal Republic and even fewer who possess detailed military knowledge.

The large American community of civilian analysts of military affairs, plus foreign policy and arms control, is sustained by two factors that are far less present on the German scene. First, the United States has a propensity to reach outside the government for policy advice, especially by contracting nonprofit research institutions, such as The Rand Corporation, or profit-making research firms, the number and size of which have burgeoned in the United States since the 1960s. By contrast, such outside institutes as the Stiftung Wissenschaft und Politik (SWP), performing research for the Federal government, are rare in Germany. Second, not only is there a large turnover in the personnel within the U.S. national security apparatus when administrations change, but also that turnover continues during the reign of a given administration, reaching well down into the staffs as even junior officials move in and out of government. This phenomenon is almost unheard of in Germany. When governments change, only the top officials change—chiefly ministers and state secretaries—and below those levels there is little movement between government and research institutions. Consequently, the national security decision-making and analytic communities constitute a single community in the United States, whereas in the Federal Republic they are separate and distinct.[4]

The lateral movement between government and research leads to a final difference that is worthy of note. American officials are often considerably younger than their German counterparts because they are able to move from outside government into senior policy positions without working their way up through the ranks—a path that is closed to their German contemporaries. (For example, the current assistant secretary of state for European affairs and the director of the Arms Control and Disarmament Agency are a generation younger than their German counterparts.) Youth has advantages and disadvantages that make themselves felt in the two national approaches to national security policy. The advantage of American willingness to consider new ideas (contrasted to the conservatism of German officials) is offset by the failure to recognize that some of these same ideas have been tried before and found wanting.

All these American and German patterns add up to distinctly different approaches to national security issues and can often contribute to German-American difficulties as much as different assessments of national interests do. For example, German complaints about the lack of consistency and calculability *(Be-*

rechenbarkeit) in American policy often stem from the American propensity to consider a wide range of policy options, to talk about them openly (or leak them), and sometimes—from lack of experience—even to choose one of the extreme ones. As another example, the heavy military-technical-analytic content of American decision making often leads to German feelings that the United States overemphasizes the military dimension of national security problems and lacks political sensitivity. Americans often despair at the Federal Republic's overemphasis on political factors and lack of understanding of military or analytic issues.

Approach

It was to help understand these problems of fashioning a common policy toward the Soviet Union and differing security approaches that The Rand Corporation and the SWP began to cooperate in 1982. Both institutions felt that discussions of research ideas, methodologies and results, exchanges of research staffs, and—from time to time—joint studies would make a small but important contribution. This book is the first product of our cooperative process. Its purpose is not to solve these two problems, but to mitigate their effects by providing a better understanding of each country's position.

The research agenda for the joint Rand-SWP study effort was almost self-evident. The circumstances prevailing in 1982 made the Soviet problem in U.S.-West German relations an easy choice. Although the conservative trends in both countries promised to reduce pressures to a degree, that did not guarantee development of a framework for coping with the common Soviet challenge. In addition, the unique nature of the two institutions also provided the researchers with a special understanding of how and why the two countries define their national security policies. As institutions with histories of interest in Soviet affairs and as American and German institutions with close connections to our respective governments, we believed that we could address both considerations.

The individual contributions to this project were not drafted in isolation, but through a cooperative process. After the two institutions had agreed on an overall research plan, the authors—together with other members of both research staffs—met in a two-day conference at The Rand Corporation, in Santa Monica. At this meeting the authors presented chapter outlines and gave an oral overview of prospective contents so that the other researchers, especially those from the sister institution, could express their views as to the likely direction of the research and its contents. Only after this review did the authors prepare initial drafts of the chapters. To facilitate continued contact between the two institutions as drafting proceeded, each chapter author was assigned a counterpart in the sister institution with whom he could discuss the draft's contents.

As a final step in the cooperative research process, Rand and the SWP sponsored a three-day conference, which was hosted by the SWP at its headquarters in Ebenhausen. The initial draft chapters formed the basis for the conference. Conference participants included the chapter authors and their institutional counterparts, researchers from other institutions, and former and present high officials from both the American and German federal governments. The purposes of this conference were to subject initial research results to constructive criticism by a wider community than the members of the study team; to open up the study process so that initial research results could be made available to a wider community, especially government officials; and finally, to use the study process as a venue for exchanges across a range of issues between Americans and Germans. Discussions at this conference greatly influenced the research, with many chapters being revised considerably as a result.

The final product—this book—is therefore not merely a collection of papers, for it rests on a long process of cooperative development between Rand and the SWP. Nevertheless, we did not require that each chapter be literally agreed on between the two institutions and among all members of the joint study team. Instead, we asked that the authors be sensitive to differing points of view and to take them into account in preparing their chapters, but not necessarily to accept each differing point. Indeed, as the reader can discover for himself, there are disagreements, sometimes sharp ones, among the chapter authors. But it was the goal of the research process that such disagreements should come out.

Although we did not intend that the chapters be distinctly "German" or "American," they have some of that flavor. Not only are German and American views discussed, compared, and analyzed in many of the chapters, but other chapters also set forth an individual's analysis of the problem he was assigned and that analysis inevitably draws on the national viewpoint and style of the author's home country. On the matter of style, it is worth noting that the variety of chapter styles reflects the differing national approaches to security issues described earlier. Even though the subject matter of this volume does not strictly lend itself to systems analysis, many of the Rand chapters attempt to rise above the debate, to categorize it and to analyze it, often through the use of alternative hypotheses, options, and models (see, for example, the Horelick, Becker, and Thomson contributions, Chapters 4, 7, and 11, respectively). In contrast, the SWP contributions generally develop a single line of analysis, building toward a conclusion (see, for example, the Schweigler, Royen, Stratmann, and Nerlich contributions, Chapters 1, 5, 8, and 10, respectively).

In undertaking this study we had two goals:

1. To identify the common ground between the United States and the Federal Republic on strategy toward the USSR and, where possible, to suggest how that common ground might be expanded through improved conclusions
2. To assess the nature of differences between the United States and the Federal Republic on strategy toward the USSR and, where possible, to suggest how they might be narrowed.

To accomplish these goals we laid out a research plan that began with an assessment of the underlying problems in German-American relations and then turned to the specific policy issues. The original plan is reflected in the organization of this book. In the first section we examine the domestic sources of commonality and differences, recognizing that it is not altogether possible to separate the domestic setting for foreign policy debates from foreign policy itself. Gebhard Schwergler of the SWP examines the domestic setting of West German foreign policy (Chapter 1), and Alan Platt of Rand looks at the domestic setting of American policy toward Germany (Chapter 2). In the third chapter John Van Oudenaren of Rand provides a comparative assessment of how the security debates in the two countries interact.

In the second section we examine the Soviet Union in view of two issues that are crucial to the construction of Western strategy toward the USSR: the prospects for change within the Soviet orbit that would alter Soviet objectives and strategy, and the nature of Soviet objectives and strategy toward the West. In Chapter 4 Arnold Horelick of Rand addresses the critical question of whether (and, if so, how) internal changes in the USSR are likely to affect Soviet external policy. In Chapter 5 Christoph Royen of the SWP examines the prospects for system change in eastern Europe and its likely effect on the USSR. Hannes Adomeit of the SWP, in Chapter 6, examines the Soviet policy toward the West.

Building on these assessments in Part Three we turn to the American-German policy agenda, examining specific policy areas as well as overall policy or grand strategy as a whole. In the seventh chapter Abraham Becker of Rand looks at East-West economic relations. K.-Peter Stratmann of the SWP follows with an examination of defense issues, in Chapter 8.

In Part Four, Reinhardt Rummel of the SWP investigates the limitations of Western political management (Chapter 9). After these assessments of specific policy areas, we introduce the political dimensions to examine overall strategy as a whole. First, Uwe Nerlich of the SWP reviews the Western record in Chapter 10, and then in Chapter 11 James A. Thomson sums up the debate with a discussion on formulating Western political strategy toward the USSR.

It is almost traditional that an analysis of an alliance stresses those problems that divide the allies, and this book is no exception. But in its analysis of the fundamental reasons for the German-American alliance—the nature of the shared values that the alliance seeks to protect and the essential nature of the threat to those values—the book also underscores the sources of commonality.

In Chapter 1, Gebhard Schweigler documents the success story of the postwar policy, first of the Western powers and then of the Federal Republic itself—to reconstruct a new state and German society along democratic lines and to anchor the Federal Republic firmly in the West. He cites various evidence about the now solid roots of democracy in the Federal Republic, especially among the young, pointing out that nondemocratic forces have been driven into the extreme fringes of the right and the left. On the more controversial question of the firmness of the Federal Republic's connection to the West, Schweigler argues that the German body politic is not seeking a point equidistant between the superpowers, but remains committed to the West and to the alliance with the United States. He also argues that what sometimes seems to be anti-Americanism among the young is a consequence of overly idealistic democratic views and a failure to understand that the United States faces the difficult task of playing the not-entirely-consistent roles of a great power with global strategic responsibilities and a great democracy with idealistic aspirations.

Schweigler is joined by other authors in directly or indirectly underscoring the broad consensus in both nations that the USSR is the chief threat to the shared values of the United States and the Federal Republic. In his chapter, Hannes Adomeit presents an assessment of the nature of Soviet objectives toward the West that was widely shared by both Rand and SWP study team participants. In addition, his assessment of Soviet progress indicates that the main area of Soviet success has been in converting Soviet military power into leverage over European political processes, or "at least successfully conveying the idea to that effect."

Hence, the basic reasons for the existence of the German-American connection remain intact—shared democratic ideals and shared views on the main threat to those ideals: the Soviet Union, especially its military power.

Notwithstanding these commonalities, this book also highlights the American-German divergences, tracing the problems of the policy agenda to their sources. In their contributions, John Van Oudenaren and James A. Thomson trace these problems to contrasting views on the appropriate priority of Western objectives toward the USSR, especially on the issue of long-term change in Europe. As Van Oudenaren points out, the American and German positions appear to have completely exchanged on this issue. In the early 1960s initial American moves toward détente with the USSR, including arms control, raised German concerns that the United States and Soviet Union might solve the problem of the division of Europe over the heads of the Germans. Now it is the Americans who are concerned about German attachment to détente and about Germany's objectives toward the East. In his analysis of the German-American debate on grand strategy toward the USSR, Thomson traces such current American and German concerns about the other nation's policies to the matter of long-term objectives. According to his analysis, Germans believe it important that Western strategy encompass the goal of a long-term peaceful change of the situation in central Europe through a favorable transformation of the Soviet system. By contrast, although Americans believe that this is a worthy objective, they tend to downplay its relevance to today's strategy, arguing that such a transformation is neither likely nor amenable to Western influence. As a consequence, Thomson argues, Americans stress the preservation of Western values, especially from military threats; Germans, although not ignoring this, also emphasize the role of cooperation with the East as a means of opening options for long-term change in Europe.

Despite the differences in policies toward the Soviet Union, in Chapter 9 Reinhardt Rummel is optimistic in suggesting certain institutional improvements in the alliance system that could enhance the implementation of a common political strategy. Given the divergent paths being followed by the United States and western Europe, Rummel concludes that NATO, in its current state, is unlikely to be able to meet today's challenges. However, such proposals as revitalizing the 1966 NATO Standing Group in

Washington, having Washington use the European Political Cooperation group more actively, and coordinating the economic policies of international organizations such as the Organization for Economic Cooperation and Development with alliance security interests are recommended as innovative ways to achieve a better consensus among the alliance members and develop a more coherent Western strategy toward the Soviet Union.

Several chapters in the book also underscore the various assessments of the nature of Soviet power that are behind such differences of long-term objectives and strategy. These fall into two principal areas: (1) Soviet progress in challenging the West and (2) the West's ability to influence Soviet policy.

A reading of the chapters that touch on the first issue highlights the fact that not only are there distinct American and German viewpoints, but also that there can be different views within each country. Hannes Adomeit's chapter examines Soviet Western policy from the perspective of six Soviet objectives. He sees Soviet progress toward these objectives as mixed at best, pointing out Soviet failure to convert the political, ideological, and economic instruments of strategy into strategic gains. As previously noted, he sees the Soviets' greatest gains stemming from the conversion of military power into political instruments.

Other authors put far more stress on the military dimension of Soviet success, perhaps on the grounds that the objectives of greatest importance to the Soviets are those most amenable to military influence—in particular, the Soviet goal to deny western Europe a viable defense option. Uwe Nerlich in his review of Western political strategy and K.-Peter Stratmann in his review of the Western debate on military strategy have dealt with Soviet efforts to deny strategic options to the West. Because of the nature of his contribution, Stratmann tends to see these efforts more in terms of Soviet military capabilities and doctrine; Nerlich builds on such military assessments to make a broader point that the USSR "has increasingly gained political control over the two developments that are central to U.S. and West German preoccupations, respectively—the East-West military competition and European détente." What these chapters show, among other things, is not a fundamental difference of assessment of Soviet progress, but a different emphasis on the relative importance of the dimensions of that progress, especially the political-military one.

The chapters by Christoph Royen, Arnold Horelick, Abraham Becker, John Van Oudenaren, and Reinhardt Rummel all address the question of the West's ability to influence Soviet policy toward the West. Christoph Royen argues that tensions between expansion and erosion are bound to increase within the Soviet orbit, most noticeably in eastern Europe. The viability of the West's political and economic system, along with credible deterrence, should induce the alliance to outwait those developments within the Soviet orbit and to encourage Eastern elites to engage in eventual domestic reforms and international interdependence through steady cooperation, particularly on the economic level.

The other contributions differ from this analysis in various ways. Horelick analyzes the relationship between Soviet internal problems and policies and external policies and finds no evidence to link internal changes with external policies. Rather, because he sees the relation as the converse—external failures triggering internal change—Horelick concludes that the West's ability to shape the Soviet view of the external environment is a far more productive way to influence Soviet policy than to attempt to induce internal changes. Becker downplays the importance of trade with the East as a lever of Western strategy, and Van Oudenaren points out that Americans see little evidence of even a potential desire of the USSR to change its policy toward the West in a fundamental and (from the West's point of view) favorable way. Finally, Rummel suggests that before change is possible, the West must present a common front against the Soviets with a strategy possessing both competitive and cooperative components.

In the concluding chapter Thomson traces how such differing assessments about the progress of Soviet Western policy and about the West's ability to influence it lead to differences about how the instruments of Western strategy should be used—that is, to differences over the specifics of the policy agenda. Abraham Becker and K.-Peter Stratmann examine many of these policy issues in the areas of economic policy toward the East and military strategy, respectively. Becker shows that the current quiescence of the debate about trade with the East may prove only a temporary respite, as the American propensity toward trade denial strategies is unlikely to find much sympathy in European capitals. Stratmann spells out the consequences for Western military strategy and capabilities of the Soviet military buildup, arguing that widely recognized military needs, especially in the area of conventional forces, are unlikely to be met because of political and economic constraints. He points out that continued differences in how these constraints are interpreted could lead to sharp German-American disputes over NATO defense efforts. To the extent that differences persist in the future, policy differences in this area could loom as well.

What does this volume have to contribute to the debate in the West about the future of the Atlantic alliance as it struggles to deal with Soviet power? *Compared with contemporary pessimism about the alliance's future, this is a basically optimistic book.* It shows that the most fundamental elements of the German-American relationship remain firmly in place. Although the book also provides a long list of serious problems in the relationship, these problems ought to be manageable. Thus we would argue that a basic restructuring of the Western alliance, and of the German-American relationship, which many are calling for, is neither needed nor warranted. Indeed, trying to tinker with the fundamentals—whether through massive American troop withdrawals from Europe, changes in defense strategy, or new modes of European cooperation on the nuclear components of security—is likely to be destructive rather than helpful. Nonetheless, this book also brings out serious problems that need to be brought under control before their domestic political ramifications in the United States or the Federal Republic trigger unilateral basic changes in the alliance structure. What is needed is more attention to these problems so that they can be better understood and a consensus can be built that is sensitive to both sides' views.

Notes

1. Alfred Vagts, *Deutschland und die Vereinigten Staaten in der Weltpolitik* (London: Lovat Dickson and Thompson, 1935), 2.

2. Such unilateral steps would tend to be detrimental to the originator and would result from folly or erratic behavior rather than from considered interest. Given the divergent role and weight of the two countries, there is, of course, an important asymmetry in the consequences of such steps: The repercussions of a breakdown in the alliance system would be more serious for the Federal Republic than for the United States. For the United States, they would primarily affect its global role, although in the longer run this would also tend to change the domestic fabric. In the case of the Federal Republic, its political system would be susceptible to external influence and change. In both countries are constituencies that associate benign consequences with such repercussions or tend to ignore them altogether, although on the American side the repercussions would be less severe. If relations with the United States seem to be more central in West German perspective than relations with the Federal Republic from an American vantage point, this derives from the asymmetry of expected repercussions. To view this difference in terms of relative power would be fallacious: Both would stand to lose on that account.

3. See Chapter 10.

4. Not surprisingly, all but one of the Rand contributors to this volume have held senior U.S. government posts; none of the SWP contributors have held German government positions.

PART ONE

The Domestic Setting of U.S.-West German Relations

Chapter 1

The Domestic Setting
of West German Foreign Policy

Gebhard Schweigler

From External to Internalized Constraints

At the end of World War II all the victorious powers agreed on
one goal: to prevent Germany from once again becoming a threat
to peace in Europe. Not all ideas conceived and presented in
pursuit of that goal were eventually realized; Germany was
neither dismembered into a number of smaller states nor de-
industrialized and "pasteurized," as the Morgenthau Plan had
proposed. Economic realities, political necessities, and the onset of the cold war combined to force a reevaluation of postwar
objectives.

Yet the main goal remained unchanged. The design, partly
deliberate and partly accidental, of the postwar political order in
Europe came to reflect that goal. Germany was eventually divided into the Federal Republic of Germany and the German
Democratic Republic (GDR); large parts of eastern Germany
were ceded to the Soviet Union and Poland; and the Republic of
Austria was reestablished, denied by treaty obligations the option of seeking unification with Germany.

The Federal Republic of Germany, comprising the bulk of the
German population and the heartland of Germany's economic
power, became the focal point of efforts to prevent a potentially
dangerous resurgence of German might. In the context of the
cold war, however, it also turned into the linchpin of efforts to
contain the further spread of Soviet power; that is, the Soviets
had to be denied influence over West German affairs, and West

Germany's political, economic, and, later, military weight had to be added to the Western alliance. Thus was the Federal Republic born into a world of conflicting goals and international pressures.

The postwar and cold war goals of Western policy toward West Germany followed two tracks. One sought to reconstruct the western part of Germany economically and politically as a new state, along with a reconstruction of German society, all with the goal of firmly anchoring West Germany politically, economically, and socially in the West. The other attempted to tie the Federal Republic down in a web of obligations and constraints that would, on their own, achieve the principal goal of postwar policy.

The formal constraints originally imposed on the remnants of the German Reich and later, after its establishment in 1949, on the Federal Republic—constraints pertaining to its buildup of military power and to policies regarding Germans as a whole and Berlin—were gradually relaxed to the extent to which they no longer seemed appropriate or necessary. The necessity for external constraints receded the more the Federal Republic internalized them, that is, the more the development of West German politics and policies, but also attitudes and orientations, conformed to Western preferences. To determine the extent to which West Germany has internalized such constraints—and in the process may have developed a new sense of identity—is the purpose of this chapter.

Attitudinal Setting: Identity and Détente

After the catastrophe of the Nazi period the Germans were faced with the task of coming to psychological terms with their terrible past. They were also confronted with the necessity of developing those orientations and attitudes without which democracy—the overriding goal of postwar West German politics—cannot flourish for long. This was no easy task, partly because a strongly felt need to forget collided with the necessity to remember in order not to commit the same mistakes again.

The development of democratic, pro-Western values represented an intended break with Germany's past. This break raised the question whether West Germans would be able to fashion a new sense of identity, a question made all the more urgent, of course, because of the division of Germany. When the Federal Republic embarked, initially under American prodding, on a policy of détente vis-à-vis the Soviet Union—a policy that at once reflected changes in West Germany's sense of identity and that was designed to help maintain an all-German national consciousness—the United States, along with other Western allies, viewed this new Ostpolitik with great suspicion. They were afraid that West Germany's unstable sense of identity would not allow it to pursue a rational policy of détente.

To most West Germans such fears seemed almost absurd. In their minds West Germany is solidly on the side of the West, its attachment to democratic values unquestioned, and its distrust of the Soviet Union as strong as ever. Because perceptions in this critical area seem so far apart, a more detailed analysis of West German attitudes concerning its sense of identity and desires for détente appears needed.

Democratic Values

The development of democratic attitudes in West Germany requires little documentation here; this success story has been more than sufficiently documented elsewhere.[1] West German political behavior in general, electoral behavior—with its high participation rate and genius in providing for stable governing majorities—in particular, and a multitude of public opinion polls specifically show that the Federal Republic need fear no comparison with other democratic countries. Democratic values have become firmly instilled; the legitimacy of the Federal Republic's political system is, in general, not questioned. Overwhelming majorities consider the present form of government the best and support its multiparty system. Most West Germans trust that their political system will be able to cope with difficult new problems; demands for changes in the Basic Law (which was never submitted for public approval through a nationwide referendum) have almost disappeared. In general, satisfaction with conditions in the Federal Republic is high. All in all, West Germans have fully adopted the political features of their new state.

Most of the surveys on democratic attitudes show that younger West Germans are even more strongly attached to democratic values than their elders. In many ways this is, of course, an encouraging finding. Fears, expressed occasionally in the United States as well as in the Federal Republic, that West Germany's youth might turn away from democracy are without foundation. There is, however, another side to the coin. It appears as if young West Germans' attachment to the ideals of democracy (perhaps under the influence of traditional German idealism) has become so strong that they are increasingly dissatisfied with the performance of the Federal Republic's political system in this regard. (Idealistic views about the nature of democracy might also have contributed to young West Germans' growing sense of disillusionment with the United States. More on this and other aspects of what has come to be known as the problem of the "successor generation" is presented later.) To the extent that such dissatisfaction is channeled into normal political processes, resulting activities are to be welcomed as important contributions to the vitality of democracy. Problems arise, however, when nondemocratic alternatives are preferred.

There is absolutely no danger that youthful (or other) dissatisfaction with the inadequacies of democratic processes could result in a significant resurgence of Nazism in West Germany. Contrary to frequently made claims, West Germans—and young ones in particular—have learned the lessons of the Third Reich. A return of another Hitler is unthinkable. Indeed, a Nazi or neo-Nazi movement has never played a significant role in West German politics (legal restrictions would have made that difficult under any circumstances). The only time a neo-Nazi movement appeared on the political scene was in the mid-1960s, at a time when a Grand Coalition of the major parties virtually eliminated effective political opposition and thus encouraged protest votes. At its height the National Democratic party appealed to some 15 percent of the electorate, although only in public opinion polls; at the elections the party never made it over the 5 percent hurdle (except in some regional elections). In the course of the 1970s the neo-Nazis disappeared; today they are of no political importance, gaining less than 1 percent of the vote in regional and national elections. Terrorist remnants, exceedingly small in number, represent an occasional and then dangerous nuisance, but amateurish as they are (a fact that at first caused authorities to underestimate their danger), they now seem to be largely under control.

Leftist-based challenges to the legitimacy of the political system have shown a more visible and longer-lasting pattern of ups and downs. Originally, the Communist party—after first having been represented in the Bundestag—was outlawed as a party not in support of the constitution (so were rightist parties). When the strong anti-Communist stance of the cold war years gave way to more relaxed—and possibly more democratic—official positions, a new Communist party was allowed to organize itself. It was never able to command electoral support, although it became active—and to some extent influential—in supporting other leftist movements.

The most important of such movements was the protest movement of the late 1960s, organized as an extraparliamentary opposition at the time of the Grand Coalition. Its main objective was to fight emergency legislation, but protest against the war in Vietnam as well as against undemocratic regimes (such as the Shah's in Iran) offered additional fuel. It was a movement for more democracy (if idealistically conceived) and had obvious counterparts in the United States and France. The youthful energies released at that time eventually contributed to the electoral victory of the social-liberal coalition in 1969 (whose goal it was, in Brandt's words, to risk more democracy). Political success of sorts having been achieved, the protest movement of 1968 petered out. But it left behind a legacy of violent terrorism.

The activities of the Baader-Meinhof gang were to occupy the Federal Republic during the following years in many ways; they constituted a serious challenge. An initial quasi-romantic appeal of the terrorists soon faded as their actions became more violent and less politically focused. But the determined effort to catch up with them and to render them harmless began to strain the political consensus, as the government felt it necessary to resort to extraordinary means (ranging from much-criticized efforts to "dry out" the presumed support network by denying employment in the public sector to persons allegedly unprepared to stand up for the Federal Republic's basic order of liberty and democracy, to restricting the lawyer-client relationship in cases of suspected terrorists). These efforts not only met with increasing resistance at home; they also became the subject of much criticism abroad.

The government felt compelled to use such means not only to eliminate a dangerous threat to its own legitimacy, indeed security (Bonn took on the appearance of an armed camp for a while), but also to protect allied installations, another target of terrorist activities. Eventually, and with a good deal of bungling leading to much controversy, the hard core of the terrorist movement was apprehended. That nightmare has, by now, largely vanished; except for a few isolated instances, terrorist activities no longer are of concern. The likelihood that they will reappear seems small; public authorities have learned how to deal with incipient terrorist movements, and—more important—the public at large will deny them what little legitimacy they might have enjoyed before.

Except for a small and militant group of terrorists, the leftist-based German protest movement, in the meantime, has shifted to new political activities in the form of groupings professing alternative life-styles and politics, support for environmental protection, and interest in peace. The "alternatives," "Greens," and the peace movement have become a recognized political force, gaining just over 5 percent in the March 1983 elections and thus being represented in the Bundestag for the first time (they had earlier gained access to a number of regional parliaments). They form the political spearhead of those who want a "different republic"—one based on more abstract ideals of democracy.

Most of the support for the Greens (to use the short term now applied to many diverse groupings) is to be found among younger age-groups, and here particularly among the well educated. We may witness here an aftereffect of the 1968 protest movement, whose adherents have, in the meantime, entered influential positions in the educational establishments and in the media. Much has been written about these young West Germans' supposed search for identity in a return to classic patterns of German (irrational) romanticism or even nationalism, about their historical uprootedness, and their angst in facing a world of insecure economic developments, frightening new technologies, and unimaginably dangerous weapons of mass destruction. All of this has made good copy and even better headlines. But wrongly so, as Josef Joffe has argued:

> There may be less than meets the headlines. For the observer, journalist, or academic, pathology is always more enticing than health. Hence the fascination with a movement that has suddenly rekindled the old German uncertainties tends to obscure some far more benign (and banal) facts about contemporary West Germany.[2]

One of these banal facts is that although the Greens barely managed to get into the Bundestag, the conservative Christian Democratic party (CDU) effected a triumphant return to power after thirteen years of social-liberal rule. In other words, the climate of opinion in the Federal Republic has generally shifted to the right (or, perhaps more accurately, returned to the center); thus the appearance of the Greens in no way signifies a tilt or even drift to the left. It must be seen as a sign of the strength and vitality of West German democracy that the Greens are now able to participate in the democratic process; to view their appearance as a threat to that democracy seems hardly justified.

The Greens could become worrisome if they were to broaden their electoral base and gain significant power (something they failed to achieve in regional elections held after March 1983). The fact that the Green movement is largely youth-based has led some observers to speculate that, as new generations come into the polity, the Greens' power will grow. This seems doubtful. More likely the fascination with the Greens is yet another fad, fed by current concerns over dying forests, unemployment, and East-West tensions, but eventually to fade as other concerns become more prominent and the demands of adjusting to adult life take precedence. In addition, the Greens will lose in attractiveness (or at least not gain) to the extent that the political system successfully addresses some of these concerns and, in the process, co-opts the Greens into the political process. Furthermore, the Greens are likely to suffer from the excesses and foibles of their representatives (witness public reaction to the blood-spilling attack on an American general or the sexual escapades of a Bundestag representative). They are, in any case, faced with the dilemma that rigid adherence to their ideology will not win them new support, whereas (more likely) attempts at engaging in compromises in order to achieve at least some of their goals threatens the support of their hard core: hardly a prescription for a successful challenge to the prevailing democratic consensus. All in all, then, West Germany's democracy continues to be solidly established and not in danger, as far as the attitudes of the West Germans themselves are concerned.

Attachment to the West

The original purpose of installing Western democratic values lay not only in helping the West Germans to lead a better life or in protecting Europe from an otherwise potentially dangerous Germany; the expectation was also that a democratically constituted Federal Republic would become part of a community of shared values and thus intimately tied to the West. This expectation appears to have been fulfilled. The values professed by most West Germans today are, allowing for some national variations, nearly identical with those prevailing in other Western nations. The Western orientation has become a firmly established part of the West Germans' identity. And their desire to stay with the West is overwhelming.

Ever since the first of almost innumerable polls was taken on this question, between 60 percent and 70 percent of all West Germans have consistently declared that they are in favor of a union of western European states. Initially, there were three main motivations for such support. One concerned the overriding goal of postwar reconstruction, namely, creating a peaceful Europe. An alliance among the western European countries would help to eliminate what used to be heart-felt enmities, particularly between Germany and France. That goal has obviously been achieved; today a return to the years of intense hostility seems inconceivable. Feelings of friendship are strong, unperturbed by occasional political or economic rivalries. The relative success of the European Community (EC) contributed to this state of affairs. It also helped to bring about the realization of a second motivation, namely, the economic recovery of Europe.

West Germans had a third and special motive for supporting a united Europe. To many of them, being a good European meant that they could rid themselves of the stigma of being a bad German; that they could dissolve, in other words, their feelings of guilt and shame in a new European identity. Besides, the mere fact of a second world war had pointed out the dangers of a Europe made up of nation-states, each fiercely nationalistic. Uniting these nations offered the hope that Europe might overcome narrow and dangerous nationalisms by creating a sense of European identity. This hope was only partially fulfilled. To be sure, the dangers of nationalism appear to have been eliminated; but Europe is still made up of nation-states and there is no sign that this state of affairs will change in the near future.

The quality of West German support for a united Europe has changed to the extent to which the need to hide one's Germanness disappeared and the Europe of nation-states reasserted itself. In general, West Germans—like other Europeans—have become somewhat disillusioned about the prospects for a united Europe; they don't really expect it any more, and they don't plead for any particular haste in bringing it about. Still, most consider membership in the Common Market a good thing and would regret it if the EC were to be dissolved. The disillusionment with the goal and process of European unification does not mean that the West Germans have begun to turn away from that part of their Western orientation. On the contrary, cooperation within the EC (indeed its enlargement) and among the European nations has become firmly internalized in West Germany's political value system. West Germans have not formed a new European identity, but the European orientation has become part of their identity.

One of the reasons a European identity never took hold has to do with the fact that West Germans could not rely on Europe to guarantee its security. Only close cooperation with the United States could achieve that goal. For that reason most West Germans never supported a Gaullist alternative to the prevailing "Atlanticist" orientation (even though the Franco-German Treaty of Friendship, concluded in 1963 by Adenauer and de Gaulle in part as a reaction against American policies under President Kennedy, met with overwhelming agreement). That preference for close cooperation with the United States as against closer European cooperation still holds, although the European option does seem to exert some occasional fascination.

The question of West German attitudes toward cooperation with the United States has, as the result of policy differences between the two countries, recently gained a great deal of attention. The suspicion is voiced with increasing frequency that West Germans are turning anti-American and that, as a result, the German-American alliance is in danger. A closer look at West German attitudes toward the United States reveals that anti-Americanism is hardly on the rise and that the danger of a collapsing alliance is vastly overdrawn; it also shows, however, that West Germans are not prepared to follow every twist and turn of American policies unquestioningly. This is particularly true for members of the younger generation, whose alleged deficiencies in this regard have caused some to express concern about this "successor generation."

In general, West Germans like Americans as a people; they always have (with a slight reduction during the years of Vietnam and Watergate). The only standard criticism about Americans is that they are too materialistic; to some extent this attitude reflects traditional western European prejudices concerning the difference between American "civilization" and European "culture." Most West Germans consider the United States the Federal Republic's best friend; an overwhelming majority believes that it ought to cooperate particularly closely with the United States. The belief that it is equally important to cooperate with the Soviet Union has, since the height of Ostpolitik, remained essentially stable despite some fluctuations.

Although the necessity for German-American cooperation is thus little in doubt, the possibility for this cooperation is another question. As William Schneider has put it: "Europeans continue to like the United States and believe it is seriously committed to their security; but they have come to distrust U.S. leadership and judgment."[3] This distrust in U.S. leadership, already evident during the Carter presidency, has increased significantly under President Reagan. West Germans were thus getting increasingly nervous about the possibility of being dragged into a conflict caused by weak—or overly aggressive—American leadership. Partly as a consequence, the belief that the Federal Republic should not blindly follow the American lead, but instead decide according to its own interests, spread correspondingly. This was one instance in which the issue of protecting national sovereignty seemed to gain in public importance.

But how important was it? The Social Democratic party (SPD) felt encouraged enough by the spread of these attitudes to base its 1983 election campaign on the slogan "in the German interest" and to argue that it would stand up against unreasonable American demands. Yet it lost that election decisively. This would seem to indicate that the issue of pursuing strictly West German interests vis-à-vis—or even against—the United States was not utmost on the voters' minds.

Yet the feeling that the Federal Republic must not slavishly follow every twist and turn of American politics cannot be neglected, not even by a CDU government (which, in some contrast to its predecessor, has begun to express stronger solidarity with the United States). Such a feeling seems a necessary component of a matured polity and society. The difficulty, of course, lies in differentiating between temporary twists and genuine policy changes on the American side and in defining West German interests. Washington cannot, therefore, always count on automatic support from Bonn; but it need not interpret every denial of support as a manifestation of anti-Americanism.

The feeling that West Germany must, at times, protect its own interests in the face of different American policies is particularly strong in regard to relations with the Soviet Union. A number of complex factors are at work. One of them has to do with the Federal Republic's security situation and its relations with other eastern European countries (especially the German Democratic Republic [GDR]). It simply cannot be in West Germany's interest to follow a strictly confrontationist policy vis-à-vis the Soviet Union, either in Europe or in peripheral areas of the third world.

Another factor derives from the fact that West Germans and Americans seem to have learned different lessons from Germany's own past (a fact that contributes to a sense of frustration on both sides). Thus for the United States, the "Munich analogy" (although discredited in Vietnam) is still strongly operative: One must not give in to the piecemeal designs of totalitarian regimes; encroachments must be resisted with determination, using strong means and, if need be, force. Most West Germans believe that such measures show little effectiveness against such regimes (and especially not against the Soviet Union). Continued relations, indeed cooperation, so the argument goes, bring better results than mindless confrontation. To many Americans this smacks of appeasement; to many West Germans the American stance seems to reflect the arrogance (if not ignorance) of a distant superpower.

These differing perceptions of the lessons of history have recently contributed to strains in German-American relations in two instances: reaction to the events in Poland and in Central America. In both cases different perceptions as to how to gain or protect democracy and human rights contributed to the transatlantic difficulties. In the case of Poland, the Schmidt government (admittedly caught in a difficult position and not always expressing itself with great clarity or good fortune) angered many Americans with its reluctance to condemn the Soviet Union and support American-initiated countermeasures. Schmidt insisted that quiet help (particularly in the form of material help for individual Poles, which West Germans provided in record volume) would be better for the Poles than public posturing and blustering. This reflected the Federal Republic's traditional approach to human rights issues, which has always relied on quiet diplomacy and significant expenditures of public funds. This, plus the fact that West German human rights efforts at times seemed too much focused on ethnic Germans, put a strain on German-American relations when the United States sought to further the cause of human rights universally through public denunciations of human rights violations.

In the case of Central America, the Federal Republic (even now under CDU leadership) is reluctant to go along with American actions against allegedly subversive regimes or in support of supposedly democratic ones. Not only does it not want to risk a confrontation with the Soviet Union over this issue (nor do many West Germans share the belief, as expressed by President Reagan, that the security of the West is at stake in that traditionally turbulent region), but it also, on the whole, is not convinced that action (and covert at that) against these regimes is a strike for democracy. (American public opinion apparently shares these convictions.)

West Germans' reluctance to condemn Soviet suppression of democratic movements and violations of human rights, while refusing to support American efforts on behalf of human rights and democratic movements elsewhere (or worse, accusing the United States of suppressing democratic movements), has led to frequent charges that West Germans were beginning to take a position equidistant between the two superpowers. Such charges received further nourishment from the refusal to take a tougher anti-Soviet line in general (and of course from the demands by some that West Germany in fact pursue a policy of equidistance). Yet such charges have little foundation in fact, particularly where they imply a moving away from the West toward the Soviet Union. To be sure, many West Germans have become sensitive to a heavy-handed exercise of American power and tend to equate such behavior with Soviet great-power behavior (President Reagan's imposition of sanctions against western European exporters of pipeline equipment for the Soviet Union was particularly unfortunate in that regard, as were overt and covert activities in Central America); the fringe of the political spectrum may well have come to see both superpowers in equally evil terms. But demands for a policy of equidistance have never become politically relevant; with the CDU back in power it is even less likely that they will.

In a way, criticism focusing on the behavior of the United States reflects a strong interest in democratic values and not an indifference to them. It is precisely those whose democratic idealism is strongest—West Germany's youth—who are most critical of U.S. behavior. Such criticism, if somewhat misguided in terms of political realism, is not indicative of a movement away from Western values. Rather the opposite is true; precisely because of the strong interest in democratic values, criticism focuses on that country which professes a higher moral quality, yet seems to violate democratic values, and whose policies can in fact be changed through expressions of public criticism. There may be some justification in worrying about the long-term effects of misguided idealism among the West German successor generation, but such worries need not focus on a loosening of their attachment to Western values. (Besides, members of this successor generation are a long way away from assuming leadership, which in West Germany takes much longer—and therefore leaves much more time for socialization processes—than in the United States. Where young West Germans are in leadership positions, they hardly fulfill the stereotype of the angry anti-American.)

Doubts concerning the quality of American leadership and the nature of U.S. democracy have not led to politically relevant efforts at distancing the Federal Republic from the United States. Neither have they, as is frequently claimed, furthered a West German propensity toward neutralism. If anything, neutralist tendencies have decreased in recent years.

Neutralist attitudes are difficult to measure meaningfully. "Neutralism" may refer to a withdrawal from the military alliance system, a move that meets with politically insignificant approval. Where questions point to the idyllic examples of Austria or Switzerland, the West Germans' liking of everything Swiss/Austrian induces a large—although apparently declining—number of them to favor that kind of neutrality. In another variation the question poses an alternative between staying on good terms with either the United States or the Soviet Union and being neutral between the two; in that case a good number of West Germans have always preferred to stay neutral. Finally, a question points out that a move toward neutralism might make western Europe safer; that meets with a good deal of approval (even in other European countries and in the United States).

What these polls—which offer something for everybody— seem to show is that the West Germans have no desire to leave the Western alliance but do have some inclination to stay out of superpower conflicts that might get them involved against their wishes or interests (the desire for neutrality has been greatest at times of international crises, such as in 1956 [Hungary/Suez] and 1967 [Vietnam]). Given the fact that perceptions of American leadership qualities have worsened in recent years, it might, after all, seem surprising that the tendency toward neutralism has decreased. In the face of a Soviet expansion of power and an inconsistent American response, West Germany has not turned neutralist, but rather reaffirmed its adherence to the West. This is evident not only in the polls; it was also the message of the March 1983 election outcome.

The National Question

Many outside observers see the greatest danger to the continued adherence of West Germany to the West as deriving from the unresolved national question of Germany. Their fears are based on the premise that no nation can be forever divided; that national frustrations must someday erupt in such overwhelming desires for reunification that almost any price will seem right. To some, the new Ostpolitik was early evidence for such a turn of events; others see their fears confirmed in recent developments.

How to achieve the constitutionally mandated reunification of Germany was the subject of intense political debate throughout the postwar years. Yet during that time, and despite these debates, that goal receded ever further in importance in the West German public's mind. Eventually, almost all hope that it might someday be reached disappeared. And although the new Ostpolitik achieved many of its objectives, that of maintaining a

sense of national cohesion remains in doubt. West Germans continue to pay lip service to the goal of reunification (although
younger West Germans much less so than older ones). Undoubtedly, the political consensus in favor of not formally giving up on
that goal is still strong (partly because many among the political
elite firmly support reunification, partly because giving it up
would require difficult changes of the Basic Law, but partly also
because that minority among the electorate that still might decide its vote on the basis of reunification issues could potentially
determine the outcome of an election and therefore cannot be
ignored). Everything considered, however, it is simply not the
case that the West Germans are so eagerly pursuing national
reunification that they might be willing to drop their Western ties
to achieve it. That was not the case in the past; it will be even
less likely in the future, if only because the younger generations
are least interested in reunification.

In recent years there has been a flood of speculations that the
West Germans' reticence in regard to the national question was
finally being shed, that a new—or renewed—nationalism was
beginning to emerge. This flood was started by the appearance
within parts of the peace movement of the argument that only a
reunified and neutral Germany could escape current security
dilemmas. It received further support by the more broadly based
argument that both parts of Germany share a special responsibility for maintaining peace in Europe (an argument picked up by
the GDR leadership in its anti-intermediate-range nuclear forces
[INF] campaign). And it certainly was not stopped when Chancellor Kohl made it a point, during his visit to Moscow in July
1983, to remind the Russians how determined the Germans are
to achieve reunification.

Yet most of these arguments did not reflect changes in attitudes or even policies, but rather were advanced as part of the
escalating propaganda campaign concerning the INF issue. Thus
some in the peace movement might have hoped that an appeal
for a reunified but neutral Germany could garner new support.
Without doubt, however, the limited appeal that the peace movement has enjoyed is not based on its calls for a reunified Germany. In fact, most of its hard core, but especially the Greens,

are opposed to any such policy. The GDR, which, through West Germany's Communist party, is supporting the peace movement more or less directly, apparently also felt that all-German feelings might be utilized in fostering anti-INF sentiments. Its subtle hints at all-German commonalities and its blatant threats that INF deployment would threaten the achievements of Ostpolitik (mainly free travel across the border) were reminiscent of similar efforts in the 1950s to stop West German rearmament and prevent the Federal Republic from joining the Western alliance. The new government under Chancellor Kohl felt compelled to counter such efforts by seeking to insulate inter-German relations from the icy climate of East-West relations and by offering the GDR a number of inducements. In essence, the Kohl government pursued exactly the kind of Ostpolitik toward the GDR that the CDU, while in opposition, had so vehemently attacked. (Most astonishing, and to its initiator, Franz Josef Strauss, politically troublesome, was an unrestricted bank loan of DM 1 billion to the GDR, in return for which the GDR eventually lowered the mandatory currency exchange, increased the number of those eligible to travel to West Germany, and dismantled automatic shooting devices along the border.) Kohl's continuity in Ostpolitik, coupled with his statements on eventual reunification, was designed with one essential goal in mind: to preempt the GDR's propaganda campaign and to blunt its potential appeal to neutralist sentiments in West Germany.[4] All in all, then, not much has changed in regard to the national question as a result of all these arguments and activities. Reunification remains only a vague goal, theoretically supported but practically little pursued. All scare scenarios concerning developments in Europe and based on allegedly strong longings for reunification rest on weak foundations indeed.

I have argued elsewhere that all the developments described so far—acceptance of democratic values, attachment to the West, adoption of the Federal Republic as a satisfactory new state, recognition of the status quo in Europe, and faded expectations of and demands for eventual reunification—indicate that West Germans are increasingly losing their all-German national consciousness and developing instead a strictly West German one.[5] A West German sense of its own identity seems to have come into existence and appears likely to increase in the future.

This new sense of national identity does, however, have some confusing elements. For instance, more and more West Germans now use the term "Germany" when they mean "West Germany," which is additional evidence for the argument that, for the West Germans at least, "Germany" is shrinking to "West Germany." However, it is not always easy to determine (particularly not for outside observers) which meaning "Germany" carries when used by West Germans; misinterpretations frequently result. This is particularly problematic in connection with another development. The emergence of a new sense of national identity, especially among younger generations, implies the development of strictly West German–focused nationalist attitudes. Much of the newly evident nationalist feeling among younger West Germans—evident in demands for greater West German control over important foreign policy decisions—is, therefore, not a sign for a rebirth of old German nationalism, but rather indicative of the development of West German national attitudes. In that sense, as well as in others, West Germany, according to this interpretation, appears to be well on the way to becoming a normal European nation-state.

That interpretation, alas, is hardly universally accepted. Many analysts continue to insist that an all-German national consciousness still does exist, and that the Federal Republic is far from being a normal nation-state. They emphasize that East Germans still cling to an all-German identity, and that therefore the national question cannot be considered settled. Some agree that the national question appears to be dormant for now but cling to the hope—or express their worries—that it might, under different national and international circumstances, become virulent again.

Yet even in the literature on this question, which recently enjoyed a boom, the emphasis has begun to change. Most of those who argue for a continuing need to settle the German problem do so from a perspective that has largely lost sight of the goal of reestablishing a unified German state. Some suggest that national longings ought no longer focus on the one German state, but instead on the one German culture (a suggestion that tends to neglect the historical fact that a strong sense of Kulturnation almost inevitably produces demands for national unification). An increasing number of observers claim that, if West Germany has not yet developed a separate identity of its own, it ought to do so in the interest of protecting liberty and democracy. In general, a new consensus seems to emerge, which emphasizes the achievement of democratic values for all Europeans at the expense of narrow national interests.

The attention of the West German elite has thus come to focus on some kind of European solution to the German problem: on the creation of a state of affairs in Europe in which the division of Germany would no longer be a problem for the Germans themselves. Frequently, this aimed-for state of affairs is described as a European peace order, in which national boundaries are transcended, old antagonisms dissolved, mutual interdependencies recognized, and military alliances (plus the weapons they pile up) made unnecessary. These hopes, and attendant problems, were eloquently expressed by Richard von Weizsäcker, then governing mayor of Berlin and prominent CDU politician:

> Our fantasy is not good enough to depict that constellation of forces which will create a new European architecture without the old, outlived structure of states, and which will overcome the border now running through the center. The division is therefore, from an historical point of view, more than a momentary creation. But to declare it permanent is unlikely to become historical truth. The center of the continent is, over the long run, as unsuitable for an empire as it is for a border. External pressures, and the goals which are brought from the outside to us, contribute to constantly new developments as much as our own ideas.
>
> Most likely for the center is change. The answers offered by the twentieth century regarding the shape of central Europe so far will not be permanent; they are not final. From an historical perspective, they will not last.[6]

How to get from here to there is the critical question. Not all observers are as reluctant as von Weizsäcker to provide answers. This leaves the field to unrepresentative voices, whose utterings, however, are taken seriously elsewhere and who therefore tend to reinforce existing prejudices concerning ulterior West German motives and designs. The simple fact is, however, that most West Germans do not support a clearly spelled-out design that envisions significant changes in the Federal Republic's current foreign policy posture. At most, the national consensus is expressed in such vague formulations as the following by Foreign Minister Genscher:

> The central element of the European policy of détente, and especially of the German policy toward the East, is the aim to establish and preserve a modus vivendi in a divided Europe—one which casts aside the basic conflict between East and West that cannot be resolved within the foreseeable future and which permits bridges of dialogue and cooperation to be spanned over the rifts formed by different philosophies and long-term goals. In this way it is intended, in the short term, to mitigate the effects of the division of Europe and, in the long term, to foster an evolutionary process in Eastern Europe and the Soviet Union itself, leading to greater freedom for people in the East and to a genuine peace order in Europe.[7]

The national consensus has shifted from achieving the immediate goal of reunification to a deeply felt wish to normalize, over the long run, those conditions in the heart of Europe that today are anything but normal. The new Ostpolitik, still pursued today, traded, as it were, West German adherence to the goal of reunification for measures designed to open the border between East and West and, in the process, to change it. Although such measures were, of course, meant to be of immediate benefit to the Germans in East and West themselves, they were not limited to them. The West Germans' interest in normalization remains larger, and deeper.

The new Ostpolitik was motivated by three concerns: to keep alive as much of a sense of national cohesion as possible; to atone for the sins of the past and come to psychological and political terms with past German behavior toward eastern Europe (a motivation symbolized by Brandt's kneefall in front of the memorial to the Warsaw ghetto); and to normalize relations with eastern Europe in general. These motivations remain strongly in force. It may be, as some argue, that a more normal West Germany has an obvious interest in normalization and may in fact be better able to pursue such a policy. But even if West Germany is not yet a normal nation-state, its commitment to a policy of normalization is not in doubt. And that is one of the reasons most West Germans continue to support a policy of détente vis-à-vis the Soviet Union.

Détente

West Germany's adherence to a policy of détente has occasionally been a subject of great controversy. Within the Federal Republic the CDU, until recently in opposition, argued (at times vehemently) against the policies pursued by Chancellors Brandt and Schmidt. In the United States the chorus of voices complaining about West Germany's dangerous "nostalgia" in regard to détente increased in volume until recently, fed in part by the Federal Republic's refusal to reduce trade with the Soviet Union or to condemn Soviet behavior in Poland. As a result of its longings for détente, so it was argued, West Germany had become "Finlandized" or, worse, "self-Finlandized." Having neglected to maintain its military power in relation to that of the Soviet Union, and being interested only in reaping the benefits of trade and improvements for ethnic Germans, West Germany, so the accusation went, had begun to cower under the Soviet threat and had broken out of the ranks of a united Western front against an expansion of Soviet power and influence.

This is not the place to present a detailed case for or against détente as practiced by West Germany since the early 1970s. It has already been argued that the Soviet Union did not succeed in its alleged goal of turning West Germany away from the West and luring it into an anti-American stance of neutralism or even pro-Sovietism. (Some more evidence in this regard is presented in the section on the military setting.) In any case it seems that the return to power of the CDU (in coalition with the Free Democratic party [FDP]) is evidence enough that the Federal Republic has not become "Finlandized." Still, even the new

CDU/FDP government has not returned to a policy of strict containment. The basic interest of the West German public in a policy of détente is too strong to be neglected; at the same time the public is by no means so unrealistic that it might force the Federal Republic into dangerous policies bordering on appeasement.

The curious mixture of a strong interest in détente with an unabated distrust of the Soviets and their ulterior motives is evident in the picture of West German attitudes that emerges from a number of public opinion polls. Thus in January 1980, after the Soviet invasion of Afghanistan, an overwhelming majority of West Germans in all age-groups and parties favored continuing the policy of détente. One year later almost equally large majorities still thought that West Germany should follow a policy of conciliation rather than a policy of firmness toward the Soviet Union. Adapting to President Reagan's tougher line regarding relations with the Soviet Union met with the refusal of a slightly smaller majority. On the whole, West Germans feel that negotiations with eastern European countries are worth the effort.

Yet the West Germans' evaluation of the achievements of Ostpolitik looks quite different. Most of them believe that, so far at least, it is the Soviet Union that has benefited from improved relations. They question the sincerity of the Soviet Union and think that the Western willingness to come to terms with the Soviet Union is being abused. Although many believe that East and West can coexist peacefully, most are convinced that the Soviet Union is basically unwilling to seek a reconciliation with the West. The belief that Russia is still dangerous and only interested in dominating western Europe does not appear to have decreased as a result of more than a decade of détente in practice.

The picture of West German attitudes regarding détente is one of an uncertain balance between high expectations and soberly realistic evaluations of past experiences. In a way it reflects a loss—or, perhaps better, continued lack—of a perspective regarding the Federal Republic's relations with its neighbors to the East. West Germans know what they want: a relaxation of tensions, an improvement in their security position, a normalization of relations (where normal is defined as the state of affairs existing in western Europe). This is what drives Ostpolitik.

Yet experiences so far tell them that Ostpolitik has not brought them what they long for. Where change seemed to take place within the Soviet orbit (change that might well have been stimulated by détente), it was suppressed by the Soviet Union in application of the Brezhnev Doctrine. This left West Germans (and, of course, not only them) frustrated and with a feeling of helplessness. How to bring about change in eastern Europe and thus changes in East-West relations? Too rigorous a human rights policy, such as once practiced by President Carter, was, on the whole, rejected, partly because it appeared to endanger East-West relations in general, but partly also because it seemed obvious that the cause of human rights could better be furthered through quiet diplomacy and continuing cooperation.

West Germany has always refused (again at the cost of straining German-American relations) to impose economic sanctions against the Soviet Union and other eastern European countries in order to force an improvement of general or specific human rights. It simply does not believe that sanctions are an effective instrument to change Soviet behavior, either by way of compulsion (to force the Soviet Union to do something it does not want to do, or to cease doing something the West does not want it to do) or by way of deterrence (to prevent the Soviet Union from doing something in the future by credibly threatening sanctions and thus changing the basis of Soviet risk-benefit calculations). The West German belief that sanctions are ineffective and the resulting policy of not imposing them have left the Federal Republic open to charges that it is interested in détente merely in order to reap economic benefits from East-West trade (and that it disregards the dangers of such trade arising from a strengthening of the Soviet Union). In fact, West Germans are aware of both benefits and dangers; the difficulty (facing the alliance as a whole) is how to combine the benefits of trade with a prevention of the dangers stemming from a transfer of advanced technologies and large sums of Western currency. But one of the benefits West Germany expects from trade with eastern Europe is political and social change, at least over the long run. For that reason, as well as for the more crassly commercial ones, West Germany will continue to engage in trade with the Soviet Union and other eastern European countries.

Trade is a part of normal relations—another reason West Germans are strongly interested in that aspect of normalization. It is normal not only for today's world of high interdependence (which causes some to worry that West Germany may get too dependent on the Soviet Union), but also from a historical point of view. In fact, there is a strong consensus in West Germany that, historically speaking, eastern and western Europe form a whole, and that it must be the goal of a process of normalization to re-create that unity. Or, as Chancellor Kohl put it recently:

> Because of our geographic situation and because of our history, we Germans are obligated to maintain good relations with West and East. For us Germans there are many historical ties to the East. We share a deep understanding of the cultural unity of Europe, in all its variety and with all its differences. We consider our neighbors in Central and Eastern Europe—not only in this cultural sense—as parts of Europe.[8]

The final—and most important—reason for maintaining relations with the Soviet Union concerns West Germany's security. It simply cannot be in the Federal Republic's interest to neglect relations with the Soviet Union, the single threat to West Germany's security; "making peace requires cooperation with the potential adversary."[9]

Ever since NATO formally adopted the Harmel report in December 1967, it has been a staple of West German political discourse to insist that both détente and defense are equally necessary requirements for a Western security policy. The new Ostpolitik was based on that assessment. Today the Federal Republic, on the basis of a broad political consensus, still pursues détente under the premises of the Harmel report. To quote former Chancellor Schmidt:

> We Europeans want to cooperate with the Soviets, especially on arms reductions. Détente seems like a dirty word in some American

circles, but I must remind you that it is official NATO language. You will not get any European government to repudiate détente. We want to live in peace without knuckling under to the Soviets.[10]

The new chancellor, in essence if not terminology, agrees

Our policy, closely coordinated with our allies, is an offer for dialogue, compromise, and cooperation. It is based on the principles written down already in 1967 in the Harmel-Report of the Alliance which we have always accepted and which for us and our friends still represent the basis for solid relations with the East: firmness and willingness for mutual understanding.[11]

West Germany's strong interest in détente—evident in the essential continuity from Brandt and Schmidt to Kohl—has, on occasion, pushed Bonn into the position of apparent interlocutor or even intermediary between Washington and Moscow. This position is not particularly relished by the West German government and much less so by American administrations. All chancellors have, therefore, denied seeking or exercising such a position. Yet in practical terms West Germany has in fact come close to playing such a role whenever it felt that its interests in détente were jeopardized by growing tensions between the superpowers. Chancellor Kohl's trip to Moscow in July 1983 (in part on a rescue mission for the INF negotiations) represented an element of continuity in that sense as well.

Worse than the charges that the Federal Republic was seeking to play the role of an intermediary (leading at one point to complaints that it was a "floating entity between East and West"[12]) are the frequently voiced suspicions that, because of its overriding interest in détente, West Germany has succumbed to the Soviets' political use of military power. Such accusations have little basis in fact. The Federal Republic has, all in all, not behaved the way it has because of some fear of Soviet power, but because of a rather broadly based consensus regarding its national interests.

West Germans, for a number of reasons, want détente; yet, as we have seen, they expect no miracles, nor do they place much trust in the Soviets. That mixture of motivations and expectations is hardly a prescription for a reckless policy toward the Soviet Union, nor one that would leave West Germany—or worse, the Atlantic alliance—a wreck. In essence, they feel helpless regarding the proper means for achieving the goal of normalization. Such helplessness does not invalidate the goal. On the contrary, it compels every West German government to keep on trying; to develop some satisfying long-term perspective on how to gain change and create new political structures in Europe embodying such change.

To get from here to there, if ever, will be difficult. West Germans have no illusion about that. The Ostpolitik announced by Chancellor Kohl reflects this:

> The Federal Republic will, in the framework of its policies for peace, continue to pursue its course of mutual understanding and compromise, of confidence-building, and of cooperation with the countries of the Warsaw Pact; it will do so tenaciously, yet without any illusions in regard to existing differences.[13]

There is no danger that, in the process, West Germany will break rank with the West. Its Western identity is stronger than any desires for an unconditional policy of détente.

Military Setting: Alliance, Arms, and Angst

West Germany's military setting is defined by its membership in the Atlantic alliance, which was designed to contain the Soviet threat while constraining a potentially dangerous German resurgence. So far, both of these goals have been achieved. West Germany has accepted the constraints and, in the process, became firmly attached to the West. And a further encroachment of Soviet power on the European continent has not taken place, not least because developments in West Germany left it no opening.

More recently, however, doubts are being voiced about Western—and here particularly West German—resoluteness in resisting further Soviet advances. The Federal Republic's strong interest in détente on the grounds that a relaxation of tensions and a reassertion of traditional ties contributes to peace (culminating in the much-maligned concept of a "security partnership" between East and West) led to fears that this might offer the Soviet Union a new opening. Such fears were fed by two factors: the failure of détente to restrain the Soviet Union globally (evident in Soviet advances from Angola to Afghanistan) and the failure of détente-related arms control agreements to contribute to a reining in of Soviet military power. Détente, so its critics argue, allowed the Soviet Union to expand militarily and, as a consequence, globally. (It also did not lead to hoped-for internal changes in the Soviet Union or the Eastern bloc—a third factor of disappointment in détente.)

Western Europe, some fear, did not and cannot escape these failures of détente; the long shadow of Soviet military power is now said to be falling across the continent. West Germany, precisely because it continues to hold on to détente, but also because it does, after all, represent the stake over which the cold war was—and is—being fought, is supposedly most affected by the political effects of Soviet military power. This argument underlies much of the uneasiness in some observers' thinking about the role West Germany is playing vis-à-vis the Soviet Union.

Alliance Issues

The case has repeatedly been made here that the Federal Republic, ever since it joined the Atlantic alliance in 1955, has remained a steadfast supporter of its essential features, particularly collective defense, allied troop presence in West Germany, and a significant West German contribution under NATO command. A neutralist stance or closer cooperation with the Soviet Union at the cost of alliance relations was never acceptable. A more detailed look reveals no different picture. If it is indeed a goal of Soviet policy to split West Germany off the Western alliance, then that goal surely has not been achieved.

Support for NATO has remained unchanged over the years, as an overwhelming majority considers NATO membership essential for the Federal Republic; only a miniscule number (approaching that of Green voters) favor a withdrawal from NATO. Most West Germans seem convinced that NATO membership has been advantageous for their country. The major advantage, presumably, is that in the case of Soviet aggression the United States would come to the defense of the Federal Republic (which willingness deters Soviet aggression in the first place). Most West Germans are convinced that the Americans are in fact prepared to help defend them.

West Germany's own contribution to NATO was originally a matter of great public debate. Still scarred by the wounds, both real and psychic, of World War II, West Germans were deeply divided when, in the early 1950s, the decision to rearm had to be made. The intensity of the public debate over rearmament was much greater than any security-related debate since. Yet Adenauer was able to make the decision in favor of rearmament stick. Approval of the Bundeswehr (the Federal Armed Forces) increased rapidly thereafter; by now the need for a German army is virtually unquestioned.

The Federal Republic's contribution to NATO has increased steadily over the years. Its share of total NATO outlays amounted to just under 5 percent in 1960, rose to over 6 percent in 1970, and jumped to almost 11 percent in 1975; by 1980 it had settled back to roughly 10.4 percent (at which time the West German contribution accounted for almost 21 percent of Europe's NATO outlays).[14] By any measure taken, West Germany's defense efforts increased during the height of détente in terms of annual percentage changes by roughly 3 percent; this increase in defense spending surpassed that of other NATO countries and certainly that of the United States (which decreased drastically between 1968 and 1975). Past West German governments have rightly pointed out that they did not neglect their responsibilities in providing for defense (and, by implication, that they were not lulled into a false sense of security by détente).

More recently, however, the Federal Republic has come under attack again for its allegedly insufficient contribution to the common defense effort. Beginning in 1979, the annual real-term increases of the West German defense budget declined to below 2 percent by 1981 and to zero by 1983; the defense budget in-troduced by the new CDU government for 1984 also showed no real increase. This slowdown in increased defense spending was mandated by the poor performance of the German economy, which—because of the large demands of social entitlement pro-grams—caused a ballooning budget deficit that, in turn, led to efforts at budget cutting, from which defense efforts could not be excluded. The West German public was in full agreement on that point.

West Germany's declining defense efforts contributed greatly to strains in German-American relations, furthered by many an acerbic exchange of arguments, both valid and cheap. On the American side there was increasing clamor for a withdrawal of American troops, given the fact (so it was alleged) that West Germans were no longer interested in defending themselves and, in any case, were selling out to the Russians (through the gas pipeline deal, for instance). The German side pleaded budgetary constraints, pointed to the fact that a stable economy (a prereq-uisite for a stable society and thus stable politics) is an important element of security, argued that it was contributing in un-measured ways to the defense efforts (from its compulsory mili-tary service allowing large reserves to providing scarce real estate for foreign troops), and claimed that some of its foreign aid (particularly to NATO member Turkey) ought to be counted as well. Given projections of future low economic growth (with attendant social problems), the Federal Republic will continue to be unable to increase its defense spending drastically. In es-sence, this has nothing to do with caving in to the threat of Soviet power.

Deterrence and Defense

One of the reasons for the West Germans' reluctance to increase outlays for conventional defense efforts substantially has to do with the basic conviction that, for West Germany at least, deter-ring war is more important than preparing to fight one. The critical question, of course, is how such deterrence can be achieved; it is the central question for the alliance. If, as many

West Germans feel, conventional defense at the central front is either undesirable (because a conventional war on German soil would leave Germany once again destroyed) or, given geographical factors and Soviet conventional superiority, doubtful, then deterrence must derive primarily from the threat of using nuclear weapons. Because the Federal Republic is barred from possessing nuclear weapons of its own and the deterrent forces of France and Great Britain offer no credible alternative, it must rely on the guarantees of the United States to use nuclear weapons in the case of an attack against West Germany. This shifts the burden of deterrence onto the United States in a dual sense: To make those guarantees credible, the United States must maintain forces in Europe equipped with nuclear weapons (and certain to be involved when war breaks out); and the United States must be willing—particularly once the Soviets gained the capability to retaliate—to risk the destruction of its own cities for the defense of West German ones.

It is understandable that the United States—in order to make that burden less heavy, but also to make deterrence more credible—should be interested in stronger conventional defense efforts. An all-out conventional effort on the part of West Germany is impossible, however: It would detract from deterrence and thus make war more likely; it cannot be afforded (neither financially nor politically); and it would require preparations for war that West Germany simply could not tolerate.[15] Thus the West German interest in deterrence and the American preference for defense were bridged in a compromise called "flexible response." It calls for some conventional defense against an attack but an early use of nuclear weapons if the Soviet attack cannot be stopped in the forward defense positions. The expectation is that the threat of an early use of nuclear weapons would deter the Soviet Union in the first place, or from further escalation, because eventually all-out nuclear war might break out; the fear is that, unless the West maintains "escalation dominance" (and that seems now denied by Soviet measures), and perhaps even then, the United States itself might be deterred from using nuclear weapons. By now the argument has come full circle, with some prominent Americans arguing for a policy of no first use of nuclear weapons (which implies a conventional buildup)[16] and equally prominent West Germans insisting on the option for first use.[17]

The various arguments in favor of raising or lowering the nuclear threshold, reestablishing "escalation dominance," preparing for "war-fighting" options, or closing a Soviet window of opportunity have by now become so arcane and among its proponents and opponents so controversial that the public is left thoroughly confused, if not bewildered—yet in a stage of agitation. Usually the West German public suffers from what might be called an "ostrich syndrome": Faced with the dilemmas of nuclear deterrence and conventional defense (which, in many ways, are indeed beyond human reckoning), it prefers not to think about these issues. Occasionally, however, it is confronted with these problems, if only by the activities of succeeding generations who have yet to learn that the dilemmas of nuclear deterrence allow no easy answers, and by the reaction of officials who must try to rationalize the unthinkable.

The debate of these issues has recently been intense, not only in West Germany, provoked by NATO's decision to deploy intermediate nuclear forces in Europe unless the Soviet Union reduces its corresponding arsenal. The controversy has gone beyond the question whether INF deployment is in fact necessary in western Europe (on which there is disagreement even among reputable experts); it has also surpassed the question whether the threat of such deployment is needed in order to induce the Soviets to agree to arms control measures, or the question whether the realization of that threat is necessary in order to show the Soviets that NATO is capable of carrying out its decisions in the face of Soviet counterefforts. The debate has come to focus on the morality of deterrence itself, on which issue the churches (in the Federal Republic as well as in the United States) weighed in with lengthy and well-reasoned documents. Massive, but peaceful, demonstrations for peace (and against INF deployment) have shown that this issue is capable of mobilizing many people. The West Germans' commitment to a posture of deterrence has thus been thrown into doubt. Yet a closer look at available public opinion data shows that attitudes have in fact changed very little during the course of this debate; only their intensity may be stronger.

All in all, a majority of West Germans agrees that a Soviet attack can be deterred if the West is adequately armed. Given the fact that only a small minority professes to being worried about inadequate defense, the assumption can be made that most West Germans consider deterrence still to be effective.

The basic dilemma of a deterrence strategy based on nuclear weapons—that one must threaten (credibly at that) to do something that, were it to become necessary, one would infinitely prefer not to do—is very much evident in West German public opinion. An overwhelming majority declares its willingness to fight against potential Russian domination, even if the brunt of such fighting were to take place on German soil. But only a minority is prepared to support fighting a nuclear war in order to maintain democracy, and even fewer would support fighting a war if nuclear weapons were to be used on German soil. Consequently, a first use of nuclear weapons by NATO has consistently found few supporters. These results likely reflect the West Germans' sense of realism (could there be a democracy after a nuclear war?) more than any sense of giving in to Soviet threats. In any case it seems doubtful that on the basis of such public attitudes the Soviet Union could have enough assurance to start a war without being opposed (where such defense implies the danger of escalation to nuclear war). The stability of these attitudes over time suggests that the Soviets have not been able to score a major impact on the West German psyche.

Angst and Peace

Many observers claim that a growing sense of angst—anxiety and fear—represents precisely such a Soviet impact on the collective psyche of the West Germans; they fear that because of such angst, West Germans may seek to gain peace at any price. Of course, fear of the Soviet threat is also a prerequisite for increased defense efforts (for which reason Western leaders at times seem eager, if unwittingly so, to do the Soviets' bidding). Expressions of angst cannot, therefore, necessarily serve as an indicator for a general willingness to appease the Soviet Union; they may also indicate a greater preparedness to seek peace through a stabilization of the military balance.

Angst, as measured by the fear of war, is not a stable condition in West German society; rather—and not surprisingly so—it appears mostly as a reaction to political events, increasing sharply at times of international crises and falling off equally rapidly thereafter. No doubt fear of war—and thus a sense of angst—increased quite drastically after 1979 with the Soviet invasion of Afghanistan, the events in Poland, American rhetoric about "going to the source" of the troubles in Central America, hints about nuclear warning shots, and the debate over nuclear rearmament. It reached its high point in late 1981 but has since dropped off again. (The beginning of arms control talks in November 1981 probably helped, as did the failure of the Soviet Union to intervene militarily in Poland.)

West German perceptions of the Soviet threat itself are somewhat less erratic than the fears of war but are still subject to the influence of external events. Firmly convinced in the early 1950s that the Federal Republic was threatened by the Soviet Union, the West Germans gradually lost that sense of threat, which reached a low point in the early years of the new Ostpolitik. After Afghanistan the feeling of being threatened by the Soviet Union increased again but declined once more in a relatively short time; however, it remained above the level reached during the détente years. On balance, then, the Soviets have not been able to convince a majority of West Germans of their peaceful intentions, but undoubtedly attitudes on this issue have become sharply polarized in recent years.

According to their own perception of the military balance between East and West, West Germans have good reason to feel threatened by the Soviet Union. In what might be considered a remarkably realistic assessment of actual trends, a steadily increasing number of West Germans have, since the early 1970s, become convinced that the East is militarily stronger than the West. It may also be a sign of realism, however, that not all who thought the Soviet Union stronger militarily felt that the Soviets were "more powerful in the world."

By fall 1983, however, the number of those who thought NATO at least equal to the Warsaw Pact was once again slightly larger than the number of those assigning superiority to the Soviet Union. (This may have been as much the result of Reagan administration boasts in this regard as owing to claims by opponents of INF modernization that an imbalance did not really exist.)

Nevertheless, given the overall strong perception of Soviet military superiority, it is hardly surprising that an overwhelming majority of West Germans believes that the Soviet Union is out to maintain or increase its superiority; nor that a similarly large majority is convinced that it ought to be the goal of Western policy to reestablish the military balance. What has surprised observers is the fact that in the face of such perceptions it has become so difficult to push through measures designed to redress the imbalance.

One reason for this reluctance—namely, budgetary constraints—has already been alluded to. Another reason seems perfectly obvious yet is fraught with great political difficulties: West Germans (and not only they) would much prefer that the imbalance be redressed through arms control measures rather than through Western rearmament. Particularly as concerns nuclear weapons—of which some 6,000 are already stored in western Europe (with some to be removed)—feelings are fairly strong that more, and more modern, weapons are not necessarily an improvement in the military balance. Less is better, and that must be achieved primarily through arms control. In addition, many fear that such rearmament might be driven by American desires for military superiority of the United States, and they worry that rearmament efforts, coupled with a reluctance to engage in serious arms control negotiations, would sustain, or even speed up, an endless and therefore dangerous arms race. The public pressure, then, was for arms control and against rearmament and, as the INF deployment date neared, increasingly so. Some analysts believe that such pressure is the result of Soviet power and attendant propaganda, or, in any case, in the Soviets' interest, because invariably a strong Western push for arms control agreements results in inadequate measures, controlling neither arms nor the Soviet Union. In the West German case, however, the evidence is by no means overwhelming that, should it become necessary, the Federal Republic will refuse to take adequate steps to improve the military balance.

One frequently mentioned example of Soviet influence on Western decision making as the result of angst is, of course, INF deployment. NATO's dual-track decision as such, i.e., to negotiate with the Soviet Union about a reduction of Soviet medium-range missiles and to deploy Western missiles should these negotiations fail, met, depending on polling organization and the wording used, either with considerable approval or with increasing skepticism. Of course, these polls revealed little about which of the two tracks was actually preferred. Other polls have never left any doubt but that the negotiating track was infinitely preferred to the deployment track.

As the negotiating and deployment deadline neared, the West German public was still overwhelmingly in favor of continued negotiations and delay of deployment. In part, this merely reflected the primary importance attached to arms control (and the dubious wisdom of linking arms control negotiations with deployment decisions under a rigid deadline). To be sure, some polls, properly worded, showed support for deployment, revealing yet again the confused state of the public's mind. But in some respects, attitudes had hardened against deployment. Thus an increasing majority felt certain that the stationing of new missiles in West Germany would endanger, rather than strengthen, peace and security. And many were convinced that neither superpower had negotiated in good faith (for which reason they supported further—and then serious—negotiations).

Yet this partial hardening of attitudes against deployment of Pershing IIs and cruise missiles came too late to be of political relevance. For the fact remains that despite apparently strong feelings against the new missiles—but perhaps also because of the public's confused state of mind—West German voters overwhelmingly voted in March 1983 for the party that had taken a firm stand on the necessity for deployment, should negotiations fail. All in all, the missile issue was not an important one in that election, despite efforts by the SPD to make it a Raketenwahl-kampf. The CDU government, which includes some who once saw in West German hesitation on INF modernization the long shadow of Soviet military power at work, was thus placed in a position to fulfill the deployment part of the dual-track decision: hardly evidence of overwhelming angst and attendant political effects of Soviet military power.

With the SPD out of power and the CDU seemingly solidly entrenched, the focus of fears concerning West German behavior in regard to the dual-track approach became the peace movement. It sprang up when that decision was taken and gained support with Ronald Reagan's election to the presidency. The 1983 election results showed that the peace movement has not become a major political force. Yet although its hard core of support is relatively small, it cannot entirely be neglected. Peace—how could it be otherwise!—is a topic of great emotional appeal, and many of the slogans of the peace movement have fallen on fertile ground. The massive demonstrations in fall 1983 showed the extent of that appeal.

Worrisome is the possibility that the hard core of the peace movement might engage in potentially violent demonstrations against the stationing of new missiles. Both sides have already prepared for this possibility, the peace movement by emphasizing the need for civil disobedience, particularly in Germany with its disastrous history in that regard (which led to a lively debate about the right to resistance against unpopular measures), and the government by strengthening laws against violent demonstrators (including some questionable provisions). It is hoped that such preparations will prove to be unnecessary. The peace movement is, in any case, faced with a dilemma. Public sympathy for demonstrations is likely to decrease rapidly if they were to turn violent; yet peaceful demonstrations, however impressive they are, will not change the government's mind. In short, the Federal Republic seems well set to weather any "hot" season produced by opposition to INF deployment. Neither angst nor fear is likely to change its military setting significantly.

Political Setting: The Primacy of Stability

Since its foundation in 1949 the Federal Republic has been politically remarkably stable; to some observers that is the real miracle of postwar Germany. In part this was achieved under the presence and guidance of the allied powers; partly it was due to West German leadership qualities; and to some extent it was probably a matter simply of good luck. The generally favorable economic climate of the postwar years, which formed the backdrop for the Federal Republic's "economic miracle," may also have had something to do with it.

Mostly, however, the political stability of the Federal Republic appears to be the result of a careful design of the political system itself and the consequent support it was given by the West German people. In this section the main features of the political system will be briefly presented, with a view toward analyzing the current political situation in terms of its likely repercussions on West German foreign policy. Its purpose is to seek yet additional answers to two related questions already mostly answered: How stable is the Federal Republic likely to be? And how stable will its foreign policy be?

One overriding element of stability has been the strong constitutional and political position of the chancellor. It is the chancellor who sets the guidelines for policies and who alone nominates or dismisses his colleagues in the cabinet. A strong chancellor can pursue his policies without too much interference from his cabinet or the Bundestag. He is also not subject to too much pressure from the public at large, as the Basic Law (drafted in such a way as to incorporate lessons learned from the collapse of the Weimar Republic) allows for almost no direct expressions of public will.

A chancellor is strong as long as he enjoys the full support of his party—and that of any coalition partner—in the Bundestag. When he loses that support (often the result of a prior loss of public support) he is liable to fall from power. The strong position of the parties, and particularly of their parliamentary representatives, allows for changes in government even without elections. Parties, such as the FDP in recent years, that have only little electoral support, but enough seats in the Bundestag to form a majority coalition, can, for whatever reasons, change coalitions and thus form new governments. Whether the relative ease with which such changes can be effected contributes to political stability or reflects, in fact, potential instability, is a much debated question. Without doubt, the FDP has played the important role of translating attitudinal changes in the public at large into political changes at the level of government, thus adding a measure of flexibility to potentially too rigid a system. At the same time the need to reach political compromises in coalition governments has also contributed to greater flexibility overall, while preventing any one party from shifting too far from previous courses; this is particularly the case in regard to foreign policy, since the smaller coalition partner has traditionally claimed the position of foreign minister for itself. It was not least for these reasons that the FDP, in March 1983, received enough (mostly intellectual) votes to push it over the 5-percent hurdle (which it has failed to surpass in a number of regional elections).

Parties elected to the Bundestag but unwilling to enter into binding coalitions represent an acute threat to political stability in cases in which a government cannot be formed without a coalition of some kind. The political system permits two answers to this problem. One would be a grand coalition between the two major parties. This was practiced once in the years 1966 through 1969; that experience pointed out the problem that such a government may be suffering from a lack of political legitimacy because it leaves no room for an effective opposition, thus causing substantial opposition movements outside of parliament. The other solution would be a change in electoral law (easily effected by majority vote in the Bundestag), providing for direct, rather than proportional, elections. On the assumption that established voting patterns continue, this would likely eliminate the small parties from the Bundestag. So far the political system did not have to take recourse to this expedient; fears that it might have to after the March 1983 elections (which brought the Greens into the Bundestag) proved unfounded.

The foreign policy orientations of the major parties are based on a broad consensus, which at times of difficult reorientations may, however, break down. This was the case during the rearmament debate in the early 1950s, during the debate over the new Ostpolitik in the early 1970s, and has now become the case with the debate over INF deployment. Past experience shows that the consensus becomes reestablished within a relatively short period, as parties out of power readjust to new realities.

The CDU is in no danger of breaking away from the established consensus. It is solidly committed to the Atlantic alliance, somewhat more interested in pursuing a harder line toward the Soviet Union (although its many supporters among West German industry prevent it from taking too hard a line), and generally more oriented toward a tight-fisted foreign policy. It was instructive to observe how easily the CDU, once again in power, adapted to the foreign policy of the previous government in its insistence on keeping lines of communication open with the Soviet Union and between the superpowers.

The party in danger of shifting to a radical stance is the SPD. Its active party membership was swelled some time ago by highly educated younger members committed to a purer kind of socialism and a more conciliatory foreign policy than pursued by the old-time membership consisting largely of representatives of the working class. The SPD thus came under internal stress between the "academic" leftists and the more practical-minded traditionalists. The SPD lost support—and eventually its hold on power—because of these internal strains, which ruined its public image and rendered it incapable of dealing with urgent political and economic problems. In addition, the very fact that it seemed to adopt a more conciliatory line toward the Soviet Union while increasing its always latent anti-Americanism cost it electoral support.

Now out of power, the SPD is under some pressure to adopt even more radical foreign policy positions in the hope of reestablishing its ideological purity and of attracting the voter potential of the peace movement. It remains to be seen whether this double strategy will prove successful. Parties out of power, although tempted to a policy of ideological purity, have generally had to learn that the road to electoral success lay not in radicalization, but in moderation. The SPD may yet be forced to learn that lesson as well. And the voter potential of the peace movement is not so large that the SPD could hope to gain more votes there than it stands to lose among its traditional supporters. For that reason, too, a formal coalition with the Greens seems highly unlikely.

Should the SPD, as now appears certain, remain in opposition for some time to come, radicalization may well be the initial response. In that case, difficult foreign policy decisions would have to be made without recourse to a bipartisan consensus. Similar experiences in the past, however, suggest that the political system is well able to tolerate such lack of consensus and make decisions stick. The only problem—and it could become a considerable one—would be if a radical SPD opposition against INF deployment were to legitimize extraparliamentary opposition and thus encourage a shift of the political debate from the houses of parliament to the streets of the Federal Republic.

The foreign policy consensus still largely prevailing is most definitely not shared by the Greens, now represented in the Bundestag with a motley collection of people and interests. It is their declared goal to withdraw the Federal Republic from the Western alliance and to follow a security policy based on a direct understanding with the Soviet Union—this apart from goals pertaining to alternative life- (and love) styles, different processes of democratic politics, and environmental protection. The limited electoral appeal of the Greens is probably based less on their foreign policy orientations—with the possible exception of their absolute stand against INF deployment—and more on their opposition to big government, big industry, waste of the environment, and opulent life-styles. Isolated as they are politically, the Greens will not be able to achieve their goals, although in some respects they may be influential in raising public consciousness regarding certain issues. In turn, through their participation in the political process, the Greens may well become socialized to it and thus rendered even more harmless politically. In that sense their representation in the Bundestag and in a number of Länder legislatures is not without some benefits.

For most of its history the Federal Republic has proved remarkably governable and its foreign policy similarly stable. Will this state of affairs continue? Undoubtedly, the general conditions will become more difficult: Lack of economic growth, increased international interdependence, and the threat of a spiraling arms race will severely tax the capabilities of the political system. Yet the Federal Republic, owing to the genius of its constitution, the consensus shared by its major parties. and the support given by its people, should be able to weather these difficulties successfully.

Notes

1. For a summary of public opinion data and innumerable studies up to the early 1970s, see Gebhard L. Schweigler, *National Consciousness in Divided Germany* (London and Beverly Hills, Calif.: Sage. 1975). More recent surveys can be found in David Conradt, "Charging German Political Culture," in *The Civic Culture Revisited,* ed. Gabriel A. Almond and Sidney Verba (Boston: Little, Brown, 1980), and Heinz Rausch, "Politisches Bewußtsein und politische Einstellungen im Wandel," in *Die Identität der Deutschen,* ed. Werner Weidenfeld (Bonn: Bundeszentrale für politische Bildung, 1983).

2. Josef Joffe, "The Greening of Germany," *The New Republic,* 14 Feb. 1983, 22.

3. William Schneider, "Elite and Public Opinion: The Alliance's New Fissure?" *Public Opinion,* Feb./March 1983, 6.

4. See "Kohls Beharren auf dem Wiedervereinigungs-Ziel ist nur ein neues Stück einer alten Linie," *Frankfurter Allgemeine Zeitung,* 14 July 1983, 5.

5. Schweigler, *National Consciousness.*

6. Richard von Weizsäcker, *Die deutsche Geschichte geht weiter* (Berlin: Siedler, 1983), 284f.

7. Hans-Dietrich Genscher, "Toward an Overall Western Strategy for Peace, Freedom and Progress," *Foreign Affairs,* Fall 1982. 43.

8. Helmut Kohl, *Programm der Erneuerung,* 72.

9. Chancellor Kohl at the Williamsburg Summit, according to "Kohl to Probe Soviets on Summit with U.S.," *Washington Post,* 1 June 1983, 1.

10. Helmut Schmidt, *IHT,* 23 May 1983. Elsewhere Schmidt argued: "The fact that we are meeting here [in Hamburg] just 40 miles from the nearest Soviet military installation will make you understand that the

Germans will never be in the forefront of Cold Warriors" ("A View Across the Atlantic," *Time,* 9 May 1983, 15, from a speech by Schmidt to a *Time* conference).

11. Kohl, *Programm der Erneuerung,* 74.

12. "Mr. Haig was reported to have told Mr. Schmidt that Washington was uncertain whether Bonn saw itself these days as part of the NATO alliance or as a 'floating entity between East and West' " ("Haig, on Eve of NATO Talks, Says He Wants Unity on Soviet Sanctions," *New York Times,* 11 Jan. 1982). Henry Kissinger complained at the same time: "It cannot go on . . . that Europeans claim to 'interpret' America and the Soviet Union to each other as if there were no moral or political difference between the two" ("Something Is Deeply Wrong in the Atlantic Alliance," *Washington Post,* 21 Dec. 1981, A21).

13. Kohl, *Programm der Erneuerung,* 74.

14. Quoted according to James R. Golden, *NATO Burden-Sharing: Risks and Opportunities, The Washington Papers/96* (New York: Praeger, 1983), 67. Golden presents an excellent survey of the intricacies of measuring defense contributions.

15. It is inconceivable, for instance, that the Federal Republic might build a network of fortifications along the border to East Germany, if only because it literally does not want to cement the division of Germany.

16. McGeorge Bundy, George F. Kennan, Robert S. McNamara, and Gerard Smith, "Nuclear Weapons and the Atlantic Alliance," *Foreign Affairs* 60, no. 4 (Spring 1972): 753–768.

17. Karl Kaiser, Georg Leber, Alois Mertes, Franz-Josef Schulze, "Nuclear Weapons and the Preservation of Peace: A German Response," *Foreign Affairs* 60, no 5 (Summer 1982): 1157–1170.

Chapter 2

The Setting of U.S. Foreign Policy Toward the Federal Republic of Germany

Alan A. Platt

The Federal Republic of Germany has occupied a uniquely important place in postwar American foreign relations. Whether or not there has existed a "special relationship" between the United States and the Federal Republic, as some have suggested, is a matter for debate. There is no question, though, that Germany has been vitally important to postwar American foreign policy interests. In political terms, the Federal Republic has been a critical factor in the formulation of America's stance toward the countries of western and eastern Europe as well as toward the Soviet Union. Economically, the Federal Republic has been the principal focus of American policy in Europe—both in terms of European reconstruction in the immediate postwar years and subsequently as West Germany's economy has played a central role in the economic growth of the West. And in military terms, particularly in light of the Federal Republic's geographic position and the importance of the Bundeswehr, the Federal Republic has been of major importance to both American and NATO defense planners.

Nevertheless, there has been a perceptible asymmetry in the place West Germany has occupied in America's postwar foreign relations as compared with the role that the United States has played in the Federal Republic's foreign relations. During most of the postwar period, America and its interests have been at the center—not near the center—of German foreign policy. Whether regarding political, military, or economic issues, American interests have seemingly played a vital role in the formulation of West Germany's foreign policy stances. Indeed, few significant postwar foreign policy initiatives have been undertaken by the Federal Republic without American counsel and assistance, or at a minimum acquiescence.

On the other hand, American concern for West German interests, although important, has not occupied an analogous position in the formulation of America's postwar foreign policies. Witness the involvement of the United States in Indochina. Or American policy toward the People's Republic of China in the late 1970s. Or U.S. policy concerning the Yamal pipeline in the early 1980s. These have all been foreign policy issues wherein the U.S. posture was primarily driven by considerations other than concern for German interests.

What accounts for this asymmetry? A significant part of the answer lies in America's view of its global interests and responsibilities in the world, as contrasted to the Federal Republic's primary focus on European affairs. Put another way, the United States frequently has had to make decisions on a variety of far-flung issues in which Germany has had only a minor interest.

Immediate Postwar U.S. Policy

The roots of these global American interests and the resulting asymmetry in U.S. and German perspectives on world politics lie in recent history. During the last stages of and at the end of World War II, many within the U.S. government, led by Secretary of State Cordell Hull, envisaged a limited American role in postwar world politics. It was widely hoped that there would be "an era of good feelings" between the United States and the Soviet Union so that the United States could go back to focusing primarily on its domestic affairs. For most people inside and outside the American government the issue in 1945–46 was not whether Soviet cooperation could be won in the postwar period, but how it could be best and most quickly ensured so that the United States could return to a highly limited role in world affairs.

This illusion was, of course, shattered as the Soviets imposed control over much of eastern Europe, including Poland, Hungary, Bulgaria, Albania, and Romania. And as the illusion of cordial relations with the Soviets progressively receded, there was a growing realization that the United States, to ensure its own security, would have to undertake to balance Soviet power and influence in various parts of the world. This meant for the United States, in essence, the adoption of a global perspective on international relations, with concern for the American-Soviet relationship at the center of the new U.S. perspective. It also necessarily meant a decline in influence in the United States on the part of both traditional isolationists, who preferred to see a complete withdrawal of American troops from Europe after the war, and those on the left, who hoped to build on the wartime alliance and forge a harmonious grouping among the allies, including the Soviets.

Concerning Germany, there was some support in the U.S. government during and immediately after the war for treasury secretary Henry Morgenthau's plan to denazify, democratize, and fragment Germany by making it primarily agricultural. In addition, there was substantial support for this plan in London and Paris, as the other allied powers hoped to make sure that Germany would not soon be in a position to again threaten the peace in western Europe. However, when President Truman and most of the leadership of the American government came to the realization that the United States would have to play the key role in containing Soviet expansionism, they quickly abandoned the Morgenthau Plan. Although there was not a consensus among the allies about how to deal with Germany in 1945–46—a fact reflected in the division of Germany into four zones—there emerged a widely held view in Washington by late 1946 that if Europe was to get back on its feet, Germany would have to be rebuilt. This viewpoint mirrored, not coincidentally, the recommendations of those individuals responsible for American policy on the spot in Germany, most important General Lucius Clay, the American deputy military governor from 1945 to 1947 and the military governor in the years 1947 to 1949.

In a widely publicized speech in Stuttgart in September 1946,

Secretary of State James Byrnes signaled this changed U.S. view
and the emerging governmental consensus on the future of Germany. In the Stuttgart speech Byrnes declared that it was vital
for American interests that Germany develop a self-sustaining
economy and build up its own capacity to export. Byrnes subsequently went on to argue that, for its economy to recover, Germany would have to be given primary responsibility for running
its own affairs.[1]

The fact that Byrnes was the official to announce this change
in American policy was not without practical and symbolic
significance. In the last stages of the war and immediately thereafter, Byrnes was among that group of advisers to President
Truman who favored the continuation of a wartime alliance, led
by the United States and the USSR, against Germany. This view
was in fact embodied in Secretary of State Byrnes' offer to the
Soviets in July 1945 to conclude a twenty-five-year, four-power
treaty guaranteeing German demilitarization, an offer that was
not accepted by the Soviets. By September 1946 Byrnes' views
had changed drastically. Now he supported Germany's economic recovery and political reconstruction and preferred to try
to incorporate America's portion of Germany into the West's
sphere of influence as a way to contain the Soviets. As Thomas
Bailey, the distinguished Stanford historian has wryly observed
about U.S. policy during this period: "The ghost of Hitler must
have laughed ghoulishly to see the West building up Germany
against Communist Russia."[2]

After the Byrnes speech a number of initiatives were undertaken by the United States to speed German economic and political recovery. Among the most notable of these measures were
the establishment of an embryonic German state, Bizonia, in
January 1947 (France was to join this British-American entity
later); the implementation of the Marshall economic aid program, which had been enunciated in a speech by Secretary of
State George Marshall in June 1947; the overhaul of the German
currency system, carried out by the U.S. military government;
the invigoration of the General Agreement on Tariffs and Trade
(GATT); and the implementation of a multifaceted effort to en-

courage Germans to play an active role in governing their own affairs.

Frustrated and threatened by these initiatives and seeking a way to undermine the growing American influence and presence in western Europe, the Soviets reacted to the new U.S. policy toward Germany by blockading Berlin in June 1948. Moreover, both the United States and the Soviet Union viewed the blockade in terms larger than just Berlin. This major Soviet initiative was an obvious test of and potential threat to America's commitment to defend Germany. In response, the United States opted to answer the Soviet challenge in a massive and ultimately decisive way. Among other things, allied planes eventually flew in roughly 13,000 tons of food and fuel daily to meet the needs of the 2.5 million Berliners. Faced with failure, the Soviets ended the blockade in May 1949, 324 days later.[3]

In putting enormous pressure on the airlift capacity of the United States, the Soviet decision to blockade Berlin—followed later by the war in Korea—had the incidental effect of concentrating American governmental and public attention on the serious political, military, and economic problems facing the emerging postwar German state. In time, this focused attention had a direct, positive, galvanizing, and wide-ranging impact on U.S. policy toward Germany. *Inter alia,* it led the U.S. government to work actively to bring about the creation of an independent German state tied to the West in the late 1940s and later full sovereignty for the Federal Republic in 1955, when the Allied High Commission formally rescinded the occupation statutes. The 1948 Berlin blockade also had the effect of solidifying American and Western guarantees of the freedom of West Berlin, whose place in the West was finalized with the conclusion of the Quadripartite Agreement on Berlin in 1971. Finally, the Soviet attempt to blockade Berlin directly led to direct American encouragement and support of European economic cooperation, integration, and independence.

In sum, it was the United States, having played a leading role in defeating the Third Reich in World War II, that defended Germany in the face of a growing Soviet threat in the immediate postwar years; that used a massive airlift to preserve the independence of Berlin; and that played an active role in helping to bring the Federal Republic of Germany into existence as part of the Western camp.

The United States, the Federal Republic, and the Soviet Union in the Postwar Era

The anti-Soviet context for the setting of American policy toward Germany in the immediate postwar years did not end with the 1949 proclamation of the Basic Law, the creation of the Federal Republic, and the preservation of Berlin. Indeed, Germany was central to the American policy of containing the Soviet Union at the beginning of the cold war in the late 1940s and this has continued up to the present. Former American ambassador to Germany Martin Hillenbrand has summarized this situation in the following way:

> The beginnings of the Cold War came out of the growing appreciation in the West and in the United States that Soviet intentions were not benign, and that the primary objective of the Soviet Union was first of all politically to dominate Western Germany, and to incorporate its economic potential in its own empire, and eventually to do that with all of Western Europe, thereby adding the strength of Western Europe to its own industrial potential. Now, I think that it is fair to say that that ultimate goal remains a Soviet objective even though the alliance has frustrated its realization for a period of more than 30 years.[4]

The creation of the NATO alliance in 1949 and West Germany's subsequent accession to membership in 1955 were, of course, central to this American and Western policy to counter the Soviet threat to western Europe, with the maintenance of a relatively large American army and air force presence in Germany being a critical element in this effort. There were numerous other initiatives, though, besides the creation of NATO and the maintenance of American troops in Germany that were pursued in Europe in the context of containing Soviet influence. Two of the most noteworthy were the formation of the Western

European Union, an organization that created for the Western allies a nonthreatening framework for German rearmament and that was pursued after the 1952–54 effort to establish a European Defense Community was thwarted by the French parliament; and the creation of the European Coal and Steel Community, which in time led to the establishment of the European Economic Community (EEC) in 1958, with the conclusion of the Treaty of Rome.

In these and other efforts American and German interests were largely complementary, although Germany was clearly the dependent junior partner in the relationship. The reality was, moreover, that for their own reasons both the United States and the Federal Republic of Germany had an interest in rebuilding Germany in economic, political, and military terms; expanding economic cooperation and integration among the powers of western Europe; strengthening the Atlantic community through the building of a strong NATO and increased transatlantic political and economic cooperation; and integrating Germany into both the European and the Atlantic communities as a full member. Accordingly, for the United States, discussions with the Soviets about a neutralized Germany were unacceptable. Germany, in America's view, was to be a bulwark in the West's efforts to counter the growth of Soviet influence and power in western and central Europe.

Although there was a close congruence of American and West German interests during the 1950s and 1960s concerning NATO, the European communities, and most bilateral issues, there were some strains in the evolving U.S.-West German relationship. These strains stemmed largely from the fact that the United States was a world power with a global perspective and global interests and the Federal Republic had more narrowly focused interests and perspectives. Most important, in the course of the 1950s there was a gradual realization in Washington that while it was important for the West to do all it could to contain the growth of Soviet influence, it was necessary at the same time to discuss with Moscow a variety of political, economic, and arms control issues. This American policy toward Moscow understandably worried many Germans inside and outside the government, and resulting German concern was frequently conveyed to Washington. For this U.S. policy was being pursued at a time when Moscow was steadfastly opposed to the two major foreign policy objectives of the Federal Republic: reunification and rearmament. And it was the German view that only firm Western strength would lead to German reunification, a "reunification in freedom" through the withdrawal of Soviet forces and the simultaneous end of the "puppet" East German government; that this reunification was an essential precondition for lasting peace in Europe; and that Europeans, Americans, and Soviets should not be allowed to get used to the division of Germany as a permanent fact of life. Accordingly, the Adenauer-led German government was at odds with the United States as to whether there should be any discussions with the Soviets about such things as European security and disarmament before reaching agreement on German sovereignty and full equality. In Bonn, but not in Washington, such U.S.-Soviet discussions were viewed as implicit recognition and acceptance of the German Democratic Republic.[5]

In time, particularly after the departure of Konrad Adenauer from the chancellorship in 1963, the German government came to accept more easily America's discussions and dealings with the Soviet Union and eastern Europe. This did not signify that the Federal Republic had forsaken its primary goal of German reunification, or that it was satisfied with reunification resulting from glacial movements of history. Rather, it suggested an evolution in thinking about how best to bring this goal about. As Anton DePorte has noted, in the course of the 1960s, "the Germans not only put up with the American switch [toward the Soviets] but creatively adapted their own foreign policy to the lessons of disappointment. Detente began to offer more tangible international rewards than cold war."[6]

After some initial *démarches* in the mid-1960s, West Germany's efforts at reconciliation with the East—the Ostpolitik—in fact began in earnest when Willy Brandt acceded to the chancellorship in 1969. Under Brandt a number of initiatives were undertaken that have provided the underpinnings of recent

German policy toward the Soviets. The major benchmarks of Brandt's policy of Ostpolitik still exist today, including the Moscow Treaty of August 1970, the Warsaw Treaty of December 1970, the 1972 Basic Treaty between the Federal Republic and the German Democratic Republic, and the Quadripartite Agreement on Berlin of 1971. Moreover, these initiatives have since been supplemented by a number of other agreements on technical, cultural, and scientific matters with the German Democratic Republic and other eastern European states.

For the U.S. government, the Federal Republic's adoption of a policy of Ostpolitik was and has been a mixed blessing. On the one hand the United States was pleased that West Germany had finally agreed to face reality and pursue a state of normal relations with the countries of eastern Europe, including the Soviet Union. For a number of years many people within the American government had thought that rigid German adherence to the Hallstein Doctrine (i.e., the West German policy of not having diplomatic relations with any nation recognizing the German Democratic Republic, with the exception of the Soviet Union) was mistaken. Further, soon after the Nixon administration came into office in 1969, it publicly proclaimed and tried to put into force "an era of East-West negotiations." Accordingly, the Federal Republic's policy of Ostpolitik was viewed in Washington as a potentially useful adjunct, if pursued cautiously, to its own policies toward the East. And this was particularly so as the Nixon-Kissinger policy of détente toward the Soviets evolved in the early 1970s.

On the other hand there was serious concern within the Nixon administration, particularly initially, that the Federal Republic under Chancellor Brandt might move too far and too quickly in its dealings with the East. Of particular concern was the possibility that either Brandt might make some unwise unilateral concessions in his dealings with the Soviets or that the Soviets would find ways to use Ostpolitik to divide the United States from its European allies. To minimize the possibility of these eventualities, the Nixon administration purposefully worked to give Brandt's policies toward the East "constructive direction."

Overall, as Henry Kissinger has tellingly remarked in his memoirs, "not without confidence, we [the United States] gave our support to Brandt's historic course."[7]

What was not fully foreseen in the early 1970s as the United States embarked on a policy of détente with the Soviets and West Germany pursued Ostpolitik was the wide disparity in the stakes that each country would accumulate in its respective dealings with the East. Since that time Germany's stakes in Ostpolitik have grown enormously—in political terms, as the Federal Republic has developed working relationships with the various countries of the East, including the German Democratic Republic; in economic terms, as German-eastern European trade and energy relations have grown; and in human terms, as networks of personal communications and relationships have flourished.[8]

For the United States, no comparable stakes have accumulated. On the contrary, as a result of the continuing buildup of Soviet military power and recent events in Angola, Afghanistan, Ethiopia, and Poland—to say nothing of the recent Soviet downing of a Korean jetliner—there has been widespread disillusionment with respect to the utility of the whole détente effort, at least as conceived during the Nixon-Ford-Kissinger era. Symbolically, the word détente has been dropped from the U.S. government's official lexicon. For a policy of seeking to moderate Soviet behavior by expanded political and economic relations has been found wanting by the U.S. government. And recent U.S. foreign policy has focused more on the competitive element than on the cooperative element in the U.S.-Soviet relationship, although nuclear arms control has been pursued—with a couple of pauses—since the early 1980s. In a speech in 1983 Arthur Burns, the U.S. ambassador to Germany, summarized this point in the following way:

> If one were to ask a typical citizen of the Federal Republic to list the benefits of Ostpolitik and detente, he could point to the normalization in and around Berlin, to improved personal contacts between the citizens of the two Germanys . . . to stronger economic ties between Western and Eastern Europe—in short, to a whole range of

developments that can be attributed to the flowering of detente in the 1970s. On the other hand, if one were to ask a typical American citizen to identify some way in which detente has affected his life, he would be hard put to respond. From a domestic standpoint, it is difficult for Americans to come up with a telling argument for detente . . . [and] when Americans turn to the international scene, they inevitably voice disappointment that their expectations from the policy of detente have not been fulfilled—that repression of human rights in the Soviet Union has not diminished—while the Soviet military buildup and its political adventurism around the globe have actually increased.[9]

The Exacerbating Role of Domestic Political Factors

In the face of (1) different accumulated American and German stakes in détente; (2) divergent U.S.-West German perspectives regarding the nature of the threat posed by the Soviets; (3) different U.S.-West German perspectives on the proper response to Soviet aggression outside the NATO area, as in Afghanistan; (4) different views with respect to the salutary effects to be expected from expanded political and economic relations with the East; and (5) the continuing centrality of the U.S.-Soviet relationship to American foreign policy interests, there are likely to be significant strains in American-German bilateral relations in coming years. Until recently in the postwar period, to the extent that American and German interests have diverged, tensions in the relationship between the two countries have been managed relatively successfully. Although there have been differences on some specific bilateral issues (e.g., trade and monetary policy, burden-sharing arrangements, nuclear nonproliferation policy), these have been passing disagreements that have not typically led to public squabbles between the two countries regarding East-West relations, as happened in 1982–1983. During most of the postwar period, as has been shown, American and German interests have been largely complementary, with West Germany being willing to follow America's lead in defining and managing the West's relationship with the East. This no longer seems to be the case, at least not in the same way as in the past. Accordingly, U.S.-West German disagreements over the Yamal pipeline, for example, must be understood as being symptomatic of a significant divergence in American and German views with respect to the West's relationship with the Soviet Union and eastern Europe. And this difference in perspective, barring a major change in international Soviet behavior, is likely to continue for the foreseeable future.

Proliferation of Actors Concerning German Policy

Coincident with this "objective" difference in perspective is the political fact that West Germany no longer occupies the same preeminent place in the minds and on the agendas of top American policymakers that it once did. Indeed, today's situation starkly contrasts with much of the postwar period, when developments in Germany were so central to American interests that the U.S. government gave more importance to German-related elements of policy decisions than to almost any other consideration. To be sure, West Germany continues to be of great importance to the United States, and we have a major stake in the U.S.-West German relationship. Yet we no longer have the same preoccupation with the Federal Republic, the same Germanocentric tilt to our policies. Now, U.S. officials typically weigh German concerns against other foreign policy considerations and other regions of the world, whether it be Asia, the Middle East, or Latin America.

Both a cause and a reflection of West Germany's changed status on the U.S. foreign policy agenda are several domestic political factors that promise to inject tension and exacerbate current and prospective strains in German-American relations. First, there has been in recent years a significant proliferation of agencies in the U.S. government that have become actively involved in the formulation of U.S. policy toward the Federal Republic. In significant part, this proliferation of policy participants reflects a perceptible diminution in the authority and role of the German Desk in the U.S. Department of State. During most of the postwar period American policy on issues affecting U.S. relations with Germany has been made by the German Desk, typically working in close coordination with the U.S. embassy in Bonn. Although involved in numerous meetings dealing with German issues, other parts of the State Department, as well as other agencies, have typically deferred to and ultimately ratified the recommendations of the German Desk, which is now bureaucratically housed within the State Department's Office of Central European Affairs in the Bureau of European Affairs.

From the point of view of maintaining harmony and minimizing discord in U.S.-West German bilateral relations, this pattern of American policymaking has been quite well suited. For the German Desk in particular and the State Department in general have consistently emphasized the importance of close, continuing consultations with the leaders of the Federal Republic and the avoidance, when at all possible, of deviating from previously agreed on positions. Further, the German Desk, perhaps not surprisingly, has seemingly been committed to retaining German interests at the head of any U.S. foreign policy agenda in Europe. It has also been the part of the U.S. government most conscious of how unpredictability in America's foreign relations might damage bilateral U.S.-West German relations. This German Desk perspective, which has dominated the U.S. governmental approach to Germany during much of the postwar period, was epitomized in the thinking and approach of former Secretary of State Dean Acheson. On this subject Acheson once wrote:

> My thesis is that in making political and military judgments affecting Europe a major—often the major—consideration should be their effect on the German people and the German government. It follows from this that the closest liaison and consultation with the German government is an absolute necessity. . . . Unexpected or unexplained action nearly always causes consternation in Bonn. Sensible action after careful consultation, even when there has been some difference in view, rarely does.[10]

Although centrally involved in internal governmental deliberations on German issues, the German Desk does not now play the kind of determinative role regarding Germany that it has played during much of the postwar period. Now there are quite a few other participants in these policy deliberations, and their respective roles typically have increased significantly as compared with their involvement and importance on these issues in previous eras. Within the Bureau of European Affairs at the State Department there are now three other offices that play important roles in helping to shape the State Department's views on specific policy issues involving Germany. There is the Office of NATO Affairs, which has primary responsibility for Atlantic political-military issues. There is the Office of Organization for Economic Cooperation and Development (OECD) and European Community Affairs, which is primarily responsible for all Atlantic political-economic issues. Perhaps most important, there is the Office of Soviet Union Affairs, which is the central coordinating point within the State Department for issues involving U.S.-Soviet relations, including those with a German component. The involvement of these three offices—and their perceptible growth in influence on issues related to Germany—in part reflects how American-German bilateral relations have been largely subsumed over time within the context of three international organizations—NATO, OECD, and the EEC. It also reflects the fact that much of postwar U.S. policy toward Germany has been reactive, with a dominant anti-Soviet orientation.

Beyond the growing involvement of these offices within the Bureau of European Affairs there are several functional (as contrasted to regional) bureaus in the State Department that now have a relatively important say on U.S.-West German issues. Most important among these are the Bureau of Politico-Military Affairs, which is the part of the State Department with primary responsibility for developing positions on the whole gamut of military issues affecting U.S. bilateral and multilateral relations with other governments; the Bureau of Economics and Business Affairs, which has primary responsibility for developing, coordinating, and implementing U.S. financial, commercial, and monetary policy; the Bureau of Oceans, International Environmental, and Scientific Affairs, which is in charge, among other things, of the State Department's nuclear nonproliferation efforts; and the Policy Planning Council, which is charged with long-range planning for the secretary of state on the entire range of issues that are likely to be of importance to future U.S. foreign policy interests. In addition to these ever more powerful functional bureaus within the State Department there is the semiautonomous Arms Control and Disarmament Agency (ACDA), which has played an important role, for example, in formulating and carrying out the U.S. negotiating position in the intermediate-range nuclear forces (INF), strategic arms reduction talks (START), and mutual and balanced force reduction (MBFR) talks. The chiefs of all three of these arms control negotiating delegations are Arms Control Agency employees. Finally, there is the quasi-independent U.S. Information Agency, which is charged with formulating and overseeing U.S. information, cultural exchange, and public diplomacy programs in Germany and elsewhere.

The proliferation of organizations and individuals within the State Department that involve themselves in U.S.-West German relations is matched by the increased involvement of other agencies within the U.S. executive branch. The Department of Defense, for example, is centrally involved in shaping American policy on a wide range of issues involving Germany—whether concerning the details of burden-sharing arrangements, or the conclusion of host-nation support agreements, or technology transfer to the East, or the appropriate level of U.S. troops in Europe. These are all political-economic-military issues wherein the Department of Defense is an important participant in the policy process in Washington.

Besides the increasing involvement of the Defense Department in U.S. policy toward the Federal Republic, there has also been noticeably more involvement in recent years of the Department of the Treasury. Reflecting both the financial stringencies of contemporary times and the growing interrelationship between economic and foreign policy considerations, the U.S. Treasury Department now plays a key role on a wide range of issues of great importance to U.S.-West German relations—from U.S. interest rate policy to the consideration of new foreign trade proposals to the management of third world debt servicing to East-West trade.

Coordinating and providing policy direction on all of these

issues is the National Security Council (NSC) staff, headed by the president's assistant for national security affairs. The NSC was created by the National Security Act of 1947 to "advise the President with respect to the integration of domestic, foreign, and military policies relating to the national security." Traditionally, the State Department has been the principal instrument of American foreign policy. Yet in recent years, as American foreign policy interests and the size of the federal bureaucracy have grown significantly, the NSC staff has proved useful to all presidents in bringing together information, identifying and evaluating issues, coping with crisis situations, coordinating governmental actions, helping to make decisions, and ensuring that executive agencies carry out the president's wishes. And given (a) the growing complexity of foreign policy issues; (b) their typically overlapping jurisdictional nature; (c) the failure of the State Department to develop sufficiently specialized expertise in such fields as trade and monetary policy or defense policy; and (d) the perceived need of presidents to have people on the White House staff working on foreign policy issues but conscious of domestic political considerations, it is not surprising that the NSC has come to play an important role in the foreign policy process in recent years.

Of course, the precise role and responsibilities of the NSC staff are different under different presidents, and it is not uncommon for the NSC staff to be more important on some issues than on others. Nevertheless, on most recent foreign policy matters, including the range of issues most central to U.S.-West German relations, the NSC staff has played a critical role in the policy process. Concerning Brandt's initial efforts at Ostpolitik, or the 1973 proposed "Year of Europe," or the ill-fated neutron bomb affair of 1977–78, or the 1979 dual-track NATO decision, the NSC staff played a central role in shaping and implementing U.S. policy. And it is highly likely that the role of the NSC regarding German policy will continue to be of prime significance in the future, irrespective of the particular president and national security adviser, for NSC staffs that coordinate policy have ways of making and implementing policies as well.

The proliferation of actors involved in setting U.S. policy toward Germany—and the associated decline in influence of the German Desk at the State Department—carries with it several general policy implications. It means that with so many more participants involved in the policymaking process, issues related to U.S.-West German relations, particularly controversial ones, are typically not decided quickly. It means that a rather broad range of institutional and personal perspectives are brought to bear on all of these issues. It means that, inevitably, there is increased policy incoherence on the part of the U.S. government regarding German policy, with different participants in the policy process voicing and holding various points of view on any particular subject. And it means that it is likely to be increasingly difficult to carry on the kind of close consultation between American and German officials that has characterized postwar U.S.-West German relations. For in the U.S. government there is a larger number of people in policy-relevant positions who do not appreciate the need for close consultation with officials of the Federal Republic, as officials at the German Desk traditionally have understood this need. As a result, from the point of view of the Federal Republic, it is increasingly difficult to divine who, if anyone save the president, speaks with the authority of the U.S. government. Moreover, this is becoming an increasingly acute problem as the average tenure of an American assistant secretary continues to drop; it now approximates roughly twenty-one months in duration.[11] Overall, the process by which the United States makes policy toward Germany is and is likely to become more fragmented, messier, more cumbersome, less predictable, and less sensitive to German interests and priorities than it has been during most of the postwar period.

Making this problem worse is a growing lack of trained American officials who are knowledgeable about German affairs. A significant reason postwar American-German relations have gone relatively smoothly and tensions between the two countries have been limited is related to the generally high level of American personnel involved in making and implementing German policy (and vice versa). At the State Department the German Desk and the Bureau of European Affairs have traditionally attracted the top people in the U.S. Foreign Service. This has had the effect of creating a continuing cadre of individuals at the top echelons of the State Department who have been sensitive to the prime importance of Germany to U.S. foreign policy interests. A relatively small number of experienced Germanists—such individuals as David Bruce, Martin Hillenbrand, and Walter Stoessel—in fact have played a key role on German issues for most of the postwar period. This is no longer the case, because these men have moved from the scene and the U.S. government in recent years has largely neglected the training and promotion of a new generation of German experts. As a result there is now and is likely to be for the foreseeable future a relative lack of people who are expert on German affairs within the State Department and elsewhere in the government, including at the highest levels. Martin Hillenbrand has ruefully analyzed this development:

> The State Department has generally neglected the problem of professional succession in the Western and Central European area and has made no attempt, systematic or otherwise, to provide for the replacement of a whole generation of highly motivated Europeanists and, more specifically, the group dedicated to German affairs. The process of decomposition was accelerated by the premature departure from the department, because of organizational failures and bad personnel policies, of some of the most talented of the Germanists who might have been expected to rise to senior positions. Although there are, of course, some very able officers who qualify as German experts, their number is small compared to the situation even a few years ago.[12]

Democratization of the Policy Process

Paralleling the decline in influence of the German Desk at the State Department and the growing lack of German experts within the government has been what might be called the "democratization" of American policy toward Germany. For much of the postwar period a relatively small group of people outside the government has exercised an important voice on U.S.-German relations. This group has generally been based along the East Coast of the United States, primarily in law firms, corporations, universities, and think tanks in Boston, New York, and Washington. Its members have typically been part of an East Coast white, Anglo-Saxon, Protestant (WASP) elite. At times, some of its members—John McCloy, George Ball, Cyrus Vance, for example—have taken leave from their normal positions and gone into the government for a few years of service, frequently at the senior reaches of the White House, the State Department, and the Defense Department. When not in government, members of this group have met in places like the New York-based Council of Foreign Relations to discuss and help shape American thinking about the heavy foreign policy questions of the day, including issues related to Germany. Overall, this group, heavily Atlanticist in orientation, has been a critical intellectual and political force for close U.S.-West German relations in the postwar era.

In recent years, to use Zbigniew Brzezinski's words, there has been a "decline of Wasp predominance in America" and this elite group is "no longer dominant either in the world or in America."[13] It is not totally surprising given recent economic and demographic shifts in the United States, for example, that the most recent American elections have brought to power Jimmy Carter, a former governor and peanut farmer from Georgia, and Ronald Reagan, a former governor and actor from California. For the WASP elite based on the East Coast has clearly lost political and economic influence in recent years on a range of issues, including U.S. policy toward Germany. This power shift away from the Europe-oriented East Coast to the Sun Belt and the virtual end of European immigration to the United States have contributed, moreover, to a diminished interest in and knowledge of German affairs specifically and European affairs more generally.

Both a cause and a consequence of this shift in influence away from an East Coast WASP elite has been the recent emergence in the United States of a more assertive, nationalistic approach to foreign relations. This approach has roots in the isolationist strain in America's political culture, which at various times in the past has played an important role in shaping U.S. foreign policy, spurring such initiatives as the Mansfield amendment during the late 1960s. This "tougher" approach, moreover, now has perceptible support in the United States across the political spectrum and has been fueled by a series of recent events—Vietnam, Watergate, an inability to rescue the hostages from Iran, U.S. ineffectiveness in responding to Soviet interventionist activities in Afghanistan and Poland, and the continuing Soviet buildup of nuclear and conventional forces in Europe and elsewhere. Taken together, these developments, public opinion polls show, have produced a "jingoism, stifled rage, and a frustrated impotence straining for an outlet."[14]

This set of emotions has found an outlet in America's approach to foreign relations in recent years and is likely to be present for the foreseeable future. Concerning Germany in particular and Europe in general, evidences of this abound. There has been, for example, a concerted effort by the United States to spend an increasing amount of money for defense to meet a growing Soviet threat and to pressure allies to do the same. There has been an effort to impose wide-ranging sanctions after the Soviet invasion of Afghanistan. There have been the Yamal pipeline issue and the associated imposition of trade sanctions. There has been less reluctance to engage in intelligence operations abroad. There has been growing support for the enactment of protectionist trade legislation. There have been new initiatives to limit the transfer of sensitive technology to the East. And there has been seemingly less patience with those allies, including Germany, that do not appear to be treating America equitably, whether in terms of the subsidization of trade, the openness of economic markets to U.S. products, or a willingness to carry a fair share of the defense burden.

The Role of Congress

This more assertive, nationalistic, sometimes parochial approach to America's foreign relations is most perceptible in the activities of the Congress, that part of the U.S. government which is closest to popular sentiments by dint of having to face the electorate every two years. During much of the postwar period, concerning foreign affairs, the president has led and the legislative branch has followed. On most foreign policy issues, including the formulation and implementation of U.S. policy toward Germany, Congress' role has generally been passive. However, largely as a result of America's experience in Indochina in the late 1960s and early 1970s, which brought about a serious reexamination of the process by which the United States makes foreign policy, this pattern of executive-legislative relations has changed in recent years.

As a result of this reappraisal, since Congress terminated American involvement in Vietnam congressional dynamism has characterized U.S. foreign policymaking. Moreover, the era of congressional acquiescence in presidential decision making in foreign affairs is probably gone forever. To understand the crucial role that Congress has played in the foreign relations of the United States in recent years, one need only look at some of the far-reaching, unprecedented foreign policy initiatives enacted by the Congress. There is, for example, the War Powers Act, passed over presidential veto, which prevents the executive branch from committing U.S. troops abroad for an indefinite period without congressional authorization. There is the Jackson amendment to the Trade Act of 1974, which ties U.S. most-favored-nation trade treatment to emigration policies in other countries. There is the Budget and Impoundment Control Act, which gives Congress a unique role in the formulation of the country's annual budget, across the range of foreign policy, defense, and domestic activities. There is the Nelson amendment, which gives Congress the ability to veto all significant conventional arms sales planned by the president. There is the Clark amendment, which terminated covert American involvement in Angola. There is the Nuclear Non-Proliferation Act, which essentially redefines American policy with respect to would-be proliferating nations. And there has been a series of other initiatives that have provided Congress with the right to approve, veto, or limit a wide range of executive branch policies—from human rights to the level of U.S. troops in Europe, from foreign aid to intelligence activities.

Three of the most important powers that the Constitution assigns to the Congress are the power to offer "advice and consent" with respect to treaties, the power to offer "advice and consent" on nominations, and the power to appropriate monies. In recent years Congress has exercised all three of these powers in ways that have been of importance to U.S.-European relations in general and U.S.-German relations in particular. In so doing Congress has made itself a critical part of the policy process, a part to be better understood and reckoned with in Germany and elsewhere. For active congressional involvement in foreign and defense matters has not only meant that the number of participants involved in the policy process in Washington has been further increased significantly. It has also meant that the president has not, in some instances, been able to go ahead with foreign policies of his choice, or in other instances, to proceed with a given policy course without extensive lobbying, compromise, and, frequently, delay.

Concerning treaties, it is the Senate, by a two-thirds vote, that has the power of approval. In the course of U.S. diplomatic history there have been few treaties concluded by presidents and subsequently rejected by the Senate. Of course, there have been some notable exceptions, such as the case of the Senate's rejection of American membership in the League of Nations after World War I. More recently, in 1979–80, the Senate refused to ratify the SALT II treaty, concluded in Vienna in June 1979 by President Carter and Secretary Brezhnev. Whether owing to "fatal flaws" in the treaty, as charged by presidential candidate Ronald Reagan in 1980, or to a highly negative reaction to the Soviet invasion of Afghanistan, or to the legislative-political maladroitness of the Carter administration, or to a combination of all of these factors, the Senate failure to ratify SALT II has seriously complicated subsequent U.S. arms control efforts. There is no question that in the future any president will have to take more account of Senate thinking than Jimmy Carter did before concluding an arms control treaty. In the meantime a number of questions important to U.S.-European security concerns are left unresolved as a result of the Senate's failure to ratify the SALT II treaty. Will the United States continue to adhere to the terms of SALT II after 1985 in the absence of

Senate action, provided the Soviets do the same? Until when? What can be done to enhance European and Soviet confidence that a future arms control agreement negotiated by the executive will be approved by the Senate? What kind of future treaty would in fact be acceptable to the U.S. Congress? In sum, in a number of important regards the status of the SALT II treaty— and a number of important associated questions—currently be- clouds and complicates U.S.-European and U.S.-German security relations in general and nuclear arms control negotiations in par- ticular.

Besides approving treaties, a second major senatorial preroga- tive is the power to confirm executive appointments. In the course of American history this power has been used sparingly by the Senate, usually more often with the intent to influence prospective executive policy than to consider actually turning down a presidential nomination, except in cases of moral tur- pitude. This situation, however, has recently changed con- siderably. In 1977, when President Carter nominated Paul Warnke to be the chief SALT negotiator and director of the Arms Control and Disarmament Agency (ACDA), there ensued a lengthy, bitter fight over his confirmation, with the outcome unclear for several weeks. In the end the Senate confirmed Warnke for both positions, although the vote on the SALT negotiator nomination was fifty-eight to forty. The forty votes against Warnke for the SALT position represented six votes more than were needed to defeat a new SALT treaty. Anti-SALT forces in the Senate, in effect, had successfully sent a message to the president and the nation at large that a substantial portion of the Senate lacked confidence in the administration's chief arms control negotiator. This, of course, later came back to haunt the Carter administration during Senate consideration of the SALT II treaty.

More recently, the Reagan administration has gone through extended, divisive confirmation hearings regarding first Richard Burt's nomination to be assistant secretary of state for European affairs and then Kenneth Adelman's to be the director of ACDA. In both cases the Senate not only delayed action on the proposed nomination for an unusually long period, leaving the ultimate outcome in doubt, but it also held extensive public hearings on the administration's and the respective nominees' detailed substantive ideas concerning European policy and arms control policy. In addition, the nominees' personal qualifications for the positions in question were subjected to intense, probing public scrutiny. Ultimately, both Burt and Adelman were confirmed. But in both cases the Senate, through the confirmation process, left its mark. By leaving the appointed positions in question vacant for an extended period, the Senate fueled foreign and domestic doubts about administration policy concerning Europe and arms control policy. It also played a decisive role in determining several other key executive appointments to the State Department and ACDA by holding the Burt and Adelman nominations "hostage" to nominees favored by individual senators. Finally, overall, it helped to ensure the sensitivity and receptivity of Burt and Adelman to prospective congressional advice with respect to European and arms control matters. The recent controversial confirmation processes of Warnke, Burt, and Adelman, among others, have been somewhat unusual in the American political context, but they are likely to become more commonplace in the future. Similarly difficult confirmation hearings before a more assertive Congress will certainly have to be anticipated by presidents in making future executive appointments to the State Department and ACDA, among other national security agencies.

The third major power exercised by Congress and shared by the Senate and the House of Representatives is what has historically been called "the power of the purse." The Constitution provides that legislative approval is needed for all governmental expenditures. This power over the appropriation of money has historically been a highly significant weapon in the hands of the legislature to influence executive policy. For it is when money is involved that members of Congress tend to be most interested in foreign policy issues and when it is easiest procedurally for the legislature to influence American policy.

Concerning Germany in particular and Europe in general,

Congress and its numerous constituent parts (committees, sub-committees, individual senators and representatives), using their appropriations power, have played an active role in shaping U.S. policy on a variety of issues in recent years. Probably most saliently, Congress has focused on the issue of burden sharing in the defense area. For a number of years members of Congress, reflecting the view of many Americans, have felt that the United States has borne an undue part of the heavy costs of NATO. Particularly given recent economic stringencies in the United States, growing American interest in Asian security issues, and the emergence of a more assertive, nationalistic approach to foreign relations, congressional criticism of European defense efforts has grown significantly since the early 1980s.

To date, congressional dissatisfaction with current burden sharing within NATO has found its most visible expression in legislation regarding U.S. troop strength in Europe. Such efforts as the 1984 amendment of Senator Sam Nunn (D.-Georgia) to reduce American troops in Europe have failed thus far. Other initiatives, though, such as those by Senators Ted Stevens (R.-Alaska) and Bill Cohen (R.-Maine) have succeeded in freezing troop levels in Europe. And as prospects grow that most European countries will not meet their pledged goal of 3 percent annual real growth in defense spending, there will undoubtedly be new legislative efforts to reduce American troop levels in Europe.

In recent years congressional unhappiness with Europe's perceived inequitable contribution to NATO has been signaled in several other ways. For one thing, Congress has periodically balked at providing the president with the necessary monies to buy equipment to be used in wartime by German reservists to aid U.S. combat units. In addition, Congress has refused to raise the limit on the storage of equipment in Europe to more than for four U.S. Army divisions. The president would like to store the tanks and other heavy equipment for six divisions at designated storage sites in Europe, but Congress has been reluctant to do this. Further, Congress has refused on several occasions to fund fully the president's request for NATO construction monies.

These and other steps have been taken by the U.S. legislature since the early 1980s in an effort to demonstrate dissatisfaction with Europe's contribution to NATO; to force various European nations, including the Federal Republic, to bear a larger share of the cost of the common defense; and, more generally, to put Europeans on notice that the United States is going to adopt a "tougher" posture in the future on burden-sharing questions.

Still another area in which Congress has actively attempted to shape U.S. trade policy with important implications for Germany concerns East-West economic relations. Here, the Congress has left its mark on policy by adding a variety of amendments to the Export Administration Act, which is the principal legislation empowering the president to expand or control exports. At the same time, hopes for a true "two-way street" on NATO weapons cooperation have dimmed considerably.

Moreover, regarding trade issues as well as other issues in U.S.-West German relations, there does not exist the kind of pro-German constituency in the Congress, among interest/lobbying groups, in the academic community, or in the country at large as exists regarding the interests of most of the other western European nations. For a variety of historical reasons, which date back to at least World War II, German-American groups in the United States (Steuben Societies, for example), are essentially cultural and social in their orientation. They tend to be inactive politically and relatively invisible, as compared with the politically active, high-profile Franco-American groups or Swedish-American groups. Further, there seems to be a relative dearth of contemporary West German studies in university curricula and published works by scholars. In this regard there has been a dramatic drop in recent years in the number of American university students studying German politics, culture, or language. As a result of these and other developments, except in the context of bolstering Western defense efforts, German interests carry little positive domestic political significance. Indeed, there is relatively little understanding in the Congress and around the United States of "what makes the Federal Republic of Germany tick." This is all particularly surprising, since more than 50 million Americans—or 28.8 percent of the population—now claim at least partial German ancestry. In the legislative context, a senior congressional staff member has summed up the situation in the following way:

> There is little active, popular support for rejuvenated American-German relations. There is little sense of what Germany represents to America and American interests except in military terms. Berlin and Germany are always everybody's [members of Congress'] top priority in rhetorical terms but that is where it generally ends.[15]

The Media

The nature of recent congressional involvement in U.S.-German relations vividly demonstrates the growing nationalistic-cum-isolationist tendencies in the contemporary American approach to foreign relations. Fueling these tendencies has been the U.S. media—television, radio, and the press. Concerning the Federal Republic, memories of the Third Reich and World War II inevitably set some of the deep backdrop for the making of U.S. policy. Television programs, late-night television films, and current movies that focus on the Third Reich, of course, rekindle those memories.

Moreover, of considerably more significance to the setting of contemporary U.S. policy toward the Federal Republic than the legacy of World War II has been the American media's recent focus on both the growth of anti-Americanism in Germany and the questionable reliability of the German commitment to the West and to democratic institutions generally. Both the policy-making elite in Washington and the nongovernmental foreign policy establishment around the United States heavily depend on the media—particularly *The New York Times, The Washington Post,* and the major television networks—for much of their information about Germany. In recent years these influential media sources have tended to cast a critical eye on the Federal Republic and its reliability as a partner of the United States, as Germany has simultaneously grown more self-questioning about its future and more independent from America on foreign policy issues. At the same time there has been relatively less discussion in the American media about the Federal Republic as a staunch ally of the United States.

This sort of media coverage was epitomized, for example, by *The New York Times'* coverage of the 1983 German elections. During the campaign *The Times* conspicuously highlighted the themes of increasing German political power and independence; growing anti-Americanism in Germany, particularly among the young; more public questioning of Germany's commitment to NATO and the West, as epitomized by the Greens and their accession to the Bundestag and the apparent leftward movement of the Social Democratic party; the growing strength of the anti-nuclear protest movement; and whether or not the Federal Republic had rid itself of undesirable vestiges of the past. In an analysis of *The New York Times'* recent coverage of European affairs, Jan Reifenberg, Washington correspondent of the *Frankfurter Allgemeine Zeitung,* has summarily noted that *The Times'* reporting about the Federal Republic has cast "a constant, nagging doubt as to whether today's Germans have really overcome a sordid past." It has also planted in readers' minds "doubts which would only tend to confirm a skepticism toward Germany that still prevails in parts of America's intellectual establishment."[16] Overall, there is little question that the Federal Republic's seemingly undemocratic dimensions elicit more attention among American audiences than its democratic features, and it is this reality that affects in important ways the American media's coverage of West Germany. Moreover, the 1983 U.S.-West German Tricentennial Celebration to commemorate the 300th anniversary of German settlers in the United States was designed in part to offset just this sort of media coverage.

Conclusions

For most of the postwar period there has been an unusually high degree of harmony in relations between the United States and the Federal Republic. This, it might be added, was not necessarily predictable given the fact that the two previous generations of

Americans and Germans had been enemies in war. This is not to deny the presence of a number of passing disagreements in post-war U.S.-West German bilateral relations. To be sure, these have existed. One need only think of prolonged negotiations concerning offset arrangements or disagreements about trade issues or the ill-fated multilateral nuclear force discussions of the early 1960s or differences on nuclear nonproliferation issues. Overall, though, postwar American-German relations—political, economic, military—have been characterized by cordiality, mutual confidence, close consultation, and common interest.

In significant part the underlying basis for this harmonious relationship has been a common understanding of the Soviet threat and agreement about the best ways to deal with it. Not surprisingly, in the course of the 1970s and into the 1980s, as Germany has grown more independent and as American and German thinking have diverged with respect to the East, tensions and strains have grown in bilateral U.S.-West German relations. Moreover, in recent years these tensions have been exacerbated by a number of continuing domestic political factors in the United States: a proliferation of officials and government offices and agencies involved in setting American policy toward Germany; an accompanying diminution in the authority of the German Desk in the Department of State, that part of the government which has historically been most sensitive to German interests; a growing lack of trained American officials who are knowledgeable about Germany, including at the senior levels of the executive branch; a decline in the influence of an Atlanticist, nongovernmental East Coast elite with respect to official U.S. policy toward Germany; the emergence in the United States of a generally more nationalistic, assertive approach to foreign relations; the growth of the role of Congress regarding a range of political, economic, and military issues affecting U.S.-West German relations; the relative absence of a pro-German domestic political constituency; and generally negative media treatment of recent political developments in the Federal Republic.

Although these factors are sure to complicate the relationship between the United States and the Federal Republic in future years by making U.S. policy less coherent and more unpredictable, they do not doom it to failure. Rather, they vividly under-score the need for heightened concern and sensitivity in the management of American-German relations in both Washington and Bonn. For such management to continue to be handled successfully, and for West Germany to develop a more self-confident and responsible approach to the pursuit of common interests, it will be necessary for both Americans and Germans to focus more attentively on the complex of issues that affect the setting of contemporary U.S. foreign policy toward the Federal Republic of Germany.

Notes

1. U.S. Congress, Senate Foreign Relations Committee, *Documents on Germany, 1944–59* (86th Congress, first session, 1959, 35–42). Also, see Daniel Yergin, *Shattered Peace* (Boston: Houghton Mifflin, 1977), 221–227.

2. Thomas Bailey, *America Faces Russia* (New York: Columbia University Press, 1950), 327.

3. For a more detailed discussion of the Berlin blockade, see John Spanier, *American Foreign Policy Since World War II* (New York: Praeger, 1977), 45–69. Also, John Gimbel, *The American Occupation of Germany: Politics and the Military 1945–1949* (Stanford, Calif.: Stanford University Press, 1968), 201–215.

4. Statement of Martin Hillenbrand on "NATO's Future Role" before the Subcommittee on Europe and the Middle East, Committee on Foreign Affairs, U.S. House of Representatives, 3 June 1982 (Washington, D.C.: Government Printing Office, 1982), 85–86.

5. Roger Morgan, *The United States and Western Germany, 1945–1973* (London: Oxford University Press, 1974), 68–82.

6. Anton DePorter, *Europe Between the Superpowers* (New Haven, Conn.: Yale University Press, 1979), 184.

7. Henry Kissinger, *White House Years* (Boston: Little, Brown, 1979), 531.

8. For a more detailed discussion of these stakes, see Melvin Croan, "Dilemmas of Ostpolitik," in *West German Foreign Policy: Dilemmas and Directions,* ed. Peter Merkel (Chicago: Chicago Council on Foreign Relations, 1983), 38–48. Also, Angela Stent, *From Embargo to Ostpolitik* (New York: Cambridge University Press, 1981).

9. Quoted in *The Washington Post,* 14 April 1983, 22.

10. Dean Acheson, *New York Times Magazine,* 15 Dec. 1963. Also, see Morgan, *United States and West Germany, 1945–1973,* 100–104, 131–135.

11. Interview with Frank Carlucci on "What Is Really Wrong with Government," *U.S. News and World Report,* 4 April 1983, 65.

12. "The United States and Germany," in *West German Foreign Policy, 1949–1979,* ed. Wolfram Hanrieder (Boulder, Colo.: Westview Press, 1980), 87.

13. Zbigniew Brzezinski, *Power and Principle: Memoirs of the National Security Advisor, 1977–1981* (New York: Farrar, Straus & Giroux, 1983), 43.

14. Lawrence Kaagan and Daniel Yankelovich, "Defense and Consensus: The Domestic Aspects of Western Security," a paper presented to the Twenty-fourth Annual Conference of the International Institute for Strategic Studies, 9–12 Sept. 1982, 5. The Soviet downing of a Korean jetliner during the summer of 1983 has perceptibly fueled these sentiments.

15. Confidential interview.

16. "*The New York Times:* Making Importance Popular," in *Reporting U.S.-European Relations,* ed. Michael Rice (New York: Pergamon Press, 1983), 40–61.

Chapter 3

U.S.-West German Relations and the Soviet Problem

John Van Oudenaren

At first glance it would seem paradoxical that the United States and West Germany are frequently at odds with each other over the very issue that impels them to maintain an alliance in the first place, namely, the Soviet Union and the threat it poses to the security of both countries. On closer inspection, however, differences between the United States and the Federal Republic on dealing with Moscow are not all that surprising given the fact—as the previous chapters have emphasized—of different historical experiences, different domestic political settings, and, up to a point, different conceptions of fundamental national interest.

Although there have always been disagreements within and between the allied countries on East-West issues, many observers now believe that these disagreements have deepened to the point where it is possible to speak of a crisis in the U.S.-German relationship. Although there are no uniform national perspectives on the causes of this crisis, many on the German side point to the sharp turn in American policy away from détente and arms control that began in the late 1970s. On the American side, in contrast, many stress the German desire to insulate détente and trade with the East from the broader issues of Soviet conduct in Poland and the third world.

Underlying these differing explanations for the "crisis" are, of course, different conceptions of what constitute the "normal" functions of the alliance. Some Germans, particularly since the arrival of the Reagan administration, have begun to ask whether the aims of a defensive alliance are served by an alliance leader that talks in terms of limited and protracted nuclear war, what they see as "economic warfare" against the East, and the ultimate collapse of Soviet power. For their part many Americans, particularly at a time when they feel militarily overextended, grow increasingly weary of Germans and other Europeans invoking the Harmel report to convince them that their principal military alliance is really an instrument of détente and arms control. They also are disturbed at a seeming reluctance to consider the security implications of East-West trade and credits and the implications for NATO of Soviet activism in the third world.

It may be useful to step back from these largely theoretical questions concerning the "normal" role of the alliance and the causes of its "crisis" and to reflect instead on the remarkable degree of consensus on dealing with the Soviet Union that has in fact existed, for whatever reasons, between the United States and Germany throughout the postwar period. Despite serious differences on particular issues, from the late 1940s until well into the 1960s German and American governments were, *in the main,* agreed on the broad outlines of a cold war and containment strategy toward the USSR. Similarly, from the late 1960s until the end of the 1970s German and American governments were broadly in agreement—again despite many particular problems—on a policy of arms control and détente with the Soviet Union. In retrospect it is clear that the sharpest disagreements between the two sides occurred at the transition points: during the Kennedy-Johnson years when, to the displeasure of the Adenauer and Erhard governments, the United States began to move toward détente, and again in the late 1970s and early 1980s, when the Carter and Reagan administrations shifted back from détente to neocontainment. One can thus point to the transitions in U.S. policy as the immediate impetus to crisis in the alliance.

In attempting to determine why so much agreement generally existed and what the prospects might be for creating a new U.S.-West German consensus, it is useful to examine American attitudes toward the Soviet Union in the postwar period and the ways in which they have changed, and then to look at why

German governments (and to a lesser extent publics) have generally acquiesced in these views and why, occasionally, they have not. The emphasis on American views is not meant to suggest that they are intrinsically superior to German, but simply follows from the fact that in the late 1940s the United States more or less already had in place a strategy for dealing with the Soviet Union into which the Federal Republic was gradually inserted, that the United States remained the "leader" of the alliance, and, finally, that both of the major changes in approach to the USSR—from cold war to détente and back to cold war again—were largely initiated by the United States.

As is perhaps inevitable in any such comparative survey of attitudes and perceptions, this chapter refers to "German" "American," and, occasionally, "European" views, without meaning to deny the great diversity of opinion that exists in all countries, or to ignore the fact that many Germans hold what in this context are characterized as "American" views, while many Americans are closer to "German" ways of thinking. Nonetheless, it is recognized that there are certain differences between what might be called the "average" or "median" view in Germany and its counterpart in the United States. The purpose of this chapter is to illuminate these differences, even if doing so on occasion requires simplifying and generalizing more than might otherwise be desirable.

The Postwar Consensus

Whatever its drawbacks and ambiguities, containment was able to unite a series of Republican and Democratic administrations with a series of conservative German governments on a general strategy toward the East. As a policy, containment drew rather sharp distinctions between what was possible and desirable over the short term in dealing with the Soviet Union, and what could and should be accomplished over the long term. In the short term it was clearly defensive. It focused on stabilizing the West by economic, political, and military means and for the most part eschewed efforts to "roll back" Communist gains, either by negotiation or by military action. Over the long term, however, it was clearly offensive in that it aimed for the eventual transformation of the Soviet state and its ruling ideology.

The combination of long- and short-term objectives posited by containment had beneficial consequences not only for the maintenance of consensus within the United States, but also for agreement between the United States and West Germany. At home, Congress and the public could support a policy that in the short term did not appear risky or aggressive, but that nonetheless held out a long-term promise that the USSR's ambitions would be frustrated, that its World War II conquests would be "rolled back," and that the United States would be able to withdraw from some of its expensive overseas commitments. For roughly similar reasons the combination of short-term caution and long-term hope appealed, if not to everyone in Germany, at least to the Adenauer government. The chancellor's "policy of strength" was a German variant of the American policy that stressed building strength in the West before attempting to reach a settlement with the East. The Adenauer policy did not foreclose reunification, but simply linked it with the successful consolidation of western Germany. (The fact that Adenauer himself may not have been particularly interested in reunification in no way detracted from the usefulness of a policy that held out the possibility.)

The success of containment in attracting broad support in both countries was owing to other factors as well. For one thing both containment and the "policy of strength" simply added an East-West dimension to policies that would have been adopted for other reasons. The United States was interested, out of humanitarian considerations and enlightened self-interest, in reviving Europe and Japan even before the Soviet threat lent a new urgency to these efforts. Similarly, the Germans had an interest in rebuilding their economy and creating workable political institutions even without being told that doing so would hasten reunification. Because of this fortunate coincidence of domestic and foreign policy objectives, many who knew or cared little about their governments' respective policies toward the USSR tacitly lent their support to them.

Moreover, even among those who considered the rationale behind government policy, containment was able to attract support by virtue of its appealing but nonetheless plausible assumptions about the Soviet Union. On the American side it was believed that if war could be avoided and the USSR contained, a process of internal change would begin in the Soviet Union that would lead to an attenuation or conclusion of the cold war. In Germany, Adenauer claimed that a long-term shift in the balance of power between East and West in favor of the latter would eventually compel the Soviet leaders to negotiate the reunification of Germany. As long as these assumptions about the Soviet Union were broadly accepted, it was possible to convince publics that the West could have the best of both worlds: that it could concentrate on its own strength and prosperity, neither provoking nor yielding to the Soviet Union, but that it could also eventually win the cold war and overcome the division of Europe.

There were, of course, significant minorities on the right and the left in the United States who rejected existing policy and did not accept the assumptions about the Soviet Union on which it was based. The right, epitomized by the Taft wing of the Republican party, argued that time was working against rather than for the United States and its allies, and that long before the Soviet Union was induced to "mellow," it would exhaust and defeat the West by instigating enough Korea-type aggressions along its periphery. Accordingly, the Taftites called for an active strategy for rolling back Soviet power. The left, epitomized by the Wallace candidacy in the 1948 presidential elections, rejected containment for even more fundamental reasons, arguing that the Soviet Union was in fact not aggressive at all and could be induced to cooperate with the West by offers of trade and economic aid.

These right- and left-based rejections of containment had their counterparts in Germany, where a small minority on the right often seemed to hint that the use of force might be necessary to bring about reunification, and where a much larger minority on the left, mainly in the Social Democratic party, was susceptible to the argument that reunification could occur by conciliating the Soviets and avoiding full participation in those economic and military organizations in which the West sought to integrate the Federal Republic. (Only from the perspective of the present does it seem significant that in the United States the most serious challenge to existing policy was mounted from the right, as the left-oriented challenge dwindled to insignificance, whereas in Germany precisely the opposite occurred.)

The left-oriented critique of containment, although it lost political importance both in the United States and in Germany, had a broader base of support than its minimal impact on policy during the cold war would indicate. Indeed, containment as a policy had been formulated only *after* the Roosevelt and early Truman administrations had experimented with the idea that conflict with the Soviet Union could be avoided if the United States offered the USSR a major role in the United Nations, economic aid, and even international control of atomic energy. The idea was that if all the privileges and benefits of participation in the international system were made available to the USSR, it would then behave like a "normal" state and abandon its aggressive behavior.

These ideas were rejected and their precise opposite was adopted. Western policymakers began to operate under the assumption that the Soviet Union would first have to offer convincing proof of its changed intentions (and this proof was often taken to mean willingness to settle the German problem on Western terms) and *then* gain the economic and political benefits it desired—trade, access to technology, and a Western willingness to treat the USSR as a political "equal." In keeping with the general attitude that it was the USSR that had to change its policies, the United States and the other Western powers regarded summit meetings not, as is the case today, as part of a "process" or "dialogue" leading toward some mutually acceptable outcome, but as opportunities for "testing" whether or not the Soviet Union had yet decided to make the fundamental changes that were seen as required of it alone.

The Kennedy administration's turn toward détente (which had clearly been foreshadowed in the Eisenhower period) marked the beginning of the West's gradual abandonment of the policy of containment. The latter really consisted of three elements: (1) a

set of prescriptions for short-term policies, (2) a set of propositions about long-term outcomes, and (3) a theoretical explanation relating the latter to the former in a more or less convincing
fashion. By the early 1960s the neat relationship between these
different elements began to break down in a way that seemed to
pull the Kennedy administration in contradictory directions that
led to conflict with the European allies.

In its short-term dealings with the Communist world the administration maintained and even strengthened elements of the
traditional containment policy. Like the Truman administration,
it stressed building strength against Communist pressure. It
therefore deepened its commitment to foreign aid and, in what
was eventually to lead to the U.S. involvement in Vietnam, its
support for countries under attack by Communist guerrillas. In
addition, the Kennedy administration in large part maintained
the cold war attitude that the USSR, by virtue of the mere fact
that it was the aggressor responsible for the division of Europe,
was not entitled to the full benefits of trade and other forms of
participation in the international system.[1]

At the same time that it resisted the idea of treating the USSR
as an equal, however, the Kennedy administration, in what was
to set a pattern for the future, began to separate arms control
from other issues in the bilateral relationship and to accord it a
unique status—one that transcended the mere political issues
that had been at the heart of East-West conflict since the 1940s.
This interest in arms control soon became a key source of friction with German governments. U.S. officials continued to stress
that precisely because arms control *was* separate from political
issues, American interest in it in no way implied a diminished
desire to find a solution to the political problem of Germany. In
Bonn, however, it was feared that the Soviets would take advantage of the new American interest in arms control to normalize
their relations with the United States without having to yield
major concessions on issues in central Europe. In addition, there
was the problem of nonproliferation, which touched in a direct
way on West German interests. German leaders feared that by
joining with the USSR in promoting a nonproliferation regime,
the United States would severely undercut West German hopes

(however unrealistic they might have been) to trade renunciation of nuclear weapons for Soviet political concessions on reunification.

In addition to separating arms control from other aspects of East-West relations, American administrations of the 1960s began to modify previously held assumptions about the nature of the Soviet system. Following certain fashions then current in the academic community, government officials declared that the USSR was possibly well advanced in a process of "deideologization" that would lead to an attenuation of the Soviet threat, and that in fact China had replaced the USSR as the main danger to global stability. What was significant about this modification of theory was that it rendered obsolete the old containment policy that had pushed fundamental change in the USSR into the indefinite future—and hence off the agenda of day-to-day policymaking. Once it was admitted that the USSR was changing in what appeared to be favorable directions, Western governments became vulnerable to the charge that they were not doing enough to hasten these favorable developments, or, even worse, that they were actually hindering them. The belief that the USSR was undergoing change undercut the earlier view that change could best be fostered by denying the USSR the benefits of trade and other forms of exchange with the West. By the mid-1960s the concept of "bridge building" had begun to incorporate in modified form elements of the left's critique of containment—the view that East-West trade should precede and encourage change in the Soviet Union, not follow and reward it.

By the mid-1960s, then, the original policy of containment had been significantly altered. There continued to be a basic consensus on the minimalist proposition that the West must not yield new conquests to the USSR and the world Communist movement. However, the simple cold war assumption that successful containment was necessary and sufficient to bring about fundamental change in the USSR was giving way to competing theories about how change could best be fostered. In place of the simple assumptions shared in the early 1950s, under which change was seen as inevitable in the long run but impossible in the short run, the USSR was brought back into a real-time relationship with the West, as day-to-day actions by Western governments came to be judged by their role in encouraging developments once believed to be largely impervious to Western influences. Finally, largely at American insistence, arms control was being established as an area of East-West relations that had a rationale of its own, divorced from those political questions that containment originally hoped to solve.

Initially, the American interest in détente and arms control led to sharp clashes with the German government, which continued to hold that détente should come only after reunification and a settlement of the German problem. Fundamentally, what developed was a conflict between the interest of the United States in managing its rivalry with the Soviet Union (which, correctly or incorrectly, was perceived by the government at the time as requiring arms control and a limited détente) and the German interest in continuing to seek a solution to the German problem. As Gebhard Schweigler has pointed out in Chapter 1, the American administration sought to resolve this conflict by encouraging the German government to change its own thinking—to explore the possibility that détente might actually lead to reunification rather than result from it.

There were in fact many in Germany who, more for reasons of their own than because they were persuaded by American arguments, were receptive to the idea of a "reverse linkage" between reunification and détente. Impressed by the unwillingness and the inability of the United States to act during periods of crisis in defense of German interests, many Germans had concluded independently that the Adenauer "policy of strength" had reached a dead end. The Soviet acquisition of nuclear capabilities against both Europe and the United States had negated hopes that a gradual shift in power would compel the Soviets to make major concessions in Europe. Faced with these realities, Willy Brandt and his adviser Egon Bahr developed the policy of change through rapprochement ("Wandel durch Annaeherung")—of attempting to overcome the status quo not by compelling the Soviets to change, but by convincing them over time that change was in their own interests. Although Brandt did not explicitly rule out reunification over the long term, he began to focus less on the German problem as such and more on the gradual construction of a "European peace order." The emergence of such order would mean a transcendence of the East-West conflict—a transformation of the European context that would not so much solve the problem of Germany's division as render the division itself irrelevant.

This evolution in German policy, combined with a continued American search for détente, made possible a new if somewhat superficial consensus between the United States and West Germany on policy toward the East. As in the period of containment, what emerged was a broad parallelism between German and American short-term policies and German and American expectations for the long term. Americans could be skeptical about the prospects for fundamental change in Europe, just as Germans could be suspicious of U.S.-Soviet détente and the specter of superpower condominium. In the main, however, Germany and the United States were pursuing broadly parallel policies toward the East—Brandt hoping to construct, through a long process of negotiation and cooperation, the European "peace order," and Nixon and Kissinger claiming to be building a "stable structure of peace." Détente thus made possible a working consensus between the United States and Germany on the matters of East-West trade and arms control.

This consensus could last only as long as both sides maintained a faith in détente. As the United States adopted a more confrontational stance toward the USSR after the invasion of Afghanistan, U.S. and West German policy began to diverge more fundamentally than at any point since the early 1960s. From the German perspective it seemed that the United States, after downplaying the Soviet challenge for the better part of a decade, had embarked on a radical and sudden shift that would endanger the positive achievements of détente. From the American perspective it seemed that the Germans had become immobilized by détente—unable, as a result of their vested interest in trade and political ties with the East, to respond to any Soviet challenge, no matter how serious.

Current Conflicts and Their Underlying Causes

By the time détente and with it much of the U.S.-German foreign policy consensus had collapsed, it was clear that the American and German governments had completely reversed the positions they had held on many East-West issues in the early 1960s. In 1959 President Eisenhower provoked a minor crisis with Chancellor Adenauer by using the term "abnormal" to describe the situation in Berlin, thus raising fears that he might join with the Soviets in solving the Berlin problem at West Germany's expense. By the late 1970s and early 1980s American governments were being castigated by their German critics for not showing enough sensitivity to West German desires to "normalize" the situation in the center of Europe. In the early 1960s German officials could protest against American and British interest in arms control talks with the Soviets; by 1980 the United States was being criticized for abandoning SALT II and was being asked to couple its NATO nuclear policy with ongoing arms control talks with the Soviets. In the early 1960s German officials feared and resented American efforts to forge a bipolar relationship with the Soviet Union; by the early 1980s German officials and party politicians seemed to go out of their way to underscore the qualitative difference between German interests and the interests of what were now called "the world powers," and to do everything possible to assure continuation of a special U.S.-Soviet dialogue.

Although these contrasts are ironic, they are not accidental. Indeed, it is not hard to detect common themes in the differences that developed between the two countries in the early 1960s as the United States was embarking on détente, and those that developed in the late 1970s, when it appeared to be abandoning it. In both cases it seemed to many in Germany that the United States, in shifting its policy toward the Soviet Union, was neglecting German interests and perhaps foreclosing the possibility of long-term change in central Europe. From the American perspective it seemed that Germany in both cases was stubbornly clinging to outmoded policies in order to sustain hopes that were, in any case, highly unrealistic, while disregarding immediate American concerns about the day-to-day management of the Soviet problem. As in the early 1960s, there was a clear incompatibility between the American focus on management of the Soviet problem and the German interest in furthering, or at least not foreclosing, change in its relations with the East.

It is also not surprising that, as in the early 1960s, arms control was at the center of the differences between the German and American sides. In the early 1960s American spokesmen could claim that lowering the risks of nuclear war through bilateral dealings with the Soviet Union was separate from the issue of the political order in Europe. Although in theory this may have been true, in practice Adenauer was correct in sensing that a bilateral détente between the United States and the USSR, even if focused on arms control, would move the German problem from the center of the international political agenda and help to foreclose its solution. In the late 1970s and early 1980s these positions were reversed, as the United States became increasingly hostile to the idea that arms control could go forward irrespective of Soviet behavior. This time it was American officials and even more the American public who sensed, like Adenauer before, that no matter how technical and "apolitical" the actual provisions of an arms control regime, its existence alone was a political reality with implications for questions outside the area of arms control. By this time, however, the West Germans, who had always been sensitive to the overall political implications of the arms control process, were committed to the reverse linkage between détente and the German question and thus reluctant to see the United States abandon the very process they once opposed.

Initially, the differences between the United States and Germany over détente were not perceived in either country as differences over basic political priorities. German political leaders in particular stressed concrete, rather mundane reasons for wanting to pursue an "islandized" détente in central Europe. For one thing, there was little faith in Europe that the United States was in fact seriously committed to its own harder policy toward the Soviet Union. Particular American leaders, especially President Carter, were regarded as inconsistent in their policy toward the East. In addition, the American political process itself, with its frequent elections and its sensitivity to media influence, was seen as inimical to continuity in foreign policy. Germans were therefore reluctant to break off détente with the Soviet Union and to endanger long-standing trade ties with the East for what might have been only a passing American mood. Such a sudden shift in German policy not only would have unpleasant international implications for the Federal Republic, but would also cause domestic political conflict, since détente helped to hold together the ruling coalition and drew the essential dividing line between the Social-Liberal coalition and the conservative opposition.

Many Americans were sympathetic to these German concerns, particularly because they themselves deplored the inconsistencies of U.S. policy and were skeptical about the staying power of the United States in a more confrontational period. At the same time, however, to many in the United States it seemed that what Germans called "inconsistency" on the part of the United States was in fact justifiable reaction to such Soviet initiatives as the invasion of Afghanistan and the systematic targeting of the American land-based missile force. Conversely, what many Germans upheld as a "continuity" in their own policy toward the East was seen as a refusal to react, even on the level of verbal condemnation, to Soviet actions in the third world and in eastern Europe.

Recognizing the legitimacy of some German complaints but rejecting the validity of others, the United States responded in two ways. On the one hand there was an attempt in the second half of the Reagan administration's first term to respond to European and specifically German concerns that were perceived as legitimate. Although they were not always successful, "Europeanists" in the administration sought to defuse conflicts over East-West trade and to tailor U.S. arms control policy to European concerns. They also managed to tone down administration rhetoric about "limited nuclear war" and, to a lesser extent, the fundamental antagonism between East and West.

On the other hand many Americans, including some of the very "Europeanists" who are most sensitive to German concerns, began to question the fundamental international orientation of the Federal Republic and the depth of its loyalty to the alliance. The center of gravity of informed American opinion thus moved closer to the school of thought, once quite small, that associates the German devotion to détente with appeasement. Many Americans also came to suspect that because of an emotional attachment to their fellow Germans in the East, the West Germans were coming increasingly into conflict with NATO. In response to these suspicions, West Germans were often quick to assert that the Federal Republic was too constrained both nationally and internationally to seriously consider reunification. In sum the question of whether Germany's international alignment and loyalty was an issue itself became an issue in discussions between Americans and West Germans. This issue has enormous potential for disruption of the alliance and deserves further examination.

Reunification Versus Change in Europe

The long-term objective of West German policy has always been to overcome, to the extent possible, the conditions imposed on Germany after World War II. During the Adenauer period and into the 1960s the main focus of German activity in this regard was within the Atlantic alliance, as West Germany sought to achieve equal political and military status in the West, while largely postponing the question of changing its political status vis-à-vis the East.

Because of this German desire to regain national sovereignty and independence, there was always something paradoxical about the relationship between West Germany and its Western partners, between the Federal Republic and the multilateral organizations in which the Western powers sought to anchor it. In joining NATO and the European Economic Community, West Germany agreed to integrate itself economically, politically, and militarily into these organizations, in so doing surrendering important aspects of its national sovereignty. At the same time, however, Germany sought to use these very mechanisms in order to recover its national sovereignty and its freedom to act as an independent state—without having to wait indefinitely for a peace treaty that might never come or, if it did, might mean the imposition by the Soviet Union of conditions less favorable than those offered under the "provisional" order that took shape after 1949.

For the most part this policy of surrendering national equality in order to regain it worked out well not only for Germany, but also for its military and economic partners. By the 1960s and Europe's full recovery from the war it would have been impossible to say whether Germany had been anchored in an integrated western Europe or whether an integrated western Europe had been created around a Western-oriented Federal Republic of Germany. The two processes were so inextricable that the distinction was hardly meaningful.

By the late 1960s Germany's work in the West had largely been completed. With regard to the East, however, there was much about Germany's situation that even the staunchest Atlanticists wished to see improved. Much the way Adenauer sought to work within allied-imposed constraints the better to regain German freedom of action in the West, Brandt seemed determined to accept the constraints of the *East-West* relationship in order to re-establish German equality and freedom of action toward the East. On one level Brandt's policy represented the final abandonment of Adenauer's policy toward the East; on a deeper level it could be said that he was only continuing by different means long-standing German efforts to overcome the effects of World War II.

That this was Brandt's objective should not in itself have been surprising to Americans. However much most Germans support membership in NATO and close alliance with the United States as the best existing course for Germany, it should not be surprising that they would also want to hold out some hope for an eventual transcendence of the "abnormal" conditions growing out of World War II. If West Germany is ever to regain fully its national sovereignty, to be able to live without nuclear weapons and foreign troops on its territory—developments that would be desirable even if there were no Germans living in the East—it must, as ever, hold out some hope for a long-term transformation of the situation in central Europe.

In principle, the United States is not opposed to change in Europe on terms favorable to West Germany. In practice, however, the German interest in policies that further long-term change—or that at least do not preclude it—has led to friction with the United States. There are many reasons this is so. First, from an American perspective this interest in furthering long-term change through détente, while acceptable in principle, leaves unanswered many important practical questions—above all the question of how realizable these hopes for change are over anything but the very long term. Most American Sovietologists see no evidence of even a potential Soviet willingness to reach an accommodation with the Federal Republic on terms that would be acceptable either to it or its Western partners. Hence there is some concern in the United States that German policy may be based less on objective analysis than on wishful thinking. Even if German officials themselves remain realistic in their assessment of Soviet motives and intentions, some U.S. observers fear that the constant rhetoric in Germany about a "peace order" and the emphasis on measures (trade, arms control, institutionalized summitry) designed to realize this order will undermine popular support for NATO and ties with the United States. More ominous from the American point of view is the prospect that the United States rather than the Soviet Union will be perceived as an obstacle to change in Europe.

Moreover, even if it were the case that American skeptics were wrong, that in fact there was a real possibility that Western policy could induce the Soviets to accept fundamental change, the United States still would face the problem of coping with the Soviet Union in the short and medium term while waiting for the expected long-term changes to occur. To the extent that trade and technology transfer—even if offered in the belief that over the long term they will moderate Soviet behavior—increase Soviet capabilities, there is a potential for conflict between the United States as the country ultimately responsible for standing up to Soviet global military power, and West Germany in its role as agent of long-term change in Europe.

Trade and Arms Control

Although German-American differences over managing the Soviet problem reflect basic differences of outlook and geopolitical position, they are usually manifested in conflicts over functional cooperation (i.e., arms control and trade) with the East. Conflicts over the Urengoi gas pipeline and over the exact counting rules to be applied in arms control negotiations are significant not primarily because of the intrinsic economic or military stakes involved, but because they reflect different political outlooks that are rarely expressed in purely political terms.

Disputes over economic issues became particularly acute in the Reagan years, as the United States embarked on a policy of not simply holding the line against Soviet power, but of actually trying to cut it back on a global basis. For example, the administration sought to block the gas pipeline in the hope that denying the Soviet Union hard currency earnings would lessen its ability to sustain its military buildup and its active global policy. In essence, the United States sought to subordinate an element of European détente to its global policy.

Not surprisingly, this approach had little to recommend it in Europe, and not simply for economic reasons. From the German perspective it is hard to imagine how even a program that *successfully* managed to cut back Soviet power on a global scale (and it was by no means accepted in Germany that the current U.S. policy would accomplish even this) could force the Soviet Union to retreat from East Germany and the rest of eastern Europe. The USSR brought this area under its control when it was far weaker than it is at present, and a cutback of Soviet global power might actually encourage the USSR to cling to its original security buffer more tenaciously than ever. Having concluded that a retraction of Soviet power in Europe can occur only with the consent of and not through pressure against the Soviet Union, West Germans find their long-term aspirations for change in Europe in direct conflict with U.S. global policy. U.S. efforts to exert pressure on the USSR through Europe for the purposes of global containment clash with German regional Ostpolitik, just as Ostpolitik, to the extent that it underwrites Soviet power by a steady flow of credits and technology to the USSR, undercuts U.S. global policy.

Arms control also became a point of at least potential U.S.-West German differences on dealing with the Soviet Union, although so far the two national *governments* have managed to work together closely and align their positions. As in the 1960s, two types of disagreement on arms control issues developed within and between allied countries: first, disagreements regarding the specific content of arms control agreements; and second, disagreements concerning the overall significance of the arms control process itself in East-West relations. Historically, disagreements about the *specific content* of arms control agreements have been less important than the differences that arose over whether or not the mere *process* of arms control was desirable from the perspective of Western interests. In the 1960s the German government had less objection to the goal of nonproliferation as such, since it had already forsworn possession of nuclear weapons, than it did to the creation of a U.S.-Soviet–sponsored arms control regime that appeared directed at the Federal Republic. In the 1970s much the opposite seemed to be the case, as Helmut Schmidt and others in West Germany had real misgivings about the actual provisions of the SALT II treaty but a deep commitment to the process of strategic arms control.

The historical pattern under which the content of arms control agreements has been less divisive than the process of arms control is now changing somewhat, as the specific provisions of particular arms control regimes—the issues of what and how to count—have become the subject of heated political debate. Still, different views on the proper role of arms control remain central to the tensions between the United States and a large share of public opinion in West Germany. At issue is the separation of arms control from political issues that was initially fostered by American governments. By the late 1970s this separation was proving untenable in the United States, as SALT II failed to obtain public and congressional support not so much because of its own real or imagined flaws than because of a feeling that the United States should not be concluding treaties with a country that had just invaded Afghanistan and that had earlier intervened with its military forces throughout Africa.

At least initially, many in Europe defended the orthodox view that arms control must be separate from politics, allying themselves with the Carter administration as it argued that SALT II should be ratified not because it implied approval of Soviet behavior, but precisely because it was separate from considerations of Soviet behavior. Once the arms control process broke down completely, however, largely because it was no longer possible in the United States to forestall a *negative* linkage between SALT and Soviet behavior, the separation of arms control from politics came under attack in Europe as well, albeit from a different direction. It began to be heard in Europe that détente had failed because it depended too much on arms control and not enough on the development of political and economic ties between East and West, the Soviet Union and the United States. Critics of American policy thus began to propose new *positive* linkages between arms control and the political and economic aspects of the East-West relationship, suggesting, for example, that in addition to reactivating arms control, the United States and the European allies ought to seek to engage the USSR in vast new economic cooperation projects.

Of these two sets of concerns—trade and arms control—the latter is by far the more serious and has the greater potential for alliance disruption. With a modicum of restraint on both sides, trade disputes can probably be kept within limits. The United States will continue to be concerned about a net flow of real resources—in the form of subsidized credits, dumped agricultural products, and inflated prices paid for gas exports—to the Soviet Union. Europeans are probably mistaken if they dismiss these American complaints as mere "low politics," or if they think that cash sales of American grain at market prices (which are, in any case, deplored by a large sector of U.S. opinion) counterbalance those European actions the United States finds so objectionable. One of the most fundamental strategic interests of the United States, after all, is to prevent the resources of western Europe from combining with those of eastern Europe and the Soviet Union. Americans cannot but grow apprehensive when they see—or imagine they see—West Germany becoming a steel mill for the Soviet Union, even if it does so while remaining under the NATO umbrella.

At the same time, however, most Americans, including those in leading positions in the administration, appear to realize that European subsidization of the Soviet economy, while regrettable, is in fact quite small. It is not on a scale to threaten American security and does not begin to counterbalance the *positive* contributions that the European countries make to American global objectives. This realization, coupled with the parallel recognition in Europe that subsidized credits are, at least in principle, not in western Europe's own interests, should permit a defusing of the trade issues in the future.

Arms control disputes may prove more intractable. Mere "agreement to disagree" is not possible in this area. The issues involved are more emotional, with European (and to a lesser extent American) publics deeply split on whether or not the NATO dual-track negotiating posture is a reasonable one. The demand put forth by critics of the U.S. negotiating position at Geneva (notably the Social Democratic party opposition) that the United States agree to count French and British forces against U.S. totals had the unfortunate characteristic of appearing sensible to large numbers of people in Europe but of being completely unacceptable to any American government. The demand that the United States compensate the Soviet Union for the existence of French and British systems does make sense if one accepts—as many in Europe have—the fundamental premise that the only basis for peace is for all sides to accept the principle of parity between the competing "world systems." U.S. refusal to accept this principle, as codified in the Soviet intermediate-range nuclear forces proposals, is thus seen by some as tantamount to a U.S. admission of a desire for global superiority and as a serious threat to world peace.

From a U.S. perspective, however, these demands are unreasonable to the point that if pressed by European governments, they would call into question the very rationale for the alliance itself. It is hard to recall an alliance in which the smaller members set as a virtual precondition for participation that its largest member compensate its main adversary for the military capabilities of these allies themselves. Such an alliance might represent more of a security liability than an asset. These kinds of demands, if adopted by European governments, no doubt would encourage a major rethinking in the United States concerning NATO. At least some Americans would conclude that the United States would be better off walking out of NATO altogether and trusting its security to a "fortress America" rather than accepting such demands for the sake of preserving the appearance of such an "alliance."

Conclusions

In the areas of arms control and East-West economic and political relations, then, there are fundamental and perhaps widening conflicts between the United States and West Germany. These conflicts reflect differences between the American interest in managing a day-to-day rivalry with the Soviet Union, and the West German interest in pursuing a policy that is stable and that holds out the promise of long-term change in Europe.

Fortunately for the alliance, these conflicts tend to be partially self-limiting, if only because both American and German leaders recognize that if they allow particular policy disputes to get out of control, they run the risk of undermining the basis of the very policies they are attempting to defend. Although American policymakers recognize that particular German actions undercut U.S. efforts to contain the Soviet Union, they also realize that West Germany is itself a vital element in the containment effort and must not be driven into close relations with the East by ill-considered American pressures. Similarly, although German leaders object to particular American actions that interfere with German détente policy, most of these leaders recognize that Germany's very ability to pursue détente is premised on a continued alliance with the West and the leverage on the Soviet Union that only it can provide. The underlying fragility of each side's preferred policy toward the Soviet Union tends to be forgotten in periods of relative harmony within the alliance or even in the early stages of a crisis. It is quickly recalled, however, when crises are deep and prolonged.

Although recognition of this fragility is useful in limiting the willingness of each side to endure a real test of wills over particular policy issues, it is clearly not the best basis on which to maintain an alliance. In effect, American policymakers tell themselves and their publics that if they do not let the Germans "appease" the Soviet Union a little, then they risk alienating Germany altogether and allowing modest appeasement to grow into outright "Finlandization." For their part German leaders tell one another and the public that if they do not go along at least partly with the American "cold war" policy, they will lose any chance of exercising a restraining influence on the United States and perhaps become victims of a war they had no role in starting. Recourse to these kinds of arguments, needless to say, does little to promote a favorable image in the public of the alliance partner.

A far more desirable basis for the alliance would be a convergence between governments, supported by their publics, on the fundamental political and strategic issues involved. Although such a convergence of views is possible, there are trends both in the United States and in Germany that make it increasingly less likely. In Germany there appears to be a rise of what might be called "parochialism" on East-West issues. This parochialism is in part a response to and in turn feeds its American counterpart, a form of "unilateralism" that might indeed be called "great power parochialism."

A growing minority in Germany seems to believe that international politics is a struggle between two "world powers" that happened to pick the center of Germany as a convenient place in which to stage their confrontation. Although the Soviet "world power" can be criticized for some of its actions, to many in Germany it seems that the United States, in that it actually tries to enlist West Germany in its rivalry with the Soviet Union, is more culpable and more dangerous. The self-adopted pose of innocent bystander in the conflict between the "world powers" is likely to prove irritating to many Americans and frustrate efforts to forge a consensus between the United States and West Germany on dealings with the Soviet Union, particularly on arms control.

One of the potential implications of such parochialism is that it feeds its American counterpart—unilateralism. Just as in Europe the passage of time and generations tends to obscure the fact that the United States did not choose to come to Europe to pursue a rivalry with the Soviet Union, but rather that it was drawn into this rivalry by events in Europe, so these same factors can make Americans forget that global rivalry with the Soviet Union was not initially an end in itself, but came about as the United States sought to extend security and a sense of security to countries on the periphery of the USSR.

American unilateralism feeds on the feeling that other countries, while too valuable to simply be conceded to the Soviet sphere of influence, are nonetheless too weak and too unreliable to join with the United States in standing up to Soviet power. The United States must therefore look for unilateral ways to strike at Soviet power without support from its own allies. "Horizontal escalation" is one example of a strategy that incorporates some of these assumptions. Unilateralist strategies, by further undermining European support for the link with the United States, may help to make self-fulfilling many American suspicions about the allies and indeed lend a certain credibility to the view that Europe can somehow extricate itself from the U.S.-Soviet struggle.

In the face of a growing parochialism in Europe, expressed as a wish to opt out of the conflict between the two "world powers," and growing unilateralism in the United States, which manifests itself in a desire to lessen dependence on the allies that are the main stakes in the East-West rivalry, hopes for restoring alliance consensus on dealing with the Soviet Union do not look promising. As this chapter has tried to suggest, interpretations of Soviet behavior tend to be highly influenced by personal and national expectations about long-term possibilities. Although political leaders often convey the impression—and perhaps themselves believe—that they and their experts seek to understand the Soviet Union by "objective," "scientific" means and then formulate policies accordingly, in reality their own a priori preferences for certain policies cannot but help determine which Sovietological theories they choose to believe.

Because many in Europe want to believe that the policy of détente can lead to the creation of a European "peace order," from an American perspective they seem inclined to overestimate the significance of the Hungarian experiment and of the effects of détente on eastern Europe. Although this particular kind of wishful thinking is not at the moment in fashion in the United States, it does have its counterpoint in the American tendency to believe that Western actions, if sufficiently tough, could force radical changes in Soviet behavior and perhaps even the collapse of the Soviet system.

Because the United States and West Germany have different hopes and aspirations for the long term, they may simply have to learn to accommodate differences on East-West issues without reaching fundamental agreement. On the German side it would be helpful if there were greater sensitivity to the day-to-day concerns of the United States as it seeks to manage, under difficult circumstances, its global rivalry with the Soviet Union. In practical terms this might mean greater German responsiveness to American concerns in the area of credits to the East, technology transfer, and arms control. On the American side it would be helpful if there were less of a tendency to regard Germany as an ally whose interests must coincide completely with those of the United States. Instead, it would be preferable for U.S. policymakers to accept the fact Germany has certain understandable and legitimate long-term aspirations in its dealings with the East, and that the United States, to the degree that it is able, should try to further the realization of these aspirations. To the extent, however, that there are fundamental clashes of national interest on some of these issues, even a will to mutual accommodation would probably only narrow but not eliminate the current divergences between the two countries.

Note

1. Declassified documents reveal that national security adviser Walt Rostow sought to block the sale of West German pipe to the USSR less because of any material advantage that it would confer on the USSR, than on the grounds that the USSR had no "right" to be treated as an equal in the international trading system. See Angela Stent, *From Embargo to Ostpolitik* (New York: Cambridge University Press, 1981), 93.

PART TWO

Change Within the
Soviet Orbit:
Implications for the West

Chapter 4

External Implications of Soviet Internal Development

Arnold L. Horelick

The image of a Soviet Union that is at once "the strongest military power in the world" yet at the same time "an economic basket case" has become one of the most popular clichés of contemporary international politics. Allowing for exaggeration in at least one if not in both parts of the cliché, the disparity between the performance of the Soviet Union in building military power and expanding its military-political influence abroad, on the one hand, and its performance in virtually every sphere of internal development, on the other, describes a paradox of enormous significance for the future of both the USSR and the world order.

Precisely what that significance may be is a question that has provoked a plethora of wide-ranging judgments from statesmen, political analysts, Sovietologists, and journalists, many of them deeply contradictory. Some have warned that the leaders of a militarily powerful but internally weakened USSR are more likely than ever to resort to external aggression, either to acquire strategically crucial new geopolitical positions and resources before a combination of their own declining domestic capabilities and more competitive Western adversaries close their "window of opportunity," or to divert with foreign successes an increasingly deprived and potentially rebellious Soviet population. Others have argued the opposite—that Soviet leaders, concerned to prevent looming domestic troubles from growing into a crisis, will perceive the need for an inward turn that will constrain Soviet external behavior and make a quiet international life more appealing to the Kremlin.

The range of predictions and speculations to which the internal-external Soviet paradox has already given rise is extraordinarily wide. As the nature of the paradox becomes more widely appreciated and publicized, beliefs about its implications will powerfully shape the way that statesmen and informed publics in the West think about the Soviet Union and about appropriate Western strategies for dealing with it in the mid-1980s. Already, those who favor a more competitive strategy argue that the Soviet Union's domestic weaknesses, if not inadvertently relieved by the West through subsidized trade and technology transfers, make the USSR uniquely vulnerable to external pressures that could compel an otherwise reluctant Soviet leadership to adopt liberalizing economic reforms that would undermine the Soviet military priority. Others who prefer a more cooperative strategy argue the opposite—that because they face a severe time of troubles at home, Soviet leaders may be more amenable than ever before to negotiating arms control agreements and settlements of regional disputes calculated to relieve external pressures and to reduce the burden of the costly competition with the West. It is clear that divergent perspectives on these issues will need to be bridged if an effective Western strategy for dealing with the USSR is to be formulated and implemented.

As important as it is for formulating effective Western strategies to understand how Soviet internal development may affect Soviet foreign policy, there has thus far been little systematic analysis of the relationship. More often than not the connection between depictions of the Soviet Union's bleak domestic prospects and the likely external behavior of its leaders is made not by analysis or close reasoning, but by casual recourse to some "immutable" law of history or freewheeling resort to maxims of social psychology or psychoanalysis.

Assumptions about the character of the Soviet internal-external nexus are still for the most part implicit or at best sketchily expounded. Now that the era of Brezhnev's generation of leaders is coming to an end in the Soviet Union, Western analyses of the Soviet future will come more and more to focus on how the successor generation leadership will address the array of severe domestic problems that it will inherit and what the implications of its approach may be for the conduct of the USSR in the world. The outcome can hardly be foreseen by Western analysts, nor for that matter by the Soviet successors. But it is important that we begin to approach the issues more thoughtfully and systematically so as to improve our understanding of the possibilities that lie ahead. Intelligent monitoring of the future course of Soviet domestic development and its interaction with the USSR's global behavior requires at a minimum some working hypotheses describing possible linkages. And the elaboration of such hypotheses is a necessary first step to understanding how Western policies may influence these outcomes.

The purpose of this chapter is to help structure the problem of defining the linkages between the internal problems and the external behavior of the Soviet Union. It proceeds by identifying the major elements that compose the Soviet internal-external paradox. Then it reviews briefly Russian and Soviet historical patterns with respect to internal-external linkages. This provides the point of departure for an exploration of some hypotheses about possible interrelationships between Soviet internal developments and external behavior. The chapter concludes with an attempt to define the sphere within which Western influence on Soviet domestic development and external behavior can most effectively be exercised.

Major Elements of the Paradox

The image of the Soviet Union as a military colossus with feet of clay evolved gradually during the 1970s, in phases, with the USSR's reputation for vast military power establishing itself first, followed, almost precisely as it peaked, by heightened sensitivity in the West to growing evidence of Soviet domestic and imperial troubles. In the early 1970s the perception of the Soviet Union as a military superpower, coequal with the United States, matured in the consciousness of the West. This perception facilitated and was in turn formalized by the signing of the 1972 U.S.-Soviet strategic arms control agreements and associated documents spelling out the mutual responsibilities of the two countries for preventing nuclear war, responsibilities that distinguished the United States and the USSR from all other states. These developments underlined the radical transformation that had occurred in both the reality and perception of Soviet military power since the Cuban missile crisis only one decade earlier, when the dramatic revelation of U.S. military superiority called into question the aspirations and the claims of Nikita Khrushchev to a global military and political role for his country.

By the mid-1970s payoffs from the huge military investments steadily pumped into the Soviet military establishment by Khrushchev's successors had begun to make themselves evident in ways that raised increasingly heated debate in the West, particularly in the United States, as to whether the USSR might not be seeking comprehensive military superiority and threatening to achieve it. On the central strategic level this concern centered on the testing and deployment of a fourth generation of heavy, MIRVed, and increasingly accurate Soviet intercontinental ballistic missiles (ICBMs), with growing capabilities for attacking the U.S. land-based ICBM forces, and of new generations of Soviet nuclear submarines carrying ballistic missiles (SLBMs) of greatly increased range that were capable of striking U.S. targets from Soviet home waters and ports. In western Europe this growing evidence that the U.S. strategic nuclear edge over the USSR had been eroded served to amplify the unsettling effects of the deployment of new, highly capable Soviet strategic systems targeted on Europe—the Backfire bomber and the SS-20 MIRVed intermediate-range ballistic missile—that many in Europe saw as threatening to decouple declining U.S. strategic nuclear power from a European theater in which long-standing Soviet conventional military preponderance was also continuing to grow. Even the massive Soviet military buildup in the Far East, seen in the 1960s as a welcome diversion bound to diminish the Soviet military threat to the West, was viewed more ominously during the 1970s, as it became apparent that the buildup in the East was not being conducted at the expense of the Western front. The Asian buildup was now seen as augmenting Soviet military capabilities to threaten Western interests in Asia, particularly in ocean and littoral areas within reach of the rapidly growing Soviet Pacific Fleet and land-based Soviet naval and reconnaissance aircraft operating out of both Soviet and newly accessible Vietnamese airfields.

A turning point in the U.S. debate over the magnitude and character of the military threat posed by growing and modernizing Soviet strategic forces came during the second year of the Carter administration, when new intelligence data revealed improvements in the accuracy of new Soviet ICBM guidance systems that exceeded expectations, accelerating by several years administration estimates of the time when the U.S. land-based ICBM force would become unacceptably vulnerable to Soviet attack. Thereafter the debate over whether an early U.S. strategic response was required was effectively ended, although controversy concerning the appropriate form of the response, including its sensitivity to political and arms control considerations, persists to this day.

Unfolding new evidence of growing Soviet military prowess and growing Western awareness of the magnitude and momentum of the Soviet military investment programs behind it, were reinforced, strongly in the United States, much less so in Europe and Japan, by a sharp increase in the assertiveness of Soviet political-military conduct in the third world. This new phase of militant Soviet engagement began in the mid-1970s—in Angola, South Yemen, the Horn of Africa, Indochina, culminating, at the end of 1979, in the Soviet invasion of Afghanistan, the first large-scale direct combat employment of Soviet armed forces in the third world. The impact of the Soviet military move into Afghanistan was greatly magnified by the sudden and dramatic collapse of the pro-U.S. regime of the Shah of Iran, which focused U.S. administration concern on the vulnerability of crucial Persian Gulf oil sources to potential Soviet coercive diplomacy, interdiction, or seizure.

As the 1970s drew to a close, parallel with sharply rising concern over the growing military might of the USSR and the potential threats associated with it, accumulating evidence also began to appear in the West that the Soviet leaders were facing bleaker prospects on the home front and in their eastern European empire. The earliest such evidence to attract wide public attention in the West were reports in 1977–78 of CIA studies of Soviet oil prospects that noted a marked slowdown in the rate of growth of Soviet petroleum output and projected a cessation of growth by the end of the decade and a sharp downturn in output in the first half of the eighties. This slowdown in petroleum output raised the possibility that the USSR would soon be obliged to seek access to Persian Gulf oil at a time when, it was then widely expected, Western dependence on Persian Gulf supplies would have grown even further. These projections also gave rise to speculation that the USSR would be unwilling or unable to continue to supply oil in volumes required to sustain the already faltering economies of the eastern European parts of the Soviet empire, raising the danger of political instability there.

These CIA Soviet oil studies stimulated a rise in analytical and subsequently public attention to other less dramatic but more pervasive evidence of slowdown in Soviet economic growth in the 1970s and even more so of prospects for accelerated decline in the 1980s. Gradual decline in the growth rate of the Soviet economy had been a well-known and long-observed phenomenon for many years before the late 1970s. From an average annual rate of 6 percent in the 1950s, Soviet gross national product (GNP) growth had declined in the 1960s to 5 percent and in the first half of the 1970s to around 4 percent. But this decline was attributed largely to abnormally high rates in the 1950s as the Soviet Union completed its recovery from the devastation of World War II and as easy gains in productivity were realized from the elimination of some of the grossest irrationalities of Stalinism, and to the general maturing of the Soviet economy. In the early 1970s GNP growth seemed adequate to sustain both a high rate of growth in military expenditures and uninterrupted, although modest, improvements in the Soviet standard of living. By the mid-1970s, however, it became clear that the slide was continuing and that the rate of decline might even accelerate, raising for the first time the question whether in the 1980s the Soviet economy could generate rates of growth required to sustain the military effort, keep improvement in the standard of living within historic parameters, and maintain a rate of investment sufficient to promote future economic growth.

Western predictions that the Soviet economy faced an acceleration in the long-term rate of decline in economic growth have been borne out by the recent record of the Soviet economy. Since 1979 yearly Soviet growth has averaged only around 2 percent. Although part of this decline can be attributed to five consecutive poor Soviet harvests, growth in industrial output had already begun to fall sharply before the streak of bad harvests, averaging only around 3 percent since 1976, compared with almost 6 percent a year from 1971 to 1975.

Until the mid-1970s economic growth was maintained by the infusion of increasing amounts of new workers, capital, land, and easily accessible natural resources. Although the effectiveness of these inputs declined steadily—capital-output ratios have risen monotonically as the rate of growth of labor productivity has declined—respectable GNP growth was still achieved by essentially brute force methods. This kind of profligate use of production inputs is no longer possible. The Soviet Union now faces a period in which the number of fresh increments to the labor force will decline rapidly, a process that began in the mid-1970s but is now accelerating. Adverse demographic trends are slowing the net growth of the Soviet labor force dramatically. It will fall during the 1980s to an average of 0.5 percent a year, down from 1 percent in the 1970s. Moreover, the more highly skilled and strategically located "European" labor force will barely replace itself in the 1980s; most of the growth will occur among the Muslim-Turkic peoples to the south and east of the country's industrial heartland. These additions to the labor force will be predominantly rural, less educated, largely non-Russian speaking, and, judging from past experience, not predisposed to move from the countryside to cities, much less to cities in the northern or western parts of the country.

Meanwhile, the vast reservoir of easily accessible raw materials, vast infusions of which, along with massive fresh inputs of labor, had fueled the Soviet economy's earlier rapid extensive growth, is now largely depleted. Thanks to the natural treasures of Siberia, the USSR remains a resource-rich country, but the costs of exploring, extracting, and transporting these resources, particularly energy, are soaring.

Although rising resource costs and a growing labor shortage reflect geographic and demographic phenomena rather than systemic or structural defects of the economy, the two categories are not entirely separable. The rapid depletion of easily accessible resources also reflects faulty strategic choices and an incentive system that systematically sacrifices future growth to current production, manifested, for example, in short-sighted oil recovery practices. The slowdown in the growth of the labor force is a critical problem primarily because labor productivity is so low and sluggish productivity is clearly a function of systemic failing; moreover, declining birthrates in the European parts of the USSR are, at least in part, a function of systemic shortcomings, especially with respect to housing and other consumer amenities, shortages of which have contributed to the increased incidence of childless and one-child families in these areas.

With the extensive brute force phase of economic development now behind the USSR, Soviet leaders must look to increases in productivity as the key to future economic growth. But returns from new increments of labor and capital have been declining for years, and the rate of decline has been progressively rising. Pessimistic forecasts of future Soviet economic performance stem largely from the USSR's poor productivity record and from the failure of the Soviet leadership to address the structural problems of the Soviet economy that underlie it: directive planning, central allocations of resources, administratively determined prices, and incentives oriented toward physical production goals. The growth of total factor productivity (output per unit of combined inputs) was low even when the Soviet economy was growing rapidly—an average of only 1 percent in the 1960s—and it has been negative in every year but one since 1973.

Thus the Soviet economy is caught in a bind. Now that the Soviet economy has matured and grown complex, the highly centralized system of planning and management that served the phase of extensive growth constitutes a massive brake on the growth of production per unit of input. But at the same time, adverse demographic and geographic factors are suddenly also slowing down the growth of basic labor, capital, and natural resource inputs into the economy. The economic system is poorly suited to make the transition from the extensive phase to the intensive phase of economic development that the USSR has entered, while shortages of manpower and cheap natural resources diminish the capacity of the system to squeeze more out of the economy in its present phase.

The key political question is whether the slowdown in Soviet economic growth is likely to have such adverse effects on the standard of living of the Soviet people as to have destabilizing consequences in the manner of Poland. A succession of post-Stalin Soviet leaders have displayed keen sensitivity to this problem. They have made sure to deliver to a population renowned for its modest expectations and stoicism in the face of adversity, a steady improvement in the standard of living, rising much more slowly than in the West and even then in most of eastern Europe, but nevertheless rising perceptibly.

Under Brezhnev, consumer welfare was protected against having to bear the full brunt of the economic slowdown. This was done primarily at the expense of future growth: The rate of growth of fixed capital investment was cut back sharply after the middle of the 1970s. Although the decision to cut back on investment may have been motivated in part, at least initially, by a desire to force improvement in the efficiency of investment and to reduce the huge backlog of uncompleted construction, the continued starving of investment appears to reflect also the leadership's concern not to arrest the growth of consumer welfare. Recent studies by the CIA indicate that the rate of growth of military expenditures, which had been running steadily at around 4 percent since the mid-1960s, might also have slowed down, to about 2 percent, after 1976, but it is not clear whether this resulted from a deliberate decision to reduce expenditures or whether it reflected a cyclical procurement lull, technological problems, or spillover into the military sector of some of the same factors that have caused a general slowdown in Soviet civilian industry.

Can Soviet leaders tolerate for very long the kind of slow growth that the Soviet economy has experienced since the late 1970s? Can they tolerate politically the changes that would have to be made in the economy to improve performance substantially? Western students of the Soviet economy see three broad options open to Soviet leaders:

1. Far-reaching economic reform aimed at decentralization of planning and management and the substantial reduction of directive targets to enterprises. This kind of reform would radically change the function and character of central planning, and inevitably make profit the dominant criterion of performance, from which price, employment policy, and other radical reforms would necessarily follow.
2. An authoritarian, more repressive (neo-Stalinist) effort to stimulate growth in productivity by attacking pervasive indiscipline and corruption in the Soviet economic system, probably including a trend to even more centralized planning and management.
3. A continuation of Brezhnev's "muddling through" approach (perhaps "muddling down" in the 1980s), not excluding some tinkering with the existing mechanism or attacks on poor work discipline, but basically a strategy of preserving the structure and not radically altering broad economic policies, in the expectation that larger increments to the work force and payoffs from Siberian energy and other large investments in the 1990s will spark a growth turnaround (or that "something else" will turn up on the next watch).

The key questions are: What are the implications for Soviet external behavior in the mid-1980s and beyond of the expected continued weakening of the domestic foundations of massive Soviet military power? In particular, what are the implications for future Soviet foreign and defense policies of the domestic choices that Soviet leaders make in response to the new time of troubles ahead?

Theory and History

Most of those who venture forecasts about the likely external ramifications of Soviet internal troubles tend to buttress their views by allusions to the lessons of history or to theories of human behavior. On closer inspection, however, neither theory nor Russian and Soviet history help much with the problems considered in this chapter. The interactions or linkages between the domestic development and the external behavior of states are not only highly complex, but also vary greatly both among states with similar political and social systems and among those with different systems. Domestic factors tend to have more immediate and direct impact on the external behavior of advanced democratic states, particularly with respect to issues involving the use of force, large expenditures of public funds, and the special interests of electoral constituencies. The external behavior of dictatorial and authoritarian states is, as a rule, less directly and immediately affected by the interests or preferences of those who are not part of the elite political class, but it is not entirely immune to domestic pressures that inevitably bear indirectly on decision makers. The capabilities of all states to conduct themselves in the international arena is inevitably constrained by the availability of relevant internal resources for use abroad; and in the most fundamental sense, the external behavioral impulses of leaders grow out of their domestic social-political systems, while their perceptions of the external reality with which they must contend are shaped largely by the ideology, political culture, values, and beliefs of their societies.

The Western social science theory literature that seeks to explain the interrelationship between domestic factors and external behavior tends either to be ethnocentric and therefore unsuitable for application to non-Western nondemocratic systems, or it attempts to escape the constraints of particular political cultures by conceptualizing internal-external linkages at a level of generality so high as to be of limited value for any particular case. Efforts to theorize specifically about Soviet or Communist systems are few and far between. The most ambitious and successful such effort by Alexander Dallin describes in broad sweep the domestic context of Soviet foreign policy, iden-

tifying a large spectrum of variables but concluding that there is
no formula or pattern of history that permits the analyst to assign
weights to the various ingredients in the mix.[1]

History teaches us primarily about the richness of the range of
possibilities but provides no confident rules for choosing among
alternatives. More specifically, Russian history is ambiguous or
ambivalent regarding the pattern of linkages between domestic
development and external behavior. Indeed, in the classics of
Russian historiography it is the impact of *external* events on
internal development rather than the converse that is seen as the
basic historical pattern.

Many renowned historians of Russia, including V. O. Klyuchevsky, have held that the goal of building and maintaining a
powerful military force both to defend Russia and to expand it
was the principal motor force driving the political, economic,
and social development of the Russian state from Ivan the Terrible to Peter the Great and on into the modern era.[2] Some Western historians and analysts of the Soviet period, notably Richard
Pipes and William Odom, have argued that militarism in the
service of external expansion has continued to be the primary
goal to which political, economic, and social development has
been subordinated throughout the Soviet period as well.[3] Although this view is contested, Russian history on the whole
provides far more cases of external failures inducing domestic
changes—from reform to revolution—than of domestic changes
generating major alterations in external behavior. As Klyuchevsky wrote:

Throughout our own history . . . a Russian war carried to a successful issue has always helped to strengthen the previously compounded order, . . . whereas a Russian war carried to a disastrous
issue invariably has evoked such a volume of popular dissatisfaction
as has wrung from the Government of the day a larger or smaller
measure of positive reform, and compelled the authorities to overhaul domestic matters. And inasmuch as, during the time it has been
doing the latter, the government of the day has always avoided external conflict, and even, for the same purpose, allowed the international position of the State to suffer, progress in Russia's political life

at home has always been gained at the price of Russia's political misfortune abroad.[4]

Russia's defeat in the Crimean War contributed much to the modernizing impulse behind the abolition of serfdom in 1862. The debacle of the Russo-Japanese war further alienated broad strata of Russian society from the czarist regime and contributed to the 1905 revolutionary outburst, and Russia's enormous losses and reverses during World War I created the massive popular disaffection from the czarist order without which neither the March nor the October revolution would have occurred. Instances of internal troubles or crises generating foreign adventures are much harder to find.

Historically, there is no precedent in the behavior of Soviet leaders since the revolution to support the proposition that leaders in that tradition would see in foreign policy adventures a remedy for domestic troubles or dangers. Indeed, the contrary has more often appeared to be the case: Domestic weakness has inclined successive Soviet leaderships to extremely cautious, even acquiescent international conduct, although such behavior has at times been covered with a belligerent rhetorical veneer designed precisely to shield from both foreign and domestic observers the underlying weakness of the regime.

The Brest-Litovsk Treaty is, of course, the outstanding instance of Bolshevik willingness to surrender major national interests to superior foreign power in the interests of protecting a weakened power base from complete destruction. The precedent of Brest-Litovsk has been repeatedly cited when circumstances have demanded Soviet retreat in unfavorable circumstances. In the immediate postrevolutionary period there was hardly any concession or promise Soviet leaders were not willing to make in order to buy time or to ease external pressures on their precarious domestic base. Precisely the same pattern of conduct can be observed during the years leading up to World War II. Stalin appeared to be acutely aware of the weakness and potential instability of the USSR after the traumas of collectivization, forced draft industrialization, and the massive purges.

Avoiding conflict, at virtually any cost, was the watchword of Stalin's foreign policy in the late 1930s, when it became clear to the Kremlin that the Western democracies were unwilling or unable to bring Hitler to heel. The logical outcome of Stalin's foreign policy was the Ribbentrop-Molotov Pact of 1939, which accelerated the onset of war in the West but bought the Soviet Union almost two more years of respite. Despite the time purchased, Stalin's inordinate fear of provoking the Germans and his lack of confidence in the regime's ability to hold the country together under Nazi attack caused him, in the spring of 1941, to disregard clear strategic and tactical warnings of the German onslaught and to deny to his military commanders opportunities to improve the USSR's defensive posture in good time to mitigate some of the crippling effects of the initial "surprise" attack.

In the postwar period the relationship between the Soviet Union's domestic predicament and its external conduct is difficult to correlate. It has been argued that in the aftermath of the war the tremendous devastation of the country required maintenance of a "war-time" atmosphere to ensure the recovery effort. The outside world had to be presented in a hostile light, and an atmosphere of militant self-sacrifice against a persisting external threat had to be cultivated. Moreover, it was essential to conceal the postwar weariness of the Soviet Union from the West and likewise abruptly to cut off even the trickle of Western contact with the Soviet people that wartime coalition conditions had necessitated. Yet despite Stalin's belligerent posturing the Soviet Union executed a rapid and massive demobilization, and Stalin's behavior beyond the confines of the Soviet zone of occupation was, on the whole, cautious, e.g., in Iran and Greece.

Stalin's successors inherited an extremely tense domestic and external environment and a deprived, beleaguered population lacking the feared and respected *vozhd'* to keep it in check. A felt need to decompress internally coincided with a sense of enormous pressure and exposure externally: The result was a calculated effort to reduce international tension and to initiate a phase of cooperative relations with the West (termination of the Korean and Indochina conflicts, the 1955 Geneva Summit conference, rapprochement with Yugoslavia, the Austrian State

Treaty). By the late 1950s Khrushchev had eliminated the Stalinist "anti-Party" group and was free to initiate a phase of extensive reorganizations and reforms at home. Now, however, improved economic performance, higher morale, and optimistic expectations about the future coincided with an assertive posture abroad, culminating in the late 1950s in a rocket-rattling threat in Berlin designed to compel legitimation of the German Democratic Republic. Thus, while changes in domestic policies do tend to be associated with changes in external policies, these changes are not necessarily in the same direction. Khrushchev's de-Stalinization and domestic liberalization were accompanied by a broad new Soviet global offensive, culminating in the Cuban missile adventure. Brezhnevite détente, on the other hand, had as its corollary the termination of de-Stalinization at home and the repression of dissidents and other potential "subversive" offshoots of détente.

Alternative Hypotheses

As noted earlier, propositions and assertions about the relationship between Soviet domestic development and the external behavior of the USSR have recently begun to appear with increasing frequency in Western political discourse. These vary widely with respect both to the external behavioral propensities that alternative Soviet domestic states are held to generate as well as to the expected impact on Soviet decision makers of Western policies designed to affect these Soviet propensities. The range of major hypotheses about the linkage between Soviet domestic development and the external policy tendencies of its leaders may be displayed in a four-cell matrix in which the rows describe alternative domestic states ("better" and "worse" from the Soviet perspective) and the columns depict alternative Soviet external behavioral propensities ("better" and "worse" from the West's perspective). (See the figure.)

Hypotheses regarding the impact of Western efforts to influence the postulated Soviet external behavioral propensities tend to be grouped along alternative "hard" and "soft" lines: "Hard" variants hypothesize that domestic stringencies and

External Behavior

	Worse	Better
Domestic Development — Worse	1	2
Better	4	3

The four cells shown in the matrix will henceforth be identified in the Russian fashion, as (1) the worse, the worse *(chem khuzhe, tem khuzhe)*; (2) the worse, the better *(chem khuzhe, tem luchshe)*; (3) the better, the better *(chem luchshe, tem luchshe)*; and (4) the better, the worse *(chem luchshe, tem khuzhe)*.

difficulties tend to make Soviet leaders more vulnerable to Western pressures, enhancing the effectiveness of denial or punitive measures or of threats to use them for compelling desired Soviet behavior; "soft" variants, on the other hand, hold that adverse domestic conditions tend to make Soviet leaders more influenceable by positive external inducements.

The Worse, the Worse

Linkages between deteriorating domestic conditions in the USSR and more belligerent or aggressive Soviet external behavior appear in several forms, all revolving around the expectation that domestic decline will trigger external behavior designed to exploit possible vanishing strategic opportunities or to relieve domestic pressures by distracting or mobilizing action abroad. In the once widely publicized "window of opportunity" case, which emerged at the end of the 1970s, especially after the Soviet invasion of Afghanistan, the prospect of imminent domestic decline threatening ultimately to diminish relative Soviet military power was seen as impelling Soviet leaders to capitalize on a possibly transient "window" of strategic opportunity while there was still time to do so.[5]

The popularity of this view declined markedly after 1980, presumably as a consequence of the generally low-key pattern of Soviet external behavior that in fact did emerge after the Soviet invasion of Afghanistan. Some observers attributed Soviet failure to act more assertively to a paralysis of leadership in Moscow associated with the aging of the Soviet leaders and particularly the progressive incapacitation of Brezhnev during his last years; persisting adverse domestic trends under a more energetic Soviet leadership would presumably resurrect the "window of opportunity" syndrome. Although such behavior has no precedent in Soviet history and appears to fit precisely the definition of "adventurism" so anathematized in Bolshevik doctrine, proponents of this view hold that the circumstances now obtaining are entirely without precedent in Soviet experience, since the combination of Soviet domestic weakness and military superiority has never existed.

A related variant of the "window of opportunity" thesis postulates aggressive Soviet external behavior in pursuit of objectives whose acquisition might relieve severe domestic strains (e.g., control of Persian Gulf oil or the exacting of major economic concessions from western Europe).

A second set of *the worse, the worse* variants sees desperate Soviet leaders lunging out externally to distract an increasingly restive Soviet population, to provide an external justification for domestic austerity and tightened social and political controls, and to preserve by external expansion the legitimacy of a regime that is manifestly failing to deliver at home. For those who adhere to this view, a belief that the Soviet Union is in deep economic and social crisis, even approaching collapse, coexists with and even fuels the paradoxical belief that the same Soviet Union grows more dangerous as it approaches its end. This thesis curiously mirrors a classic Bolshevik image of the declining West, still occasionally displayed in the USSR, which holds that imperialism becomes more dangerous precisely as it approaches its inevitable doom.

Policy implications drawn from Case 1 scenarios have both softer and harder variants. Adherents of the softer view warn against the danger of triggering desperate Soviet external reactions by threatening the Soviet Union and foreclosing the possibility of reduced competitive pressures at a time of severe domestic troubles. Others draw the opposite conclusion—that more aggressive Soviet behavioral propensities associated with domestic decline will place added strains on deterrence, which must therefore be reinforced accordingly. The West must build its military strength more rapidly and maintain a tough posture so as to raise Soviet estimates of the costs and risks of attempting an external "breakout" or diversion. This view, which was especially influential in U.S. official circles in the last year of the Carter administration and the first year of Reagan's, was not widely shared in western Europe. Divergent perspectives on this matter contributed to the U.S.-allied debate about NATO defense spending growth targets and out-of-area security issues, especially centering on the Persian Gulf, which was widely believed in Washington in 1980–81 to be an imminent target of Soviet aggression or coercive diplomacy.

The Worse, the Better

A sharply opposed set of hypotheses holds that domestic adversity is more likely to cause Soviet leaders to exercise restraint in their external behavior, perhaps even to seek opportunities for retrenchment or retreat from overextended or costly foreign positions, and to comport themselves so as to promote accommodation with their most powerful adversaries. The motivation most commonly attributed to Soviet leaders on this view is a perceived need to alter the state's priorities, to reduce the flow of resources devoted to external and security matters so as to free up resources and political energies for a period of sustained concentration on internal needs. On this view a Soviet regime that has turned inward to work on the society's long-neglected domestic problems will seek a quiet life externally in order to (1) relieve the strains and demands on its resources and attention imposed by the external environment, and (2) to create an external political climate conducive to desired imports of technology, grain, and credits from abroad. This kind of linkage between adverse domestic development and restrained external behavior may be attributed to either conservative or reformist Soviet leaders, with conservatives seeking to avoid the necessity for structural reform and reformists to facilitate it by reducing competitive external pressures and promoting an expanded flow of resources from the West.

Again, there are two Western policy variants, harder and softer, of this case. The softer variant holds that the Soviet propensity toward external restraint postulated in this case is best cultivated by providing positive incentives, including a relaxation of tension and of competitive pressures, in order to shape an external environment conducive to a turning inward and to reform in the Soviet Union. A tense international environment in which Soviet leaders perceived the West as poised to exploit Soviet internal weakness would, on this view, rule out far-reaching reform efforts at home or any substantial weakening of the military priority. Hypotheses captured in this variant of Case 2 reflect most of the same assumptions about the relationship between Soviet domestic development and Soviet external behavior held by the classic détente school (Case 3), notwithstanding marked differences in the points of departure for the two cases—1969–71 versus the early 1980s.

During 1982, as contentious East-West trade issues came to the fore in the alliance and Soviet economic performance continued to decline, U.S. official thinking about the Soviet internal-external nexus shifted from Case 1 *(the worse, the worse)* to a hard variant of Case 2 *(the worse, the better)*, in which the operative hypotheses of Reagan administration policy toward the Soviet Union, at least during much of its first term, appear to reside. The essential argument is that the Soviet Union confronts a domestic crisis so severe that if the West does not permit Soviet leaders to escape the burdens of their own shortcomings by gratuitously relaxing competitive pressures or imprudently subsidizing the Soviet economy, they will have no realistic alternative but to adopt far-reaching and inevitably liberalizing economic reforms. Such economic reforms are bound to have a pluralizing effect on the Soviet polity, which will necessarily weaken the traditional priority position of the military sector. Such a Soviet Union would be a more restrained and reasonable international actor.[6]

It is acknowledged that no Soviet leaders would willingly adopt economic and social reforms that they perceived as generating potential threats to the very core of their political power and to the guiding principles of the Soviet system itself. Yet only far-reaching structural reforms have the potential for pluralizing the political system and ending the lopsided priority on amassing military power and expanding the Soviet empire at the expense of domestic well-being. Adherents of this view see the ending of that priority as the only basis for genuine accommodation between East and West. In the hard perspective, Soviet leaders can only be *driven* to the risky course of reform and only if other plausible alternatives for averting economic collapse or domestic instability have been foreclosed. Denying such easier alternatives, on this view, requires from the West (a) termination of subsidies for East-West trade and of easy Soviet access to Western technology such as might feed Soviet hopes that shrewdly managed use of imported Western resources could make it possible to restore momentum to the Soviet economy without liberalizing economic reforms; and (b) maintenance of competitive military buildup pressure so that Soviet leaders must pay an ever-increasing price if they insist on preserving their present military advantages, much less seek to enlarge them. The theory is that if Soviet leaders are thus obliged to bear the burdens of their own domestic shortcomings, they will ultimately be compelled, in order to avert imminent disaster, to accept the potential risks to their political power that far-reaching liberalizing reform would entail.

The Better, the Better

Hypotheses describing linkages between improved domestic conditions in the USSR and Soviet external behavior are now seldom articulated because most observers are preoccupied with current internal trends in the Soviet Union that are seen as negative. Case 3, however, remains important because it captures the major hypotheses of the "classic" détente period of the early 1970s, which continue to inform the thinking of many regarding the likely external ramifications of deteriorating Soviet domestic conditions.

In general, Case 3 hypotheses hold that improving domestic conditions in the Soviet Union and moderate Soviet external behavior tend to be mutually reinforcing phenomena and that over time their interaction can lead to progressively greater Soviet leader preoccupation with economic well-being and a greater stake in the international economic and political order. Extreme versions of this interpretation, advanced against the Soviet Union by the Communist Chinese in the early 1960s, hold that the preoccupation of the Soviet leaders with consumerism ("goulash Communism") was leading to the "embourgecise-ment" of its foreign as well as its domestic policies.

Policy implications derived from this détente model of the Soviet internal-external nexus vary primarily in accordance with the mix of "carrots" and "sticks" implied. Most adherents of this view acknowledge the necessity for the West to maintain a mixed cooperative-competitive relationship with the Soviet Union under conditions of détente.

The Better, the Worse

One school of thought holds that any improvement in Soviet domestic conditions serves only to make additional resources and energies available to the leadership for external expansionist purposes and to reduce the domestic strains that the regime's priority development of military power inevitably entails. Only an amelioration of domestic conditions that resulted from systemic change so extensive as to alter the fundamental political order of the society is held likely, in this view, to produce more acceptable Soviet external conduct. To the extent that the Soviet political system remains essentially what it is, on this view, improved domestic conditions only reinforce the capacities and determination of Soviet leaders to persist in the amassing of military power and the conduct of global expansion. Case 4 clearly is the complement of the hard variant of Case 2 *(the worse, the better)*.

Scope for Western Policy

The historical record is sufficiently complex and diverse to provide at least some evidence in some time frames to support each of the hypotheses examined in the preceding section. But, as observed earlier, no systematic pattern can be discerned that reveals consistent linkages between improved or worsened Soviet domestic conditions, on one hand, and particular external behavioral propensities of Soviet leaders, on the other. No particular hypothesis among those examined seems so much more plausible or analytically powerful than the others as to command great confidence for predictive or policy guidance purposes.

The conceptual approaches embraced by these hypotheses tend to assume a relationship between Soviet domestic development and Soviet external behavior that is more direct and immediate than seems likely to occur under complex real world conditions. There are many intervening variables that can and do complicate the internal-external interaction and muddy the distinction between the two spheres. For example, the Soviet leadership succession process has in the past and may again in the future develop a policy dynamic of its own profoundly affecting both the internal and external spheres, but in a highly uneven manner reflecting the diverse personal or factional interests of contenders rather than the more coherent thrust of larger domestic political, economic, or social imperatives. Major shifts in Soviet foreign policy in the years of the Stalin succession struggle (1953–58) sometimes sprang from the deliberate manipulation of external issues in Khrushchev's struggle against Malenkov and the "anti-Party" group rather than from a purposeful strategy developed as a foreign policy complement to the "thawing" of the USSR domestically after the tyrant's death. To the extent that factional conflict erodes the consensus politics approach of the Brezhnev era, Soviet external behavior is likely to be increasingly sensitive to the possibly uneven course of the Chernenko succession struggle.

Furthermore, efforts to explain or predict Soviet external behavior in terms of influences from the internal environment tend also to ignore or underestimate the extent to which exogenous factors in the external environment may drive Soviet foreign policy decision making, overriding domestic considerations that might otherwise point Soviet policy in different directions externally, and even compelling changes in internal policy to accommodate external exigencies. Far-reaching changes in the external environment have in the past and could again in the future dominate Soviet decision making in both the foreign and domestic spheres. The rise of the Nazi threat during the 1930s dominated the conduct of Soviet foreign and military policies throughout a decade that was marked by massive internal disruptions and sharp changes in domestic policy directions. Indeed, to some extent Stalin's assessment of the gathering external menace conditioned his strategy and tactics for dealing with domestic issues and served as a justification and probably a spur for his murderous purges of the Soviet political and military elites.

In present circumstances there is an additional conceptual problem associated with scenarios that project major external behavioral changes from Soviet internal weaknesses. These scenarios start with the assumption that Soviet leaders perceive the country's domestic condition to be so grave as to compel them to make major alterations in the Soviet internal order or in their external behavior, or both, that they would otherwise regard as unacceptable.

It is highly unlikely, however, that Soviet leaders will see their economy or their society in such desperate straits, or that they will perceive the alternatives before them as starkly as some Western observers do. This is not because the elements of weakness and decline identified in Western analyses have gone unnoticed in the USSR. Almost every item on the Western list of Soviet troubles may also be found in the speeches of Soviet leaders and in detailed articles by specialists: Gorbachev, like Chernenko and Andropov before him, has warned about widespread labor indiscipline and the chronic lag of productivity behind demand for consumer products; Brezhnev in his time expressed deep concern about the food problem, acknowledging it to be a political as well as an economic problem; Soviet economists have warned about steadily rising capital-output ratios and about the slowness of Soviet industry to generate and absorb technological innovation; and Soviet demographers have written extensively about declining national birthrates, reductions in increments to the work force, and the special problems associated with trying to bring central Asians into the industrial work force. But these elements do not add up to a picture of pervasive decline or weakness. There is lacking in the Soviet depiction of the country's troubles the sense of acute urgency that one would expect from leaders concerned about an imminent crisis.

Under Brezhnev, the Soviet leadership seemed prepared to ride out the slowdown, leaving intact existing institutions and structure and adhering generally to the basic policies of the early Brezhnev years. They attempted sporadically to cope with aspects of this slowdown by making relatively minor adjustments in the system of planning and management, and by experiments with piecemeal decentralization and incentives that never managed to be generalized into national reform.

Brezhnev's successors have been under stronger pressure to improve Soviet economic performance and, during Andropov's fifteen-month tenure, proceeded somewhat more energetically than during Brezhnev's declining years. During the brief Chernenko interregnum, there was a widespread perception in the Soviet Union of reversion to "business as usual." And while the selection of Gorbachev as Party General Secretary in February 1985 aroused expectations of a more vigorous attack on the USSR's economic problems, there is still no clear evidence that Gorbachev and his colleagues are laying the groundwork for comprehensive economic reform. Soviet press discussion of possible innovations in economic planning and management is neither as widespread nor as animated as it was in 1965, after the ouster of Khrushchev. At the same time there has been a persistence and even intensification of warnings, stimulated earlier by Polish events, about the dangers of "consumerism," anticollectivist attitudes, and of "whipping up problems long since solved."[7] Whether Andropov, had he lived, would have moved much more aggressively to reform remains a debatable, if moot, question. The major themes of his domestic policy were on balance more authoritarian than reformist: restoration of order and discipline and curbing of corruption.

In any case the behavior of Soviet leaders since Brezhnev's death, while not indicating complacency, does not suggest that they live in fear of economic collapse or political upheaval arising out of food or other consumer goods shortages. They are not likely to be more pessimistic about their prospects than the CIA, which reported to the Congress shortly after Brezhnev's death that, on its current trajectory, the Soviet economy is not losing its viability; that an economic "collapse"—defined as a sudden and sustained decline in GNP—is not even a remote possibility; and that without major structural reforms or substantial reallocation of resources from defense to investment, GNP growth would remain "slow but positive."[8] New Soviet leaders, like their predecessors, will place the supreme domestic priority on the maintenance of political control, and they will not consciously jeopardize it in order to gain a percentage point or two of GNP growth.

Moreover, Soviet economic performance in 1983–84 shows measurable improvement over the record of the final Brezhnev years, with GNP growth in the probable range of 3 to 4 percent, as compared with an average of only 2 percent growth over the 1979–82 period. Most of this improvement is probably accounted for by the work discipline campaign initiated by Andropov that may have contributed a small one-time gain in labor productivity and by a probably temporary increase in the rate of investment growth in 1983. This recent improvement does not reflect any change in the adverse secular trends slowing down Soviet economic growth or in the underlying structural problems plaguing the Soviet economic system, and improvement is unlikely to be sustained without more far-reaching changes in economic policy or institutions. But the 1983–84 upturn will diminish internal pressures for risking such changes by alleviating, at least temporarily, politically sensitive food shortages, relieving some industrial bottlenecks, and providing ammunition for conservatives who contend that the Soviet economic system still possesses vast "reserves" of growth factors that harder work and stronger discipline can tap without recourse to risky and alien experiments and reforms.

Not only do Soviet leaders probably not perceive their domestic situation to be as severe as depicted in the West, their commitment to protecting long-standing external priorities against internal demands runs very deep. In the Brezhnev era, military and other external priorities were clearly central. The Brezhnev succession leadership was dominated precisely by the men who managed the Soviet Union's national security apparatus during the period of its greatest growth (Andropov, long-time KGB head, as General Secretary, and Ustinov and Gromyko heading the defense ministry and the foreign policy apparatus). Having brought the Soviet Union so far so quickly in the world power arena, leaders such as these will not willingly retreat from the international role they have cultivated so assiduously and at such great cost. Their impulse will be to insulate their foreign policy from their domestic travails, particularly in the face of what they perceive as an implacably hostile adversary seeking to reverse their historical gains.

Soviet responses to domestic troubles are almost certain to be more cautious, measured, and incremental than is assumed in scenarios that link domestic policy shifts to major changes in Soviet external behavior. The USSR is now far too complex, institutionalized, and bureaucratized a society, and its international commitments, obligations, and expectations are far too great to permit any set of Soviet leaders to contemplate massive fundamental changes in the domestic order that would inevitably be highly disruptive. In any case, barring a radical discontinuity in Soviet politics, decisions on how to respond will be those of an oligarchy, not of a single dictator, like Stalin, and they will reflect the hedging and the compromises required to secure and maintain consensus or to contain factionalism. Economic policy changes are more likely than profound structural reforms. A decision to reduce even further the rate of growth of military expenditures would have the most direct implications for Soviet external behavior, but the impact should not be exaggerated. Unless reduction took the form of large cuts in military manpower, there would be a long time lag between a reduction in the growth rate of military expenditures and some perceptible change in deployed Soviet military forces. The great momentum imparted to Soviet military programs by past military investments would continue to be felt well into the decade. Moreover, even a gradual reduction in the rate of growth of Soviet military capabilities would not in and of itself require major alterations in Soviet external behavior.

Within the more modest limits of internal change that seem likely in the Soviet leadership's response to worsening domestic conditions, the implications for Soviet external behavior are, for the most part, marginal, ambivalent, or indeterminate. Indeed, it is perhaps just as likely that Soviet perceptions of the prevailing external environment will influence Soviet internal decisions as that internal change will affect Soviet foreign policy. To the extent that this is true, the opportunities for the West to influence Soviet domestic development reside chiefly in the impact that Western policy can have on the external environment of Soviet policymaking.

Whether a new Soviet leadership will substantially alter the priorities of the Brezhnev era, and make a prolonged inward turn, will depend not only on how gravely they assess the domestic costs and risks of preserving the old priorities, but also on the character of the external environment they perceive. If that environment promises to reward persistence in global assertiveness with lucrative gains at acceptable risk, then change is not likely. The most important variables include the strength and cohesion of the Western alliance; the position of China between the United States and the USSR; and the incidence of third world conflicts that the West is unable to mediate or pacify and of revolutionary social change to which the West proves unable to relate constructively. If promising external developments occur against a backdrop of military trends that continued to favor the Soviet Union, assertiveness and interventionism could appear almost obligatory to any Soviet leaders. In such a propitious external environment it would be difficult, even for a leader predisposed to reform, to enforce a major reordering of priorities.

At the other extreme it is not difficult to imagine Soviet leaders perceiving an intensely hostile and threatening environment in which an increasingly cohesive West, under American leadership, is mobilizing to exploit Soviet vulnerabilities, to isolate the USSR, and to wage a general counteroffensive against Soviet positions worldwide, regardless of Soviet behavior. In such a grim environment any major change of domestic policy or reform of structure—already risky internally to the political monopoly of the party—would almost certainly seem much too dangerous and even adventuristic, particularly in the face of a Western strategy explicitly oriented on compelling domestic Soviet reform. Scope for effective and constructive Western policy influence on Soviet domestic choices lies in international environments that fall somewhere between these extremes.

In his "Letter to Soviet Leaders," written shortly after he was banished from the USSR, Alexander Solzhenitsyn called on the Kremlin rulers to concentrate more on making the Soviet Union a great country rather than a great power. It is the vision of precisely such an inward turn that accumulating evidence of Soviet domestic decline has conjured up among hopeful observers in the West. Whether Soviet leaders eventually do reverse their priorities depends on their perception of the urgency of the need for new departures to rebuild the sagging domestic foundations of their country, and on the political costs and risks, both internal and external, of attempting to do so.

The Western world can affect the external environment of Soviet policymaking much more directly and effectively than it can manipulate Soviet leaders' choices among alternative domestic policies. Efforts directed from abroad to drag Soviet leaders by the ears to liberalizing reform and thereby to transform them into respecters of the international status quo are even less likely to be successful than earlier efforts to induce such a transformation by the offer of economic benefits that was not balanced by credible Western will and capability to deter Soviet expansionism. Moreover, a Western domestic influence strategy aimed openly at *forcing* a transformation of the Soviet internal order has a high probability of backfiring, promoting not liberalization at home and cooperation abroad, but domestic xenophobia and heightened external belligerence. Western policy can contribute more effectively and reliably to promoting an eventual shift in the balance between Soviet internal and external priorities by affecting the Soviet leaders' calculation of the *external* costs and risks of an inward turn. We can do so by working to shape an international environment that is increasingly less hospitable to Soviet aggrandizement, but that is also not so implacably hostile as to signal that Soviet self-restraint would remain unreciprocated.

Notes

1. Alexander Dallin, "The Domestic Sources of Soviet Foreign Policy," in *The Domestic Context of Soviet Foreign Policy,* ed. Seweryn Bialer (Boulder, Colo.: Westview Press, 1981), 380–381.

2. V. O. Klyuchevsky, *A History of Russia,* vol. 4 (New York: Russell & Russell, 1960), 57–60.

3. Richard Pipes, "Militarism and the Soviet State," *Daedalus,* Fall 1980, 1–12; William E. Odom, "Whither the Soviet Union," *Washington Quarterly,* Spring 1981, 30–49.

4. Klyuchevsky, *History of Russia,* 214.

5. See particularly Edward Luttwak, "After Afghanistan, What?" *Commentary,* April 1980, 40–49. Also, Colin S. Gray, "The Most Dangerous Decade: Historic Mission, Legitimacy, and Dynamics of the Soviet Empire in the 1980s," *ORBIS,* Spring 1981, 13–28.

6. This view is developed in Richard Pipes, "The Soviet Union in Crisis" (Mimeographed: n.d.). Also, Richard Pipes, *Survival Is Not Enough* (New York: Simon & Schuster, 1984).

7. See, for example, R. Kosolapov, "Socialism: Organic Integrity of a Social System," *Pravda,* 4 March 1983.

8. Statement of the Honorable Henry Rowen, chairman, National Intelligence Council, CIA, before the Joint Economic Committee, Subcommittee on International Trade, Finance, and Security Economics, "Central Intelligence Briefing on the Soviet Economy," 1 Dec. 1982.

Chapter 5

Change in Eastern Europe: Implications for Soviet Policy and the Scope for Western Influence

Christoph Royen

What Kind of Change Are We Looking for?

Eastern Europe is the area in which the Soviet Communist challenge to the outside world has resulted in the first significant expansion of Soviet communism after World War II. Consequently, eastern Europe was regarded by the Western world as the most obvious field for various counterstrategies to contain and erode Soviet power.

Two considerations appear fundamental in the Western attitude toward eastern Europe:

1. *The moral aspect:* The people of eastern Europe were the real victims of World War II. First, the German Third Reich deliberately destroyed the independence of *Zwischeneuropa,* won only after World War I. Then the Western democracies were unable to prevent their Soviet ally from cashing in the prize of the common victory over Germany: eastern Europe's inclusion into the expanded Soviet empire. Thus the societies of western Europe, above all the Germans in the Federal Republic, maintained or regained their freedom and new prosperity, leaving the eastern half of the European continent to Soviet domination.
2. *The aspect of "realpolitik":* If it can be shown that the political development of eastern Europe continues to have an impact on the structure of the Soviet empire, elementary

self-interest of the Western democracies in defending themselves against Soviet power and working simultaneously
for a change of that power's systemic nature demands permanent Western concern for the future of eastern Europe.
Only this dimension of "realpolitik" provides for our understanding of the task's full complexity. The merely moral
impulse to support the people of eastern Europe to regain
self-determination can easily mobilize public opinion in the
West. Moreover, Western governments may find it necessary or instrumental to respond to eastern European conditions or actual crises in strong terms. But as the history of
Western reactions to the various popular revolts against the
imposed political system in eastern Europe shows, moral
impulse quickly loses its momentum as soon as it is confronted with the prospect of a protracted, drawn out struggle.

Change in eastern Europe has happened over time and with
visible results. It can take various directions in the future. One
way or the other it will always result from an interplay between
internal pressures for change, Soviet interests in maintaining
control, and efforts on the part of the regimes concerned to cope
with a given situation. Western policies and attitudes may have
but marginal influence on the origins or pace of developments in
eastern Europe. Yet both Western stakes as well as repercussions of change on East-West relations rule out Western indifference. Western policies and responses may vary with the nature
of the challenge—the country involved, the role of the Soviet
Union, the potential for internal disruption, and the prospects
for spillovers into East-West relations. There also tends to be a
differential of Western interests, restraints, and responses according to distance and contiguity, conflicting interests and commitments, and actual versus long-term stakes.

Although Western attitudes, policies, and responses to change
in eastern Europe will always result from many considerations,
instant concerns should not blur long-term requirements for internal change in eastern Europe as a precondition for peaceful
change in East-West relations. Given the implications of change

in eastern Europe for the Soviet Union, this is a tall order. The pace of change thus will be determined by both Soviet chances to control outcomes and Soviet perceptions of the need to be responsive.

Any Western policy of peaceful change in European East-West relations will have to cope with internal pressures and existing regimes in eastern European countries and the interplay between the two and Soviet behavior. Basically, this offers two types of choices to the West: (1) increasing internal conflict pitting the Communist regimes against societies in an uncompromising struggle until one or both warring sides are exhausted, and (2) conscious striving of the regimes to win their nations' confidence by adapting Communist rule to society's traditions and ambitions.

Both approaches have their constituencies in the West. Because they tend to be irreconcilable, this often creates tensions within the West over how to deal with eastern Europe. Such tensions occur within western Europe and within the United States, but more recently they are particularly obvious between governmental policies in Washington and major western European capitals. West Germany is seen to be most exposed in this regard. Whereas reasons for the former approach result on an ad hoc basis from tactical and moral considerations, the second approach is based on long-term considerations that are difficult to integrate into operational policies.

This chapter sets out to describe the underlying reasoning for the second approach. This perspective may be most characteristic of West Germany's current policies toward eastern Europe, but it reflects, to a degree, other West European approaches as well. Some better understanding of it could help to coordinate Western approaches—a task that ranks high on the U.S.-western European agenda. This is all the more important if Western policies toward eastern Europe are expected to influence outcomes there and to promote change as part and parcel of a long-term process of peaceful change in European East-West relations.

Any exertion of influence contributing to conditions of the first kind is bound to have undesired consequences: Western support for the regimes against their unrestful populations obviously would run counter to the West's principal political values. Yet, on the other hand, to encourage the nations of eastern Europe to disobedience and rebellion would only aggravate the dangerous general tension between East and West, while there is no guarantee that such encouragement will advance the cause of self-determination. On the contrary, it might well be that it would become even more difficult to reach that goal and that the Communist rulers' system-conserving entrenchment will be reinforced.

To work for evolutionary change certainly does not offer a safe prescription to achieve desirable change either. But a more expedient political strategy does not seem to exist. As long as the West can proceed from the observation of permanent self-made insufficiencies in the Communists' method of promoting their countries' material and spiritual welfare, it can expect the Communist leaders to search themselves again and again for suitable ways to overcome their failure. This search can be encouraged from outside with an attitude that appeals to the Communists' own interest to base their rule on more acceptable foundations.

The Role of Eastern Europe in Soviet Empire Building

Eastern Europe—A Field for Soviet Economic Exploitation?

According to a widely held popular view in eastern Europe, the Soviet Union is exploiting the economies of the people's republics very much in the traditional colonial powers' fashion. The roots of this conviction rest in the immediate postwar period. Not only the Soviet zone of occupation in Germany, but also the other countries of eastern Europe, including Poland, which had suffered most from both Germany and the Soviet Union, were forced to contribute to the reconstruction of the USSR. These acts of exploitation, however, hardly brought an equivalent gain for Soviet economy, because Soviet economy was unprepared and Soviet infrastructure was unable to handle all the incoming goods.

Moreover, for a number of years it has been the Soviet Union that sold especially energy products to its East European allies below world market prices. In return, it bought products that could hardly be sold on the world market. Meanwhile, the eastern Europeans succeeded in exporting some of their most competitive products to the West. Thus, even if at present the ruble price for oil is approaching the level of the dollar price in the international market, the subsidizing effect of not forcing the East Europeans to pay in hard currency remains remarkably high. True, a number of Polish writers affiliated with the movement of "renewal" argued in 1980–81 that the Soviet Union was still exploiting the Polish economy by letting the Poles import certain items from the West for hard currency and then buying the products manufactured (e.g., ships) with these items from the Poles for transfer rubles.[1] However, this pertains to only one segment of Polish-Soviet economic relations while ignoring others, where the Soviet side appears as subsidizing the Polish economy.[2]

A similar pattern emerges from the efforts to impose uniform economic principles on the new bloc. This imposition led to the relative decline of higher developed countries like Czechoslovakia and East Germany and prevented the others from gradually joining the competition in the world market. Hungary can be adduced as the best example. Yet, again, by keeping the smaller allies below their performance capacity, the Soviets failed to increase their own competitive strength. Therefore, Soviet "exploitation" of the East European economies is really of a political nature: By making them weak and dependent on Soviet support, the USSR gained a lever to secure Moscow's predominance in the Eastern "alliance."

The Military-Strategic Function of Eastern Europe

To Western eyes, the most obvious function of eastern Europe in the Soviet empire is still that area's traditional value as a safety perimeter for the rulers of Russia, who lived with the constant trauma of insecure borders open for foreign invaders. As a consequence, the czars expanded their empire beyond the territories inhabited by Russians and other members of the eastern Slavic family (like the Ukrainians) so as to compromise, ultimately, the Baltic nations, the Poles, and the Moldavians. After 1945 the fresh memory of human casualties and material damage incurred until German invaders finally had been defeated provided Stalin's claim to a zone of "friendly regimes" in eastern Europe with plausibility, even among his Western war allies.

However, just as the czars encountered early perennial unrest among the non-Russian populations, so the new safety perimeter in eastern Europe was founded on the repression of all forces striving to regain their previous autonomy as independent nations. The "alliance" of Socialist states thus carried from the beginning the stigma of being imposed on the eastern Europeans together with the domestic political system they were forced to adopt.

Moreover, there is no longer a European enemy in sight who might consider an attack against the Soviet mainland. The strategic importance of eastern Europe hence rests in Soviet designs to intimidate the western Europeans with superior military power. Yet the common Western wisdom that sees military power as the best trump card in Soviet foreign policy does not correspond to the Soviet mind. For the Soviets, strategic considerations are but one component in Soviet-style military, political, economic, and cultural integration with eastern Europe.

The Link Between Soviet Hegemony in Eastern Europe and the "German Question"

A more general key to understanding eastern Europe's role in Soviet foreign policy might consist in the unsolved "German question." The possession of East Germany and East Berlin gives the Soviets the material lever in co-determining any future political shape of central Europe. Geopolitical logic, then, suggests that the Soviets cannot conceive of safely holding on to those foreposts if they were separated from the USSR by a neutral or even hostile belt of other states.

Yet this argument merely begs the next question: What is the

Soviet design for central Europe? It is here where the deeper reasons, both for the Soviet attitude toward the German question and for the need to prevent the eastern European belt of people's republics from gaining autonomy, will come to the fore. It is these roots that generate the challenge of Soviet communism to the community of Western democracies and their pluralistic societies.

The Extension of "Real Socialism" to Eastern Europe: The Relevance of Soviet Communist Ideology's Central Tenets

Western interpretations of Soviet power often ignore or reject ideology as a meaningful factor. This approach fails to recognize the specific setting of Soviet power.[3]

Political power can be defined as the capacity to induce others to act according to the powerholder's will. A fundamental distinction exists between mere coercion and the acceptance of the ruler's will based on goal-consensus with the subordinates as legitimate.

Pluralist democracies provide their governments with legitimacy by consent through periodic elections. Monarchies draw their legitimacy from religious or other sources of unquestionable charisma. Dictatorships can win voluntary cooperation only by promising their followers to deliver material or immaterial satisfaction to be gained from the conquest of other countries or from the suppression of those domestic groups that possessed earlier wealth and prestige. Dictatorships of the familiar nationalist or racist type are almost from the outset confronted with the dilemma between ever-increasing hostility abroad or— if they devote their power to repression and redistribution at home—the prospect of diminishing returns. Unable to escape from that dilemma, their lifetime is always restricted.

The Bolshevik revolutionary dictatorship, however, could at least mitigate that dilemma with a specific program based on the theoretical teachings of Marx and their adaptation to political practice by Lenin. The essence of that program comprises the following elements:

- Marx discovered an objective law of world history's development: Capitalism is just one formation in a sequence of such formations during the historical process. It will ultimately be substituted universally by a final formation: socialism.
- Lenin, by applying this law—somewhat contrary, though, to the original concept of Marx—to backward, semifeudal Russia, had to develop the concept of the leading role of the revolutionaries' party. It installs a guiding, ruling elite of "cadres." They alone are armed with the full insight into the nature of the historical process. Therefore, they have the right and the duty to repress all tendencies and forces adhering to false ideas and endangering the revolutionary party's historic role.
- This claim to the exclusive possession of truth within the first socialist state had its logical extension into the outside world: In order to defend the revolution and the construction of socialism against every attempt "to turn the wheel of history back," an unrelenting struggle against the outgoing formation of capitalism is unavoidable. Hence the antagonism between "opposing systems" is irreconcilable.
- At the same time, socialism—contrary to other claims of a "historic mission," like nationalism or racism in their various forms—offers mankind around the globe the fulfillment of eternal hopes for justice, equality, and brotherhood. Wherever this mission is understood and accepted, the "proletarians of all countries" unite in true "internationalist" spirit around the motherland of socialism.

The most important practical consequence of these central contents of Marxist-Leninist ideology was twofold: On the one hand the hostility of the outside world was to be countered with the support of friendly outside forces as well. On the other hand the conviction to be invested with a monopoly of truth and to act according to a scientifically founded, objective law of history freed the rulers of the young revolutionary state from the pressure to "deliver" the fruits of their rule fast enough, before competing forces could outdo them in promising more. They thus gained the flexibility and the long breath necessary for a grand strategy to be carried out.

The effectiveness of this ideological arsenal was soon to be seen: Measured by conventional standards, the Bolsheviks stood a poor chance to consolidate their power. Yet they prevailed in the civil war against domestic and foreign forces. They survived the dangers inherent in Stalin's policy of industrialization and in his forced collectivization of agriculture, as well as the purges of the Soviet military elite. Finally, they proved able to bring the German assault to a halt and to emerge from the war as the dominant power on the European continent. All these victories confirmed the Soviets' belief that, no matter how formidable opposing forces appeared, the course of history had vindicated the unique destiny of the Soviet state. The fact that in all these critical times the outside world had underestimated the Soviets' capacity to remain in control could only add to this conviction.

Admittedly, by now the rise of the USSR to world-power status might suggest that the former relevance of ideology as a power source has been replaced by the self-confidence and assertiveness of a "normal" power. Thus one encounters frequently the impatient objection: How can one possibly still try to explain the present structure of the Soviet empire by referring to a concept recognized even by most Communist rulers as nothing but a habitual propaganda device, kept intact only by bureaucratic routine and indolence?

Yet one can. Indeed one must. The question is not whether the present Communist rulers still "believe" in the theoretical, philosophical truth of their ideology's claims. In fact, they may not. But they know clearly that once they would give up their claim of possessing the unique truth and would allow free competition of different *Weltanschauungen* and political programs, the tested foundation on which the legitimacy of their power was built would crumble without a suitable and reliable substitute available.

Therefore, they are constantly forced to keep intact the dogma of historical progress to socialism at home and throughout the world, because the practical validity and usefulness of that

dogma have been confirmed by experience. In the domestic context this requires the all-pervasive mandatory contribution, even
if it is largely lip service, of every official Soviet institution to the
maintenance of the central dogma's validity. In foreign affairs
the cardinal sin would be the explicit or implicit admission that
victorious socialism can be replaced again by a return to pre-
socialist conditions. Hence to state that ideology can be used to
justify any conceivable direction of Soviet domestic or foreign
policy, and that it has, consequently lost its perspective and
motivational force, fails to recognize the value of that ideology's
central principles as immaterial power components of the Soviet
political system.

The implications for Soviet politics in eastern Europe are obvious: The creation of "people's democracies" in that area and
the officially enunciated construction of socialism in these countries serve as the first tangible proof that world history really is
taking the course predicted by Communist ideology and followed by Soviet political practice.

The six[4] eastern European states, which are the only Socialist
countries participating with the USSR both in the economic integration of Comecon and in the political-military integration of
the Warsaw Treaty Organization, serve an additional important
function during the further Soviet expansion into other regions
of the world. They form the Soviet extended empire's inner
nucleus, compared with the increased number of successful
Socialist revolutions in countries far away from the USSR and in
societies whose cultural heritage differs radically from familiar
European patterns. In this outer periphery of the "Socialist
Commonwealth" *(sotsialisticheskoe sodruzhestvo)* it is more
difficult to protect the dogma of "irreversibility" of established
socialism against reversal by successful counterrevolutions.

The existence of such a nucleus appears even more necessary
with regard to those cases in which revolutionary movements
have entered the "path of noncapitalist development" or—as
this stage is usually called in more recent years—the intermediary formation of "Socialist orientation." Realism requires
that the Soviet leaders deal flexibly with demands for Soviet
assistance and commitment. But in order to refuse such de-

mands for active Soviet support in dubious cases, the yardstick of irreversible "real socialism" as established in eastern Europe may be used to justify Soviet noncommitment or to reprimand overzealous newcomers to the Socialist creed.

Thus, although eastern Europe's "real socialism" is not a model to be followed elsewhere, the inflexible maintenance of strict Soviet control in eastern Europe provides for flexibility during the further expansion of the empire still under construction—a paradox of Soviet expansionism that is elaborated on in subsequent sections.

"Socialist Internationalism" in Eastern Europe: A Road to Eventual Incorporation into the USSR?

The joint intervention by five Warsaw Pact members into Czechoslovakia in 1968 made it clear for the first time that the sovereignty of a Socialist state does not prevent the other members of the Socialist Commonwealth from exerting their right and duty to defend the "revolutionary achievements" *(revolyucionnye zavoevaniya)* by intervening in a Socialist country threatened by counterrevolution. Shortly afterward Soviet efforts to intensify cooperation within the Warsaw Pact and in the Comecon became visible, and the former Soviet rejection of the term "integration" was discontinued. The new emphasis on "Socialist integration" was accompanied by Soviet claims that "Socialist internationalism" and the process of *sblizhenie* (rapprochement) among the nations and nationalities within the USSR had actual significance for the further development of the Socialist Commonwealth too.

Therefore, some Western observers began to wonder whether the conscious use of identical terms for domestic and foreign relations was an indication of a Soviet design for gradual *sliyanie* (merger) of the eastern European countries with the USSR.[5] In hindsight, such concerns appear rather far-fetched: Maybe for a short while Soviet leaders were impressed with the apparent upswing of western Europe's integration after the European Community summit at The Hague in December 1969. But Soviet authors pointed out early that *sliyanie* belonged to a distant future, when the construction of communism would have been achieved wordwide and when the role of the state would begin to diminish. The Soviet Constitution of 1977 refrained from using the word *sliyanie* even in the domestic context. Andropov, in his speech at the sixtieth anniversary of the USSR, mentioned *sliyanie* only once to remind his audience that this was Lenin's ultimate vision, but not an assignment for the present generation.[6] Instead, *splochennost'* (cohesion) has become the generally preferred key word in describing the task for the Eastern alliance system.

There are good reasons for such caution: Internally, the Russians are concerned with demographic trends that tend to reduce their numerical weight in a multinational federation. Any attempt to extend that federation to eastern Europe would add new dimensions to this problem. Externally, the prospect of an emerging supranational empire on the Eastern side would merely challenge the western European and the Atlantic communities to strengthen their cohesion. In addition, the maintenance of an alliance of nominally independent, equal states serves their implementation of Soviet foreign policy goals. Experience shows that the six eastern European allies with their specific potentials and profiles can be entrusted with various responsibilities where direct Soviet involvement would be less effective. Thus Poland, with its ties to the West, proved to be useful in advertising détente among the Western states. Czechoslovakia, and later the German Democratic Republic, assumed important auxiliary functions in the third world. Hungary's economic policy helped to persuade Western businessmen and governments that Socialist economy may be more reformable and more open to Western standards of efficiency than is commonly thought. Bulgaria could be trusted to represent Soviet interests in the multifaceted Balkan subregion. And even Rumania's often seemingly defiant or deviant behavior occasionally played into Moscow's hands—be it by preventing a common front of the smaller allies at sessions of the Warsaw Pact or of Comecon, or be it by impressing the West with the appearance of the Soviet Union as tolerating different views in the Socialist alliance.

Hence for the foreseeable future we can safely proceed from

the recognition that the eastern European states will continue to possess at least the formal capacities and instruments of independent actors in international politics.

Conclusion

One conclusion follows from this discussion of the nature of the connection between the Soviet Union and eastern Europe: Designs or plans to "free" eastern Europe from Soviet domination will not succeed unless they either free the people of the Soviet Union, too, from their Communist rulers, or the nature of Soviet Communist power changes enough to render conceivable less hegemonic relationships between the eastern European nations and their big neighbor.

The Potential for Systemic Change in Eastern Europe

The Crucial Role of Communist Elites

The West does not possess the strength to force the Soviets to retreat from eastern Europe. Nor are there any signs that the Soviet political system will change to a degree that would allow them to discard control over eastern Europe as a frustrating, superfluous burden. Yet both these truisms address extreme ultimate solutions of eastern Europe's fate. They do not help to evaluate a third perspective, in which Soviet expansion and control over eastern Europe produce themselves the seeds of emancipation and demands for autonomy in that area. This built-in mechanism deserves most careful attention in the West because it would militate against the dangerous perception of the East-West conflict as one to be decided by the victory of one camp over the other—a perception intrinsically linked to Soviet ideological concepts of history's course, but alien to the Western democracies' striving for conflict solutions acceptable to all parties concerned.

On first glance, of course, emancipatory autonomous development of eastern Europe's political system appears inconceivable under continued Soviet hegemony. Time and again it has been proven that the majority of the population in the eastern European "people's democracies" regards the new system imposed after World War II as contrary to national traditions and ambitions and therefore as illegitimate. Every attempt of various Communist rulers in eastern Europe to bridge that gap between themselves and their nation failed either because of their own timid halfheartedness or because of Soviet intervention. Even allowing for considerable differences in the degree of oppressive rule and in the intensity of resistance, the overall political situation in eastern Europe appears characterized by a principal dichotomy pitting the "regimes" and their Soviet "overlords" against the majority of the population.

Yet this alleged irreconcilability of Soviet hegemony and autonomous change initiated and guided by the Communist ruling elites in eastern Europe requires a closer look. In a way it fits too well with preconceived notions of the Communist system. The present Polish crisis provides abundant illustration in this context.[7] But it might be precisely the peculiar mechanism of the Communist system that conceals from outsiders' eyes the fact that "unanimously" announced decisions were preceded by intense soul-searching debates. Moreover, focusing on that fundamental dichotomy in the societies of eastern Europe and on the general failure of the regimes to win the legitimizing consent to their rule tends to overlook or to minimize the internal systemic significance of small, albeit insufficient, improvements won in a hard struggle among competing factions at home and with suspicious skeptics in the politburos of "brotherly" parties abroad.

Because of these failures and setbacks, the problem of achieving authentic legitimacy remains. After almost forty years of Communist rule in eastern Europe, the time has definitely passed when eastern European leaders could rely on coercion as their main source of power to destroy the structures of the old society and to erect the foundations of the new formation. In order to meet the growing demands of the populace for tangible improvements of life under the allegedly "superior" new system, to steer the complicated network of division of labor in a modern society, and to keep abreast in the international competition with other actors, the gradual winning of domestic approval and consensus is required. The present generation of leaders in eastern Europe is virtually condemned to confront that task or else they reduce the perspectives of Communist rule to a permanent internal and external state of siege—a condition that would be increasingly costly for the Soviets to maintain also. Mere extrapolation from the past's well-documented poor record of systemic change in eastern Europe, therefore, misses the essential point of departure in evaluating the full potential of future development.

Divergent Interests Between Eastern European and Soviet Leaders

Economic Differences. As stated before, Soviet hegemony prevented the eastern European countries from fully developing their economic potential because it kept them in an inferior class of international competition. However, the mere existence of that hegemony did not exclude improvements of performance, nor did it strangle all endeavors to overcome the flaws in the mechanism of Socialist economy. In fact, the debate on how to "reform" the economic system has been the most constant subject of discussion in every eastern European country and also in the Soviet Union.

This is not the place to review the well-known story of economic reforms in the Socialist countries. It suffices to focus on the reasons why the rather successful Hungarian example was not imitated by other Socialist countries and why even the Hungarians have not gone further. Eastern European economic experts in their majority seem to concur that, although there may be a number of serious problems of a strictly economic nature that militate against the introduction of comprehensive reforms across the board, the room for maneuvering so far has not really been exhausted anywhere. Hence the advocates of more reforms were stopped on the political level. The fear that the "leading role" of the party might be jeopardized by the introduction of market-type steering elements into the economy was crucial, since that would demonstrate the limited competence of the party. To be sure, this concern is met in every ruling Communist party. But it makes a difference whether the Communist Party of the Soviet Union (CPSU) is clinging to this assessment of its power base, or whether the governing Communists in eastern Europe repeat it. The latter's power base is narrower and more precarious and would therefore more urgently require remedies to economic stagnation.

When Comecon's first blueprint for integration deserving its name was adopted in 1971 (the so-called Comprehensive Program), it also contained the postulates of reformers for reestablishing money's function as the only suitable instrument to compare economic efficiency and to measure the benefits or losses of mutual economic cooperation, thus introducing into Socialist economy the prerequisites for joining the universal division of labor. Yet as soon as the oil crisis of 1973 created the impression that the Western economy was facing another "general crisis," whereas the Soviet Union would rise in status as an economic power, those reformist parts of the "Comprehensive Program" became virtually dead letters.

Another controversy can be adduced in this context: the rather explicit resistance of the smaller eastern European countries to Comecon's extension to Cuba and Vietnam or other potential candidates in the third world. The reason is obvious: The eastern European countries would have to contribute to pay the bills without drawing equivalent benefits from the extension.

How serious these differences are can be gauged also from the apparent difficulties to convene the summit conference of Comecon members' top leaders, first announced by the late Leonid Brezhnev at the Twenty-sixth Party Congress in February 1981 but postponed several times since then before it finally took place in June 1984.

Opportunities and Costs of Military Integration. What has been pointed out for economic integration in Comecon is also true for the military integration of eastern Europe with the Soviet Union in the Warsaw Treaty Organization (WTO): Costs and benefits are distributed unevenly. This is in part attributable to military expenditures, since Soviet expenditures calculated in absolute and relative figures are undoubtedly higher than those of the smaller WTO allies.[8] More importantly, however, in view of the safety eastern European countries gain from their expenditures and the extent of their influence on the destination of their contribution to the military strength of the Eastern alliance, the share of Soviet allies has to be considered as disproportionately small.

Strategically the eastern Europeans remain hostages of Soviet concepts for a potential military conflict in Europe: In case of a conventional military conflict the eastern European countries would be the first targets of NATO's attempt to stave off Communist aggression. In case of a nuclear exchange, the Western "flexible response" of gradual escalation is also likely to cause major damage earlier in eastern Europe than in the Soviet Union. Therefore the smaller allies are compelled to join in the Soviet variant of "forward defense" by carrying every conceivable military conflict into the enemy's territory as early as possible and to decide it there.[9]

Moreover, apart from the dangers of actual armed conflict, the eastern European countries have almost no control of political developments that might lead to an outbreak of war, especially if those developments originate outside Europe. Thus far the Soviets have not openly pressed to expand existing bilateral and multilateral treaty obligations to include active participation of the WTO allies in "out-of-area contingencies." Yet at least some, albeit small, contingents of various eastern European troops have been on duty in third world conflicts. Only in the case of the German Democratic Republic did such involvement serve that country's leaders' own interest in winning further prestige in an area where they had achieved their first successes in the struggle for international recognition.

Another field where the utter dependence on the Soviet Union is felt in eastern Europe is the area of arms control and disarmament negotiations. Nowhere else are the smaller allies parroting Soviet propaganda so slavishly—occasional superficial defiance by the Rumanians notwithstanding. The only other country that engaged for many years in genuine proposals for disengagement and disarmament in Europe, i.e., Poland, had to learn the bitter lesson that authenticity will not be rewarded if—like in the case of Adam Rapacki's proposals for a nuclear-free zone in central Europe—the Western addressees recognize behind the Poles' sincerity less sincere Soviet designs.

The Scope for National Distinctive Features of Eastern European Socialism. The famous "Basic Principles for the Construction of Socialism" *(osnovnye zakonomernosti),* enunciated at the Moscow conference of twelve Communist parties in November 1957,[10] reflect primarily the Soviet concern for systemic cohesion of the extended empire. But the same document states that the *osnovnye zakonomernosti* should not be interpreted as to neglect the "specific national conditions" in the construction of socialism in the individual Socialist countries. Thus the eastern European Communist leaders possess at least a commonly agreed platform legitimating attempts toward more meaningful independence.

Looking back over the past twenty-five years the significance of this reservation for "specific national conditions" is not restricted to the perennial search for ways to improve Socialist economic performance by introducing market elements. The constant struggle between cohesion and diversification can also be observed in the sphere of domestic politics. A brief survey may suffice to indicate the existing scope for modification of the Communist system in eastern Europe. All of the following modifications concern the introduction of pluralist components into a principally antipluralist system:

- Under the headline of developing "Socialist democracy" intensive debates have taken place in most eastern European countries and have produced, for example, improved controls of the administrative organs by the judiciary. Hungary recently initiated changes in the electoral system to allow voters a broader choice between competing candidates within the National Front's integrated slate. In Poland, early in 1984, similar steps for the system of local elections were publicly discussed but ultimately rejected by the regime as too risky at present.
- Parallel discussions have evolved regarding the practice of

the party's supreme constitutional principle: "Democratic centralism." The most promising relevant development in Poland has been interrupted by the imposition of martial law in December 1981. But the new party statute, adopted a few months before and providing for more attention to the opinion of the rank and file, has not been repealed, only temporarily suspended.[11]

- The sometimes surprisingly unorthodox opinions expressed in the Polish press and on Hungarian radio and television are already something like a hallmark of these countries' socialism. The reformed Polish law on censorship, adopted in summer 1981, was toughened again two years later. But the earlier version has set a standard that is likely to outlast the present crisis.

- The former monopoly of "Socialist realism" as the only permissible form of artistic expression ceased to exist many years ago in most eastern European states, including those with a notoriously tough regime, like the German Democratic Republic. Even in the Soviet Union, cultural pluralism has made considerable inroads into officially licensed cultural life.

- Contrary to Western stereotypes, the treatment of dissidents and the general state of the classic human rights are characterized by wide margins of difference. Political prisoners practically do not exist in Hungary. And under Gierek, the Polish leadership could pride itself on its lenient tolerance in dealing with the strongest and broadest opposition movement in eastern Europe. Even the repressive measures of martial law conditions remained far below the level of ruthlessness to be expected from Communists in comparable situations elsewhere.

- Not to be neglected, finally, is the general increase of freer movement for people and ideas across the systemic border between eastern and western Europe. A good part of the existing restrictions are caused by nonpolitical reasons like the foreign currency shortage and underdeveloped infrastructures for foreign tourists. But on the whole, the decade

of détente and cooperation in Europe has brought a new
level of mutual acquaintance among Europeans from both
halves of the divided continent.

True, only two countries, Poland and Hungary, show a
broader record, and some of Poland's distinctive features, in
particular the special position of the Catholic Church and the
dominance of private farming in Polish agriculture, will remain
exclusive peculiarities of that country. But the mere fact that
these two members of the Socialist Commonwealth have already
been able to test the system's flexibility for a considerable period
of time should warrant acknowledgment, even if the crucial
point of no return is nowhere in sight.

One can compare the distances separating the present eastern
European reality from the reign of Stalinist terror on the one
hand and from pluralist democracy on the other to reach a
clearly negative verdict on the reform potential of eastern
Europe. Yet to apply such yardsticks to measure the progress of
systemic reform may be useful to remind Western public opinion
of how different the Soviet empire is—and will be for a long time
to come—from our Western world; at the same time these comparisons convey the perception that the Communist system can
be changed exclusively by unrelenting pressure from below and
from outside. They thus tend to play into the hands of those
groups and forces in the Socialist countries that insist on maintaining the undiminished contrast between the pluralist and the
antipluralist parts of the world.

The forces of gradual reform and change among the Communist elites in eastern Europe suggest, however, a different approach: Their vision of progress is based on the conviction that
"Real socialism" cannot be freed from its obvious shortcomings
and failures as long as the Communist leaderships cling to their
polarized view of the global class struggle.[12] Surely these reformers' intimate familiarity with the inner fabric of Communist
policymaking makes them quite aware of why they accomplished so little so far. But they may also know best how to
criticize the system's performance and to suggest improvements
without overstepping the limits of tolerance beyond which the

system's top managers feel threatened by uncontrolled "revisionist" or outright "counterrevolutionary" tendencies.

Western analysts should consider this sober and thoroughly realistic approach in evaluating the record and the perspectives of systemic change without naive optimism or preconceived pessimism, but with the adequate sensibility both for the objective necessity of such change and for the amount of obstacles precluding change's uninterrupted advance at a faster pace.

The Western Role in the Process of Change in Eastern Europe

Results of Western Influence

The question then is how much influence Western policy can have on the process of change in eastern Europe. Obviously, scarce information on internal processes of Communist policy-making does not allow the establishment of causal links between Western behavior and Eastern reactions. Any answer thus will be based on plausible assumptions rather than on hard evidence.

It is not surprising, then, that direct explicit connections between Western pressure or Western inducement and respective positive results for the process of change in eastern Europe are difficult to ascertain. Probably the most solid case for such a connection can be made by pointing to West German experience with so-called *menschliche Erleichterungen,* i.e., easing conflicts of individuals with their Communist governments, which were virtually "bought" by the Western side in an open or barely veiled quid pro quo agreement. The United States and other Western governments have had comparable experiences. The results of these bargains mostly consisted in winning the freedom to emigrate and, in some instances, the relaxation of prosecution or punishment. In addition, one can cite examples where public Western protests or high-level diplomacy helped to ease the fate of more or less prominent victims of Communist repression.

Although in all these cases the significance for the individuals concerned was high, they had no visible bearing on the overall practice of Communist regimes. As soon as the Western side began to demand explicit quid pro quos of a more general nature, the Eastern side remained adamant, following the precedent set by the USSR regarding the famous Jackson-Vanik amendment.[13] The reason is manifest: Open, explicit concessions are viewed by every Communist leadership as detrimental to their monopoly in determining their style of rule.

Therefore, a less obvious linkage approach might seem more promising. A good example is provided by the Federal Republic of Germany's treaties with the Soviet Union, Poland, the German Democratic Republic, and Czechoslovakia between 1970 and 1973. All of these treaties centered around the German recognition of the postwar territorial status quo and did not contain any equivalent concessions by the Eastern partners. But by concluding the treaties, the Federal Republic of Germany effected the lasting depreciation of a favorite instrument Communist governments used to employ in order to discipline their populations with the specter of German "revisionism" and "revanchism."

Another example can be adduced from the impact of the Helsinki Final Act on Polish domestic policies under Edward Gierek. Gierek's interest in fostering among Western creditors and politicians the image of a liberal, modern Polish society living in accordance with Western standards, expressed in the provisions on human rights and in "Basket Two" of the Final Act, appeared for some time to confirm Western expectations that economic dependence of a Communist country would open it gradually to systemic change. Today, however, after Gierek's fall from power, the sixteen months of "renewal," and the subsequent period of martial law, Poland presents itself to many in the West as only the most recent symbol of Communist repression and immobility, whereas Poland's neighbors see reconfirmed their distrust toward the West as well as their own insistence on a policy of "no experiments with opening our system."

The two examples, thus, provide us with a mixed, ambivalent result. The German treaties confined themselves to depriving the Communist leaderships of a device to detract from internal deficiencies. But they did not suggest specific solutions to those deficiencies. By contrast, the Final Act's endeavor to prescribe certain forms of Communist power exertion contributed to reviving the Communists' fundamental problem of remaining in control of change after it had seemed temporarily manageable.[14]

On balance, even the indirect Western approach to systemic change encounters early obstacles or generates backlashes. There remains thus as possibly the most potent and at the same time the most durable outside agent of change the West's ability to defend itself against outside challenges to its security and systemic integrity. Above all, Western democracies display how to meet and solve constantly arising new problems of development. Without the successful reconstruction and integration of western Europe after World War II, the eastern European Communists would not have felt the same urgency to search for suitable ways to win more domestic legitimacy by improving their rule's benefits for their nations.

Communist ideology and propaganda have invented the slogan of "peaceful competition between the systems." The Western democracies would be well advised to accept this challenge as their own guiding principle in promoting change on the Eastern side.

Some Conceptual Conditions for Lasting Support of Evolutionary Change in Eastern Europe

Peaceful systemic change in eastern Europe thus cannot be promoted by explicit Western demands, since they run against the Eastern leaderships' concern to remain in control of their political system's evolution. Therefore, "slow," "meager," "unimpressive" progress at best, if not stagnation and recurrent interruptions of change, are to be expected. Premature frustration over the prospects of peaceful change could be the consequence. This in turn may lead to a prevalance of deliberate antagonism in Western politics versus the entire Soviet "bloc," or, alternatively, to the equally counterproductive hectic search for symbolic token agreements. To evade consequences of this kind, a long breath embedded in a confident long-range perception of the Communist system's development is required.

Such a long-term confidence, however, should start from an assessment of all dimensions of the conflict. Tendencies to view the Soviet empire as a "normal" empire with the aspirations and tools of a "normal" superpower will lead astray because they focus on outside appearances rather than on structural conditions of Soviet power. What is necessary, instead, is the recognition of ideology's central tenets as the engine behind Soviet expansionism as well as the cause behind the erosive, centrifugal tendencies preventing the Soviets from achieving cohesion in a stabilized empire.[15]

This recognition of an inseparable nexus between ideology's expansive and erosive effects, then, allows for our appraisal of eastern Europe's pivotal function in the future of the Soviet empire: Socialism in eastern Europe is both an affirmation of the Soviet system's "internationalist" self-legitimation, yet at the same time the most important inner challenge to the empire's cohesion, thus making eastern Europe a visible refutation of internationalism's claim.

From here one can proceed to take a critical look at three frequent fallacies in Western perceptions of eastern Europe: First, meaningful differentiation and change in eastern Europe do not only set in once the Soviets themselves are ready for real reforms. Before that stage is reached they can always provide obstacles to a dangerous process of reform in an eastern European country or intervene to stop it altogether. But Soviet leaders are sufficiently realistic to see that mere repression of the forces of change in eastern Europe will not do and that repression has increasing costs. Therefore, the limits of tolerance for divergencies have to be constantly redefined and, thus, tend to become more flexible in general. What was tolerated in Poland in 1980–81 would have been still intolerable ten and certainly twenty years earlier.

The second fallacy rests in the idea that since the Soviet Communists show no sign of leading their allies onto the path of reforms and change, Western policy should concentrate its energy on bringing about "Finlandization," neutralization, and finally the liberation of eastern Europe. This idea, however, neglects the impact the continuous internal pressure for systemic change in eastern Europe can have on the Soviet Union if the links between both areas are not severed. It is here where Helmut Sonnenfeldt's famous notion of an "organic relation" comes in—not, as it was generally misunderstood when he coined it, as a mere complacent or timid approval of the existing status quo, but rather as the expression of a constant deficit acting as a dynamic challenge from within to Soviet hegemony over eastern Europe.[16]

The third fallacy to be countered consists of an insufficient understanding of the dilemma with which the national Communist leaders of eastern Europe have to struggle. To see them as nothing but Soviet "satraps" or as a Communist kind of "Gauleiters" and to regard intellectual dissidents or a mass movement like the Polish Solidarność as the only forces working for systemic change from within may be in accordance with our natural sympathies. Yet it reinforces and perpetuates rigid attitudes toward the East-West conflict that see that conflict in black-and-white terms and can conceive of it exclusively as a zero-sum game.

All these various conditions for a sustainable concept with regard to the goal of systemic change in eastern Europe must ultimately be related to a general concept of the Western alliance to meet the Soviet dual strategy of the "international class struggle" and "peaceful coexistence" with an adequate response.

Actually, the Western alliance did make an attempt to formulate such a response in 1967 in the so-called "Harmel Report,"[17] even if at that time the main purpose of the document was to manage imminent frictions in the alliance rather than to develop guiding principles for a common long-term political strategy.

Two points deserve particular emphasis in this context:

1. Since systemic change in eastern Europe and, to be sure, in the Soviet Union requires a rather extended time perspective, Soviet Communist antagonism will be a constant source of danger for the West's security. A credible collective military defense, therefore, is indeed, as the report says, a "stabilizing factor in world politics."
2. Yet the report also says unequivocally that credible deter-

rence is a "condition" for "effective policies directed toward greater relaxation of tensions." Because we are
surely entitled to interpret the words "greater relaxation of
tensions" as including the promotion of a change involving
not only symptoms, but also the roots of the East-West
conflict, we have in front of us two modalities of Western
policy defined in the report as the "complementarity" of
"military security" and a "policy of détente."

The outstanding significance of these formulations lies in their
clarification of the relation between defense and détente as two
constant requirements, each existing in its own right and yet
forming an inseparable unity of purpose. This significance becomes manifest particularly in dealing with the unsatisfying record of the West's working for systemic change in eastern Europe.
If Western policy can operate on the solid base of being
sufficiently protected against Soviet aggression or blackmail, the
West's capacity is strengthened to accompany the slow process
of that change, including its phases of stagnation and temporary
setbacks, with the necessary perseverance and flexibility. The
West will not be under pressure to achieve a breakthrough
quickly enough in order to preempt by an intervening peaceful
change of the Soviet Communist system that system's capacity
to use its military power against the West.
Thus we can constantly demonstrate readiness to broaden the
fields for détente and cooperation instead of promising such a
peaceful engagement merely as a reward for far-reaching change
already completed. To treat cooperation with the Communist
system like a faucet to be opened and closed again deprives
Western potential for cooperation of its real political value.
Those who tend to see the political value of such a cooperative
Western attitude only in the possibility to withhold cooperation
and to allow it only as an instrument to nudge the Communist
leaders into the desirable direction may underrate the degree to
which the need for change is recognized among eastern European Communist elites. What is lacking is a viable way to leave
the vicious circle of frustration oscillating between the growing

insight into the urgent need for change on the one hand, and the equally important need to control such change on the other hand.

In order to encourage the open and latent internal forces of reform and change to amend their critical appraisal of their system's intrinsic shortcomings with the appropriate consequences, and to risk finally the first experiments with meaningful change, a minimum of Western cooperation must be a stable factor in the reformers' calculations. Yet Western cooperation can become such a stable factor only if it is perceived with the established confidence based on experience, not promises, that the West is not out to exploit the opportunity arising when the Communist system appears weakened internally during the difficult phase of that system's intensive soul-searching, by destabilizing from outside the leadership's capacity for control.

Western readiness for cooperation, especially in the economic field, is, of course, not sufficient to produce political change in eastern Europe. One of the lessons to be learned from the 1970s is to recognize that the eagerness of Western businessmen and governments to increase just the volume of economic East-West transactions tends to be used by the Communist regimes in order to cover the negative results of their socioeconomic policies and to avoid the necessary reforms. In the meantime, though, East and West had already to face the disastrous consequences of neglecting the conditions for sound Western credits and investments in the Eastern economies. Therefore, far from giving the Communists in eastern Europe another "free ride," Western continued offers for stable cooperative relations will be possible only if the Eastern partners can demonstrate their self-critical reappraisal of the past and if they engage in creating the favorable framework for lasting economic cooperation.[18]

On the domestic level this means primarily to enter some honest dialogue with society, free from self-righteousness of the party and from shortsighted attempts to bribe the masses into political conformity with unsolid promises of more welfare and consumption. On the international level the Communist leaders have to show their increasing awareness of the self-defeating effects caused by threats against the fundaments of the Western societies' stability.

Failure of the Communist regimes in eastern Europe to understand these imminent conditions and to act accordingly thus restricts economic cooperation to a cash-and-carry type of exchange. On the other hand it seems that explicit sanctions by Western governments demanding systemic change are not only ineffective, but in addition they tend to obscure the fact of how much it lies in the Communist leaders' own interest to come to grips with their rule's shortcomings.[19]

Future Perspectives of the Soviet Role in Eastern Europe

Whether and how the constant inner pressure for systemic reform in eastern Europe will produce forms of government accepted by the eastern European societies and welcomed by the West ultimately depends on the Soviet attitude. Soviet resistance to such change certainly will be the main obstacle for the foreseeable future. However, the periods of respite won by recurrent suppression of change's progress are likely to become shorter every subsequent time. The underlying causes of the eastern European quest for overcoming the separation from the Western half of Europe will reassert themselves with ever-increasing vigor.

To take just an actual illustration: The Polish crisis and with it the general problem of eastern European debts to the West, combined with Western sanctions, have inspired a debate on the Eastern side, whether more autarky should be sought after the previous opening to the Western economies had ended with disastrous or, at best, with disappointing results. If this debate would end with the advocates of more autarky prevailing, this would not remove the reasons for which the previous opening was sought in the first place. "Reorientation" could only temporarily cure some symptoms, while the disease would spread further.

Hence, although it is well-nigh impossible to predict approximately the time when mere shoving problems under the rug has exhausted its tranquilizing capacity, at some juncture in the future a sufficient number of Soviet leaders will, instead of letting the empire rot still further, search for a viable alternative from the following three choices:

1. To get rid of the eastern European "burden of empire"
2. To start addressing themselves to the causes of the empire's predicament
3. To break out of the dilemma with open threats to use Soviet military power against the competing system of the Western democracies.

The third alternative presupposes, above all, a clearly weakened Western ability to deter a Soviet military threat. As long as the Western community of states shows itself determined to maintain the conditions under which a Soviet threat would fail to impress the Western nations and their governments, since it entails grave risks for the Soviet empire too, only an extremely desperate Kremlin's assessment of adverse trends would bring the Soviets to engage in such a reckless course nevertheless.

Hardly less desperate a perspective of the future would be required before the Soviet Communists would admit the failure of their internationalist empire building and, as a consequence, would allow the nations of eastern Europe to determine their own political system. Moreover, apart from the fatal blow to the Soviets' image of their historic role in shaping their international environment, it would be difficult to limit the renunciation of the concept of *sblizhenie* to the nations of eastern Europe, while insisting on its undiminished validity for the nations and nationalities within the USSR.

Hence, just as the eastern European Communists appear condemned to find a solution to their domestic legitimacy problem, the Soviet Communists will have to justify their claim to lead the Socialist Commonwealth with a model of partnership that satisfies all of its participants. To reach this goal the Soviets will have to do something about that "unorganic" relation with their eastern European allies. The claim according to which all the brotherly Communist parties within the alliance are contributing to the "collective wisdom" of "Real socialism" would then have to be more than a mere slogan or a curtain veiling Soviet dominance. The former role of the CPSU as the highest authority, therefore, will have to be amended to a greater extent by a practice whereby the Soviet Communists can learn from their eastern European partners as well.

A first step into that direction was made already by Leonid Brezhnev at the Twenty-sixth Congress of the CPSU, when he emphasized explicitly cases in which the traditional "master–pupil" relation appears to be reversed.[20] The same theme was, albeit less outspokenly, touched by Yuriy Andropov in his first major ideological treatise after he had become Brezhnev's successor.[21] Behind these modifications of the CPSU's erstwhile interpretation of its role as *primus inter pares* we have to recognize at least some awareness among the Soviet leaders that to maintain the prospect of making their empire competitive in a peaceful international competition too requires partnership, not domination of allies.

What has prevented the Soviets until now, and is likely to do so for considerable time still, from developing such a model is their overconfidence first in their revolutionary, then in their military, strength, combined with the often-described Russian lack of experience with political domestic and international relations based on mutual trust. Therefore, the prospects for peaceful, evolutionary change in eastern Europe are inseparably linked with the Soviet ability to learn to live in an interdependent world.

This leads us back again to the Western potential to influence and support a Soviet *aggiornamento*. Modest as that potential may be—to maintain that the Soviet political system is inherently unreformable, or even that the civilized world ends at the Western borders of the USSR[22]—will only discourage the Soviet leaders from a search for a more constructive role in global and regional politics. Instead of offering them only confrontation or capitulation, "the democratic nations have," as Seweryn Bialer put it, "until the end of this century and probably even beyond no choice but to face the conflict with the Soviet Union, while at the same time striving to cooperate in the mutual interest," "to pursue a policy of 'containment, détente and confrontation' towards the Soviet Union."[23] If those three elements would form inseparable parts of a Western concept for peaceful change, it would in turn provide eastern Europe, its nations and their Communist rulers, with a long-range perspective worth working for without being torn between illusory hopes and bitter disappointment of attention and support from the free part of the world.

Notes

1. Cf. the assessment by Marian Rajski, "Współpraca gospodarcza Polska-ZSRR," *Kultura* (Paris), 1981, no. 11 (410): 146–158, which found a broad echo in the Western press.

2. Prominent Soviet spokesmen view these subsidies as a burden that has to be reduced. Cf. Oleg Bogomolov, "SEV—ekonomicheskaya strategiya 80-kh godov," *Kommunist,* 1983, no. 7: 73–84. An attempt to measure the amount of Soviet losses and to ascertain the future of Soviet subsidies for the economies of eastern Europe is presented by Michael Marrese and Jan Vanous, *Soviet Subsidization of Trade with Eastern Europe: A Soviet Perspective,* Institute of International Studies, University of California, Research Series no. 52 (Berkeley, Calif.: University of California, 1983). See, however, also the critical evaluation of that attempt by Paul Marer, "The Political Economy of Soviet Relations with Eastern Europe," in *Soviet Policy in Eastern Europe,* ed. Sarah Meiklejohn Terry (New Haven, Conn.: Yale University Press, 1984), 171–180.

3. Christoph Royen, *Die sowjetische Koexistenzpolitik gegenüber Westeuropa—Voraussetzungen, Ziele, Dilemmata,* Stiftung Wissenschaft und Politik, Internationale Politik und Sicherheit, Band 2 (Baden-Baden, 1978), 20 ff., 157 ff.; Christoph Royen, "Sicherheit und Entspannung in Europa vor dem Hintergrund der polnischen Krise," in *Kontinuität und Wandel in den Ost-West-Beziehungen (Moderne Welt—Jahrbuch für Ost-West-Fragen),* ed. Boris Meissner and Axel Seeberg (Köln, 1983), 251–284; cf. also Hannes Adomeit, "Ideology in the Soviet View of International Affairs," in *Prospects of Soviet Power in the 1980's,* ed. Christoph Bertram (London, 1980), 103–110.

4. Albania's breakaway from the Soviet bloc in 1962 does not invalidate the dogma of irreversibility. First, the Albanians never claimed a return to pre-Socialist conditions. Instead they accused the Soviets of treason to Socialist ideals. And second, the Soviets always regarded Albania as an annex to Yugoslavia, which had never come under Soviet hegemony.

5. A good overview of Soviet literature and a balanced appraisal is offered by Teresa Rakowska-Harmstone, " 'Socialist Internationalism' and Eastern Europe—A New Stage?" *Survey* 22, no. 1 (Winter 1976): 38–54 and no. 2 (Spring 1976): 81–86.

6. *Kommunist,* 1983, no. 1 (Jan. 1983): 6.

7. For an attempt to give a less polarized assessment of the Polish situation, see Christoph Royen, "Polish Perspectives After the Suspension of Martial Law," *Aussenpolitik* (English ed.) 34, no. 2 (1983):155–170.

8. Cf. the figures in *The Military Balance 1984–1985,* ed. International Institute for Strategic Studies (London, 1984).

9. This point is made in particular with regard to the Polish military by A. Ross Johnson et al., *East European Military Establishments: The Warsaw Pact Northern Tier* (Santa Monica, Calif.: The Rand Corporation, 1980), R-2417/1-AF/FF, v–vii, 65–67.

10. Russian text in *Izvestiya,* 23 Nov. 1957.

11. Cf. Józef Cegla, *Polityka,* 6 March 1982, 1/9.

12. A recent Polish example is provided by the transcript of a discussion organized by the Polish Institute of International Affairs, in which the participants seemed to agree that, contrary to the standard formula, peaceful coexistence should *not* be accompanied by an unrelenting ideological struggle. Cf. *Sprawy Międzynarodowe,* 1983, no. 6: 117–134.

13. For the consequences of this amendment concerning Jewish emigration from the USSR see the figures compiled by the Soviet Jewry Research Bureau in *Human Rights—Soviet Union: Markup Before the Committee on Foreign Affairs and Its Subcommittee on Human Rights and International Organization,* House of Representatives, 97th Congress, 2d Session, 3 Feb. and 1 April 1982 (Washington, D.C.: U.S. Government Printing Office, 1982), app. I.

14. Nevertheless, in September 1983 the Eastern states agreed to renew the commitment of the Conference of Security and Cooperation in Europe to human rights in the concluding document of the Madrid follow-up conference in rather unequivocal terms.

15. Cf. Royen, *Die sowjetische.*

16. Helmut Sonnenfeldt explained his view extensively in *United States National Security Policy vis-a-vis Eastern Europe (The "Sonnenfeldt Doctrine"): Hearings Before the Subcommittee on International Security and Scientific Affairs of the Committee on International Relations,* House of Representatives, 94th Congress, 2d Session, 12 April 1976 (Washington, D.C.: U.S. Government Printing Office, 1976).

17. Text in *The North Atlantic Treaty Organization—Facts and Figures,* 10th ed. (Brussels: NATO Information Service, 1981), 288–290.

18. This point is emphasized by Friedemann Müller, "Der Zusammenhang von politischem Klima und Wirtschaftsko-operation," in Friedemann Müller et al., *Wirtschaftssanktionen im Ost-West-Verhältnis—Rahmenbedingungen und Modalitäten,* Stiftung Wissenschaft und Politik, Aktuelle Materialien zur Internationalen Politik, Band 1 (Baden-Baden: Nomos, 1983), 130–144.

19. A different conclusion might be warranted with regard to those sanctions whose primary purpose is to demonstrate Western concern for the sanctity of universal international law or to protect vital Western interests against undermining threats; cf. Christoph Royen, "Wirtschaftssanktionen in einer langfristigen westlichen Strategie für die Gestaltung des Verhältnisses zur Sowjetunion," in ibid., 209–234.

20. *Izvestiya,* 24 Feb. 1981, 2.

21. Yuriy Andropov, "Uchenie Karla Marksa i nekotorye voprosy sotsialisticheskogo stroitel'stva v SSSR," *Kommunist,* 1983, nc. 3: 9–23 [21/22].

22. Cf. Vice-president George Bush's speech in Vienna on September 21, 1983, in *Wireless Bulletin from Washington,* no. 173 (22 September 1983): 21–29, for a judgment along that line.

23. Quoted from Seweryn Bialer, "Die Sowjetunion und der Westen in den achtziger Jahren," *Europa-Archiv* 38, no. 18 (25 September 1983): 539–550 [550].

Chapter 6

Soviet Policy Toward the West: Costs and Benefits of Using "Imperialist Contradictions"

Hannes Adomeit

American-Western European Policy Disagreements: Scope for Soviet Influence?

Politics, in the Marxist-Leninist view and in Soviet practice, is the craft of conflict; it consists of the skillful management of contradictions. Even a "more powerful enemy," according to one of Lenin's most basic statements on strategy and tactics,

> can be conquered by exerting the utmost effort, and by *necessarily, thoroughly, carefully, attentively and skillfully taking advantage of every, even the smallest, "rift" among the enemies, of every antagonism of interest among the bourgeoisie of the various countries and among the various groups or types of bourgeoisie within the various countries, by taking advantage of every, even the smallest, opportunity of gaining a mass ally, even though this ally be temporary, vacillating, unstable, unreliable and conditional. Those who do not understand this do not understand even a particle of Marxism, or of scientific, modern Socialism *in general*.[1]

The utilization of conflict *between* capitalist countries ("interimperialist" contradictions) and conflict *in* capitalist countries ("intraimperialist" contradictions) seems to hold out greater promise of success for Soviet foreign policy than ever before. The capitalist economies are experiencing lower growth rates and higher unemployment figures than at any time since World War II. All new and old remedies for restoring economic dyna-

mism—Keynesian, monetarist, or "supply-side economics"—
have failed. Projections made by Western economic research
institutions point to unabatedly high or even rising unemployment for the rest of the decade and beyond. High figures of
government indebtedness with the perceived need for saving run
up against major government commitments (some of which are
legally binding) for maintaining a costly social security network
and an unfavorable age structure of the population (higher ratios
of old-age pensioners to the actively employed). All this may
lead to sharper domestic conflicts over distribution of income
and resource allocation. Defense, in this context, could very
well be regarded by the electorate as the prime sector for extensive cuts.

Such development may appear all the more probable as
pacifist—mainly antinuclear—and neutralist currents ("peace
movements") have increased in strength in the late 1970s, particularly in western Europe. Because the United States is the
strongest military power of the Western alliance, with global
commitments that could involve western Europe in a military
conflict with the Soviet Union, these currents more often than
not are also anti-American, or at least quite critical of American
policies. Such attitudes, moreover, are by no means limited to
Communist parties, ecologists, or Marxist and other groups at
the fringe of Western society, but extend to the major churches,
non-Communist labor unions, and Social Democratic parties.

At the governmental level, too, there appears to be wider
scope for the utilization of contradictions by the Soviet Union.
Disagreement between the United States and western Europe on
matters of substance has become severer, the tone of the exchanges more acrimonious. Many problems are at issue, including the scope of defense efforts, equitable burden sharing,
protectionism in trade, and the level of interest rates on domestic money markets. But they are all overshaded by and intertwined with one problem of major importance: relations with the
Soviet Union.

Whereas in the past, too, attitudes and policies toward the
Soviet Union were often characterized by disagreements both
within and among the western European countries and the

United States, the late 1970s and early 1980s present an entirely different situation. In the perception of both western Europeans and Americans, the dividing lines run much more sharply defined between western Europe and the United States. Additionally, the differences in attitude and policy toward the Soviet Union are regarded on both sides of the Atlantic as encompassing a much broader range of issues than ever before.

Irritation accumulated under the Carter administration (caused in the western European view—right or wrong—mainly by vacillation, unpredictability, and lack of firmness of this administration) burst into resentment over how to react to the Soviet intervention in Afghanistan, notably, over how to evaluate this Soviet move and Soviet intentions; how to deter the Soviet Union from future expansionism; whether to use sanctions and, if so, whether to apply them across the board of political, economic, financial, scientific, and cultural contacts or only in selected areas. Resentment has deepened under the Reagan administration, whose ascent to power and policies appear to many European policymakers and analysts as one of the many shifts in U.S. policy from one extreme to the other. At issue continue to be policies that seem to aim at "managing the decline of the Soviet empire" or making sure that this empire goes under with a "whimper" rather than with a "bang"; the utility or, as the case may be, disutility of arms control negotiations with the Soviet Union; the scope of modernization for NATO's theater nuclear forces; the validity of charges that western European foreign policies reflect dependence and deference to Soviet power; the degree to which Soviet policies are responsible for instability in the third world; and, finally (back to square one after Afghanistan), how to react to the "internal intervention" in Poland.

As summarized by Charles Wolf, the countries of western Europe—by and large, and with some differences among and within them—have concluded that

détente, and its underlying premise about the "web of economic relationships," were valid and useful in the 1970s and remain applicable in the 1980s. By contrast, we in the United States—by and large, and also with differences among us—have concluded that détente and its premise "have been weighed in the balance and found seriously wanting." We have concluded that we should envisage drastic changes in our relations with the Soviet Union in general, and in our economic relations in particular. We have concluded . . . that the policy of seeking to influence and moderate Soviet behavior by encouraging expanded economic relationships has failed badly— so badly that its underlying premise should be discarded.[2]

Before, if at all, embarking on drastic changes of policy toward the Soviet Union, it is appropriate to take a closer look at *Soviet* policy toward the West. For this purpose it is necessary to lay a framework of analysis by clarifying that the Soviet view of antagonist contradictions has not remained static, but has significantly changed over time; that Soviet policy toward the West cannot be regarded as a simple one-way street—as a straightforward implementation of a Soviet plan to create dependence—but as a more complicated process of managing interpenetration and interdependence; and that the Soviet attempts at fostering differences between the United States and western Europe are not a goal per se, but are subordinated to larger Soviet objectives. The probable objectives are then described in more detail. The following, main part of the chapter deals with the evolution, forms, instruments, and foci of Soviet policy toward the West. And the final part analyzes the effectiveness and likely degree of success of this policy.

"Contradictions" Between the United States and Western Europe: Changes in Soviet Perception and Policy

Changes in Perception

Even under socialism serious contradictions are admitted by Soviet spokesmen and scribes to exist, but they are regarded as being "non-antagonist" and hence, in principle, open to solution.[3] This is different from three other types of contradiction: (1) the fundamental antagonism between the two opposed socio-economic systems, socialism and imperialism; (2) conflicts *between* capitalist countries ("interimperialist" contradictions); and (3) conflicts *in* capitalist countries ("intraimperialist" contradictions). These types of contradiction are seen as "irreconcilable." They are bound to disappear only with the disappearance of the capitalist system.

Because the resilience of that system may continue to confound Soviet analysts in the coming years, it is of considerable interest for any examination of Soviet objectives and policy toward the United States and western Europe to note that formalized Soviet ideological perceptions of the three types of antagonist contradiction have changed significantly. "How else," Lenin asked during World War I, "can the solution of [interimperialist] contradictions be found, except by resorting to *violence*?"[4] Wars for the redistribution of power and influence, colonies, markets, access to raw materials and cheap labor, and so on, he reiterated after the war, "are absolutely inevitable."[5] Furthermore, given the nature of the capitalist system, Lenin was also convinced that "a series of frightful collisions between the Soviet Republic and the bourgeois states will be inevitable."[6]

Until the last stage of Stalin's rule it was never clearly stated which of the existing antagonist contradictions were more likely to lead to war, those between capitalist states or those between capitalism and socialism. Clarification was provided shortly before the Nineteenth Party Congress in 1952. "War with the USSR," in Stalin's view, would "certainly put in question the existence of capitalism itself."[7] To that extent, such war was not as probable as war between capitalist states for mere realignment of power. "Outwardly," he explained,

> everything would seem to be "going well": the USA has put Western Europe, Japan, and other capitalist countries on rations; [Western] Germany, Britain, France, Italy, and Japan have fallen into the clutches of the USA and are meekly obeying its commands. But it would be mistaken to think that things can continue to "go well" for "all eternity," that these countries will tolerate the domination and oppression of the United States endlessly, that they will not endeavor to tear loose from American bondage and take the path of independent development.[8]

Khrushchev was less impressed with the sharpness of conflict between the United States on the one hand and the countries of western Europe and Japan on the other. To be sure, when he stated—at the Twentieth Party Congress in 1956—that "war is not fatalistically inevitable," he referred to war between the two opposed world systems. Yet at the same time war among capitalist states was no longer a topic for him—not surprisingly as cooperation in the Atlantic alliance increased steadily in the 1950s and as a new factor difficult to reconcile with traditional Marxist-Leninist precepts was to arise: capitalist integration.

The European Economic Community was initially interpreted very much in the light of Lenin's criticism in August 1915 of the slogan of the United States of Europe (USE), which held that alliances under imperialism could only have a "temporary" and "reactionary" character: Internationally, USE could be designed only to reapportion colonies and markets in competition with the United States and Japan; domestically (i.e., in Europe), it would be used to check the advances of socialism; but in any case the whole experiment could not last. The modern equivalent of USE, however, *did* last and has been regarded by Soviet analysts as by and large quite successful.[9]

Whereas this view of relative success has stayed constant until recently, Soviet analysis of the economic and political implications of western European integration has evolved in several stages. First, at the foundation of the Common Market it was thought that this venture of capitalist integration was directed primarily against the Soviet Union. In the second stage, in the 1960s, integration was seen primarily as a device by the western European countries to assert themselves against the *défi américain*. In the third stage, in the 1970s, Soviet experts came to the realization that the western European "power center" *(tsentr sily)*[10] was not developing as much in the direction of autonomy and independence from the USA as they had previously thought.

Finally, the "current economic and political situation in the capitalist world system," according to one of the foremost Soviet analysts on Western integration, is characterized "by—in the post-war period—unprecedented sharpening of imperialist contradictions between the USA, the Western European countries of the EEC, and Japan." It is a stage, to summarize the argument, that consists of a counteroffensive by the United States against the background of loss of economic power to the other two main competitors and a further weakening of its "political hegemony."[11]

As these shifts in interpretation show, formalized ideological perceptions and international relations analyses have reflected fairly accurately actual trends. In general, these interpretations almost invariably are couched in combative language and—in line with Communist "group-speak"—they tend to dramatize aspects of threat to the Soviet Union and of conflict among the capitalist "power centers." It takes some courage and standing in the Soviet political forum, therefore, to deviate from this pattern and, moreover, completely stand Leninism on its head by arguing that

> the strengthening of the international positions of the world socialist system, the successes of the national-liberation movement in the "Third World" and the sharpening of social antagonism and the growth of the democratic and working class movement in the capitalist countries put *clearly recognizable limits to the development of the competitive struggle and rivalry,* the implementation of an autarkic policy by imperialism, grim protectionism, and trade and currency wars, not to speak of such extreme measures as inter-imperialist wars.[12]

These interpretations are quite significant. Growth of power of the Socialist and developing countries, in Leninist perspective, can have but one consequence: the creation of severe *constraints* on the export of capital and the possibilities of making "super-profits," and hence the *sharpening* of interimperialist contradictions up to the increased likelihood of violent conflict, rather than the "setting of limits to the competitive struggle and rivalry." Nevertheless, the author sticks to her point. Even though in her view, too, "American-West European contradictions have never been sharper in the post-war period than today," she also clarifies (in the introduction to a round table discussion on problems of western European integration at the Institute of World Economy and International Relations [IMEMO]) that "these two regions of the capitalist world [the

United States and western Europe] are linked by a close network of capital, growing interdependence of economic development, and alliance obligations."[13] Yet another warning
against exaggerated perceptions of rivalry among the "power
centers" of imperialism (rather than legitimate dramatization for
maximum political effect) is contained in her observation that
"Western Europe, *as the world as a whole,* is to a certain extent
living through a critical period."[14]

The implications are obvious: If western Europe and the
United States are objectively closely linked, and if, furthermore,
important problems exist that affect the capitalist countries as
well as the Socialist countries and the third world, there are
significant limits to which it can be considered useful from the
Soviet point of view to fuel divisions in the West. Enhancement
of contradictions beyond a certain point could ultimately be
counterproductive for the solution of problems facing the USSR.

Utility for Soviet Policy

To that extent by no means is it safe to assume that the differences of perception and policy between the United States and
western Europe are the result of deliberate and successful Soviet
diplomacy, propaganda, and clandestine operations rather than
of self-inflicted pain. Second, by no means is it correct to proceed from the assumption that the Soviet leadership is inexor-
ably and singlemindedly trying to maximize conflict between the
United States and western Europe rather than attempting to unite
Western policymakers behind certain policies favorable to the
Soviet Union.[15]

Time and again it has been shown that as long as one particular country or "power center" "A" proves unresponsive to over-
tures by Moscow, the Soviet leaders use indirect approaches to
change its course. By demonstratively engaging in atmospheric
improvements, offering political concessions, and placing economic orders in countries "B" or "C" responsive to Soviet over-
tures, they hope to produce a spillover or bandwagon effect on
"A." This technique could be seen at work during the period
from 1965 to 1969, when Soviet-French relations were designed

to accelerate the pace and broaden the scope of the incipient West German Ostpolitik. Similarly, Moscow's practice of selective détente (with strong dosages nevertheless of warning and pressure) vis-à-vis western Europe since the end of 1979 can very well be interpreted as an attempt at blunting the edge of American hard-line policies toward the Soviet Union and inducing the United States to realign its policies with those of western Europe.

This purpose of Soviet policy is evident in Moscow's dialectical view concerning the divisibility of détente. The "concept of the divisibility of détente," according to N. Portugalov, "does in our view correspond to a certain extent to political reality." It does apply in the sense that "the events of Afghanistan must not, under any circumstance, put in danger détente in Europe." And it remains valid as long as the United States attempts "to shelve détente policy, resume the cold war, put pressure on the USSR and work towards its isolation, etc." Détente, on the other hand, is "indivisible on our continent, as well as in other regions, in quite a different sense. One cannot, as some politicians in NATO countries do, support the continuation of détente in Europe and at the same time, and not only verbally, act in solidarity with American policy which is directed at undermining it."[16]

Soviet attitudes toward the divisions between the United States and western Europe, therefore, are transcended by standard operating assumptions and procedures that posit a perennial "struggle of two tendencies" in capitalist countries. On the one hand there are said to be the "sober" and "realist" forces acting in recognition of objective tendencies and in line with the *Zeitgeist (dukh vremeny)*. They are pitted against, on the other hand, the "reactionary" and "ultra-rightist" forces, the "madmen" who want to turn back the course of history. Such divisions pose the task for Soviet policy, to paraphrase Soviet arguments, of encouraging the progressive against the reactionary tendencies and to make sure that the former "triumph" over the latter.

Divisions of a similar kind—into more accommodating or uncompromising leaders—may exist in the Soviet Union too; and it may very well be true, as reported by a prominent West German journalist after a trip to Moscow, that there are exponents among the Soviet middle-level party officials and higher-ranking international relations experts who regard the exploitation of American-western European differences as a matter of principle and as a goal per se, and those who caution against such a course of action.[17] As for the latter, "we are realists," V. Zagladin is reported as having said, "and it would not be a realistic goal to drive a wedge between Western Europe and America."[18]

Similarly, as two Soviet international relations experts write, people in the West who claim that the Soviet Union is trying to drive a wedge between the United States and western Europe "do not see or do not want to see the difference between a dialectical-materialist approach to foreign policy and narrow-minded politicking *(melkoe politikanstvo)*." The main criterion on which the USSR bases its foreign policy, they argue, is not the degree of unity or absence thereof among the Western powers, but "the extent to which [they] cooperate in or, conversely, oppose the solution of important international problems."[19]

The emphasis on the "objective" nature of interimperialist contradictions and the view that exacerbation of such differences from the outside would be shortsighted raise the problem of the extent to which such arguments reflect *genuine* policy or attempts to *deceive* the West. This requires close examination of the costs and benefits, as well as the objectives, of Soviet policy toward the West.

Objectives of Soviet Policy

Whatever the degree to which individual functions of ideology may have been eroded, Soviet concepts of international relations still proceed from the "fundamental contradiction between the two opposed socio-economic systems" as a basic fact of life.[20] On the opposing side—despite relative gains in economic power and political influence by Japan and western Europe since World War II—it is the United States that is regarded as the by far most powerful country. Whereas western Europe and Japan (and China too) are looked on as regional powers, the United States is seen as a global power whose strength or weakness ultimately decides the outcome of the historic struggle between the two systems.

Western Europe in this global competition has correctly been regarded by the Soviet leadership as the single most important region. It is, from the Soviet point of view, both a *lever* and a potential *prize*. This is due to a number of facts. Western Europe has a much more developed infrastructure and a much more developed technological and industrial base than the USSR. It is culturally more highly developed, and its societies are more dynamic and more adaptable to change. Despite all the frictions, the European Community is still functioning, attracting new members and broadening into political cooperation. All this has repercussions in the smaller countries of eastern Europe. It reinforces the traditional affinities between the two halves of Europe. It makes the western half a center of attraction and emulation for a significant portion of the population in the eastern half, and hence it poses problems for Soviet control. Western Europe, beyond that, is an important political, economic, cultural, and, last but not least, military bridgehead of the United States on the Eurasian landmass. Obviously, if this bridgehead were to be denied to the United States, its global power position would decisively be weakened.

Taking into consideration these facts of life, and looking at published Soviet analyses and the twists and turns of Soviet political approaches since World War II, it is possible to postulate the following six objectives of Soviet policy toward the United States and western Europe:[21]

1. To win recognition of the *territorial and systemic status quo* in eastern Europe.
2. To make sure that the western European countries adhere to the Soviet definition of "peaceful coexistence," i.e., that *they observe a certain code of conduct* in their relations with the Soviet Union, maintain "friendly" relations with the USSR, abandon "policies from positions of strength," refrain from "interference in the internal affairs" of the USSR and the eastern European countries, etc.
3. To retain and, if possible, broaden *access to Western tech-*

nology, know-how, and credits so as to overcome the Soviet Union's perennial economic and technological inferiority vis-à-vis the West.

4. To *limit as much as possible Western political cooperation* in the frameworks of the European Community and NATO.

5. To *deny to western Europe any viable defensive option* and to make sure that the western Europeans are acutely aware of their military vulnerability in relation to the USSR.

6. To *transform the pluralistic systems of western Europe* by encouraging and supporting the Communist parties and other "progressive" and "peace-loving" forces.

When looking at these probable Soviet objectives in more detail, care needs to be taken not to fall into the analytical trap of invariably and unquestioningly fitting each and every Soviet move, including moves of embarrassment, probing, or blunder, into a coherent strategic design. Care also needs to be taken not to neglect the possibility that Soviet objectives may be mutually contradictory. After all, international politics is a complex web of actions and reactions, challenges and responses, and naturally anything the Soviet Union does in one particular direction may contain the seeds of failure in another.

To take some examples, success in furthering "revolutionary transformations" in western Europe would probably weaken the economies of the countries of this region and would be a bonus in promoting the Soviet Union's self-image as a historical agent of undiminished ideological zeal. But assuming that such transformations would take place in Italy or in France, the net effect could very well be a much closer alliance between West Germany and the United States. Depending on the internal makeup of any given western European regime in which local Communist parties were represented, such success would, as during the assumed rise of "Eurocommunism," put in doubt more strongly the relevance of the Soviet Union as a model of development in advanced industrial countries. It would probably also create a much more unstable situation in Europe than hitherto.

To take another example, growth of Soviet military power, the creation of further imbalances in the correlation of military forces between the Warsaw Pact and NATO in Europe, vigorous support for "peace movements" in the western European countries, and the refusal to make substantive concessions at the negotiating table in Vienna and Geneva could very well enhance the western European sense of vulnerability and further erode NATO's strategy of "flexible response." The adoption of this course of action, however, could increase the burden on the Soviet economy and diminish the prospects of successful economic reform. The continued emphasis on military power (domestically and internationally) would certainly not make the Soviet Union more attractive in western European perceptions and—despite an increased sense of vulnerability and inadequate defensive efforts—would not necessarily make western European countries more cooperative and more amenable to Soviet demands. It could, more dangerously from the Soviet point of view, harden American attitudes even further and transform the U.S.-Soviet arms competition into a real arms race that the USSR in the foreseeable future—as in the past—could still lose by a significant margin. The prospect of engaging the United States in large-scale economic ventures for the development of Soviet natural resources or of gaining access to U.S. technology and credit would practically vanish.

A third example of potential dilemmas in Soviet policy toward the United States and western Europe concerns the problem of "Europeanism" (European foreign policy autonomy and economic integration) versus "Atlanticism" (cooperation of western European countries with the United States). If Soviet pressure or autonomous developments were to lead to disintegrative processes in the European Community, the net effect of this development could very well be the establishment of closer links between individual western European countries and the United States. This version of Atlanticism would not be in the interest of the Soviet Union. (Thus, during the period from 1965 to 1969, at a time when De Gaulle opposed enlargement and in-depth integration in Europe, the USSR was loudly decrying the "formation of a military, revanchist axis FRG-USA.") Conversely, if the Soviet leaders were to make liquidation of the U.S. military presence and political influence in western Europe their main objective, they may in the process (accidentally or by design) encourage closer western European cooperation, including *military* cooperation up to and including the formation of an independent western European nuclear force (with West German participation?). Such a "Europeanist" development evidently cannot be regarded as desirable by the Soviet leadership.

This dilemma between Europeanism and Atlanticism did exist in the past. But whether or not it will continue to exist in the future is an entirely different matter. It is not at all implausible that the Soviet Union envisages a western Europe that is politically fragmented, in which U.S. forces have been thinned out, in which U.S. political influence has been reduced, and in which doubts prevail about the credibility of U.S. security guarantees.

If this were indeed a major long-term Soviet objective (which would create the necessary conditions for "Finlandization"),[22] it still poses the problem for the Soviet Union of how best to go about achieving it and how to do so without defeating the other important objectives mentioned earlier. It raises the problem for the Soviet leaders of whether they should adopt in their turn a primarily Europeanist (anti-American) or Atlanticist approach (cooperation with the United States to shape European affairs).

Implementation of Objectives: Attempts and Approaches

Europeanism versus Atlanticism

The Stalin Era: "U.S. Go Home!" Soviet diplomacy and propaganda since World War II has vacillated between the Europeanist and the Atlanticist approaches. But even when one approach is dominant and played forte by the Soviet orchestra, one can always discern in the background (as if waiting, in turn, to become dominant) the countertheme played piano or pianissimo. In the immediate postwar years, as the grand alliance quickly disintegrated over questions such as quadripartite control and administration of Germany and Japan, reparations, the Ruhr, free elections in eastern Europe, and Soviet designs—presumed or real—in Greece, Turkey, and Iran, Stalin shifted to an anti-

American stance. Several years of strident "U.S. Go Home!" campaigns were to follow.[23] Burdened with the legacy of Lenin's inevitability-of-war thesis, verbal aggressiveness, and anti-American rhetoric, the Soviet Union blundered into the blockade of Berlin only to find that if it wanted to avoid war in conditions of U.S. nuclear monopoly, and if it desired to find a solution to the German problem, it had to appeal to the theme of "after all, we are still allies."[24] Given the circumstances, such appeals were, of course, in vain. The blockade enhanced the impetus for closer Atlantic defense cooperation, checked to some extent, at the popular level, by a Soviet-supported peace movement.

Yet Soviet foreign policy soon recovered from the setback of the Berlin crisis. The explosion of the first Soviet nuclear device in August 1949, the victory of communism in China, and the nationalist, anticolonialist uprisings in the French and British territories in Africa and Asia apparently induced a new sense of Soviet strength and helped to precipitate the Korean War. But it also defeated the purposes of the peace movement, undercut neutralist currents in western Europe, led to the rearmament of West Germany, and provided the impetus for the reintroduction of sizable U.S. forces in Europe. Thus there was no confirmation of Stalin's idea, quoted earlier, concerning the alleged western European (and Japanese) desire "to tear loose from American bondage."

The Khrushchev Era: Contours of Condominium. Under Khrushchev, the other approach was dominant. Claiming (prematurely) that the possession of nuclear weapons and intercontinental means of delivery and other attributes of power established rough military parity with the United States, he asserted political equality as well. It was as simple as that: "Where there are equal forces, there must also be equal rights and responsibilities."[25] On various occasions, moreover, he stressed that "history has imposed upon our two peoples great responsibility for the destiny of the world," and that as regards the two countries "our interests do not clash directly anywhere, either territorially or economically."[26] Apparently not yet affected by the change at the apex of Soviet power in October 1964, Soviet writings on U.S. foreign policy and U.S.-Soviet relations continued to see a "community of national interests" between the United States and the Soviet Union and state that "their national interests do not collide either globally or anywhere regionally."[27]

Soviet détente strategy thus assumed the contours of Soviet-American condominium, or dyarchy, in international relations. The superpowers, according to this approach, would demarcate their respective areas of vital interest, define their area of common interest, delineate the status quo to be preserved, and establish rules of conduct to govern their competition.[28] Furthermore, the primary focus of competition was not to be military power, but ideology and economic performance. Bilateral summitry (see, for instance, Khrushchev's meetings with Eisenhower in Camp David in September 1959 and with Kennedy in Vienna in June 1961) and personal contacts at lower levels were to be the primary means of reaching agreement.

Yet the logic of a relationship in which a power ideologically committed to achieving "victory" and bent on *changing* the status quo is bound up with a power dedicated to *defending* world order is quite obvious. The power called on by "history" to change the status quo will be tempted to use the special relationship as a protective umbrella under which to expand its power and influence. It will tend to interpret the agreed-on code of conduct not as a mutual obligation, but as a constraint on the freedom of action of the adversary. It will have an inevitable bias toward regarding its own sphere of influence as irreversible and that of the adversary as open to revision. The likely effect of a condominium, or dyarchy, thus imposed on the allies of the status quo-oriented power is to make them suspicious and insecure so they can no longer be sure whether their own vital interests will not be sacrified. The danger of such a bilateral relationship, finally, is recurrent misperception and misunderstanding about the "rules of the game" actually agreed on. It is not surprising, therefore, that "big two-ism" under Khrushchev did not exclude (or even substantially contribute to?) serious international crises, including the Berlin and the Cuban missile crises.

The Brezhnev Era and Beyond: Détente and Its Defects. Khrushchev's successors tried a change of tack—at least initially. For this change to occur several developments coincided. The United States was militarily and politically preoccupied with the Vietnam War. Western European government reaction to the U.S. engagement ranged from lukewarm support at best to thinly veiled opposition. Left-wing student unrest was using the war as a rallying point for anti-American demonstrations. De Gaulle was calling for his *Europe des patries* and for a reduction in the role of the "peripheral" powers (the United States and the USSR) and of the two military alliances in Europe. His withdrawal from NATO's military organization seemed to herald the beginning of a dissolution of the Atlantic alliance in the long run.

The stage was thus set for the Soviet leadership, under Brezhnev in 1965 to 1969, to try to mobilize western European sentiment against NATO, against participation of the United States and Canada in the "all-European" security conference, for 'independent" foreign policies, and for the dissolution of the military blocs. It was set, in short, for an attempt at fragmentation of Europe and separation of Europe from the United States. Thus Foreign Minister Gromyko—at the Twenty-third Party Congress in April 1966—was to reminisce in sorrow and in anger: Roosevelt had assured Stalin at the Yalta conference that U.S. troops would not stay in Europe much longer than two years after the war. However, "ten times two years have elapsed since then, but the American army is still in Europe and, by all signs, claims permanent status here. But the peoples of Europe are having and will continue to have their say on this score."[29]

Even more assertively, the "main document" adopted by the latest (and last?) world conference of Communist and workers' parties in Moscow in June 1969 proclaimed that peace and security in Europe meant "guaranteeing the European peoples their sovereign right to be masters of their continent without interference from the USA."[30]

But in the same year another set of factors converged to induce a change of approach in Soviet Westpolitik. First, as de Gaulle left office and Brandt formed a left-liberal coalition government, France's role as Moscow's *interlocuteur privilegié* diminished. The evolving Ostpolitik of the new West German government, not least because of the problems of Berlin, intra-German relations, and the borders, required quadripartite participation, i.e., inclusion of the United States in the negotiating process. Second, with the removal of Dubček from all positions of power, "normalization" in Czechoslovakia had come full circle and provided Moscow with new freedom of maneuver to launch a Peace Program. Third, the Ussuri clashes had transformed Sino-Soviet relations from latent to overt conflict; some initiative was needed to forestall U.S.-Chinese security cooperation. Fourth, the conviction had grown in the United States that it would be impossible to find a military solution to the Vietnam War and that Soviet "restraint" and good offices were needed to achieve "peace with honor" (in essence, a decent interval before the collapse of South Vietnam); Soviet promises of mediation between Hanoi and Washington to work out a political solution of the Vietnam War would be worth U.S. concessions on other issues, e.g., European affairs or East-West trade. Finally, the Soviet leadership had been unable to reverse the trend of declining growth rates in the Soviet economy and to cope successfully with the necessary transition from extensive to intensive growth. As economic reformism had been at the root of much of the political revisionism in Czechoslovakia, reform as a means of enhancing economic performance in the Soviet Union had been much discredited; as a consequence, large-scale import of Western—including American—technology and access to know-how and credits began to look like an attractive alternative.

Thus on all levels of East-West interaction—political, legal, military, and economic—U.S. participation became a *conditio sine qua non.* This precondition was made even more stringent by the West in the further evolution of the bargaining process when two sets of linkages were made explicit: (1) no ratification by West Germany of the Moscow treaty and the treaties normalizing relations with the German Democratic Republic, Poland, and Czechoslovakia without quadripartite agreement on Berlin; (2) no agreement by the West to the Conference on Security and Cooperation (CSCE) without Soviet consent to talks on mutual, balanced forces reductions (MBFR).

It is not surprising, therefore, that the Soviet leadership in 1970 gave up its opposition to U.S. participation in the European security conference. It is, similarly, less surprising in retrospect that Brezhnev, in his speech in Tbilisi in May 1971, consented to talks on MBFR even though NATO could not conceal the fact that the "Reykjavik Signal" of 1968, formalized in Rome in 1970, was in essence an appeal to the Soviet Union to help the West alleviate the pressures exerted by the supporters of the Mansfield amendment for unilateral withdrawal of American troops.[31] The Soviet leadership had decided on a *comprehensive* management of East-West relations and a *negotiated* withdrawal of U.S forces. Their all-European security system was apparently designed to transcend the constraints of both Europeanist and Atlanticist approaches. Rather than—as in the first phase of Brezhnev's policy toward the West from 1965 to 1969—trying to achieve fragmentation of Europe and separation of Europe from the United States by pressure and head-on propagandist campaigns to isolate West Germany and exclude the United States from European affairs, the Soviet leadership in this phase of policy allocated to the United States the noble task of presiding over a *voluntary* curtailment of its influence in Europe.

Brezhnev's détente strategy, therefore—in contrast to all previous phases of Soviet policy—did contain new elements. They included (a) the unprecedentedly broad scope of East-West agreements ranging from general rules of conduct to cooperation in space, from the prevention of nuclear war to environmental protection, and from strategic arms limitation to cultural and scientific exchanges; (b) the unprecedentedly large scale of Western commitment envisaged for the expansion of East-West trade and the development of the Soviet and eastern European economies; and (c) the inclusion of the western European countries as well as the United States in the overall approach, i.e., the limitation of the traditional attempts at playing off one power center of imperialism against another and one capitalist country against the next. These are undoubted improvements to which Chernenko or his successors may eventually revert.

There were, however, a number of negative (from the Western point of view) features, too, some of which were mentioned earlier in the context of Khrushchev's condominium-cum-collusion approach. Foremost, Soviet ideology with its formalized perceptions of global systemic antagonism and the "tactical" nature of compromise persisted, thus casting serious doubt on Soviet intentions and fueling mutual distrust. Second, the Soviet leaders continued to apply a double standard as regards the "rules of the game" and the commitment to maintaining the status quo in Europe: Whereas they were determined not to allow any relaxation or tension to undermine the ideological, political, and socioeconomic system of the Soviet Union and eastern Europe, they continued to actively support and encourage "progressive" forces in western Europe to change the political map of that region. Third, they adopted a similar double standard as regards East-West competition in the third world: While claiming that the Soviet Union was consistently pursuing a "policy of peace and friendship among nations" (i.e., détente), they also stated unambiguously that the USSR would "continue to conduct a resolute struggle against imperialism" and "give undeviating support to the people's struggle for democracy, national liberation and socialism."[32] In practice, this stance meant expansionism at limited risk in areas of the third world (mainly through arms deliveries and Cuban and Vietnamese interventions) from Angola to Cambodia and (with Soviet forces) in Afghanistan.

Fourth, they early on succumbed to the temptation of trying to use even the semblance of U.S.-Soviet dyarchy against the allies of the United States. This is shown, among other things, by the proposals made by Brezhnev and Gromyko to Secretary of State Kissinger in the fall of 1972 to the effect that the two superpowers conclude a secret agreement to provide, in the event of war, for the use of nuclear weapons on the territory of their allies only.[33]

Fifth, the Brezhnev leadership embarked on a consistent buildup of Soviet military power to strategic parity with the United States, a further enhancement of its conventional superiority over NATO in Europe, and modernization of its medium- and intermediate-range nuclear delivery systems in the same region.

These features of Soviet policy largely explain why the proclaimed Soviet aim of "making détente irreversible" failed to be achieved. To some extent these features are self-generated. They spring from the Soviet domestic political context. However, as Arnold Horelick has argued (see Chapter 4), domestic conditions do not in and of themselves push or pull the Soviet leadership in any one particular direction. The *external* environment, too, is quite important for shaping Soviet foreign policy. Hence Western attitudes and policies in the 1970s probably influenced Soviet Westpolitik to a considerable extent and contributed to the demise of détente.

Among the factors to mention in this connection are, first, Western impatience with the slow pace of change in the Soviet Union. This concerns the almost complete lack of awareness for the perceived need of the Soviet leaders to make sure that opening to the West would not lead to a rapid crumbling of their control at home and in eastern Europe. Given the ideological and institutional limitations to major reform inherent in the Soviet system, change can occur only as a result of a long-term evolutionary process. The loud trading of Western demands concerning human rights on the open market of East-West relations, therefore, could only turn out to be counter-productive.

Related to that is the failure of East-West economic interaction to increase in line with the possibilities for expansion—and with probable Soviet expectations. This is a development that was undoubtedly triggered by the Jackson-Vanik and Stevenson amendments and the concomitant refusal by the United States to grant to the USSR most-favored-nation status, and the limitation of government-guaranteed credit to a measly $75 million a year (a sum completely inadequate to contribute to the development of the Siberian resources of the USSR). Some of the external Soviet policies (e.g., the resumption of weapons deliveries to Hanoi after 1974, with their decisive contribution to the collapse of South Vietnam) can arguably be regarded as a backlash to the passing of U.S. trade legislation.[34] The lack of Soviet restraint on this issue, in turn, set in motion an action-reaction pattern whose consequences are still with us.

Yet other facets of Western policy conditioning Soviet responses in the 1970s are the evolving U.S. perceptions about the diminishing utility of military power in the nuclear age, the curtailment of executive power (Watergate), the playing of the "China card," and, last but not least, the slow and inadequate reaction by the alliance to the Soviet arms buildup and arms control approach. This reaction, with the emphasis on various aspects shifting over time, has consisted in the overloading of arms control negotiations with expectations of rapid improvement in East-West political relations. It has seen the burdening of these negotiations with the notion that in and by themselves they would cause a slowing down of the Soviet arms effort and alleviate the urgency of meeting the West's own defense problems. In short, there was little appreciation for the dual-track approach by the Soviet leadership: to stress the necessity of détente and arms control on the one hand while embarking on a significant armament program on the other, and to use this approach as an instrument with which to influence West-West relations.

How much importance are the Soviet leaders attaching to this approach? Answering this question necessitates a review of both this and other instruments used by the Soviet leaders to achieve their objectives, and of the likely degree of success or failure they themselves perceive to have had.

Instruments and Their Effectiveness: Success or Failure of Soviet Policy?

The Status Quo, Codes of Conduct, and Western Pluralist Systems: Political and Ideological Dimensions. Contrary to some pessimistic assessments made in western Europe and (more so) in the United States, Soviet policy toward the West has not been an overall success story. The record suggests that success and failure have been evenly mixed, the failures lying primarily in the socioeconomic realm (i.e., in the attempts at achieving objectives 1, 2, 3, and 6 listed earlier), and the success, in undermining Western political and security cooperation and eroding the credibility of NATO's doctrine of "flexible response" (objectives 4 and 5).

To look at some of the issues in detail, considering the Western emphasis on basket 3 in Belgrade in 1977–78 and in Madrid in 1980–82; taking into account, furthermore, the activity of various Helsinki "observer groups" in the Soviet Union and in eastern Europe in the latter half of the 1970s; and taking note of the increased impetus for greater internal autonomy in eastern Europe (notably in Poland) induced by the Helsinki process, it is difficult to remember that it was the Soviet Union that from the mid-1960s to the mid-1970s vigorously advocated convocation of the CSCE, and that it was this very conference, which— according to the Soviet agenda—was to lead to the recognition not only of the territorial but also the systemic status quo in Europe.

The territorial status quo engrained itself more deeply into the collective consciousness of the Helsinki participants. But even this development cannot be regarded as a major gain for the Soviet Union. On the one hand the true guarantee of the postwar map has always been Soviet military power. Nothing changed in that respect. On the other hand the borders in Europe are merely regarded in the CSCE final act as "inviolable," not as "immutable" or "unchangeable." This, from a legal point of view, means leaving open the possibility of German reunification or other voluntarily agreed on territorial changes. (In fact, the formulation chosen was adopted precisely on West German insistence.) Finally, as this qualification concerning the status quo implies, neither the final act nor the follow-up conference ever did legally codify or politically legitimate the existing socioeconomic order in Europe. Even more important, they never did endorse the kind of political and military control the Soviet Union is exerting in eastern Europe.

If, from the Soviet perspective, further proof of this was needed, it was amply provided by the Western responses to the developments in Poland after July 1980. These responses included the open support for Solidarność across the whole political spectrum, from left to right, in western Europe and the United States; the ill-concealed hope for an undoing of the "shameful surrender" to Stalin at Yalta; the earnest belief in the "Finlandization" of Poland as a realistic prospect; and, finally, after the restoration of Communist control in December 1981,[35] the demands put forward by Western governments individually, as well as by the European Community and the NATO Council of Ministers collectively, for (a) the lifting of martial law, (b) release of all internees, and (c) resumption of the dialogue between the authorities and Solidarność. These demands were backed up by sanctions, more substantive and severer in the case of the United States and less stringent and more symbolic by the western European countries.

Thus neither the western European countries nor the United States adhered to the code of conduct applicable, according to Soviet interpretations of the CSCE final act, to the events in Poland: "non-interference in the internal affairs of sovereign states." Rather than cooperating with the Soviet Union in codifying the status quo in Europe, they had, in the Soviet view, tried their best ("worst") to change it.

But even assuming a *willingness* on the part of western European governments and the public to observe a Soviet-defined code of conduct, the very existence of (relative to eastern Europe) economically successful, ideologically diverse, socially adaptable, and politically autonomous systems would continue to be a constant challenge to Soviet control in eastern Europe. This points to the failure of Soviet diplomacy to achieve yet another of the objectives enumerated earlier: transformation of the pluralist systems of western Europe by winning a greater degree of control over their domestic policies and channeling them in a pro-Soviet direction.

In fact, all empirical evidence runs counter to the view that "bonds of sympathy and a community of interests are developing as rapidly between Western Europe and the Soviet Union as they are dissolving between Western Europe and the United States."[36] Obviously, it is necessary to make a distinction between calculated adaptation to Soviet power (a problem that will be dealt with shortly) and favorable images of the Soviet Union. Growth of Soviet power, it stands to reason, does not necessarily lead to improvements in the Soviet image. Indeed, the former may very well damage the latter.

To illustrate the point, recent public opinion polls show that a significant majority of *West Germans* believes that the aim of Soviet policy is to achieve not peaceful cooperation with the West, but the domination of western Europe, and that they feel *more* threatened by the Soviet Union now than they did in the late 1970s. Perhaps predictably, these very same polls also show that West German opinion of Russia has become *less* rather than more favorable.[37]

Similarly, even without detailed poll data, it is evident to any casual observer that there has been a spectacular deterioration of the Soviet image and influence in France. This was true even before the imposition of martial law in Poland and in all likelihood has increased since. Concurrently, there has been broad support in France for Mitterrand's hard-line policies toward the Communists at home, toward relations with the Soviet Union (e.g., the mass expulsion of Soviet agents in the spring of 1983), and on defense.[38] Britain in the past decade has been particularly immune to an increase in Soviet influence. At the same time it has set a standard that has been emulated by other western European countries. Despite high unemployment figures, the country remains eminently "governable" and even retains an electorate that is prone to vote center-right rather than center-left or left.

The Communist parties, needless to say, have been the prime instruments in the Soviet attempts at transforming the domestic system of the countries concerned as well as their foreign policy orientation. In line with the declining attraction of Soviet ideology among Western intellectuals, however, the effectiveness of the Communist parties in promoting Soviet influence has decreased. More often than not, the impact that can be made by various "peace" campaigns on domestic politics in western Europe crucially depends on their organizers being able to refute the charge that they are acting on behalf of the Soviet Union. Similarly, voting strength and electoral support for Communist parties in western Europe in recent years have almost inversely been correlated with pro-Moscow orientation (although in many instances anti-Soviet positions do not help either).

Thus the "new internationalist" Communist party of Italy (CPI), whose pro-Soviet wing under Cossutta was thoroughly defeated at the Seventeenth Congress of the CPI (March 1983), was able to poll an impressive 30.4 percent of the votes in the 1979 parliamentary elections. (Still this result represented a drop of 4 percent from their showing in the 1976 elections.) In contrast, the abandonment of, even though ambiguous and half-hearted, "Eurocommunist" positions by the French Communist party (CPF) and the concomitant realignment of the party with Moscow, among other factors, resulted in a significant reduction of CPF voting strength from the traditional one-fifth of the electorate to a mere 15.3 percent—the worst performance since 1936—in the second round of the 1981 presidential elections. In all other western European countries the Communist parties play a limited and, in general, declining role at the margin of the political mainstream. This is true also, after a more promising start initially, for the Communist parties of Spain and Portugal—and even for "Finlandized" Finland.

If increase in the standing and influence of the Communist parties were to be taken as a measure of successful penetration of the political systems of western European countries, the recent record in West Germany must be considered particularly disastrous by the Soviet leadership. The pro-Soviet German Communist party (DKP) managed to poll an abysmally low 0.2 percent of the vote in the March 1983 parliamentary elections—a result too embarrassing to be mentioned by any of the Soviet newspapers in postelection reporting.

The consequences for Soviet policy toward western Europe are not difficult to reconstruct. First, although continuing to use the Communist parties wherever possible as an agent of influence, the Soviet leadership has increasingly come to rely on "front" organizations (the World Peace Council, the World Federation of Trade Unions, the Christian Peace Conference, etc.), which are not always immediately recognized as a tool of Soviet foreign policy, and non-Communist political forces (e.g., Socialist, Social Democratic, and other political parties; labor unions; and student groups), which may disagree on long-term goals with the USSR but that nevertheless tend to join in "practical action against imperialism."

Second, as the Soviet leadership is no longer able—as it was during the period of the Comintern and the Cominform—to control the major western European Communist parties and use them as "transmission belts" of Soviet foreign policy, it must increasingly rely on persuasion, inducement, incentives, and coordination of policies with these and other political parties. This makes policy implementation much more complex and more difficult for the Soviet leadership.

Third, even more than before the Soviet approach is aimed primarily at making tangible economic and foreign policy gains rather than trying to achieve ever more elusive revolutionary transformations of the domestic political systems of the western European countries. This warrants a closer look at the economic and military-political objectives and the more immediate and tangible benefits the Soviet Union may hope to gain from its policies toward the United States and western Europe.

The Economic "Lever": Dependence Versus Interdependence. "We [the Soviets]," Andropov said in his first speech to the Central Committee as general secretary in November 1982, quoting Lenin, "are exerting the greatest influence on the world revolutionary process through our economic policy."[39] This observation was as untrue in Lenin's time as it is today, under Gorbachev. What is, of course, indisputable is the fact that a dynamic, varied, and efficient economy is an important asset in the global competition between the two opposed systems. It provides foreign policy with wide possibilities of exerting influence. In fact, influence and control based primarily on military power, if not strengthened by ideological, cultural, and economic bonds, must be regarded as inherently unstable. At the same time the ever more rapid pace of military-technological innovation and modernization of the armed forces requires a sound scientific-technological and economic base.

However, as Abraham Becker shows in Chapter 7, the economic base of the Soviet Union has been faltering. The USSR has failed abysmally in its attempt, still part of the official 1981 Party Program, to "catch up with and overtake" the United States in production by 1970. It did not achieve its aim of overcoming the perennial technological inferiority vis-à-vis the West (see objective 3). Its structure of trade with the Organization for Economic Cooperation and Development (OECD) countries is still very much that of a developing country: It is importing finished products (machinery and equipment) in exchange for raw materials and energy supplies (notably oil and gas).

For a time, in the first half of the 1970s, the USSR was successful in achieving its goal of broadening access to Western technology, know-how, and credit. This soon began to change, however. A number of economic and political factors converged and set in motion an action-reaction process, part of which was described earlier. Such factors include (a) the burdening of Soviet-American trade with *political preconditions* (Jackson-Vanik and Stevenson amendments), leading to a tendency for the Soviet Union preferentially to place orders in western European countries and Japan; (b) the development of serious *imbalances* in Soviet-American trade (e.g., Soviet imports from the United States by 1976 amounted to $2.3 billion as compared with $221 million for Soviet exports); (c) the overall *slowdown in the rates of growth of the Western economies* in the wake of several "oil shocks," resulting in cutbacks of orders from Comecon countries; and (d) the *change in the role of commercial credit* from being an important driving force of East-West trade to becoming a brake on its development.

Taking into account these developments, considering the important role of the trade with Comecon as a bone of contention among the "imperialist power centers" and the damage the issue is doing to the political relations among them, bearing in mind that U.S. economic sanctions in response to the Soviet intervention in Afghanistan and the imposition of martial law in Poland elicited only lukewarm support in western Europe (and Japan), and remembering furthermore that U.S. attempts at preventing the Soviet-western European oil, pipeline, and credit ("Yamal") project failed—is it correct to assume that the Soviet leaders have finally achieved the best of all worlds: "business as usual" with the West (minus the United States) *and* enhancement of divisive tendencies in the Western alliance?

Whereas the latter is true up to a point (more of this later), the former undoubtedly is not. Of course, for maximum political effect, Soviet analysts and propagandists are claiming that even the use of "economic weapons of mass destruction" by the United States did not and will not divert the western Europeans from taking care of their vital interest in trading with the East and that it will not arrest the decline of U.S. power.[40] Trade statistics are gleefully presented by them to show that economic relations between the countries of Comecon and those of the EEC "were one of the most dynamic areas of world trade" and that "whereas, in 1970–79, the volume of foreign trade of the USA, for instance, rose by a factor of 3.4, the trade between Comecon and the EEC [increased] by a factor of 3.9."[41]

Is there no impact, then, made by U.S.-Soviet political relations on Soviet-western European (and Soviet-Japanese) trade? There is. In stark contrast to the perceived dynamism of Comecon-EEC trade, the very same author just quoted frankly acknowledges that *"economic relations between Eastern and Western Europe are closely connected with American policy."*[42] This admission expresses as clearly as is possible in current Soviet analyses that East-West economic relations are dependent on East-West political relations. Even though western European governments may have been reluctant, for sound political reasons in their view, to embark on explicit "linkage" and economic sanctions, the fact remains that linkage between politics and economics is inescapable. This certainly is true for the medium and long term. It would, indeed, be difficult to believe that anyone with responsibility for East-West affairs in Moscow has failed to make the very same observation made recently by *The Economist:* "The conduct of East-West trade has altered fundamentally from the days of the détente-led boom that preceded the Russian invasion of Afghanistan."[43]

Although there have been some increases in the value of Soviet-western European trade, caused mainly by the significantly higher prices charged for Soviet oil, the share of the Comecon countries in overall OECD trade fell from the mid-1970s to the early 1980s and has remained constant ever since. The share of Comecon in West German trade, too, fell in the mid-1970s to the early 1980s and has increased only slightly after 1981 (see Figures 1 and 2).[44] East-West credit relations conform

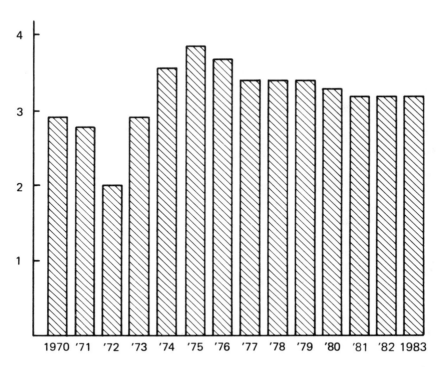

FIGURE 1. Share of CMEA (Comecon) in OECD foreign trade, 1970–83 (in percent).

to this pattern. Although it is understandable that, for financial and economic reasons, the eastern European countries have increasingly come to be regarded by Western banks as a credit risk, this should be different with the rating of the USSR, which possesses huge gold reserves and natural resources, and the foreign indebtedness of which is quite low. Yet its creditworthiness, too, has suffered significantly. Net financing flows from Western banks to the Soviet Union have decreased to a trickle. As this decrease cannot convincingly be explained on economic grounds, it must be due to political reasons, i.e., to the general atmosphere of tension and uncertainty prevailing in East-West relations.

Political uncertainty and unpredictability of Western supplies are undoubtedly a factor in Soviet calculations. Yet judging from

Soviet statements and policies under Andropov and Chernenko, the Soviet leaders are unlikely to set the course of Soviet economic policy in the direction of autarky, probably even despite a growing realization that the solution of difficult economic problems must lie in mobilizing internal Soviet resources. It will, in all probability, remain interested in retaining and expanding access to Western technology and know-how, agricultural products, and credit and continue to look for Western participation in joint ventures for the development of Siberia.

The Soviet leadership, for all of these reasons, must be quite aware of the fact that on matters of East-West trade, it is more of a *demandeur* than the Western countries. This undoubtedly provides the West with some leverage. It would be naive, however, to believe that Moscow is so dependent on trade with the countries of western Europe that it "might not [consider it] very sensible to seek to destabilize them,"[45] or that "in exploiting the differences between Europe and America over East-West trade

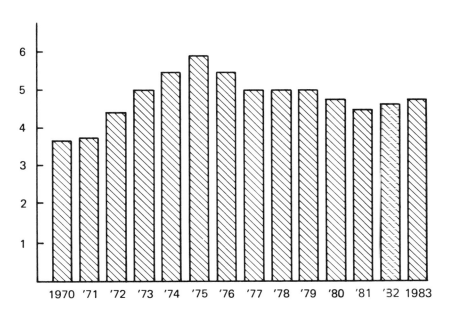

FIGURE 2. Share of CMEA (Comecon) in West German foreign trade, 1970–83 (in percent).

the principal Soviet motive is to preserve that trade as far as possible, not to break up the Atlantic alliance."[46] The policy options for the Soviet leadership are, in essence, quite different. They do not present themselves in these extremes of "either/or," but in terms of "more or less." For the Soviet leaders, then, it is necessary to decide not between trade *or* destabilization of the western European political systems, and trade *or* breakup of the alliance, but to choose between more or less trade and more or less improvement in East-West political and security relations.

The Military Instrument as a Source of Soviet Influence. In contrast to the East-West competition in economic, ideological, and cultural affairs, the Soviet Union has been more successful in the East-West military competition. This is indicated by (a) the achievement of strategic parity by the USSR, (b) the modernization of its intermediate-range and theater nuclear forces, (c) further improvement of its conventional preponderance in central Europe, and (d) the buildup of forces capable of power projection and intervention at and beyond the periphery of the Soviet Union.

In the Khrushchev era the primary focus of competition between the two opposed world systems was declared to be ideological and economic. This was amply reflected both in the Seven-Year Plan of 1959 and in the Party Program of 1961. But starting from the Berlin crisis of 1961 and the Cuban missile crisis of 1962 the focus began to shift. Increasingly, the central sphere of competition between the two opposed world systems came to be military. This was perhaps not a conscious decision taken by the leadership under Brezhnev. But as the adversary superpower itself seemed to place such a great emphasis on military power as a decisive power in international relations, and as other Soviet means of influencing world events turned out to be relatively ineffective, this reorientation became ever more pronounced.

This reorientation, however, poses a difficult question: How, in the nuclear age, can the Soviet leaders hope to transform military power into political influence? On the surface this seems an almost impossible task. Even given disparity in various categories of military power in favor of the Soviet Union, any major military clash in central Europe would involve the conventional forces of the nuclear powers—the United States, Britain, and France—and carry with it the risk of escalation to nuclear war. The Soviet leadership, ever since the crises in Iran (1946) and Berlin (1948), seems to have acutely been aware of this risk. Soviet "victory" in nuclear war, therefore, may still figure in Soviet strategic writings for reasons of maintaining morale and for underpinning the privileged position of the military in the domestic struggle for the allocation of resources. It may also occur in ideological treatises to convey the erroneous impression that nuclear weapons do, after all, adhere to the class principle. It is extremely doubtful, however, that it is regarded by the Soviet political leadership as a valid operational concept.

Transformation of military power into political influence, therefore, can only work through perceptions—or, more precisely, through a process of interaction between changes in the power relationship and their recognition. If a power can convincingly demonstrate that the opposing coalition has no viable defensive option, political accommodation of the latter is likely to set in. Such a process could be enhanced if the use or threat of force by the former at the flanks were to add to the latter's political, economic, and military constraints. In such circumstances, opposition to a power bent on changing the status quo would appear as increasingly risky. This kind of perception would open the way to the political exploitation of military vulnerabilities.

The Soviet Union has attempted to travel this very road. It has tried to convey the idea that war in central Europe—conventional or nuclear—is not only thinkable, but even probable; that there is, as Andropov told American commentator J. Kingsburg Smith, "a mounting threat of war."[47]

This thesis is supported by other Soviet spokesmen and sources, and their claim that arms races in the past have sooner or later, but inevitably, led to war and that, in current conditions, this danger took concrete shape in "Washington's stubborn unwillingness to seek ways of reducing the nuclear confrontation in Europe."[48]

Yet other arguments used in this context are that the risk of war is heightened by the danger of "horizontal escalation," i.e., the likely spillover of military conflict from one region to another; that political leaders in Washington could lose control of the "force of events"; and that the world, as in 1914, could accidentally "stumble" or "slide" into war.

In order to prevent such a development toward war it may, and does, appear advisable to some sections of western European public opinion to be more accommodating to Soviet demands than in the past, or at least to support policies of equidistance from both the USSR and the United States. Obviously, such a drift can be accelerated by American reactions: the more stridently anti-Soviet the rhetoric and the more unbalanced the emphasis on meeting the Soviet challenge purely on the *military* level of the East-West competition, the more politically effective the Soviet argument.

There is a second point of entry that the Soviet Union has tried to use in order to transform military power into political influence. This is by attempting to erode the confidence among the western European public and political leadership in the U.S. security guarantees, in the viability and credibility of NATO's doctrine of "flexible response," and in the willingness of the United States to put its own territory at risk for the defense of Europe. To such a process yet another correlation is applicable: the wider the gap between Soviet offensive military capabilities in Europe and NATO's ability to defend itself by conventional means, and the stronger the movement toward "no first use" of nuclear weapons in European NATO countries, on the one hand, the deeper the insecurity and anxiety about American security guarantees, and the stronger the tendency among some sections of western European public opinion to look more favorably on Soviet interests on the continent, on the other.

Thus, whether by design or default, the Soviet choice of making the military sphere the main "arena" of East-West competition, and using shifts in the East-West military "correlation of forces" to induce changes in West-West political relations, must appear to the Soviet leadership as having been correct and promising for the future. Military competition, after all, is best suited to a centralized command economy in which military industry has been allocated a privileged position and national security receives top priority. Conversely, military competition is the sphere that is most controversial in Western pluralist systems. It is the sphere in which they are most vulnerable. Consequently, claims for a higher or even constant share of defense expenditures against the trend in almost all Western countries of cuts in government spending and rising unemployment are likely to lead to domestic polarization.

But the emphasis on military competition is bound to lead to intra-alliance polarization as well, for three reasons: (1) in western Europe the size of the military sector in the national economy is smaller than in the United States (i.e., the military-industrial complex is economically and politically less influential); (2) western Europe has a more extensive and costly social welfare net; and (3) it has strong Social Democratic parties committed to its protection.

The skillfully chosen point of departure by Soviet spokesmen and scribes for enhancing this double polarization is their assertion that the reactionary forces currently at the helm of U.S. foreign policy are bent on "gaining military preponderance" and "achieving world domination." Western Europe, they claim, is to be used in these plans as an instrument with which to conduct economic warfare against the Socialist countries (not least by accelerating the arms race to such an extent that the USSR will collapse). Western Europe, they charge, is to make available to the Pentagon war planners the territory on which to build a new strategic threat, and it is to consent to becoming a nuclear launching pad for a first strike against the Soviet Union.[49]

Even more sensitive parts of the intra-alliance fabric are touched when Soviet military and political leaders portray Western arms efforts and political détente in Europe as irreconcilable. This, in fact, is the stance they have adopted toward NATO's double-track decision. In essence, they have made East-West relations in Europe hostage to nonimplementation of the alliance's decision to deploy intermediate-range nuclear systems. They have done so by repeatedly warning that détente will not survive deployment and that "the Soviet Union will reply [to

NATO deployment], both militarily and politically, and the consequences will be very grave indeed."[50]

The effectiveness of these threats is enhanced by Soviet sources correctly reminding the western Europeans that they have a much greater stake in political, economic, scientific, and cultural contacts and in tourism between the two halves of Europe, and perhaps not so correctly charging that the current U.S. administration is prepared to see these contacts disrupted within its overall strategy of attempting to maximize social, economic, and political instability in eastern Europe, thereby "accelerating the decline of the Soviet empire."

Obviously, suspicions that there may be a large grain of truth in these Soviet allegations are politically most damaging in West Germany and to German-American relations. West Germans, perhaps more than other western Europeans, are worried about negative repercussions on intra-German relations (and indeed such worries are being fueled by East German leader Erich Honecker's warning about a new "ice age" to begin in the relations between the two German states if NATO missiles were deployed).[51] They are concerned not only about the prospect of SS-21, SS-22, and SS-23 missiles being deployed in the German Democratic Republic and Czechoslovakia—and perhaps even, as reports from eastern Europe indicate, in Rumania and Bulgaria—but also by pressures that may be exerted by the Soviet Union on the smaller members of the Warsaw Pact to increase their defense expenditures and agree to closer military integration. They are, in short, apprehensive that the Soviet leaders may become prisoners of their own inflated rhetoric and sharply limit the eastern Europeans' scope of maneuver. If this were to occur, the very rationale of the Ostpolitik since the late 1960s (as adhered to also by the new conservative coalition since March 1983) would be undermined.

To a large extent, of course, the Soviet threats are deception and bluff. But in order to safeguard West German and western European interests against all eventualities, arms control negotiations have come to assume an important role in East-West relations in Europe. In fact, this role has steadily gained in significance and at present has even become the dominant issue

in these relations. However, because East-West military disparities have been growing, and because (as noted) so much
opposition exists in the civilian-oriented western European
societies to engaging the Soviet Union in the military competition, there are considerable asymmetries of bargaining power
between East and West. These asymmetries are amplified by
widely held ideas in the West that the arms race serves no one,
including the Soviet Union, and that hence the USSR, too, must
have a vital interest in successful arms control negotiations.

Such perceptions are at variance with a more complex reality.
They are at odds most of all with the fact that the Soviet arms
buildup, the Soviet stance in arms control negotiations, and the
Soviet support for the "antiwar movement" in western Europe
are closely integrated in an overall political design. In due recognition of the disparities in bargaining power in favor of the
USSR, Soviet arms control negotiations are not primarily meant
to enhance Soviet security (which is probably seen by the majority of Soviet military and political leaders as being safeguarded
mainly by strengthening Soviet military preponderance in
Europe), but to *increase the Soviet influence in the domestic
political process of the western European countries and on security relations between western Europe and the United States.*[52]

Thus, perhaps paradoxically, arms control negotiations concerning Europe have done much to worsen the very military and
political disease they were intended to cure. Rather than supple-
menting sound programs of defense they have often stood in
their way. And rather than supporting sound policies of détente
they nowadays tend to defeat their very purposes. Indeed, the
West has managed to get trapped in a vicious circle. First, Soviet
arms control proposals are made against the background of rising Soviet military capabilities, and they give rise to Western
expectations that, somehow, the Soviet Union can be persuaded
to help in alleviating Western defense problems. This, of course,
will not happen, and predictably the negotiations do not produce
any result, or only inadequate solutions, necessitating further
negotiation. But in the meantime the Western negotiating position has again weakened owing to additional Soviet armaments
and more insistent demands by an impatient western European

public for more comprehensive agreement. This, in turn, leads to the next round of arms control negotiations from a worse starting position for the West.

Soviet diplomatic and propagandistic skill, western European government vacillation and procrastination, and the strength and Soviet support of the "peace" movement have driven this vicious spiral. Undoubtedly, it received a major impetus during the campaign against the enhanced radiation weapon (the neutron bomb) in 1977–78. This campaign provided a major rallying point for the mobilization of pacifist, environmentalist, religious, and other groups opposed to nuclear weapons, and it laid the groundwork for the campaign against the deployment of Pershing II and cruise missiles. According to the chief of the International Department of the Hungarian Communist party, Janosz Berecz (the Hungarian counterpart to Boris Ponomarev), it was "one of the most significant and most successful [campaigns] since World War II."[53] Most likely it was similarly regarded by Soviet political leaders and analysts. They apparently drew the conclusion that the Soviet-supported "peace" campaign had *decided* on major issues of Western defense policy in their favor and that they would be able to do so again in the future.

As these developments show, it is not outright military aggression by the Soviet armed forces, nor even clearly stated ultimatums and blackmail, that hold the greatest promise for Soviet foreign policy and, conversely, the greatest danger for the Western alliance. It lies rather in the Soviet Union's successfully gaining leverage over western European political processes, notably on security matters, or at least successfully conveying the idea to that effect.

Lessons and Prospects

The principle of *divide et impera* has for centuries been used to good political effect. Applied to Soviet policy toward the United States and western Europe, this principle, as well as the traditional Leninist "operational code," would seem to make use of "contradictions" between the "imperialist power centers" a straightforward affair. Yet, as the present examination has shown, the enhancement of divisions between Europe and

America cannot be regarded as a fixed goal of Soviet foreign policy per se. It is rather to be seen as an *instrument* with which to achieve larger Soviet objectives.

A probable spectrum of Soviet objectives has been postulated here, but it is by no means clear how the individual goals in the spectrum are related to one another. Because of ever-changing international and, to a lesser extent, domestic conditions in the USSR, the goals may change in importance, and they may contradict one another.[54]

In pursuing its objectives, Soviet diplomacy has vacillated between three approaches in the postwar period: (1) Europeanism, that is, encouragement of tendencies toward neutralism, foreign policy autonomy, and independence of western Europe with an anti-American bias; (2) Atlanticism, that is, Soviet-American cooperation, collusion, or condominium directed at "solving," jointly with the United States, European and other world problems; and (3) pan-Europeanism, a combination of the two, consisting of the abandonment of crude endeavors of either forcing the United States out of Europe or trying to settle matters bilaterally with America at the expense of Europe. It consists instead of an attempt at persuading the United States to consent to a reduction in its European role and encouraging among the Europeans an "all-European" consciousness.

This last approach is probably the most important one because it is best suited to achieve what may be called the overriding, long-term Soviet goal: political fragmentation of Europe and elevation of the Soviet Union to a status of dominant power on the continent.

None of these attempts and approaches, however, has proven entirely successful. This has much to do, first, with the community of values and interests between western Europe and the United States, no matter how deep the policy disagreements on specific issues. Whereas the United States is as much as western Europe part of the Western cultural heritage of the Renaissance, Reformation, and Enlightenment, czarist Russia was not, and the Soviet Union has selected only certain aspects of these secular movements to merge with Marxist-Leninist ideology (in many ways thereby linking up with the Russian Byzantine tradition).

It has, second, something to do with what Soviet analysts call the "political economy" of Atlantic relations: the, despite all the alleged antagonist contradictions, "closer international interconnectedness," the "internationalization" and "cosmopolitanization" of capital, and the formation of "transnational military-industrial complexes" embracing big corporations on both sides of the Atlantic.[55]

Third, it is connected with the fact that the slogan peddled by the Soviet Union's traveling salesmen—"It is time that Europe be returned to the Europeans"—has a major deficiency: it does not include Soviet readiness to accept viable western European defense cooperation, including nuclear cooperation.[56] Instead, adoption of the slogan would leave the Europeans, East and West, defenseless in the face of Soviet military power.

Yet a fourth set of factors contributing to relative failure of Soviet policy toward the West consists in the deterioration of the Soviet image in western Europe; the erosion of the power and influence of the Moscow-oriented Communist parties; the decline in the effectiveness of Soviet ideology; and the significant problems faced by the Soviet economy, including declining overall growth rates, negative increases in factor productivity, falling rates of investment, underdevelopment of the economic infrastructure, adverse demographic trends, exhaustion of oil reserves in the European parts of Russia, labor shortages, low competitiveness of Soviet products in the world market—in short, inability to achieve a successful transition from extensive to intensive growth.

These deficiencies in the economic sphere make it safe to assume that the more modern and more industrialized western European countries have, relatively speaking, just as much as or perhaps even more political "leverage" than the Soviet Union. Certainly, it is not safe to assume that the Soviet Union has, or that the Soviet leaders think they have, achieved a relationship of dependence.

The conclusion is warranted, therefore, that the main area of success in Soviet policy toward the West has been the sphere of military competition. What seems to have begun, at the start of the Brezhnev era, primarily as a quest for strategic parity and political equality, as well as deterrence of American intervention in the third world, has turned into a major effort at gaining military preponderance and led to Soviet military intervention, directly and by proxy, in the third world. At the same time the USSR has more assertively used its newly developed military capabilities for political purposes in Europe, trying to convey the impression that the current disarray in the Western alliance is a direct result of its activist "peace policy." It has haunted Western governments with the specter of their inability in the future to implement agreed-on defense programs in the face of combined pressure by the Soviet Union and the "peace" movement. It is for this—political—reason that NATO's dual-track decision on the deployment of Pershing II and cruise missiles must be regarded as an important test case for the effectiveness of Soviet attempts at transforming military power into political influence.

It is also for this and other reasons that Soviet policy toward the United States and western Europe has arrived at a crucial juncture. On the one hand, given the tremendous Soviet investment in arms production since the mid-1960s and the apparent strength of opposition in western Europe to the deployment of intermediate-range nuclear missiles—in fact, to any reliance on nuclear weapons in peace or war—there is evidently a strong temptation for the Soviet leadership to "cash in" on its investment. This could mean, in practice, ever more threats of new deployment of weapons; intransigence in arms control negotiations; further fueling of divergencies between the United States and western Europe; and continued reliance on domestic pressures in NATO countries to erode Western security policies.

On the other hand unceasing emphasis on military power does nothing to alleviate the Soviet Union's social and economic problems. It strengthens the role of the military and of the orthodox political and ideological forces in the Soviet system, making decentralization and other reforms even more difficult to achieve. The unbroken priority for military production and the military instrument in foreign policy does nothing to improve the efficiency of Soviet control in eastern Europe. It serves to undermine even further the legitimacy of this control among most eastern Europeans. It further enhances the image in western Europe of the USSR as a repressive garrison state founded on a rigid and antiquated ideology. Most important, it carries with it the risk of the Soviet leaders overplaying their hand, because since—with or without an arms control agreement— new intermediate-range nuclear systems are being deployed by NATO as scheduled and backed by strong defense-minded governments (Kohl in West Germany, Thatcher in Britain, and Mitterrand in France), the peak of the "peace" movement could very well have passed. Perceptions as to the effectiveness of Soviet pressure and the Soviet Union's ability to control the course and outcome of Western security policy could significantly change, and the utility of the military instrument for Soviet policy decrease.

Such prospects may be strengthened by more basic facts of life in East-West relations. As Brzezinski has written, "neither side can be certain about the consequences of a military engagement, even less so about the consequences of quick preemption. Nor can either side count on effectively intimidating the other through the use of military power as a threat."[57] Proper Western responses demonstrating to the Soviet leaders the limited utility of military pressure for influencing the perceptions and policies of the alliance, thus, could induce yet another shift in approach by the Soviet Union. Such shifts, as shown, have happened before—and sometimes with surprising speed. But for such a development to occur it is necessary for the West not to have disrupted in the meantime all important channels of communication and economic cooperation. Preferably, the more complex and differentiated dual-track approach adopted by the Soviet Union vis-à-vis the West should be met by an equally differentiated response in the West.

Notes

1. V. I. Lenin, *Left-Wing Communism, an Infantile Disorder: A Popular Essay in Marxian Strategy and Tactics* (New York: International Publishers, 1969), 59 (emphasis in the original). The essay was written in 1920.

2. Charles Wolf, Jr., statement before the Senate Foreign Relations Committee, 12 Aug. 1982 (unpublished mimeograph).

3. Andropov, for instance, warned that contradictions in Socialist countries should be taken seriously lest they lead to "grave collisions"; see his "Uchenie Karla Marksa i nekotorye voprosy sotsialisticheskogo stroitel'stva v SSSR," *Kommunist* 3 (Feb. 1983): 9–23, esp. 21. For a more detailed discussion of the problem of Socialist contradictions see A. P. Butenko, "Protivorechiya razvitiya sotsializma kak obshchestvennogo stroya," *Voprosy filosofii,* 1982, no. 10: 16–29.

4. Quoted from Lenin's essay, *Imperialism: The Highest Stage of Capitalism* (New York: International Publishers, 1969), 96–97, written in Zurich in the spring of 1916. (Emphasis in the original.)

5. Ibid., 10, preface to the French and German editions, 20 July 1920.

6. V. I. Lenin, "Report to the Eighth Congress of the Communist Party, 18 March 1919," *Selected Works,* vol. 8 (New York: International Publishers, 1943), 33.

7. J. V. Stalin, *Economic Problems of Socialism in the USSR* [a collection of comments on a draft for a new textbook on political economy written between February and September 1952, i.e., shortly before the Nineteenth Party Congress (October 1952)] (Moscow: Foreign Languages Publishing House, 1952), 39.

8. Ibid., 38–39.

9. One of the foremost Soviet experts on Socialist integration, for instance, frankly acknowledges in comparative perspective EEC-Comecon that "the level of the division of labor in CMEA [Council for Mutual Economic Assistance] does not satisfy the requirements of the countries participating in it. . . . CMEA lags behind the Common Market in that respect. Foreign trade quotas show that the European socialist countries . . . have as yet not attained the intensity in the international division of labor typical of the Common Market countries, although as regards such objective factors as the population figure, the capacity of the domestic market etc., both the former and the latter greatly depend on foreign markets." M. Senin [director of the International Institute for the Study of Economic Problems of the Socialist World System at CMEA], *Socialist Integration* (Moscow: Progress Publishers, 1973), 178. Although published in 1973, Senin's appreciation of the relative differences in the depth of economic integration achieved by the two economic organizations remains valid. One of the most recent indications of this was repeated the postponements of the summit conference of the Comecon countries until June 1984.

10. See, for instance, Brezhnev's report to the Twenty-fourth Party Congress in which he stated: "By the early 1970s, the main centers of

imperialist rivaly have become clearly visible: these are the USA—Western Europe (above all, the six Common Market countries)—Japan. The economic and political competitive struggle between them has been growing ever more acute." *The Twenty-fourth Congress of the Communist Party of the Soviet Union, March 30, April 9, 1971: Documents* (Moscow: Novosti, 1971), 20.

11. Juri Schischkow, "Rivalität der drei Zentren des Imperialismus und der USA-Konfrontationskurs," *Deutsche Außenpolitik* [East Berlin], 1983, no. 2: 49–56, esp. 49 and 53. For a more detailed examination of Soviet perceptions of western European economic integration see Hannes Adomeit, "Soviet Perceptions of Western European Integration: Ideological Distortion or Realistic Assessment?" *Millenium: Journal of International Studies* (London) 8, no. 1 (Spring 1979): 1–24.

12. M. Maksimova, "Kapitalisticheskaya integratsiya i mirovoe razvitie," *Mirovaiya ekonomika i mezhdunarodnye otnosheniya,* 1978, no. 4: 14–24, esp. 19.

13. M. Maksimova, Introduction to a Round Table Discussion of MEiMO, "Problemy Zapadroevropeiskoi integratsii," ibid., 1982, no. 11: 107–111, esp. 111.

14. Ibid., 110.

15. This is a point well made by Kenneth Pridham, "The Soviet View of Current Disagreements Between the United States and Western Europe," *International Affairs* (London) 41, no. 1 (Winter 1982–83): 17–31.

16. TASS commentary, published in *Neues Deutschland,* 9–10 February 1980. N. Portugalov is a senior Soviet journalist who writes on West Germany and European security issues and apparently is on the staff of, or otherwise attached to, the CC Department on International Information (see *Le Monde,* 2–3 March 1980).

17. Theo Sommer, "Wollen die Russen Krieg?" *Die Zeit* (Hamburg) 11 (March 1983): 9–10. Zagladin is first deputy head of the International Department of the Central Committee.

18. Ibid.

19. S. Madzoevskii and D. Tomashevskii, "Rost mezhdunarodnoi napryazhennosti i Zapadnaya Evropa," *MEiMO,* 1982, 11:42–51, esp. 50–51.

20. See Hannes Adomeit, "Ideology in the Soviet View of International Affairs," in *Prospects of Soviet Power in the 1980s,* ed. Christoph Bertram (London: Macmillan, 1980), 103–110.

21. This summary of Soviet objectives draws on Christoph Royen,

Die sowjetische Koexistenzpolitik gegenüber Westeuropa: Voraussetzungen, Ziele, Dilemmata, Series Internationale Politik und Sicherheit, ed. Stiftung Wissenschaft und Politik (Baden-Baden: Nomos, 1978). Although written in 1977–78, such changes as have occurred in the meantime have not gone far enough to make this summary in any way outdated.

22. Concerning "Finlandizaton" as a possible Soviet objective, see Hannes Adomeit, *The Soviet Union and Western Europe: Perceptions, Policies, Problems,* Center for International Relations, Queen's University, Kingston, Ontario, National Security Series, No. 3/79, 9–14; see also George Ginsburgs and Alvin Z. Rubinstein, "Finlandization: Soviet Strategy or Geopolitical Footnote?" in *Soviet Foreign Policy Toward Western Europe,* ed. George Ginsburgs and Alvin Z. Rubinstein (New York: Praeger, 1978).

23. More detail on this is provided by Pridham, "The Soviet View," 19.

24. Such appeals are documented in Hannes Adomeit, *Soviet Risk Taking and Crisis Behavior: A Theoretical and Empirical Analysis* (London: Allen & Unwin, 1982), 67–182.

25. Khrushchev, in a speech to graduates of Soviet military academies, *Pravda,* 9 July 1961.

26. *Pravda,* 31 Dec. 1961.

27. Institut Mirovoi Ekonomiki i Mezhdunarodnykh Otnoshenii, ed., *Dvizhushchie sily vneshnei politiki SShA* (Moscow: Nauka, 1965), 507.

28. This summary of Khrushchev's détente strategy follows Vernon Aspaturian, *Process and Power in Soviet Foreign Policy* (Boston: Little, Brown, 1971), 780. On Khrushchev's détente policies vis-à-vis the United States and their effect on western Europe, see John Van Oudenaren, *The Leninist Peace Policy and Western Europe,* Research Monograph, Center for International Studies, MIT, Jan. 1980, 8–9.

29. *Pravda,* 3 April 1966. Roosevelt, in fact, was even more gloomy on this subject than Gromyko cared to remember. "I can get the people and Congress to cooperate fully for peace [Roosevelt said], but not to keep an army in Europe for a long time. *Two years would be the limit.*" U.S. Department of State (ed.), *Foreign Relations of the United States: The Conferences of Malta and Yalta* (Washington, D.C.: U.S. Government Printing Office, 1955), 628 (italics added).

30. Text of the document as published in *Problemy mira i sotsializma* (June 1969).

31. The NATO ministerial meeting in Reykjavik in June 1968 called for discussions on mutual, balanced forces reductions. This call was formally reiterated at the NATO ministerial meeting in Rome in May 1970; for the context of the offer and the Soviet response see Lothar Ruehl, *MBFR: Lessons and Problems,* Adelphia Paper No. 176 (London: International Institute for Strategic Studies, 1982), 6–8.

32. Quoted from Brezhnev's report to the Twenty-fourth CPSU Congress, 30 March 1971, *Pravda,* 31 March 1971.

33. Henry Kissinger, *Years of Upheaval* (London: Weidenfeld & Nicolson, 1982), 276–279.

34. See, for instance, Frank Snepp, *Decent Interval: An Insider's Account of Saigon's Indecent End* (New York: Vintage Books, 1978), 138, as quoted by Gebhard Schweigler, *Von Kissinger zu Carter: Entspannung im Widerstreit von Innenund Außenpolitik, 1969–1981* (Munich: R. Oldenbourg, 1982), 206.

35. The choice of words is deliberate. It is, in my view, a dangerous illusion to think that in Poland the established Communist party "collapsed completely and had to be replaced with a military regime," *Foreign Policy,* no. 49 (Winter 1982–83): 3–19, esp. 8. What did take place, in my view, rather than some kind of Latin-American–style military coup, was restoration of control by the Soviet Union and the Polish Communist party *through* the military and the security police— hardly a novel means of recourse by a Communist party under challenge.

36. This is the view expressed by CBS News correspondent David A. Andelman, "Struggle over Western Europe," *Foreign Policy,* no. 49 (Winter 1982–83): 37–51, esp. 37. Unfortunately, this biased view is not an isolated one: However much one may deplore the changes in the West German Social Democratic party on defense issues, it is surely inaccurate to speak, as James H. Billington (director of the Woodrow Wilson Center for International Scholars) does, of an "increasingly pro-Soviet drift" of the SPD (*International Herald Tribune,* 26–27 Nov. 1983).

37. See Elisabeth Noelle-Neumann, *The Germans: Public Opinion Polls, 1967–1980* (Westport, Conn.: Greenwood Press, 1981), 428–430; for more detail on the evolution of German attitudes see Chapter 1, by Gebhard Schweigler. The deterioration of the Soviet image in West Germany was measured on February 1977 and January 1980 and hence reflects the impact of the Soviet intervention in Afghanistan. It is doubtful that the events in Poland have in any way improved the Soviet image.

38. See Michael J. Sodaro, "Moscow and Mitterrand," *Problems of Communism* 31; no. 4 (July–Aug. 1982): 20–36.

39. *Pravda,* 23 Nov. 1982.

40. Schischkow, "Rivalität der drei Zentren," 56. This main line of argument is adhered to also, among many others, by I. D. Evgrafov, "Uroki razryadki: Vashington i vostochnaya politika FRG," 1983, no. 3: 27–37, esp. 35–36.

41. Yu. Andreev, "Ekonomicheskie otnosheniya Vostok-Zapad," *MEiMO,* 1982, no. 12: 93.

42. Ibid., 94 (italics added).

43. *The Economist,* 30 Oct. 1982, 69.

44. These graphs were compiled by Friedemann Müller in the context of a project on the role of sanctions in East-West relations conducted at the Stiftung Wissenschaft und Politik, Ebenhausen, in 1982–83; see Friedemann Müller et al., *Wirtschaftssanktionen im Ost-West-Verhältnis: Rahmenbedingungen und Modalitäten,* ed. under the auspices of the Stiftung Wissenschaft und Politik, Series Aktuelle Materialien, vol. 1 (Baden-Baden: Nomos, 1983), 130–44. The statistical data are drawn from OECD Trade Statistics, Series A.

45. Pridham, "The Soviet View," 28.

46. Ibid., 30. With the exception of this faux pas concerning the role of East-West trade in relation to other Soviet objectives, as well as the possibilities of their realization, Pridham's analysis is one of the best on the subject of Soviet policy toward the West.

47. *Pravda* and *Izvestiya,* 31 Dec. 1982.

48. Editorial in *Pravda,* 27 Dec. 1982.

49. Some of the more recent statements of that effect are contained in Andropov's first official reaction to the shooting down of the Korean airliner over Sakhalin ("Zayavlenie General'nogo sekretarya . . . ," *Pravda,* 29 Sept. 1982), and the articles by Yu. Zhilin and D. Kraminov in *Pravda,* 15 Aug. and 24 Oct. 1983, respectively.

50. General and Deputy Minister of Defense K. Mikhailov, in an interview with the West German newspaper *Frankfurter Rundschau,* 3 Nov. 1982.

51. As quoted in *Der Tagesspiegel* (Berlin), 16 Oct. 1983.

52. These ideas are developed further in Hannes Adomeit, "The Political Rationale of Soviet Military Capabilities and Doctrine," in *Strengthening Conventional Deterrence in Europe: Proposals for the 1980s,* Report of the European Security Study (ESECS) (London: Macmillan, 1983), 67–104. More specifically, it is a dangerous misperception of Soviet aims in Europe to assert, as Raymond Garthoff does,

that "there is considerable indirect evidence" to the effect that the Soviet Union did *not* "see an opportunity to gain political-military advantage and leverage *vis-à-vis* Western Europe by the SS-20 deployment" ("The Soviet SS-20 Decision," *Survival* 25: 3 [May/June 1983]: 113). Certainly, the political implications of the deployment decision were repeatedly pointed out to Moscow by various Western leaders, starting with Chancellor Schmidt in London in 1977.

53. Quoted in Permanent Select Committee on Intelligence, U.S. House of Representatives, *Soviet Covert Action (The Forgery Offensive)*, Hearings Before the Subcommittee on Oversight of the Permanent Select Committee on Intelligence, House of Representatives, Ninety-sixth Congress, Second Session (Washington, D.C.: U.S. Government Printing Office, 1980), 75.

54. Prospects as well as constraints, and chances as well as limitations, of Soviet policy are stressed in Edwina Moreton and Gerald Segal, eds., *Soviet Strategy Toward Western Europe* (London: Allen & Unwin, 1984), by the editors themselves and in the contributions by Hannes Adomeit, Karen Dawisha, R. A. Mason, Lawrence Freedman, Angela Stent, and Jane Sharp. The book makes the claim to express a distinctively western European view of Soviet interests, goals, and tactics.

55. All of these terms are used by S. Men'shikov, "Politekonomika 'Atlantizma,' " *Pravda,* 9 May 1983.

56. According to a report of Agency France Press from Moscow, unidentified "usually well informed Soviet sources," in addition to the inducement of "Europe ought to be returned to the Europeans," suggested that the western European countries should also "provide for their own defense" (as quoted in *Frankfurter Allgemeine Zeitung,* 4 March 1982). Such sources, it stands to reason, form part of the traditional Soviet endeavor of raising the level of uncertainty in the West about Soviet aims in Europe. They are not to be taken seriously.

57. Zbigniew Brzezinski, "A Deal for Andropov," *The New Republic,* 13 Dec. 1982, 14.

PART THREE

East-West Issues and Western Policy Changes

Chapter 7

East-West Economic Relations: Conflict and Concord in Western Policy Choices

Abraham S. Becker

East-West economics became the smoldering focus of Atlantic relations in the year 1982. No other issue generated as much heat or as much transatlantic diplomatic shuttling (the one being the generator of the other). In sharp contrast 1983 was largely devoid of conflict on this issue. Instead, intermediate-range nuclear forces (INF) deployment and arms control became the hinge of alliance politics. The Versailles economic summit of June 1982 was dominated by two subjects: U.S. interest rates and East-West trade. In May 1983 the Williamsburg summit communiqué devoted three sentences to East-West trade, and the press reports do not suggest that much time was spent composing them.[1]

Mais ou sont les orages d'antan? to reframe François Villon's melancholy question. What explains the Sturm und Drang of 1982 and what happened to it in 1983? Has the explosiveness of East-West economics as an alliance problem been permanently defused? It might be argued that the storms of 1982 were associated with a unique conjuncture of events—the Polish crisis and the concluding phases of the gas pipeline deal. Yet if this particular conjuncture was unique, the events were bound up with recurrent issues. So it was in the past and so it seems likely to be in the future. Are we then witnessing only a temporary lull,

An earlier version of this chapter appeared in the *Atlantic Quarterly* 2: 1 (Spring 1984).

to be quickly succeeded by fresh tempests? Probably not. True consensus seems as remote from achievement as before, but the critical issues of the alliance are political-military, not East-West economic. On the latter the safest weather prediction is occasionally threatening overcast, rather than imminent downpour.

Background: Disarray in the West; New-Old Uncertainties in the East

To understand what happened in 1982, what did not happen in 1983, and what might happen in the near future, a context seems necessary. It seems useful, therefore, to sketch out the political-economic background of alliance considerations of these issues at the beginning of the eighties.

An economist is inclined to start with the second half of the hyphenated term. Among the economic factors the most important affecting relations among members of the Atlantic alliance, not just with regard to East-West economics, but in almost all aspects of their interconnection, was the worldwide major recession, arguably the most serious one of the postwar period. In reaction, governments sought, frantically at times, to maintain income and employment levels by a variety of means—among the most traditional was the search for sales outlets in external markets. As the recession deepened, protectionist sentiment and the threat of increasing trade barriers grew apace. Both of these interconnected trends—the increasing sensitivity to domestic unemployment levels and to the foreigner's (never one's own) unprincipled trading behavior—conditioned reaction to American attempts to control East-West trade.

The crisis of income and employment in the Western economies was joined with a crisis of the international credit market. Few non-bankers doubted that this was directly a consequence of the uninhibited expansion of credit that had taken place in the mid- and late 1970s, fueled by the vast influx of petro-dollars. As debt levels rose to seemingly astronomic heights, it was feared that default, inadvertent or intended, would spread and bring down the international financial system—like a house of cards or a row of dominoes; the preference for game metaphor varied.

One of the early-warning signals of this threat was seen in the Polish debt crisis of 1980–82, which became a major focus of the controversy over East-West policy. The Polish debt problem drew attention to possible flashpoints elsewhere in eastern Europe, particularly Rumania and Yugoslavia, as well as to various parts of the third world.

At the other end of the East-West connection, the 1970s witnessed the acceleration of the retardation in Soviet economic growth that had begun in the late 1950s. The retardation was gradual and uneven for the better part of two decades, but from the mid-1970s on that decline steepened. A related development was a fall in the growth rate at current prices, and perhaps even in the real level, of Soviet imports of technology from the West, accompanied by an increase in the importance of food imports. This combination of developments raised questions about future Soviet trade policy with the West and the dependence of the Soviet economy on external supply, particularly of agricultural products and other foodstuffs as well as capital equipment and know-how. Economic weakness and internal social-political strains, in the context of a leadership succession process, gave rise to Western debates about the vulnerability of the USSR to external pressure.

In the political-military domain in the West, the NATO alliance was being stressed by security issues—dilemmas of arms control versus missile deployments, debates over strategy and doctrine, the increasing militancy and vociferousness of the European peace movement. These issues are dealt with at length in other chapters of this volume. At the same time the divergence of American and European views on the meaning of détente, its past success or failure, and the degree to which it represents a viable strategy of East-West relationships, became increasingly prominent in public discussion.

To these general contextual developments we should add two international crises, erupting virtually simultaneously at the end of 1979, that provided tests of the alliance's ability to develop consensus on the application of economic sanctions. The first was the Iranian hostage crisis, in which the United States sought international cooperation in enforcing sanctions against the

Khomeini regime. The most important action was the freezing of $12 billion of Iranian assets under American control or access. This involved the use of extraterritorial controls, which aroused considerable misgivings even among America's allies, pre-figuring the far stronger reaction when extraterritoriality was applied in the wake of the Polish crisis two years later. In the Iranian case the allies cooperated, although somewhat grudg-ingly. They did not apply sanctions of their own to reinforce those imposed by Washington.

The second crisis centered on East-West relations and was therefore more significant as a test of the allied consensual mechanism. In general, reaction in the United States to the Soviet invasion of Afghanistan in December 1979 was con-siderably stronger and more ideologically colored than was the reaction in either western Europe or Japan. The sanctions in-stituted by the Carter administration—notably, the boycott of the Olympics and the grain embargo—received a mixed recep-tion. The Olympics boycott was in itself, of course, only a sym-bolic gesture and received some support in allied capitals (most emphatically in Bonn). However, the grain embargo was largely circumvented by the noncooperation of other major grain pro-ducers—Canada, Australia, and, especially, Argentina—as well as the European Community. These episodes provided a fore-taste of the still greater difficulties to come in relations between the United States and its allies over response to the imposition of martial law in Poland and to Washington's attempt to restrict what it believed was Western aid for the Soviet military buildup.

The East-West Follies of 1981–82

In the course of the first two years of the Reagan administration a raging cross-Atlantic controversy developed over the several issues of East-West economic relations, which became the cen-ter of debate on East-West issues generally. The alliance seemed strained at the seams before a lid was placed on the conflict in the fall of 1982.

The focus of the clash was the Soviet gas pipeline to western Europe. Long in preparation, the project had excited western

European interest because of the magnitude and the duration of the expected contracts. During the years of rising energy prices the pipeline deal promised new sources of energy and a reduction of European reliance on OPEC. At the same time the Soviets would buy pipe, compressors, and associated equipment and services to lay the pipeline. This aspect, the up-front sales of pipe and equipment, became especially important as the recession came and deepened in western Europe.

Initially, U.S. opposition (back to the Carter administration) centered on the question of European dependence. The share of western Europe's total energy supply that was to come from Soviet gas in 1990 was about 5 percent, whereas the share of total gas supply was to be roughly 20 percent; for the Federal Republic of Germany the Soviet gas share would be higher, perhaps 30 percent.[2] In European capitals these numbers were judged relatively low, but U.S. leaders felt that a dependence on the Soviet Union would be created that could provide Moscow with political leverage, especially in crisis periods. Subsequently, Washington's opposition shifted to two other aspects. First and foremost was the size of the hard currency stream that would flow to Moscow as payment for the movement of gas westward. Washington worried over the likely enlargement of the Soviet capability to import Western technology. The second, but minor, theme was U.S. opposition to the export of "high" technology to the Soviet Union in the form of gas compressors and associated equipment. After some early hesitation the Reagan administration fought hard to turn the Europeans off the deal.

The opposition to the pipeline became part of a much more general issue at the end of 1981 with the repression of Solidarity and the establishment of martial law in Poland. Reaction to the pipeline deal was now coupled with Western response to Soviet backing, if not actual initiation of the Polish repression. In December 1981 President Reagan levied a series of sanctions against the Soviet Union that included a ban on the export of energy technology. There was considerable difficulty in securing allied response to support those measures.[3]

Earlier the same year the Polish debt became a front-page

issue. The sharp decline of the economy in 1980–81 brought on a catastrophic shrinkage in Polish trade and in Warsaw's ability to service its debt. In March 1981 the Polish government declared an inability to pay and demanded a rescheduling of its public and private debt with the West. How to deal with the Polish debt crisis in the context of the simultaneous political crisis became a subject of heated debate on both sides of the Atlantic. However, the lines of division within the U.S. government on this issue were almost as sharp as those between the U.S. government and western Europe on the gas pipeline.

During the presidential campaign of 1980, Ronald Reagan had promised to resume grain sales to the USSR. On assuming office he hastened to fulfill his campaign promise. When the Polish crisis broke and sanctions were applied against the Soviet Union for its complicity in the repression, the grain embargo was conspicuously absent. Thereafter, this became an albatross around the administration's neck in trying to win allied cooperation on sanctions. Few European discussions of East-West economics neglected to point to the failure to reinstitute the grain embargo as an indication of the selfishness or lack of seriousness of the American effort. The administration's arguments that there were substantive differences between sales of grain and sales of technology were dismissed as sophistry.[4]

In June 1982 the annual economic summit of Western leaders convened at Versailles. Within days of its conclusion, the paper consensus was shredded by acrimonious charges and countercharges, particularly between the United States and France.[5] Whether in connection with these events or not, President Reagan decided to extend the December 1981 controls on the export of energy technology to the Soviet Union to sales by branches of American companies operating abroad and by wholly owned foreign companies using licensed American technology. This extraterritorial extension of the controls threatened the front-end European benefits from the gas pipeline deal, but it was also perceived as a gross infringement of national sovereignty; on both counts the U.S. action caused a furor in western European capitals. It seems fair to say that the U.S. decision in

November 1982 to suspend the attempt at extraterritorial control was largely in response to the European reaction.

Even before martial law in Poland there was a sense in Washington that Western, especially European, trade with the East was laced with open and hidden subsidies in the form of favorable credit terms and government guarantees. Subsidization was seen as strengthening the Soviet economy, particularly the military buildup. After martial law in Poland, subsidization came to be regarded as an open scandal, and it emerged as one of the major subjects on the agenda of allied negotiations on East-West issues that were so salient a feature of 1982.

Control of technology transfer has been a perennial of Western discussion, although the intensity and tenor of that discussion have varied with the temperature of East-West relations. In the heyday of détente, under the explicit encouragement of trade expressed in the 1969 U.S. Export Administration Act, the controls were applied much more flexibly. The deterioration of détente led to a strengthening of restrictions in the 1979 Export Administration Act, which sought to regulate exports so as to ensure national security safeguards and consideration of U.S. national policy goals. It was under the authority of this act that the sanctions of 1980–82 were applied.

With the lifting of the extraterritorial controls allied conflict over East-West trade controls diminished substantially. Some unhappiness continues to be expressed in Europe with the changes being considered in the Export Administration Act, whose renewal is still bogged down in congressional disagreement; the enforcement of technology transfer, which the Reagan administration has been pursuing vigorously at home and abroad, undeniably causes frictions in the alliance. But Secretary of State Shultz was able to declare at the end of a harmonious ministerial-level meeting of the Organization for Economic Cooperation and Development (OECD) in the spring of 1983 that the East-West issue "just isn't that controversial at this point. There aren't any sore points in this area."[6]

No doubt controversy has waned, but it is not so clear that the "sore points" have disappeared. The pipeline controversy was resolved by the decision to study the major East-West economic issues. It seems hardly doubtful that this was a thinly disguised victory for the Europeans, who, not surprisingly, felt vindicated in their general opposition to the vigorous U.S. sanctions policy. By the same token the Reagan administration appeared to gain little from the episode.[7] There was a widely shared view on both sides of the Atlantic that alliance relations had been embittered and that only the Kremlin emerged a net gainer.

The fundamental issues remained unresolved—not just energy dependence or technology transfer, but the more general, tougher questions: Is there a major security dimension to East-West trade, and in which of its aspects should that be taken into account? (The Williamsburg summit declared that "East-West economic relations should be compatible with our security interest"; fortunately, the summiteers were not obliged to spell this out.) Should trade be used in the furtherance of foreign policy, specifically, to punish Soviet or eastern European aggressiveness? On what basis should East-West economic relations be conducted? It is, therefore, to these larger issues that we now turn.

The Big Picture: Objectives and Grand Strategy

The transatlantic controversy over the fundamentals of East-West relations tends to be cast in simple dichotomies—typically, pro- or anti-détente. For all its oversimplification such a categorization conveys some meaning. But it may be useful to consider the controversy in the framework of three additional, interrelated pairs of distinctions between (1) normalization and containment as grand strategies of Western relations with the USSR, (2) the objective of transformation of the Soviet system versus that of managing the conflict, and (3) pessimistic and optimistic views of the extent and structural embeddedness of Soviet hostility to the West.

There is clearly a basic agreement among Americans and Germans on the general need to deter Soviet expansion and aggression, although as other chapters in this volume indicate, the implementation of the principle leaves room for dispute. But is deterrence the sole or ultimate goal? Here there is a marked bifurcation of general approaches, with several branches within each of the two principal groups.

To most Germans, but also to most Americans, it seems self-evident that deterrence of Soviet power must be complemented by various forms of cooperation. Deterrence alone is insufficient and dangerous, because if the military competition proceeds unchecked, it may end in military confrontation and nuclear disaster. Thus arms control becomes an article of faith. But in Germany particularly the perceived necessity for cooperation is not limited to the requirement for arms control. There is a sense that Western security depends on changing the entire tenor of East-West relations.

The desired state of relations has been characterized variously. The Harmel report, a NATO document that receives homage more often in the Federal Republic than almost anywhere else on the continent, speaks of "a final and stable [European] settlement" and "a just and lasting peace order in Europe" as the ultimate purpose of the alliance.[8] A characteristic European, particularly German, image of the needed change is "normalization," although the current German government is uncomfortable with the implication that relations with the Soviet state can ever be placed in the same category as those with the Federal Republic's Western neighbors. An alternative term might be "regularization," which conveys the sense of instituting rules of behavior according to prescribed or consensual norms. This term might be understood more narrowly, in the spirit of the 1972 Soviet-American "Declaration on Basic Principles of Relations,"[9] or more broadly, linking up with the Harmel language. It is in the sense of regularization that the more common term, normalization, is used hereafter.

Economics and geography powerfully impel Germans in this direction. Former Chancellor Schmidt appeared to be adducing a historical lesson when he stated, "We Europeans have done business with the Russians for centuries." That he was really talking economics was evident in what followed: "If we wanted to trade only with democracies we would certainly ruin our economies very quickly."[10] German involvement in East-West trade is, of course, far larger than that of the United States. The Federal Republic's imports from the Soviet Union in 1981 and 1982 were nineteen and twenty-five times larger than U.S. imports. Despite the large volume of U.S. grain and food shipments, German exports to the USSR were 58 percent and 37 percent, respectively, larger than the U.S. volume. The Federal Republic remains, by a considerable margin, the Soviet Union's largest export market among all the non-Socialist countries; as a seller to the USSR it was a close second to Japan in 1982 but far ahead in 1983.[11] West German trade with eastern Europe is similarly much more extensive than that of the United States. As many German observers are quick to point out, these trade volumes are small relative to gross national product (GNP) or even to trade with the rest of the world. But the share of trade with the East in total trade is four times higher in the Federal Republic than in the United States, and the German Eastern-trade: GNP ratio is eleven times higher than the American counterpart.[12]

More potent still is geography. When the superpower adversary is camped on Germany's doorstep, normalization seems an *objective* devoutly to be desired. In an earlier era American power alone was believed capable of leading ultimately to that goal. But the Soviet achievement of parity (or better) made normalization appear to many as the only prudent *strategy* as well.

The issue that integrates historical, geographical, and economic elements is the special relationship West Germany feels with East Germany. This tie seems composed of varying parts of hope for reunification, family connections, and the sense that the Federal Republic has an obligation to try to make life easier for its unfortunate compatriots on the other side of the Iron Curtain. Under Adenauer, reunification was to be achieved through Western pressure on the Soviet Union and was therefore effectively relegated to the back burner. The realities of Soviet power preclude a direct approach to reunification; but since the mid- or late sixties the hope for change has rested on cooperation rather than confrontation: "If there is a way towards the unity of the nation," Foreign Minister Walter Scheel declared in 1972, "then it is only through a general relaxation of tension in Europe which can bear the burden of pushing into the background everything that separates us from the GDR."[13] It has been argued, indeed, that the driving force behind the new direction of Ostpolitik pursued by Willy Brandt was disillusionment with Adenauer's reunification strategy and hope of overcoming the increasing estrangement between Germans of the East and West.[14]

Normalization is, however, foreign in its essence to the thinking of the Reagan administration and that of a great many other Americans, who see Soviet expansionism as deeply rooted in the Soviet system. The administration is more naturally attuned to the notions of containment that developed out of George Kennan's historic 1947 article. The original concept of containment carried with it the expectation that countering the Soviet Union's expansionist impulse all along its Eurasian perimeter would force the Soviet pressures back inward and result (eventually) in the transformation of the system.[15] Thus containment had two essential elements: the strategy of countervailing power and the objective (or hope) of transforming the Soviet Communist system so as to eventually resolve the conflict.

Juxtaposed against contemporary controversies, containment seems rife with paradoxes. For example, it was born in a more "optimistic" era, in which Soviet malevolence, but not its power, was viewed as unlimited. For all its sense of urgency in military buildup, part of the Reagan administration—the White House and the Pentagon, particularly—seems to have similar views. This view is, of course, acutely concerned with growing Soviet power, but it believes that the social-economic foundations of that power are ultimately rotten and that containment can turn the pressures back on the regime.[16]

Another paradox revolves around the goal of transforming the Soviet system. The transformationist zeal of cold war containment seems a typical product of the American political imagination, characteristically impatient with complexities and diplomatic niceties. It seems born of the American need to have definite terminal points in sight to undertake a prolonged national burden. It is not in the U.S. temper, it is often said, to accept a problem as insoluble. One would think it a more characteristic European pattern of mind to seek the management and thus the taming of a conflict. In this sense one may think of normalization as a natural European inclination to direct great power conflict into channels in which it can be controlled by diplomacy (updated forms of conventional nineteenth-century politics, to a mid-American view) and bought out by the live-and-let-live currency of quid pro quo. This would be opposed to the American sense that the conflict with the Soviet Union is *sui generis.*

Strangely, it would then appear, a number of Europeans, and Germans in particular, also rest their hopes on transformation of the Soviet system. The major rationale stretches back to the theme of Egon Bahr's landmark speech at Tutzing in 1963, "Change Through Rapprochement" *(Wandel durch Annaherung),* which advocated relaxation of tensions and cooperation as the means to exorcise the Soviet threat. A related line of thought sees transformation as not only desirable, but also absolutely essential, if the *conflict* is to be contained. In part this is perhaps because it is recognized that the conflict is indeed *sui generis,* at least for now, and therefore dangerous. Because it involves a structural hostility that makes it a specialized conflict, there is the ever-present danger that deterioration of the balance of power could lead to armed confrontation.

The controversies over East-West relations also feature a clash of two tempers. One, pessimistic, sees Soviet military power rooted in systemic hostility to the West. Another, optimistic, sees Soviet military power as the unavoidable trappings of a large industrial state burdened by long land frontiers. But in another paradox there is no necessary alignment between temper, grand strategy, and objective. To the pessimistic outlook, containment is a strategic imperative of survival, whereas to the optimistic view, containment, in its narrowest sense of deterrence, is at most a necessary, although not a sufficient, condition of stabilization. But the goal or hope of transformation, as we have seen, arises from both containment and normalization perspectives. On the other hand, thoroughly pessimistic "containors" see little hope for resolution of the conflict and count only on managing it. Yet optimistic "normalizers" believe that the process will stabilize through transformation.

The ultimate paradox is that for all those who seek transformation of the Soviet system—from whatever direction they start out, whether cold war containment or 1970s-détente—and for all those who believe that only management of the conflict is possible—whether they are "normalizers" or "containors"—for all of them, economics rather than politics is taken to be the operative force. The choice of economics is not surprising. It is obvious to most that military force, in this era of supernuclearization of the superpowers, is not a flexible tool for the long-term competition between the two systems. Because political power, it was once said, comes out of the barrel of a gun, this instrument, too, seems flawed. Thus economics wins out by elimination. However, divergent approaches to general East-West objectives and strategies effect sharply different views on what constitutes appropriate trade strategy and policy.

East-West Trade Strategies

One may distinguish three logically possible strategies of East-West economic relations. The first seeks to use trade and credit as inducements. Under the names of linkage or leverage, an inducement strategy formed the economic foundation of the theory of détente in the 1970s. The aim was to create a network of interdependence with the USSR through the extension of trade and credit ties in order to tame Moscow's expansionist impulse.[17]

Partisans of détente believe that it is still a viable mode of dealing with the Soviet Union, perhaps the only reasonable one. This view has several variants:

- Détente never really died, it was just misinterpreted as applying to the third world where it was never intended to and cannot apply.
- Détente could have worked had the West not lowered its defense guard. Détente depends on a two-track approach—cooperation and deterrence—and in the 1970s the first was in full operation, while the second was allowed to lapse. If the West can achieve a credible deterrent posture in the

1980s, it can re-create the fundamental conditions necessary for the success of détente.

• Détente failed in the 1970s because the West did not try to make it worth Moscow's while to participate in cooperative international arrangements. For example, in the United States the Jackson-Vanik and Stevenson amendments denied the Soviet Union major economic benefits, which, apart from the diminution of the danger of nuclear war, were to be the USSR's primary stake in détente. Hence the Soviet Union found no profit in détente with the United States.

The alternative view, held most strongly in the White House and the U.S. Department of Defense, is that détente was tried in the 1970s and failed. The West subsidized Soviet and eastern European development, and for its money bought the invasion of Afghanistan, intervention in Angola and Ethiopia, and Soviet expansion in every part of the third world in which opportunities allowed; détente bought Polish martial law, the crushing of Solidarity, and the repression of dissent in the Soviet Union; perhaps most important, détente bought the Soviet military buildup.[18] Where, then, is the Kremlin's sensitivity to trade ties that was supposed to stay its hand, as the theory of détente had proposed? No, the only viable strategy was to make East-West trade policy consistent with East-West political-military policy and serve the function of deterring Soviet expansionism. Trade policy must seek not to subsidize the Soviet economy, but to impede the Soviet military buildup, at least not to contribute to it.

This second basic strategy tends to take a jaundiced view of the argument that trade should be unrestricted. It is inclined to paraphrase Clausewitz and say that "trade is a continuation of foreign policy by other means." Bernard Brodie interpreted Clausewitz to mean that "war takes place within a political milieu from which it derives *all* its purposes" (italics in original).[19] The Reagan administration would not be prepared to substitute "trade" for "war" in Brodie's phrase, even with a restriction to trade with Communists: Witness the lifting of the grain embargo. Nevertheless, it believes that trade with the Communist world has a significant military security and foreign policy dimension that must be governed by the corresponding interests of the West.[20]

In principle, there ought to be a third strategy insisting that trade defines its own value without connection to political objectives of any orientation. This view would indeed be laissez faire, laissez passer. It would suggest that trade be left to the market-place. However, it is difficult to identify live specimens of this genus. Those who decry the politicization of trade are most often adherents of détente policies, "normalizers," or even cherishers of hopes for transformation. They are opposed to constraints but not to government intervention in behalf of East-West trade, which is institutionalized and deeply rooted in Europe. Insistence on pure market justification of East-West trade seems a hallmark of the contemporary anti-détente school, but in fact its adherents wish to apply the market test only where security is not involved. The domain of "safe" trade, however, is shrinking, as the list of technology transfers considered to have security implications grows.

The two antagonistic strategies of East-West economic relations have been defined in general terms, but there are specific trade policies that attach to each of them. However, before considering the trade policies it would be useful to examine the needs and behavior of the Soviet Union. The controversy is, after all, largely about trade and credit relations with the USSR. Let us therefore turn first to this set of issues.

The Soviet Economy and the Role of Trade

There is a new leadership in the Kremlin once again, but it confronts old policy dilemmas. These have, however, become sharper since the late 1970s. As noted, the general growth retardation already visible in the 1960s accelerated in the second half of the 1970s. The prospects for the 1980s are that GNP will grow at annual rates of 2 percent to 3 percent. Low growth is still growth; even stagnation or absolute shrinkage of the economy would not necessarily bring on a counterrevolution. Most contemporary societies are under stress, and even those under serious stress often show remarkable resilience. The drop in Soviet average growth rates from levels of 6 percent in the 1950s to 2 percent or 3 percent in the eighties does not in itself impel the conclusion of imminent crisis.

Nevertheless, the decline in growth prospects aggravates the policy problem of allocating resources among competing claims for defense, investment, and consumption. In 1980–81 voices were heard in the Soviet Union implying that the leadership decision to cut back the growth rate of investment, for the second straight five-year plan, was a serious mistake.[21] In fact, investment was stepped up from 1981 to 1983.[22] Western calculations may show continued increases in Soviet per capita consumption on the average, but in 1979–82 there was evidence of widespread, intermittent food shortages, especially in quality foods like meat. The network of specialized distribution systems developed to protect the privileged elite but also large sections of the industrial worker class has surely meant shifts in the distribution of income to the detriment of unprotected elements of the population, particularly pensioners.

There is little doubt, therefore, that the regime senses it has a significant problem. Andropov was frank in acknowledging that; so was Chernenko. Gorbachev's policy options will be essentially the same and just as unappetizing as those Brezhnev had.[23] One is tempted to call them the three Rs: Reform, Reallocation, or Repression.

Moscow is periodically alive with rumors about impending major reform. Andropov's alleged association with Hungarian reform was a chief topic of Western media speculation in the early days of his accession. Much of the air went out of that balloon as the months passed, but his long-term commitment to reform could not be tested. It is still too early to determine which way the Gorbachev Politburo will eventually move, but what some Western observers regard as the kind of reform required to stir the economy out of its doldrums—major devolution of decision making, reliance on prices for resource allocation—is hardly likely. Reforms of a minor sort, representing small-scale changes of the system at the margins, are not only acceptable, but are also constantly being talked about and even instituted. But they also provide correspondingly marginal results.

Reallocation of resources from military to civilian uses also has restricted possibilities. Western simulations with mathematical-economic models of the Soviet economy suggest that substantial resource shifts are required over a prolonged period to make a significant dent in the long-term Soviet growth problem.[24] For a regime whose major support appears to be in the military-security sector, which sees itself in serious military competition with a formidable adversary, such drastic cutbacks in military spending probably would not even get on the agenda of discussion. The flattening of the weapons procurement curve that the CIA estimates took place in 1976–82 may still be in progress.[25] Such smaller scale changes may even help ease particular bottlenecks, but they cannot in themselves provide the stimulus Soviet leaders are so obviously searching for.

On accession to power, Andropov's first reaction (the policeman's instinct?) was, indeed, to crack the whip: "Although everything cannot be reduced to discipline, it is with discipline that we must begin, comrades."[26] Perhaps the more favorable output growth claims made by the Central Statistical Administration for 1983 relative to 1981 and 1982 even attest to some tangible effects of this minicampaign. But it is difficult to believe that indiscipline was simply the result of slipshod Brezhnevism, or that the measures adopted by Andropov and partly continued under Chernenko are likely to have a permanent and positive impact on worker and management effectiveness. Will Gorbachev attempt to intensify the enforcement of discipline? How far can this be carried? Do Soviet leaders have the stomach for the brutality of real neo-Stalinism? Even if they do, it is doubtful that present-day Soviet society is as manipulable as it was under Stalin. In any case, the productivity effects of such atavism are not self-evident.

In short, the options for resolving the Soviet Union's growth dilemma—the inability to maintain extensive output growth as factor input growth declines, and the inability to launch intensive output growth, held back by systemic barriers to productivity increases—are all mediocre. The economy's prospects have not suddenly brightened because of Brezhnev's departure.

What is the role of East-West trade in a possible Gorbachev policy package? Probably not unlike its place in the Brezhnev platform, if the rest of this analysis is essentially correct. In the 1970s the Soviet Union was much more heavily involved in international trade than it was in the past. The calculations of Treml and Kostinsky indicate that total imports revalued at domestic prices accounted for roughly a fifth of Soviet net material product in 1980.[27] The dependence on Western trade alone is, of course, considerably smaller. At a lower level of aggregation it is clear that Western machinery and equipment played a significant, although not dominant, role in Soviet investment activity. Bond and Levine estimate that imports from the West varied between 30 percent and 40 percent of all Soviet machinery imports in the last half of the 1970s and accounted for 8 percent to 10 percent of Soviet investment in producer durables.[28] Industry case studies suggest that the impact of Western technology in selected branches of the economy was greater than these aggregate figures indicate.[29]

In the mid-1970s a pattern of Soviet trade with the developed West emerged in which, to simplify somewhat, the USSR exported primarily energy and raw materials (as well as arms) and imported Western technology. In the late 1970s, with the increasing difficulties experienced in Soviet agriculture, food and grain began to dominate the Soviet import picture. At the same time Soviet imports of Western technology fell off, arousing intense speculation in the West about the reasons. Evidence from the Soviet press suggests various possibilities: a deliberate policy decision to curb Moscow's technological dependence on the West; resentment by Soviet research and development institutions and skepticism of the benefits gained from imports; problems of "digesting" imported technology; and balance-of-payment pressures.[30] In any case, imports of machinery and equipment from non-Socialist countries have increased since then: In current prices, the 1983 level was 51 percent higher than that of 1979.[31]

In the near and medium term, shortages of domestic investment resources may point to a renewal of Soviet interest in larger-scale technology imports. It was arguable that the Soviet investment ratio was too high in the mid-1970s and that benefits would be experienced from allowing the capital:labor ratio to stabilize or even decline. However, the sizable cutbacks in investment growth rates in the tenth five-year plan (1976–80) and again in the eleventh (1981–85) have not been accompanied by visible improvement in productivity. Some sectors are clearly "starved" for investment as scarce funds under the eleventh plan are being hoarded primarily for agriculture, food, and energy.

It is important to be clear about the issue. It is not whether technology imports were historically a major contributor to Soviet economic growth; or whether foreign technology can be effectively diffused in the Soviet centralized economy, in the sense of accelerating technical progress and growth. The issue in the mid-eighties is likely to be whether the economy can "muddle through"; Western machinery and equipment may well appear to provide a sorely needed supplement to the slowly growing domestic production. The fact that the West's technology is considerably more productive than Soviet counterparts, even after allowance is made for the much higher Soviet staffing requirements, adds to its attractiveness.

Moscow's ability to pay for large volumes of Western technology imports depends, in the main, on two factors. Both Andropov and Chernenko committed themselves to pursuing Brezhnev's "food program," but unless there are unusual improvements in both average weather patterns and the organization of Soviet agriculture, grain or food imports will intermittently get first priority in allocation of foreign exchange. Thus the state of Soviet agriculture is likely to be the first constraint on the permissible volume of capital imports from the West. The second is Soviet ability to continue to sell abroad the mainstays of its hard currency–earning capability. In 1982 there were sharp increases in Soviet exports of oil—apparently, also, in arms. Together with a decrease in the rate of growth of imports from the West, this resulted in a significant improvement in the Soviet hard currency balance.[32] An actual drop in the dollar value of

imports from the West in 1983 maintained the gain.[33] It is likely
that energy, gold, arms, and other raw materials will continue to
be the staple means by which the Soviet Union will earn the
wherewithal to import its food and technology requirements.
Estimates of the likely time pattern of change in this earning
capacity vary, depending in part on the trade and domestic production scenarios envisaged.[34]

The improvement in the Soviet balance-of-payments position
since the late 1970s and in the standard indicators of balance
"health"—ratios of debt service, debt to GNP, and the like—
imply that, by bankers' standards, the Soviet Union is a good
lending risk. Political sensitivities appear to be the main reason
deterring U.S. banks from seeking out the Soviet loan market,
but Europeans are less affected by such considerations.[35] In
1981–82 the Polish debt crisis and the danger of possible defaults
in other eastern European countries brought about a spasmodic
curtailment of Western bank loans to Socialist countries. In the
latter half of the 1980s, bankers may reconsider the utility of
lending to the USSR.

Alternative Trade Policies

What opportunities or constraints does the Soviet domestic economic and foreign trade position create for the West? Dependencies are not necessarily vulnerabilities; even vulnerabilities do
not guarantee success in exerting pressure. Between dependency and vulnerability lie the characteristics of buyer and seller
and the state of the market. Dependent but monopsonist buyers
fare well against competitive sellers. Soviet dependence on imports for grain has been heavy, but because of the structure of
the international grain market, Moscow's vulnerability in 1980
proved low. The factor of difference between vulnerability and
successful external pressure is politics, the political will of those
exerting and those resisting pressure. The West's "opportunities" can be understood only in the setting of the debate on
alternative East-West trade policies, which are outlined later.
The discussion attempts to link trade policies to the strategic
orientations from which they emerge and stresses their indi-

vidual perspectives on the meaning of Soviet economic developments for trade policy.

When the Reagan administration assumed office, it offered a developed perspective linked to well-defined trade policies: (1) Military power and its political uses lie at the core of the Kremlin's self-image and world view; (2) the Soviet military buildup will continue at rates more or less like those of the past decade or two; (3) the West will have difficulty catching up with the cumulated level of Soviet military capabilities or keeping pace with the Soviet buildup; and (4) yet, astonishingly, the West continues to contribute to the accumulation of Soviet military forces, through overt and covert trade. Hence the Reagan administration policy is one of denial of resources likely to aid the military buildup. Soviet access to specific key goods, technology, and know-how ("critical technologies") should be reduced to the maximum. Further, the West should not subsidize Soviet acquisition of food, consumer goods, and advanced technology by cheap credit and government guarantees that help reduce the cost of the military buildup. Parts of the administration, particularly the Defense Department, favor a more general denial policy, which would constrain the general flow of resources to the USSR from the West, to make it more difficult for Moscow to resolve its resource allocation dilemma, while keeping the priority of military spending intact. The constraints on key goods and services are reflected in the effort to strengthen COCOM (the Paris-based Coordinating Committee) and the controls on technology transfer generally; the hypothesized connection between West-to-East resource flows and the Soviet military buildup justified the opposition to the gas pipeline deal and is the rationale for pressures to eliminate government subsidies to the East. However, the administration does not oppose all trade; the policy is one of limited denial.

Thus much of Washington sees the Soviet economy in a "time of troubles," vulnerable to external pressure. Soviet economic difficulties are an opportunity to complicate Moscow's resource allocation dilemma and thereby limit the resources that can be funneled into the military sector. Evidently, this is a form of classic containment strategy, in which Soviet pressure outward is to be turned back on itself. Does the administration also take the next step, believing that contained pressures must result in systemic change? The White House and the Pentagon seem to incline to that view;[36] the Department of State is, by nature, oriented to conflict management.

The U.S. government's limited denial policy is characterized by a certain self-limitation of expectations. There is no effort to secure, by threats of denial, overt Soviet behavioral concessions, which are believed unobtainable as long as Soviet power is unconstrained; carrots are, of course, conspicuous by their absence. There is only a belief that if the resource flow to the Soviet Union can be dammed, the military buildup will be impeded, and that alone serves Western policy objectives. Much of this effect is to be obtained by reliance on market forces rather than by administrative regulation, on the assumption that the market assesses the risks of East-West trade high and the benefits low relative to trade with other regions. However, controlling technology flows, a high-priority objective in Washington, is the major exception to a market approach.

If the expectation of Soviet behavioral change in the U.S. limited-denial policy is modest, so, too, is the likelihood of actual impact on the Soviet military buildup. It is hard to appraise the effectiveness of the campaign to control the covert export of militarily relevant technology from the United States ("Operation Exodus"). The parallel effort to secure allied cooperation is bound to be difficult too.[37] As for the attempt to constrain general resource flow, the gas pipeline deal has gone through (but the alliance has agreed to avoid excessive dependence on a single supplier and to pursue development of secure alternatives). Intra-West negotiations will not have much effect on Soviet hard-currency earnings from sales of oil—certainly not on sales of arms. Even in principle the connection between restricting resource flow to the USSR and a change in the rate of growth of Soviet defense spending that would not otherwise have taken place is highly indirect. The Kremlin need not play the game by the rules drawn up in the White House. If the Politburo chooses to cut back on consumption rather than defense, is that good or bad for the West?

The polar opposite of the Pentagon's approach to East-West trade policy cannot be identified with a particular capital, but it is more strongly and widely held in the Federal Republic than anywhere else.[38] This "neo-détente" outlook, to give it a name, accepts (at least in principle) the necessity of the countervailing-power strand of containment, but only with respect to Europe and the strategic nuclear balance. (Its enthusiasm for "out-of-area" forces is minimal, to say the least.) But its most important characteristic is an optimistic temper with respect to Soviet objectives and a disposition to see real possibilities for systemic transformation in eastern Europe and the USSR. For neo-détentists, the problems of the Soviet economy are not vulnerabilities to exploit: They suspect the Reagan administration of harboring a desire to wage economic war against the Soviet Union, which is viewed as both fruitless and only a step away from shooting war. Instead, they believe, the Soviet economic difficulties should be seen as an opportunity to assist the Soviet Union to reform its economic system. Such a reform, and the spirit of cooperation that would make it possible, would contribute to the development of a more pluralistic society, the basis for a durable peace in Europe.[39]

Ideas of linkage or leverage are absent from this formulation too; it is not interested in establishing the nature and rate of the exchange between aid to the USSR and moderation of Soviet behavior. This may be rationalized with the argument that the beneficial effects of cooperation will be manifested only after a considerable time. There are variants of neo-détentism, however, that do worry about linkage and leverage. These variant viewpoints are equally concerned about the need to develop cooperative modes of relations with the USSR, but they aspire to use the West's economic power "offensively": They would offer economic aid and interdependence with eastern Europe for the promise of improvement in political-security relations, including arms control at substantially reduced levels of balance, and liberalized economic reform. Thus this outlook, too, is transformationist, but its temper is less optimistic than that of the pure benefaction variant.

Neo-détente abhors Pentagon-style denial (especially in cari-

catured form) as provocative and dangerous, or deems it impo-
tent. The less optimistic variant of neo-détente thinks denial
alone is insufficient for "behavior modification," for reasons already indicated—a possible Soviet decision not to play the
West's game. But the causal connections between Western attempts to exert leverage and Soviet behavior are, if anything,
even more tenuous than those between denial policies and
Soviet military spending. Apart from technical problems in
defining the terms of linkage/leverage, there is the overriding
political problem of the lessons of the 1970s. The implementors
of linkage/leverage then were supposed to carry sticks as well as
offer carrots; at least they were supposed to be able to withdraw
the carrots. As Josef Joffe put it, "linkage requires the freedom
to cut links."[40] Economic détente in the 1970s proved to be a
ratchet propelling the West in one direction. At least this was so
in Europe, where domestic and alliance politics seemed to dis-
criminate consistently in favor of East-West trade, despite the
rapidly changing international environment.[41]

Is there a middle way? Those who think so may perhaps be
characterized best by what they are not: They cannot make
themselves believe in the reality of transformation (except
through long-term internal evolution over which the West can
have little effect), and they are not optimistic about Soviet intentions. They tend to share the neo-détentists' disbelief in the
power of general trade denial to change Soviet resource allocation policy and the anti-détentist's lack of reverence for the
behavior-modification possibilities of linkage/leverage. They
are, of course, skeptics, but one might think of them also as
upholders of "modified containment." The essence of their outlook is concern with the threat of Soviet power, globally, not just
in Europe. At the same time, but also because of this central
concern, they are adherents of arms control (although not at any
price) and political dialogue. In East-West trade policy this posture would tend to support strict controls on militarily relevant
technology and "true" (as opposed to government-disguised)
tests by the marketplace of the profitability of East-West trade to
the West. In effect, the views described take the middle ground
between the trade encouragement of parts of the U.S. Depart-

ments of State and Commerce and the trade constraint of the Pentagon and the White House.

The Special Case of Eastern Europe

This discussion has focused on policy to the Soviet Union. Trade policy to eastern Europe does not automatically derive from policy to the USSR. The Federal Republic has made clear that it cannot be indifferent to the fate of compatriots in the German Democratic Republic. The concern to maintain an open line between the Germanies moves Bonn, irrespective of the party or coalition of the power, to make periodic conciliatory efforts. But more than any other of its alliance partners, the Federal Republic has also been sensitive to developments in eastern Europe as a whole, particularly those affecting the connection to the Soviet Union. Of course, this is also related to the central role of inter-German relations in Bonn's foreign policy outlook. For many Germans, détente means, in good part, a relaxation of tensions in eastern Europe that makes possible increased contacts with their German Democratic Republic cousins. They fear that when the rhetoric of Soviet-American relations turns harsh, the openings to East Germany begin to close. It is this more than any other factor that conditions Federal Republic views on trade policy to eastern Europe.

Other considerations come into play too. Physical proximity alone would make the Federal Republic, more than its Western allies, sensitive to tremors in Prague, Budapest, and Warsaw. In the Polish crisis of 1980–82 Bonn at times referred to history and the special responsibility of Germans, as well as their alleged special knowledge, in attempting to explain a cautious reaction to the fast-paced events of those years. Reform or revolution in eastern Europe, symbolized by Hungary after 1968 and Poland in 1980–81, has given rise to hopes for the evolution of reform-minded, less Soviet-dominated regimes, which would directly improve the prospects for stability in Europe and indirectly contribute to the same goal by stimulating reform tendencies in the USSR.

For all these reasons there is a strong inclination in Bonn

to preserve flexibility for economic cooperation with eastern
Europe. The U.S. government, too, is interested in the development of independent-minded regimes in eastern Europe.
To a limited extent Washington is willing to encourage that possibility by economic measures (International Monetary Fund
[INF] membership for Hungary, for example). But the U.S. government's policy is one of differentiation, between the USSR
and eastern Europe and within eastern Europe itself. Even in its
favorable disposition to one or two countries, Washington is not
prepared to subsidize eastern European development. In both of
these aspects of policy, coordination between the United States
and western Europe will be difficult to achieve. U.S. faith in the
potential of trade and aid to effect lasting political change in
eastern Europe is far more limited than is the case in West Germany.

Prospects

In the second half of the 1980s the West's national and alliance-
wide policy choices alike will probably be affected by national
economic conditions but even more by political events and perceptions. The recession in Organization for Economic Cooperation and Development (OECD) countries played an important
role in strengthening their reluctance to allow trade to become
"politicized," by which term they really meant undercutting the
politics of trade encouragement. The Soviet contracts were useful at politically sensitive margins not only in Germany (e.g.,
Mannesman or AEG-Kanis), but also in the United States (conspicuously, the farm bloc). If recovery is general and prolonged,
these pressures are likely to diminish. If recovery is partial and
short-lived, there may be a return to the environment of 1981–
82. Even under the more favorable scenario, however, the
transatlantic asymmetries in the importance and structure of
trade with the East would maintain a standing differential bias—
in favor of the trade in Germany and western Europe generally,
and more or less opposed (grain remaining the significant exception) in the United States.

That is, provided East-West trade is maintained at levels at least as high as those of the 1970s. The earlier discussion of Soviet economic prospects noted the important constraints on the flexibility of Moscow's trade policy—the dependence on imports of grain and the limited hard-currency earning power—but it also pointed to the possible importance of capital imports from the West in allowing the Kremlin to cope with its resource dilemma. It is highly unlikely that the Western dissension on East-West trade will be resolved by Soviet withdrawal from the world market. In any case, eastern Europe probably does not have such a choice, given the extent of its dependence on trade with the West, although the volume of trade may be lower than in the 1970s. The Western policy problems connected with this part of East-West economic relations will remain.

The second, political set of factors could make a considerable difference. By far the dominant issue in Europe in 1983 and 1984 was INF deployment and arms control. The outcome of the policy debate, the nature of Moscow's reaction, and the effects on western Europe all have the potential to change the environment of East-West relations. A European perception of global military balance, the American nuclear umbrella still extended over Europe, plus Soviet concessions in arms control negotiations would be likely to at least ease the alliance's internecine problems on both political and economic fronts. On the other hand, if Europe comes to believe generally in the peace movement's image of Washington policy, resistance to American East-West trade initiatives will surely harden. If the Soviets break off the arms control negotiations and succeed in fastening the blame on Washington, trade denial will not get much of a hearing in European chancelleries. The experience of 1980–82 notwithstanding, the Reagan administration would probably look to economic, rather than military, weapons again in reaction to a future Soviet outrage. That outrage would have to be egregious indeed, however, to elicit a different alliance response.

Despite appearances to the contrary, East-West trade policy was only in part an independent issue between Bonn and Washington or between Washington and other allied capitals in 1980–82. This chapter has argued that trade policy is interlinked with strategy at various levels of generality, a part of the changing debate on East-West relations between members of the alliance. Behind the conflict over missile deployment in the "hot" autumn of 1983, the basic identity of the Federal Republic seemed to be at stake. East-West economics casts a small shadow in this potentially fateful conflict.

If the game will not be fundamentally changed and East-West economic relations will still matter, are there prospects for improved intra-West cooperation?

Perhaps the closest the allies came to consensus on a principle in 1982 was on the issue of technology transfer and the strengthening of COCOM. The present American administration is convinced that there has been a major contribution of Western technology to the Soviet military buildup, obtained from both licit and illicit sources. Most of the alliance seems prepared to agree on the need for somewhat stricter controls and for updating the controls in line with technical progress. The consensus begins to dissolve when the issue is control over technology whose application to military use is indirect, or when there are, in fact, dual uses. The Pentagon perspective, which tends to consider most technology transfers to the Soviet Union as disadvantageous, will come head on against a general European viewpoint that although (legal) transfer aids the Soviet economy, it may also be profitable to the West. On balance, there may be some progress in finer screening of militarily relevant technology transfer,[42] but different outlooks on the relative value of trade are likely to prevent the development of full cooperation here as in other aspects of East-West trade.

Twice in 1982 the major Western leaders enjoined themselves to behave "prudently" in East-West trade—the first time at Versailles and again in the November agreement allowing the revocation of extraterritorial application of energy equipment controls. Presumably, that meant fewer government subsidies and guarantees. The minimum interest rate on government credits to the USSR has been increased, but one may reserve judgment on whether future loans will be granted at or below market rates, given the traditional use of export incentives in international trade and European fears about the erosion of their international competitive position. The Kremlin will continue to play on the fears of the individual countries that their reluctance to provide a better deal will only result in somebody else grabbing the whole basket. Even where trade and credit agreements appear uneconomic, political considerations may dominate, as they often did in the past.[43]

There may be somewhat better prospects in the next decade for agreements on alliance energy policy, particularly if demand continues slack, even allowing for the increases attendant on economic recovery, and if the currently touted opportunities with respect to Norwegian gas or greater use of coal turn out to be practical.

The most useful thing the West can do is to institutionalize study and discussion of East-West economic issues, creating the framework, staff, and facilities for continuous updating, as needs may require, of the component issues. The studies begun in the fall of 1982 were assigned to different agencies—COCOM, the International Energy Agency, and OECD, as well as NATO—in part because no such mechanism now exists within the alliance. Also, some of the issues involve nonmembers of NATO, such as Japan. There is little support in NATO for extending the organization's purview to East-West trade, and it would probably be infeasible to attempt to create a single organization with the responsibility for developing and managing all Western study and discussion of East-West economic issues. Nevertheless, even with several forums and without development of immediate cooperation or coordination of policies, ability to keep these issues under systematic review would in itself represent an important gain for the sanity of Western discussions.

Parts of the U.S. government appear hopeful that there has been a meeting of minds with the allies on basic questions of East-West trade policy—technology transfer, subsidies, energy dependence, and general sensitivity to the security dimension. But no American administration can fail to be aware of the ambivalence Europeans, and especially Germans, feel about East-West relations—on the one hand, consciousness of the dangers in the security terms underscored so often by Washington; on the other, desire to defuse bloc tensions by cooperative arrangements. Nowhere is that ambivalence as strong as in the Federal Republic, for which both Ostpolitik and loyalty to the Western alliance have been foundations of its external relations. In a period of recrudescent superpower hostility the Federal Republic's policy dualism becomes an antinomy with the potential for generating sharp conflict in the alliance.

To sum up, taking account of the asymmetries in position and the sharp divergences of view, modest expectations of Atlantic harmonization are in order. Perhaps the best to be hoped for is a damage-limiting, incremental progress strategy for alliance policy on East-West economics. The strategy is damage-limiting in the literal sense of attempting to minimize the likelihood of further destruction of the alliance's fabric. It is one of incremental progress because the conflict of national interests and national perceptions is profound. The strategy seems appropriate because the alternatives have such poor prospects. The ability of the Western alliance to play on Soviet economic dependencies and vulnerabilities is severely limited by political weakness; its ability to force cutbacks in Soviet military spending by resource denial is dubious technically as well as politically.

The dominating problem of alliance consensus dictates the likelihood that only small changes will be effected. The safest prognosis in the foreseeable future is for only marginally successful denial and spasmodic linkage with little effective leverage. That sounds pessimistic, but it is probably only realistic. If, in the process, better means of communication and consultation on East-West economic issues are developed, that would constitute grounds for justified satisfaction.

Notes

1. For the communiqué, see *New York Times,* 31 May 1983.
2. Figures vary according to the source. For the U.S. government view in the fall of 1981, see *Soviet Energy Exports and Western European Energy Security,* Hearing Before the Subcommittee on Energy, Nuclear Proliferation, and Government Processes of the Committee on Governmental Affairs, U.S. Senate (Washington, D.C., 1982), 61. The counterpart view from Europe is summarized in *East/West,* no. 277 (30

Sept. 1981). See also Jonathan P. Stern, "Specters and Pipe Dreams," *Foreign Policy,* no. 48 (Fall 1982): 23–24.

3. See, for example, the action of the European Community on March 10, 1982, weakening the sanctions against the USSR, agreed to on February 23 (*Washington Post,* 24 Feb. 1982; *The Economist,* 27 Feb. 1982, 49–50; and *New York Times,* 12 March 1982).

4. It remains an open question, however, whether European cooperation would have been substantially greater even if the president had maintained the grain embargo in force. For a discussion of the embargo and subsequent U.S. policy on grain sales, see Abraham S. Becker, *Economic Leverage on the Soviet Union in the 1980's,* R-3127-USDP (Santa Monica, Calif.: The Rand Corporation, July 1984), section IV.

5. See the interview with President Mitterand in the *Washington Post,* 16 June 1982, and the American reactions in the following days.

6. *Wall Street Journal,* 11 May 1983.

7. In Washington it was claimed that western Europe and Japan now had a much better understanding of the issues and of the U.S. government's seriousness in attempting to limit the contribution of East-West trade to Soviet military power. (The resemblance of the American pipeline action to that of hitting a mule on the head with a wooden plank to get its attention was not lost on either Washington or the allied capitals.) On the outcome of the studies that constituted the apparent European concession, see the discussion in the section on prospects.

8. "The Future Tasks of the Alliance (Harmel Report). Report of the Council. Annex to the Final Communique of the Ministerial Meeting, December, 1967," reprinted in *The North Atlantic Treaty Organization Facts and Figures* (Brussels: NATO Information Service, 1981), 289. The Harmel report distinguishes between the creation of a "climate of stability, security and confidence" between East and West, which requires maintaining a balance of forces, and the effort to achieve "a more stable relationship in which the underlying political issues can be solved." The former is the prerequisite for the latter (ibid., 288).

9. For the text see U.S. Arms Control and Disarmament Agency, *Documents on Disarmament 1972* (Washington, D.C., 1974), 237–240.

10. *Newsweek,* 30 May 1983, 68. Willy Brandt's motivations for the revision of Ostpolitik on his accession to the foreign ministry included a domestic economic component: "We had to safeguard employment and open up new fields of economic opportunity." Angela Stent, *From Embargo to Ostpolitik. The Political Economy of West German-Soviet Relations, 1955–1980* (New York: Cambridge University Press, 1981), 176.

11. Ministerstvo vneshnei torgovli, *Vneshniaia torgovlia SSSR v 1983* (Moscow, 1984), 9–14.

12. United Nations, *Monthly Bulletin of Statistics* 37, no. 7 (July 1983): Special Tables D (national product), I (East-West trade), Tables 52 (German and American total trade), and 62 (exchange rates). In 1983 Federal Republic imports from the Soviet Union were still twelve times larger than U.S. imports from the USSR and exports to the Soviet Union were more than double the U.S. level (*Vneshniaia torgovlia SSSR v 1983* 9–10). Americans often hear Europeans, particularly Germans, arguing at different times that the Eastern trade is both relatively insignificant and of considerable importance. The former claim is intended to refute the charge of dependence; the latter is used in defense of interests challenged by American sanction proposals.

13. Cited by Stent, *From Embargo to Ostpolitik,* 185.

14. See Gebhard Schweigler, "Whatever Happened to Germany?" and Michael Kreile, "Ostpolitik Reconsidered," both in *The Foreign Policy of West Germany: Formation and Contents,* ed. Ekkehart Krippendorff and Volker Rittberger, German Political Science Studies, vol. 4 (London and Beverly Hills, Calif.: Sage Publications, 1980), 103, 127, respectively.

15. "The United States has it in its power to increase enormously the strains under which Soviet policy must operate, to force upon the Kremlin a far greater degree of moderation and circumspection than it has had to observe in recent years and in this way to promote tendencies which must eventually find their outlet in either the breakup or the gradual mellowing of Soviet power" ("X" [George Kennan], "The Sources of Soviet Conduct," *Foreign Affairs* 25, no. 4 [July 1947]: 582).

16. See below, note 36.

17. The goal was common to proponents of both linkage and leverage. However, Nixon and Kissinger, with whom linkage policy is most closely identified, saw linkage both as an objective reality and a policy means of applying leverage. In this sense they attempted to have trade improvements follow rather than precede political progress. See Henry Kissinger, *White House Years* (Boston: Little, Brown, 1979), 129, 153.

18. About two of every three West Germans think the West did at least as well out of détente as the Communist countries; only one-third think the West did worse. In the United States these proportions are approximately reversed. *The Economist,* 27 Feb. 1982, 18.

19. Bernard Brodie, *War and Politics* (New York: Macmillan, 1973), 1.

20. Henry Kissinger empathized with a Clausewitzian view of trade

but had in mind a different trade strategy: "If the Soviet Union can enter our markets for credit or goods on the basis of purely economic criteria, all political leverage disappears" (Kissinger, *White House Years,* 153).

21. See Robert Leggett, "Soviet Investment Policy in the 11th Five Year Plan," in Joint Economic Committee, U.S. Congress, *Soviet Economy in the 1980's: Problems and Prospects,* part 1 (Washington, D.C., 1982), 145–146.

22. The final draft of the eleventh plan provided for only a 6 percent increase in 1983 over 1980 in state capital investment (*Pravda,* 20 Nov. 1981). The actual growth was 14 percent (TsSU, *Narodnoe khoziaistvo SSSR v 1983 g.* [Moscow, 1984], 355).

23. Abraham S. Becker, *The Burden of Soviet Defense: A Political-Economic Essay,* R-2752-AF (Santa Monica, Calif.: The Rand Corporation, Oct. 1981), 59–72; an abbreviated version was published as "Sustaining the Burden of Soviet Defense: Retrospect and Prospect," in *The Soviet Asset: Military Power in the Competition over Europe,* ed. Uwe Nerlich (Cambridge, Mass.: Ballinger Publishing Co., 1983). (The reference in this note is to pp. 256–264.) Also, idem., "Sitting on Bayonets? The Soviet Defense Burden and Moscow's Economic Dilemma," in a special issue of *Soviet Union,* "The Soviet Calculus of Nuclear War," vol. 10 (1983), parts 2–3.

24. These studies are reviewed in the papers identified in the previous note.

25. Joint Economic Committee, U.S. Congress, *Allocation of Resources in the Soviet Union and China—1983* (Washington, D.C., 1984), 214, 230–232; "Statement by Robert Gates, Deputy Director for Intelligence, Central Intelligence Agency, on The Allocation of Resources in the Soviet Union and China—1984, Before the Subcommittee on International Trade, Finance, and Security Economics of the Joint Economic Committee, U.S. Congress," November 21, 1984.

26. *Pravda,* 1 Feb. 1983.

27. Mimeographed update of Table 1, from Vladimir G. Treml and Barry L. Kostinsky, *Domestic Value of Soviet Foreign Trade: Exports and Imports in the 1972 Input-Output Table,* Foreign Economic Report No. 20 (Washington, D.C.: U.S. Bureau of the Census, Oct. 1982).

28. Daniel L. Bond and Herbert S. Levine, "The Soviet Machinery Balance and Military Durables in SOVMOD," in Joint Economic Committee, *Soviet Economy in the 1980's,* part 1, 307.

29. Philip Hanson, "The Role of Trade and Technology Transfer in

the Soviet Economy," in *Economic Relations with the USSR: Issues for the Western Alliance,* ed. Abraham S. Becker (Lexington, Mass.: Lexington Books, 1983), 39–43.

30. Ibid., 30–39.

31. Calculated from Soviet official data on the commodity structure of imports from the world and from Socialist countries in annual issues of *Vneshniaia torgovlia SSSR.* However, the increase was largely for the Siberian gas pipeline.

32. Wharton Econometric Forecasting Associates (WEFA), "Soviet Foreign Trade Performance in 1982," *Centrally Planned Economies Current Analysis* 3: 28/29 (21 April 1983).

33. WEFA, "Soviet Foreign Trade Performance in 1983," *Centrally Planned Economies Current Analysis* 3: 22/23 (9 April 1984).

34. See Gregory Grossman and Ronald L. Solberg, *The Soviet Union's Hard-Currency Balance of Payments and Creditworthiness in 1985,* R-2956-USDP (Santa Monica, Calif.: The Rand Corporation, April 1983).

35. Judy Shelton, "Would U.S. Banks Like a Loan Market in Moscow?" *Wall Street Journal,* 8 Jan. 1985.

36. Perhaps the clearest expression of that view was provided in a speech in West Germany given in late 1982 by the former director of East European and Soviet Affairs of the National Security Council, Richard Pipes, entitled "The Soviet Union in Crisis." See also Pipes, *Survival Is Not Enough* (New York: Simon and Schuster, 1984).

37. For an administration view of the central problem and the efforts made to cope with it, see Stephen D. Bryen, "Strategic Technology and National Security," *Journal of Electronic Defense* 25 (May 1983): 45–52. For a skeptical view, see Joel Brinkley, "U.S., Despite Technology Curbs, Sees No Big Cut in Flow to Soviets," *New York Times,* 1 Jan. 1985.

38. At an American conference on East-West economic relations, a French participant remarked that with two polar views of the Soviet Union in NATO, the Pentagon's view and that of the SPD, the French government shares the American view but behaves like Germany in East-West economic matters.

39. Helmut Schmidt's comment in 1978 on the signing of a twenty-five year Agreement on Long-term Cooperation with the USSR is in a similar spirit. He lauded the agreement as providing "an orientation . . . for long term peaceful development which presupposes that the people in both countries acquire a permanent interest in one another's economic welfare." Cited in Stent, *From Embargo to Ostpolitik,* 205.

40. Josef Joffe, "Mixing Money and Politics: Dollars and Detente," in Becker, ed., *Economic Relations with the USSR*, 17.

41. However, the Soviet share of western Europe's trade fell and rose between 1975 and 1982; the net gain of 2 to 2½ percentage points resulted largely from the second wave of energy price hikes in 1979–81.

42. Paul Lewis, "Allies Curb Computers for Soviets," *New York Times*, 17 July 1984.

43. The Schmidt government was doubtful of the economic justification of the 1978 long-term agreement with the USSR, but in Angela Stent's words, "its positive political effects were considerable and outweighted the economic disadvantages of Soviet-West German trade" (Stent, *From Embargo to Ostpolitik*, 206).

Chapter 8

Strengthening NATO's Deterrence in the 1980s

K.-Peter Stratmann

General Problems

NATO is confronted with a military challenge posed by the continuously growing capabilities of the Warsaw Pact. This development has taken place at the intercontinental-strategic level, in the field of conventional and nuclear forces in Europe, and in strategically important regions outside Europe. The security policies of Western nations have come under increasing pressure because of this shift in the balance of forces, and NATO has entered a difficult and contradictory process of seeking to adapt to the deteriorated military situation. In particular, two aspects stand out:

1. The backlog of military programs and simultaneous new challenges in many important military fields place requirements on the financial and personnel resources of Western countries available for defense that cannot be met. Because of this mismatch of programs and funds, it is now necessary to redefine and, in part, shift priorities.
2. The change in the military situation has triggered a process of intra-Western criticism of NATO's current strategy and military posture that may be described as a "credibility crisis." The solution to this crisis is highly controversial and has been opened to public debate. Divergent interests, differences of opinion, and tensions appear in the domestic politics of Western nations and among NATO countries. Even though these strains are less visible at the govern-

mental level than in public opinion, they have notable repercussions on the motivations and constraints of alliance
governments and parliaments, especially those in Europe.

The resulting political situation limits the options available to
governments to improve Western military capabilities. These
constraints partly lie in the veto positions held by strong political
minorities and, more generally, in the growing unpopularity of
military tasks that, in conjunction with the effects of the present
poor economic and budgetary situation, will complicate or even
prevent essential defense initiatives in the foreseeable future. In
addition, this situation contains the potential for friction among
NATO nations and for weakening consensus among the allies.

This trend has resulted in a widening gap between defined
objectives and actual programs that NATO governments will be
able to implement. This gap is most prominent in two key areas:
modernization of NATO's nuclear forces and improvement of
NATO's conventional defense capabilities in central Europe.

Reasons for and Impediments to NATO Defense Improvements

Modernization of NATO's Theater Nuclear Force Posture in Europe

Since the 1970s, Soviet regional nuclear armament efforts have
led to a quantitative buildup and considerable qualitative improvements. Both developments have run parallel to the
strengthening of Soviet intercontinental-strategic capabilities up
to parity with the United States. Owing to these developments,
the Western military-strategic concept, especially its nuclear
component, is being exposed to multiple pressures. The credibility of the concept of nuclear escalation is strained by the loss of
American strategic superiority. The credibility of linkage between the U.S. strategic nuclear forces and the defense of Europe
(extended deterrence) has been increasingly questioned in
public, not least in the United States, and even declared obsolete. Such assessments necessarily lead to a perception of Soviet
nuclear escalation dominance vis-à-vis western Europe.

Concerns about the U.S. strategic nuclear guarantee are aggravated by the quantitative and qualitative development of Soviet regional nuclear forces. Since the late 1950s the Soviet Union has had the ability to destroy western Europe and to threaten important military targets in the region with medium-range bombers and intermediate-range missiles. Moreover, since the 1960s the Soviet Union has been capable of providing nuclear support for offensive operations through the employment of short-range missiles and fighter-bombers. However, during this period Soviet nuclear capabilities appeared to be neutralized by U.S. strategic superiority and constrained by their inflexibility. More important, the extreme vulnerability of Soviet medium-range forces probably would have forced massive use only in the event of war. In view of the high weapon yields, such use would have amounted to indiscriminate destruction of western Europe, i.e., to politically and strategically nearly absurd consequences. Moreover, it would have probably triggered the initiation of general nuclear war. For these reasons the employment of the Soviet regional nuclear forces could be envisaged only within the scope of "general nuclear war" scenarios.

However, the situation has become very different since then. Because of the loss of U.S. strategic superiority the West has tended to attach considerably more importance to the Soviets' destructive potential against western Europe. Against this background the improved nuclear operational flexibility, achieved by the Warsaw Pact through modernization, gains additional importance. After the introduction of modern mobile SS-20 missiles, Soviet intermediate-range forces are less vulnerable, permitting the selective employment of these systems. Improved accuracy and lower yields allow for effective selective engagement of military targets while reducing collateral damage to the civilian environment. This means that the Soviet leadership today can employ a strategy of controlled nuclear escalation and thus also discourage such operations on the part of NATO. In addition, Warsaw Pact forces may initiate nuclear escalation and, protected by their superior regional massive counterstrike potential, destroy key components of NATO's defense systems. As for the operational and tactical level of nuclear employment, the Soviets must be credited with increased flexibility. In conjunction with their offensive operational concept for the European theater and with their superiority in conventional force strength, the Warsaw Pact's regional nuclear war-fighting capability has become impressive.

Since the early 1970s NATO has been analyzing requirements for modernizing theater nuclear forces (TNF). However, since the 1977 enhanced radiation weapons (ERW) controversy, the process of modernization has been subject to political debate in some European NATO countries. NATO's second approach to TNF modernization, the deployment of U.S. intermediate-range nuclear forces (INF) in Europe, has even prompted a fierce and politically effective protest movement. At the same time, NATO announced the reduction of its nuclear stockpile by 1000 warheads. Thus a paradoxical situation has developed. As announced in a spectacular manner, the Warsaw Pact has embarked on a further buildup and modernization of its regional nuclear potential, whereas on the Western side the decision was made to further reduce NATO's nuclear weapons deployed in Europe. Obviously, there were substantive reasons for this decision, although the need to mollify antinuclear protests was clearly an important motive too. Influential political elements in western European nations tend to look more favorably at radical proposals, such as NATO's waiving the concept of nuclear first use or creating a zone in Europe that is free from nuclear weapons. In this debate most western European governments have been driven into a defensive political stance. By adopting a rather soothing rhetoric, they have tried to mollify public opinion and to defuse the situation. In some cases this has even resulted in official statements that appear to support the arguments of the antinuclear protest movement, e.g., by depicting the nuclear arms race as the prime danger and by heralding the goal of complete nuclear disarmament. Rarely have attempts been made to stand up and firmly defend NATO's valid strategy in public. Rather, the current tendency is to abstain from any measures that could prompt another public controversy over nuclear strategy. Western European governments and parliaments seem to be effectively deterred from taking political action in favor of nuclear modernization.

The crucial question is whether this condition should be regarded as being temporary or of lasting duration. Risks in the latter case are manifold. In the United States, above all in Congress, resistance against the allocation of further funds for TNF modernization would grow. Negative votes in this respect have already served as a welcome means for legislators to demonstrate understanding for the American freeze movement without being compelled to vote against nuclear arms projects, which are crucial to U.S. national security. In view of the skepticism concerning the role and the value of TNF in Europe that has been noticeable for a long time in many political camps of the United States—from the left-liberals to the ultraconservatives—and because of diverging preferences on the part of the U.S. armed services, any persistence of this negative European attitude would most likely result in a revival of political pressures and demands to withdraw nuclear weapons from Europe, not least because the protection and maintenance of these weapons entail extensive manpower requirements and relatively high costs. If such tendencies in the United States and the pressure by antinuclear movements on western European governments were to interact, any effective resistance to such demands would collapse.

Even today the armed forces of some western European nations tend to opt for the reduction of nuclear operational tasks and assets rather than give up conventional capabilities, if they are forced to economize. In short, if the present state of affairs continues, NATO's system of nuclear sharing will be in danger of eroding and the perspective of those who favor nuclear freeze regimes and unilateral reductions would prevail. The loss of nuclear operational flexibility and willingness to share the nuclear risk would destroy the psychological and material basis of NATO's nuclear strategy. In that case the enlarged spectrum of the Warsaw Pact's nuclear and nonnuclear offensive capabilities could only be countered by the threat of nuclear escalation through U.S. "strategic" delivery means, most of which would be deployed outside Europe, a threat whose credibility would have to be rated as relatively low under the prevailing conditions.

However, political problems would not only arise in the long- or medium-term. In the short term the Nuclear Planning Group and other NATO committees could lose their meaning and importance unless NATO governments overcome current constraints. Unilateralist attitudes in the United States would gain strength if consultation and coordination in the alliance on questions of nuclear strategy, armaments, and arms control were primarily to act as a transmission belt for domestic political pressures on western European governments. The same effect would occur if decisions taken jointly were to become noncommittal because they could not be enforced by these governments. American reservations vis-à-vis European suggestions to link or merge START (Strategic Arms Reduction Talks) and INF negotiations at times seemed to spring from the interest to deny western European governments, which were considered too weak, any direct leverage on U.S. strategic policy vis-à-vis the Soviet Union.

All in all, there is hardly any doubt that the task "of coping with Soviet military power and of strengthening Western deterrence" in the regional nuclear force balance demands a reversal of current policy trends. Otherwise, Soviet superiority in this domain is bound to grow and NATO would have to conduct negotiations from a position of inferiority. Such negotiations could only end in the political recognition of Soviet regional predominance.

Thus the key question is how to remove the psycho-political barriers that have developed in western Europe because of the deterioration of the nuclear force balance, its impact on diverging national security outlooks, and the irresponsible and self-destructive manner in which the debate on Western nuclear strategy has been conducted in the United States and in western Europe. The distortions, miscalculations, suspicions, and fears that have resulted from this process stand in the way of a rational discussion and the restoration of consensus and political support. Unless they can be tackled successfully the Western alliance will be hard put to keep its nuclear strategy viable. The points at issue, especially those involving the United States and the Federal Republic of Germany, are addressed later in this chapter.

Strengthening NATO's Conventional Defense Capability in Central Europe

The urgent need to strengthen NATO's conventional defense capability in central Europe has long been recognized and stressed time and again within the alliance. This recognition reflects the results of numerous analyses and the contents of several joint programs, most recently of the Long-term Defense Program. However, current political awareness of this aim has increased as a result of growing disenchantment with the nuclear component of NATO strategy. There is broad consensus in all political camps in the United States and among governments and opposition parties in almost all European countries that NATO should enhance its conventional capabilities in order to reduce its present dependence on a possible early nuclear first use. If pertinent press publications could be believed, such efforts would seem just short of decisive success. However, such optimism appears superficial and premature. Rather, NATO's problems in this area, too, are likely to increase in the coming years.

One reason for this is the continuous development of the offensive capabilities of the Warsaw Pact's conventional forces in central and eastern Europe since the early 1970s. In particular, the USSR has enhanced the combat efficiency of its ground forces by providing them with more and better-quality major equipment. Moreover, the capability of the Warsaw Pact's air forces to conduct offensive operations into the depth of the NATO area and to provide direct support for the ground forces' offensive has considerably increased during the years of modernization.

For NATO this constitutes a new, more critical situation insofar as it must prepare itself for the possibility of an attack by the Warsaw Pact after a short preparation phase. In view of the USSR's superior mobilization and reinforcement capability, NATO's main problem has long been that its forces would only suffice for a conventional forward defense of limited duration. True, it could be assumed that NATO would be able to build up such a defense and maintain it successfully for at least a few days, but there is the danger that the resistance of the Western forces would break down, at the latest, under the onslaught of the Soviet follow-on forces from the Western military districts.

However, because of the changes in the air threat to NATO's air and land forces and the strengthening of the combat efficiency of the Warsaw Pact's first echelon forces, which are being maintained in high readiness, even these expectations have been called into question. The Warsaw Pact's armaments development, the reorganization of its air and ground forces, and the development of its operational and tactical doctrines reveal the Soviet interest in securing the option of a conventional offensive that may be carried out almost from a "standing start." Given the dependence of NATO's conventional defense capabilities on mobilization, which is relatively time-consuming and susceptible to interference, and on initial deployment and preparation of its units in the envisaged defensive areas, this option of conventional "surprise attack" would offer the Warsaw Pact forces the possibility to attack a NATO forward defense not yet completely established. Because in such a situation the bulk of Western units actually earmarked for main defense would have to be used in a delaying battle, and because combat in the defensive areas would be hindered by excessive stretching of frontage widths, by insufficient battlefield preparation, and by a lack of operational reserves, relatively rapid enemy breakthroughs and thrusts into the depth of NATO's rear combat zone would have to be expected. The concept of using highly mobile operational maneuver groups, as developed and improved by the Warsaw Pact, is optimally suited to this specific objective.

This concept, part of the effort to perfect the Warsaw Pact's conventional offensive capabilities, confronts NATO with the following difficulties:

- its strategic concept of *forward defense,* which is of decisive importance, especially to the Federal Republic of Germany, may be negated;

- its ability to conduct effectively at least a coherent conventional *initial defense,* to interrupt the momentum of attack, could be jeopardized.

Thus the military prerequisites for NATO's ability to support its forward defense with tactical nuclear operations would be lost as well. At the same time the political-strategic preconditions for successful implementation of its concept of controlled nuclear escalation would largely cease to exist.

For the reasons stated, NATO, in this situation, would lose the flexibility needed to respond in a politically responsible and militarily effective manner. Its overall strategy would be successfully undercut by the Warsaw Pact. Western governments and parliaments would be faced with the dilemma of either accepting a probably irreversible military defeat in central Europe or resorting almost immediately to massive nuclear first use against the enemy's offensive potential in the battlefield area or against lines of communication in eastern Europe. The only other military option remaining would consist of bringing on the imminent danger of a strategic nuclear war. Much speaks for the possibility that such strain would cause NATO to lose its freedom of action and to disintegrate politically, not only in the event of war, but even in a serious crisis.

Hence, if the NATO nations, in keeping with their repeated declarations, wish to raise the "nuclear threshold" or only prevent its further lowering, they must at least acquire sufficient conventional forces to enable them to counter a Soviet short-warning attack and to secure the stability of their initial defense. However, even the fulfillment of this minimum requirement for the viability and feasibility of NATO's strategy of flexible response raises considerable difficulties. The process of strengthening the Warsaw Pact forces' first strategic echelon is not yet complete. After some delay the modernization of non-Soviet units after the Soviet model has begun. Moreover, the Warsaw Pact's improved capability of conventional "surprise" exploits *structural weaknesses* in NATO's defense posture. For instance, although NATO's air defense systems have been designed to maintain a relatively high level of readiness, their total capability still has significant deficiencies and could be swamped by a major Warsaw Pact air offensive. These air defenses are vital to the protection of army units engaged in forward defense against attacks by enemy aircraft and helicopters, to the survival and combat readiness of the Western air forces, and to the air defense of numerous warning and command and control components, support sites, lines of communication, etc.

Strengthening NATO's ground forces, which are capable of being used on short notice in central Europe, is no less important. This mainly applies to active combat and combat and service support units, but also to reserve units capable of rapid mobilization. Approximately four or five additional division equivalents consisting of suitably located, sufficiently combat-ready troops will be necessary to enable effective delaying operations near the border after only short preparation, and to assume and stabilize main defense operations with the minimum of tactical and operational reserves required. However, such active army units (or near-full-strength units) are expensive because of their manpower requirements and most difficult to sustain in peacetime. This explains the present general tendency of most western European governments to gradually increase, rather than reduce, the dependence of their ground forces on mobilization measures owing to lack of money and personnel.

The significance of another weakness of NATO, which would also have serious consequences in the event of an "unreinforced attack," is frequently overlooked. It involves accomplishment of the tasks of the Federal Republic's territorial and civilian defense, primarily that of supporting NATO-assigned forces in central Europe by securing their operational freedom, their supply, and their protection in the rear area. The assets required for this task would, if at all, be available in sufficient numbers only about two days after the beginning of mobilization. Thus the possibility could not be excluded that, in the initial phase of a "surprise attack," sufficient control over mass refugee movements by the German police might be impossible. Important military installations could be protected only initially against covert and commando operations in a selective manner. Damage caused by bomb attacks or sabotage could be repaired only with delay. Essential support services would have to be dispensed with initially.

In view of the possibility of a short-warning attack these tasks, on which the military responsiveness of NATO depends to a considerable extent, properly should be taken care of by active service military and civilian personnel. The inability to meet this requirement leads to a state of permanent vulnerability, and the consequence would become more critical the more additional support and even combat support tasks would have to be taken over by German territorial forces under "wartime host nation support" arrangements or as substitutes for U.S. forces being used outside the NATO area. The improvement of relevant German capabilities is without a doubt appropriate and in part even possible. In terms of funds and personnel, however, such improvements would compete with the task of maintaining the level and readiness of NATO-assigned Federal Armed Forces divisions and the activation of additional reserve combat units (home defense brigades).

Another critical problem concerns the ability of NATO air forces to support the ground forces' operations. Air force commands have traditionally attributed prime importance to the battle for air superiority, i.e., the engagement of enemy air forces on the ground and in the air. Compared with the latter tasks, battlefield interdiction and close air support have ranked second up to now. NATO's dilemma lies in the fact that the operational urgency of both tasks is growing simultaneously. Under the conditions of an attack after short-warning time, which would probably be initiated by a large-scale air offensive on the part of the Warsaw Pact, Western air forces initially would have to secure their survival through air warfare operations of their own. In doing so their aircraft assets capable of attack would be almost entirely tied down (and probably decimated considerably). Under these circumstances, simultaneous, sufficiently effective support from the air, vital to the army units spread thinly across a wide area while engaged in forward defense, would not be possible in the critical initial phase of operations. This obviously opens another wide range of expensive and difficult tasks, such as the development and increased procurement of efficient, specialized delivery systems, target engagement systems, modern types of ammunition, means and procedures for engagement of enemy air defenses, and the coordination of air operations on the battlefield, including the use of air defense and artillery support of friendly ground forces.

In the years to come what are the chances that the Western alliance can meet this fundamental challenge to its conventional defense capabilities? If one takes a look at the points of main effort visible in the present medium-term defense planning of NATO countries that are most important to the central European situation, such as the United States, Great Britain, France, and, not least, the Federal Republic of Germany, the same paradox appears as in the nuclear area. In contradiction to the existing and widely proclaimed necessity to strengthen conventional defense capabilities, another problem, may be that fundamental weakness looms in the second half of the 1980s.

The U.S. administration assigns political priority to the dynamics of its armaments and research and development programs in the domain of nuclear-strategic competition with the USSR. The ambitious naval expansion program seems to enjoy a comparable level of support. The strengthening and modernization of globally deployable general-purpose forces ranks second. As the buildup of these components is effected without a commensurate increase in the peacetime level of U.S. forces, the necessity arises to realign forces and to change operational missions. As is already recognizable, the lowering of the defense budget growth rates originally planned by the Reagan administration will make cutbacks and delays inevitable. For national strategic and domestic political reasons, they will primarily affect the U.S. ground forces, probably primarily the stationing forces and reinforcements committed to or earmarked for the defense of central Europe. There are already some clear indications to this effect.

All in all, the impression prevails that priorities in strategic thinking under President Reagan are shifting at the expense of the stronger commitment to conventional defense in Europe as advocated under President Carter. This appears to correspond to the mood prevailing in Congress and also in the U.S. military establishment. Reflections on the possible critical consequences of such a shift in strategic thinking are overruled by the currently perceived urgent need to respond to the nuclear strategic threat against the United States and to the challenge posed by possible conflicts in Southwest Asia and in Central America, whose likelihood appears greater than that of a war between the Warsaw Pact and NATO in Europe. Moreover, there is a tendency to parry the consequences of this change by requesting the European NATO countries (and specifically the Federal Republic of Germany) to offset such consequences by enhanced own-defense efforts.

The development of British and French defense policies shows a similar perspective. The governments of both countries assign priority to their respective national strategic nuclear forces. Both are planning expensive modernization programs, each seeking to achieve growth in this area in order to maintain the effectiveness of their national retaliation potentials even under conditions of an intensified Soviet-U.S. armaments competition that could lead to the buildup of improved antimissile systems. Both countries also spend considerable resources on ensuring their military capabilities for limited intervention in regions outside the NATO area.

The economic and monetary situation of both countries is relatively poor, and there is no hope of rapid improvement. Despite drastic cuts in social programs, both countries have tried to protect their defense budgets. Great Britain has even managed to sustain real growth, but it has been additionally burdened with expenditures following from the Falkland War. It is true that the decision, long feared, to reduce substantially the British Army of the Rhine has so far not been made. Instead, as decided in 1981, cuts will continue to center on the British surface fleet, even if in a mitigated form. However, most informed observers consider further medium-term cuts in the conventional area as inevitable. By the end of the decade the budget situation of Great Britain should further deteriorate because of declining North Sea oil output. Thus any realistic prognosis should be based on the premise that the British forces in the Federal Republic will by no means be reinforced in the course of the eighties, but, on the contrary, may be expected to be reduced if the government of Great Britain sticks to its present strategic priorities.

The French government has already decided on concentrating required cuts on the country's conventional ground forces. Two divisions will be disbanded. The heavy units of the First French Army have long been suffering from delays in the modernization of their equipment and from atrophy on the part of their combat support and supply elements. This leads to limitation of their freedom of action in their role as a strategic reserve, which is important to NATO. The organization of the air-mobile Force d'Action Rapide (FAR), which is earmarked for missions outside and inside Europe and supposed to be built up from already-existing units, can only partly offset this weakness. As this multipurpose force absorbs assets of heavy army units, such as their helicopter regiments, and is given preferential treatment in equipment and personnel, army divisions in the reserve role will be further weakened. On the other hand, France would acquire the military ability to support NATO, given the appropriate political decision, in the initial phase of a conflict with highly mobile operations within forward defense. This highly welcome prospect, however, cannot cover up the fact that the total strength of French conventional forces will continue to decrease.

The prognosis is as pessimistic for other western European NATO countries, whose army units are supposed to participate in the forward defense in central Europe with corps or divisions of their own. In the face of looming national bankruptcy, Belgium sees itself compelled to effect additional reductions in its already-diminished military contributions. The Netherlands plan to downgrade further the operational readiness of their forces. These tendencies give rise to concerns that the concept of NATO's defense in central Europe as a multinational, integrated forward defense shared by German, Dutch, British, Belgian, and U.S. corps (with Danish, Canadian, and possibly French support) will continue to lose in substance. The maintenance and modernization of the multinational, integrated air defense belts on the soil of the Federal Republic of Germany in its present form poses problems of a comparable nature.

What is particularly disturbing is that these erosive tendencies in the respective countries are not meeting with determined public resistance. The scarcity of funds and the politically more pressing interests of each in solving its own economic and social problems are leading to a generally felt, increasingly "national" attitude toward defense policy, i.e., an attitude strongly deter- mined by domestic political criteria. Protectionism in the field of defense production and procurement is gaining further ground. In these circumstances, defending the performance of "inte- grated tasks" in NATO, possibly with armed forces stationed on foreign soil, has not found a strong political lobby.

In addition, there is a growing opinion—not only in the U.S. Congress, but also in Great Britain, the Benelux countries, and elsewhere—that the Federal Republic of Germany could and should rely more heavily on its own forces to satisfy its defense needs and compensate for possible withdrawals of allied forces for their employment elsewhere. The Federal Republic is seen as a relatively rich country with a large untapped pool of reservists, a country that enjoys an excellent military reputation and that should have a greater interest than any other in an effective, close-to-the-border defense of its own territory. Such expecta- tions and assessments, however, are regrettably sharply at odds with the problems looming ahead for German defense policy at the end of this decade, problems that may affect primarily the army. Because of the sharp decline in the number of male youths coming of military age, the Bundeswehr will be less and less able to meet its manpower requirements after 1987. Computations indicate that, accordingly, the peacetime strength of the armed forces would in the 1990s have to be reduced by at least 50,000 men despite various planned countermeasures, as, for instance, extending the draft to eighteen months and increasing the per- centage of longer-serving volunteers and full-career soldiers. Be- cause the air force and the navy have comparatively less personnel, the bulk of the reductions will be at the expense of the army. Because the territorial defense forces of the Bundes- wehr—despite the impending expansion of their tasks—have al- ready had to surrender some of their personnel slots to NATO- assigned formations, in the wake of the latest structural reorganization of the army, and these assigned formations are even now organized at various levels of readiness, a reduction of the peacetime strength by the figure mentioned would thus necessarily mean increased dependency on mobilization measures.

Without the compensatory actions mentioned the situation would become much worse. However, because they increase the personnel cost share of the defense budget, these measures will aggravate the already-difficult financial situation of the Bundeswehr as far as its equipment plans are concerned. These plans suffer from the fact that, up into the late 1980s, all the funds expected to be available, and more, have already been committed to the current, extensive modernization programs of the air force, the army, and the navy.

Therefore, only limited funds will be available for unscheduled new acquisitions, for instance, for weapon systems, advanced types of ammunition, and support components in the category of the so-called emerging technologies. The squeeze is likely to become tighter the earlier and more rapidly the cost of personnel increases. Certainly, this gloomy forecast also hinges on political preconditions. The prospect of stagnating or even decreasing economic growth obviously was responsible for abandoning the goal of real defense increases over the medium term. The political priority of the current government, so far, aims at the consolidation of the federal budget and the reduction of the federal debt. Growth in defense—for which, in the present political mood in the Federal Republic, there is no strong, organized support—will remain subordinate to this goal. Even if the financial scope for defense planning was widened in order to ensure some modest real growth for the critical years ahead (something that ought to be considered imperative in view of the situation of the Federal Republic), an increase in the size of the Bundeswehr, and thus the possibility of compensating for possible further reductions in the armed forces of the allies in central Europe, would remain out of the question. As things stand it would even have to be considered a success if the present strength of the Bundeswehr could be more or less maintained.

The prospect that NATO's conventional defense capability in Europe against a possible short-warning attack could become even weaker, urgently calls for political action. Otherwise, there is not much hope that the credibility of NATO's military strategy and its political support can be maintained. The proclaimed objective, to raise the "nuclear threshold," thus would have to be reflected in the guidelines for medium-term defense planning of the major NATO countries, which at present it is not. The necessary revision to this effect must be based on a sober assessment of the national strategic priorities of the United States, Great Britain, and France and their implications for the NATO defense in Europe. What would also have to be determined are the limits of the Federal Republic's capability to unilaterally offset, through increases in its defense efforts, both the growth of the conventional offensive capability of the Warsaw Pact *and* a possible reduction of the land forces that Germany's allies have deployed in Europe. Such a review would have to take place at the highest political level and would have to include a number of domestically highly controversial problems: adjusting the peacetime strength of the armed forces in accordance with the expansion of the operational tasks and a changed military threat; using the draft to reduce personnel costs; assuring the requisite real growth in budget planning; and saving costs through increased specialization and division of labor in defense research, development, and production as well as in the discharge of various operational tasks.

To help provide the necessary information for this political debate, the responsible military staffs of the alliance should, as concretely as possible, identify their force requirements and specify the military risks in case these goals are not met. In particular, they should identify the qualitative and quantitative force requirements for the indispensable assurance of an effective conventional initial defense in central Europe. These data should also and especially be made available to the public in order to facilitate an informed debate.

Without wanting to anticipate the outcome of the studies recommended here, it is safe to say that, because of the limitations and trends shown, NATO will not attain an exclusively conventional defense capability to countervail the conventional capability of the Warsaw Pact in the foreseeable future. If only for this reason, NATO must stick to the nuclear component of its compound strategy and win public support for it. Furthermore, using scarce resources to build up a capability for sustained and extensive conventional warfare might endanger the feasibility of the more important initial defense of central Europe. Another important aspect relates to the character of the debate on the future strategy of the United States and NATO, a debate that is determined, above all, by the stimuli received from the United States. This debate serves a necessary function in the attempt to adapt the military tool and the operational doctrine of the Western alliance to changed military conditions. Still, it would be important to abandon unequivocally concepts of a "strategic renewal" that are obviously unrealistic, deflect attention from the most urgent military problems and tasks, or seem to call into question valid political premises of the NATO strategy.

It is necessary, therefore, to put the Western strategy debate back on a materially and operationally more realistic footing and at the same time to secure adequate influence for the dictates of political wisdom and reason. Otherwise, the frictions between NATO countries from reciprocal misassessments, disappointments, and reproaches may become more serious. In this context the American-German relationship is critical for a number of reasons.

Security Policy Problems Existing Between the United States and the Federal Republic of Germany

The Importance of the German-American Relationship to NATO

The chances of NATO to respond effectively to the earlier described conventional and nuclear challenge posed by the Warsaw Pact depend, in a positive as well as in a negative respect, on future developments in German-American relations in the areas of defense and foreign policy. In this regard the following aspects play an important role:

- The basic structure of German security policy is influenced to a considerable extent by the behavior of the United States. This strong dependence means that any changes in

American policy that deviate, or seem to deviate, from German security interests are bound to put an immediate strain on the stability of German policy.

- On the other hand, the policy of the Federal Republic, for several reasons, holds a key position for the stability of the U.S. military commitment in Europe. The Federal Republic is the most important host country for U.S. forces stationed abroad. Its armed forces contribute considerably to the defense of western Europe, and its political and economic development has become a symbol for the significance and the success of American postwar policy in Europe. From the American standpoint it is, above all, the policy of the Federal Republic that is taken as the yardstick for the willingness of "the Europeans" to ensure the security of western Europe with the United States as an ally.
- This special position, which, from the German point of view, is more of a burden than a boon, is underscored by the fact that a number of smaller nonnuclear NATO countries in western Europe orient their policies according to the developments in the Federal Republic.

For these reasons any drastic deterioration in the German-American relations must be regarded as more than just a bilateral problem. Because of the mutual, if differing, dependence of both countries, and because of their respective political strategic key positions within NATO, such deterioration would lead to a crisis within the Western alliance.

During the turbulence of the late 1970s and early 1980s such fears remained by no means hypothetical. As a result of a dramatic deterioration in East-West relations and because of a drastic reorientation of U.S. foreign and military policy, German security policy was put under considerable pressure. Dilemmas and traumas related to the German security situation, which were kept dormant for a long period, now became the subject of emotionalized debates in the Federal Republic. The speakers and organizers of the powerful antinuclear protest movement accused American policy and NATO, allegedly controlled by the former, of being a serious threat to the security and the survival of the Federal Republic. It is safe to assume that the picture of this "peace movement" and its anti-American propaganda in the media have negatively influenced the way in which the Federal Republic is seen by the political elites in the United States. Another fact was that Bonn, being under domestic political pressure and motivated by tactical considerations, kept pressing for changes in U.S. policy that were regarded as inexpedient in Washington, which in turn led to increasing resentments.

It is not the objective of this chapter to reconstruct every detail of the intricate history of this mutual irritation. Attention should be paid, however, to all those factors and circumstances causing confusion and posing an obstacle to this very day. It is necessary to identify these factors in order to eliminate existing misconceptions and reestablish a consensus with respect to basic political strategic issues. Only on this condition can we hope to curb the now customary abuse of military strategic issues and the subject of arms control policy as a means of the domestic political struggle for power and political direction, and to regain the political freedom of action for the necessary measures of adjustment.

"Security Essentials" of the Federal Republic and "Strategic Renewal" of American Policy

The basic precepts of German security policy are a result of the actual strategic location of the Federal Republic. In the event of war its overall territory would presumably become the theater of operations. The defense against the attacking main forces of the USSR, a military superpower, would have to take place on its territory whose narrow space, high population density, and high degree of industrialization make it extremely susceptible to war damages. The catastrophic consequences of a large-scale war have the effect that, in the opinion of the Federal Republic, security depends on the successful prevention of war, but that it could not be guaranteed by the ability to defend itself successfully in the event of war. The significance of this ability, consequently, lies in its contribution to the prevention of war and to its fastest possible termination—should it break out in Europe.

The Federal Republic's exposed position and vulnerability were the governing factors in simultaneously leading its security policy in two complementary directions. With the aid of its NATO allies it seeks to prevent the leadership of the Soviet Union, through effective military deterrence, from using military force against the alliance and at the same time tries, through a policy of détente and East-West cooperation, to pursue crisis prevention and eliminate possible reasons and causes for conflicts. This was a major underlying factor in concluding the Eastern treaties. Ostpolitik was also meant to open up new avenues of development for Europe, avenues that could relieve the Federal Republic (and the German Democratic Republic) of playing the role of a central arena for political separation and military confrontation.

Despite its vital importance, the policy of military deterrence has, for a long time, been burdened with fundamental problems for the Federal Republic. From the German point of view, a sufficient deterrence of the superpower USSR requires the capability and the willingness to put the very existence of the USSR at risk, if necessary. But this can be achieved only through the threat of strategic employment of nuclear weapons, even against targets on Soviet territory. Consequently, all notions of a "limited war" whose politico-geographical escalation barriers would keep the territory of the USSR as a "sanctuary" were firmly rejected. From the German viewpoint, such a strategic concept would be bound to weaken the effect of military prevention of war considerably and expose the Federal Republic to a politically unacceptable singular risk.

As a result, the German side has always interpreted and depicted the NATO strategy of "flexible response," first and foremost, as a strategy of nuclear deterrence that is based on the concept of a gapless nuclear escalation and the coupling of the U.S. strategic nuclear arsenal to the defense of Europe. There is no need, here and now, to elaborate on the fact that U.S. policy did not share this interpretation but, on the contrary, sought to develop alternatives to the reliance on the "extended strategic deterrence" and the concept of nuclear escalation.

The plausibility of the German version of the NATO strategy, however, was not only called in question by the developments in the American strategy debate, but it also suffered from unresolved inherent contradictions. These became increasingly apparent the more the West became aware of the extent and the consequences of the Soviet nuclear and nonnuclear buildup. For a long time the dominant line of reasoning in the Federal Republic was: The buildup of too strong a conventional arsenal by NATO would be bound to be taken by the Soviets as a refusal to use nuclear weapons, and thus weaken the effects of nuclear deterrence. A "low nuclear threshold" was considered expedient. Thus the significance of nuclear theater weapons was seen in this connection. However, NATO was not to restrict possible nuclear missions to military support of NATO's battlefield-level defense efforts, but to make the Soviet leadership aware, as quickly as possible, of the risk of an escalation into a strategic war in order to induce the Soviets to make the political decision of stopping the aggression and retreat. This interpretation of the NATO strategy as a nuclear deterrence strategy was thus characterized by two elements: NATO being coerced into an early nuclear first use and a strong emphasis on a rapid escalation.

It was doubtful, however, whether the actual application of such a strategy would really satisfy German security interests, should deterrence fail. Use of nuclear weapons inside the theater of operations by NATO and the Warsaw Pact based on military decisions could quickly lead to the total destruction of the Federal Republic, thus reducing to absurdity the very goal of its defense. It may be assumed, consequently, that in a war an effort would be made on the German side, too, to conduct defense as much as possible with conventional weapons alone. This is suggested at least by the obviously divided attitude in German strategic thinking with regard to use of theater nuclear weapons. Moreover, because the cataclysm of a general nuclear war serves no one, one may presume that the leadership of the Federal Republic, too, would have an interest in working toward limiting war and having nuclear escalation controlled.

The existential character of these dilemmas and their potentially demoralizing and politically destabilizing effect have induced the Federal Republic of Germany to adopt specific forms of adaptation:

- All sensitive military strategic problems have for decades been deliberately kept away from public debate, particularly those involving nuclear doctrine and operational planning, but also generally all military operational aspects and requirements of European deterrence and defense. This policy encouraged official portrayals of NATO strategy as a "political strategy to prevent war" in contrast to the scorned notion of a "strategy enabling the conduct of war." Deterrence was thus derived from relatively abstract postulates and concepts, such as "triad interaction," "gapless escalation," the commitment to joint "forward defense," etc. The required concomitant military operational substratum for these concepts, however, was never made a subject of consideration to the general public. The very possibility of war was banned by way of definition. The feasibility of deterrence appeared to be achievable independent of—indeed, even as a contrast to—the ability to conduct war.
- This view corresponded with a political mentality that perceived the defense of the Federal Republic of Germany, above all, not as a national task, but as a mission of NATO. The reason for this attitude was that the Federal Republic of Germany is inherently incapable of autonomous self-defense. Moreover, most of its active armed forces have been assigned to NATO. Operational planning and command and control in the event of war are thus tasks incumbent on the integrated NATO staffs.

   It is true that the German federal government, through its defense ministry, has brought to bear considerable influence in military matters on the development of NATO's overall doctrine, its procedures, situation assessment, operational doctrine, and operations plans. However, this process was mostly internal, without awareness and participation of the body politic. The long-time broad political support for the Federal Republic's security policy in NATO had been for the official portrayal of this policy and had thus in effect been accepted by resorting to exonerating simplifications and dismissals. This consensus was bound to turn fragile once the problems suppressed became the subject of public controversy.

- The result of the development just outlined was that the general public in West Germany was neither aware of developments in the nuclear doctrine and the operational concepts of NATO that had evolved since the 1960s, nor recognized the implications stemming from the systematic increase of the Warsaw Pact's military capabilities. The consequences of this were twofold: First, no possibility existed for an appreciation to develop of the factual reasons for the American policy that urged increased armaments efforts of its allies, considered new conceptual initiatives, and criticized the results of the security negotiations between East and West that had been conducted up to then. Second, releases about operational concepts and ideas of NATO even then produced the impression among the public in the Federal Republic of Germany that this information signified a fundamental change and violation of NATO strategy, when in reality it was in conformity with that strategy and the operational practice of the alliance.

- In addition, the importance of military operational issues to the security of Europe was for a long time balanced by the perspective of the gradual improvement of the political relations between East and West. The visible advances of the process of détente caused the perception of a military threat to be thrust into the background. The fact, however, that successes in the arms control negotiations between East and West failed to materialize attracted little attention because the German public contented itself with the political and symbolic effect of the negotiation process as such. Military operational objectives and criteria for success were, for the reasons mentioned, afforded only a minor role in the public mind. The prevailing idea of political "confidence building" through negotiations was more closely associated with the domain of emotion than with strategic calculation in negotiations. In addition, the German public was, to a large extent, denied a sobering insight into the Soviet idea of the policy of "peaceful coexistence." One reason for this was that the "German policy of peace and détente" had assumed a great importance as an electoral campaign strategy in the domestic struggle for political power. To prevent the unmistakably continued antagonistic traits of Soviet practice in the "international class struggle" and in the domain of arms and negotiation policy from impairing the persuasiveness of the German Ostpolitik, these aspects were largely hushed up, downplayed, or rationalized in public by the political parties in power.

These tendencies became more pronounced when, in the late 1970s, Soviet-American relations deteriorated and a conservative reorientation became apparent in American foreign and security policy. In Bonn there developed a highly complex political game between government and conservative opposition as well as inside the Social Democratic party (SPD), then in power, in which tactical interests and fundamental political goals and considerations combined in inseparable interaction. The government, in the light of the crises in Iran and Afghanistan, in dramatizing manner emphasized the purportedly increasing danger of war in order to substantiate the importance and indispensability of its "peace and détente policy" (which by then had become the only attractive campaign topic). A primary role in this, apart from the imperative of staying in power, was played by the fear that the emerging shift in the direction of U.S. policy would kill the possibility of a policy of détente vis-à-vis the USSR and eastern Europe. So the idea was that by arousing the German population, it would become possible to cling to the continuity of this policy even in the face of pressure from the United States.

As it turned out, however, the governmental wing of the SPD lost its grip on the control of developments. Although Federal Chancellor Schmidt, by walking a difficult tightrope, continued to strive to maintain the continuity of both components of German security policy and make a contribution to the stability of NATO, both amid the controversy over INF and with regard to bolstering conventional capabilities, this policy was attacked with ever more effect from inside the SPD. The fear of war among the German public, which in some quarters rose to the extent of hysteria, was guided, above all, against the strategy and armament projects of NATO and the United States, which were branded as destabilizing and as a danger and obstruction to détente. An emotional debate was unleashed by the mouthpieces and organizers of the "peace movement," which touched the most sensitive aspects, until then banished from the public mind, of the military security dilemma of the Federal Republic. Their exaggerations and the false information they spread met with such response in a general public unprepared for this and largely ignorant of the matter concerned that the government found itself pushed more and more onto the defensive. To alleviate the rampant fear it found itself compelled to exalt the few remaining elements of visible communication between the American and Soviet leadership to the status of evidence of a continued willingness of both sides for negotiation and détente. With regard to the difficult and intricate problems revolving around the development of the nuclear arsenals, the operational doctrines, and the planning of objectives in the East and the West, it attempted to sidestep a detailed debate and stick with the time-honored soothing rationalizations.

The feasibility of politicizing such topics is a symptom of the peculiar burdens from which the Federal Republic's military security policy suffers. Its inherent paradoxes necessitate the complementing of military deterrence and defense by a policy of cooperation and conflict avoidance that, in Europe, would work toward a state of political stability. The fact that this combined strategy matches up with the Federal Republic's national security interests became apparent at the latest when, after the change of government in Bonn, the Christian Democratic Union/ Christian Social Union also adopted a stance of support for continuity in the Ostpolitik.

However, this double-track strategy encountered obstacles that were hard to overcome after the Soviet invasion of Afghanistan, the assumption of office by President Reagan, and the beginning of the INF deployment. Although the Federal Republic tried to maintain continuity, the two superpowers were determined to prevent it. Soviet and American policies influenced the German public and the Federal government in opposing directions in order to prompt it to abandon its established policy line. The influence exerted by both was designed to bring the Federal Republic's interests in military security in the Atlantic framework in opposition to its interests in détente and political stability in Europe, that is, to destroy the complementary coherence of this policy.

The Soviet side put pressure on the Federal Republic to object to the renewal of American containment policy, the armament projects of NATO, and, above all, the stationing of INF in Europe. Otherwise, the Soviets indicated, the Federal Republic would lose the fruits of détente and see itself exposed to a considerably increased military threat, even including the danger of a preemptive nuclear destruction.

From the American side, the Germans were urged to stop their efforts toward détente and cooperation with the Soviet Union in questions of trade relations, in the Conference on Security and Cooperation (CSCE) process, and in the boycott of the Olympic Games in Moscow, and to share in solidarity the military burdens of the global containment policy envisaged by the United States.

Consequently, Bonn saw itself compelled to prevent the impending collapse of the existing German security policy on which the feeling of security and the political consent of the population have so far been based. It is not surprising, however, that the insistence on continuity had to assume voluntaristic features in a situation in which, in contrast, both the USSR and the United States sought to demonstrate in their relations the very fact of discontinuity. Faced with the loss of the familiar political perspective and confronted with the choice between alternatives that promised less security, uneasiness and frustration began to spread in the public of the Federal Republic. The forced discussion of questions regarding a fundamental reorientation led to a polarization of domestic policy. Political tactics overshadowed and distorted the discussion of the controversial problems in the way indicated earlier.

There were several reasons, some of which have been mentioned already, for the fact that in this debate it was primarily American policy that was blamed for the deterioration of the situation; for instance:

- the "blind spots" and rationalizations in the public political consciousness with respect to the political and military strategy of the USSR and the development of its arms buildup since the sixties
- the lack of information and understanding in the public in regard to critical operational military requirements and problems of Western security policy
- the partial incongruity between internal assessments and political activities of the government and their representation and perception in the public (examples for this are Chancellor Schmidt's internal basic criticism of the American policy in the SALT II negotiations notwithstanding his firm support in public for the ratification of the SALT II treaty, which was referred to as the key element of the détente process; furthermore, the coexistence of diverging justifications for the deployment of modern INF in Europe and for the respective negotiating goals)
- the restriction of the German security policy perspective to the European area and here mainly to the situation in central Europe.

Because of this selective blindness the role of Soviet policy in the deterioration of the East-West relationship was substantially underrated. An understanding as to what degree the U.S. policy *reacted* and *had to* react to intensified objective challenges to the Western alliance could not develop. As a consequence, the new security issues that plagued the Federal Republic seemed to be mainly the result of arbitrary American initiatives. This produced favorable conditions for the effect of the disinformation campaign that was initiated by the propagandists of the anti-nuclear protest movement. Large segments of the political public began to perceive the Reagan administration as the actual threat.

It should not be underestimated, however, to what decisive extent the American policy itself has contributed to this alarming negative perception. During the Carter presidency, the discussion about American foreign and security policy had intensified considerably. Issues concerning military strategy and armaments policy became the focal point in the struggle for power. They were voiced and exploited primarily in the propaganda campaigns for and against the ratification of the SALT II treaty. The conservative opposition dramatized in its general attack the military weakness of the United States vis-à-vis the USSR; with its theorem of the "window of opportunity" it even insinuated a Soviet need for preventive war. This was explained by the assertion that the Soviets would have to bring to bear their superior nuclear counterforce capability before the American countervailing armament programs would close this "window." In addition, the allegedly growing dependence of the Soviet energy supply from the oil of the Persian Gulf area was stated to the same effect. The revolution in Iran and the Soviet invasion of Afghanistan served as proof for the correctness of this expectation. As an answer to this "clear and present danger" the conservatives demanded a departure from the previous practice of security negotiations with the USSR and a major, comprehensive arms buildup by the United States. After the election of President Reagan this platform program continued to determine the new administration's policy, and it was specified in a series of ambitious strategy concepts and armament programs. The necessity to mobilize the people for this effort that would entail considerable sacrifices gained an essential influence on the attitude and rhetoric of the American leadership vis-à-vis the opposing superpower whose military aggressiveness and political-ideological hostility and wickedness were described in a colorful style.

Actions or signals in the dealings with the other side that could have effected a less dramatic impression of the situation were initially not appreciated.

In retrospect one will be inclined to belittle the importance of these reminiscences. After the report of the Scowcroft Commission, the deflation of some of the military fantasies in the conventional field, and the moderation of the political language of the president and his advisers, many of these things appear to have been an expression of political tactics and deliberate rhetoric that, however, were perceived as authentic at that time. No doubt an insufficient understanding of the special workings and customs of the American political system was also a contributing factor, particularly in Europe. However, this factor alone does not suffice as an explanation. On the contrary, even well-informed unprejudiced European observers could, on the basis of their reading of the situation, arrive at alarming assessments of American policy. In the Federal Republic the following aspects gained particular significance:

- the perception of a growing expectation on the part of the American leadership that it will come to a military confrontation with the USSR, and an apparent willingness to accept this risk (as well as the exact mirror image at the Soviet end)
- the perceived determination to integrate NATO in the intended American global strategy and adopt a concept of horizontal escalation. This concept would require a NATO military capability to offensively threaten the Soviet position in eastern Europe from western Europe in case of out-of-area conflicts (DoD Annual Posture Statement—FY 1983). This, of course, would imply a fundamental change of the political character and the strategy of NATO.
- the perceived intention to actively speed up the arms competition with the USSR in those fields in which there is an American edge—i.e., in the military application of high technologies—in order to overstrain Soviet resources and, in this way, to force a change of the Soviet foreign and military policy and to exacerbate the internal crisis in the Warsaw Pact system
- the perceived intention to conduct arms control negotiations after the alleged Soviet pattern, i.e., as a supporting operation with a primarily propagandistic purpose, as a means of the "ideological struggle" without, however, letting such negotiations constrain the objectives and conditions of U.S. national strategic policy.

Some of these perceptions that seemed to be plausible at that time on the basis of official and semiofficial sources have since lost their bearing (others probably remain relevant). In any case, from the Federal Republic's point of view, it was fatal that these actual or supposed political-strategic guidelines formed a perspective that, in toto, was in sharp contrast to German security needs. Political and military trends appeared to indicate a growing likelihood of war. What made this constellation even more alarming were the effects of a burst of conceptual-strategic activism in the American defense community that reflected a feeling of "setting out to new shores." The resulting controversial reverberations in the U.S. media, which were reflected in an even more distorted form in the German TV and press coverage, contributed to a growing sense of shock and confusion.

There is no need at this point to describe in detail what echo the repeated public application of perfectionism to the thinking about nuclear warfare—be it in terms of "central nuclear exchanges" or in regard to the "integrated conventional-chemical-nuclear battlefield" of the Airland Battle doctrine—had to evoke in a country whose troubling military security dilemmas have so far been evaded by suppression. What else can be expected than rejection and revolt from citizens who have to learn from authentic maps in publications of the U.S. army or from American telecasts that their town has been designed as ground zero of a nuclear warhead for illustrative purposes.

In this connection it is unfortunate that the unrestrained discussion of the whole range of nuclear and conventional warfighting options was conducted in the American public without giving due consideration to the overriding political-strategic objective of preventing war by means of deterrence. Rather, a mere infatuation with technical and tactical problems of military operations is frequently noted. Or one even gets the impression that the effectiveness of deterrence had become so brittle that preparation for the conflict to come should be pursued with urgency.

Furthermore, in the American defense debate demands for increased military efforts within NATO have been repeatedly justified on the basis of strategic concepts that had to stir up concerns and objections in the Federal Republic. This, for example, holds true for the recurring inclination to advocate improved nuclear war-fighting capabilities in the European theater as a more credible alternative to the concept of extended strategic deterrence, which allegedly had become implausible. This line of reasoning must inevitably produce the traumatic fear on the German side that it might become the prime victim of a suicidal nuclear war that would be limited only in geographical terms. This is a perspective against which German policy has tried to hedge through NATO's concept of deliberate nuclear escalation, which in turn hinges on the capability and willingness of the United States to sustain strategic coupling. However, the prospect that the German government will succeed in winning political support for any steps in TNF modernization against determined opposition will be negatively affected to the extent that this central element of NATO's strategy is made to appear obsolete in the American debate.

Another important example is the association of the debate on improving Western conventional capabilities (particularly pertaining to "deep attack" concepts, for instance, Airland Battle, Follow-on Forces Attack [FOFA], Deep Strike, Counterair 90) with American considerations to change current NATO strategy by providing for a major offensive capability on the ground vis-à-vis eastern Europe. The perception of such a connection resulted from the notion of "horizontal escalation." It was reinforced by information on the indiscriminate espousal of the principle of the offense in the development process of the U.S. army's Airland Battle doctrine and the initial advertisement of this operational concept. In the Federal Republic this perception became an important controversial topic of discussion and has been exploited politically ever since, despite the fact that meanwhile the American government has clearly dissociated itself from such views. Consequently, the above-mentioned conventional defense improvement initiatives have met widespread reservations and sometimes even outright rejection.

These examples illustrate a basic problem: Public hypersensitivity in Germany regarding any issues of actually fighting a war, which is perfectly understandable, is interacting with an almost total insensitivity to this unique condition. The American defense debate is largely self-centered, beyond political control, and often it is rather careless in the handling of sensitive information that could embarrass allies. Moreover, competitive innovation, which goes hand in hand with permanent "overselling," is reigning supreme. Certainly, this situation cannot be changed fundamentally. It would be helpful, however, if political control could at least be established over such official activities within the U.S. government that may critically have an effect on the policies of other NATO countries. This demanding task could be facilitated if the United States, together with its European allies, could work out explicit political-strategic goals that would have to be specified by "conceptual frameworks." In this way it would be possible to counter the misunderstandings and reservations referred to earlier: first, in respect to the political motivation to create and exploit such phenomena, and second, in regard to the possibility of doing so successfully.

The German government is now facing the difficult task of gradually familiarizing the public with military reality and complex problems without jeopardizing political support for its security policy. However, the possibility of achieving this adaptation, which is essential for the political acceptance of increased defense efforts and conceptual innovation in this field, requires avoidance of any impression that Germany's security essentials will be threatened by this process. Unless this requirement can be met, Germany will maintain a conservative and essentially defensive attitude with regard to any quest for modification.

PART FOUR

Reducing Inconsistency in Western Approaches Toward the Soviet Union

Chapter 9

The Institutional Impediment: Improving the Implementation of Political Strategy

Reinhardt Rummel

Throughout the history of the Atlantic alliance the United States has been its leading manager and the dominant partner in the European-American relationship. Today, however, from a European perspective the Atlantic alliance is in trouble because a self-centered America is unwilling to protect the interests of a willful Europe. On the U.S. side the Atlantic alliance is seen to be in trouble because of the unwillingness of a declining Europe to follow and support adequately the leadership of an assertive America.

America's striving for leadership and Europe's dynamics cause tensions between Washington and the European capitals that normally are not discussed openly, yet form the hidden background of many of the disputes within the transatlantic relationship. These tensions are present in West-West relations, but they are of particular importance in the West's policies toward the Soviet Union and eastern Europe. It will probably not be feasible and may not even be useful to address these tensions squarely. Rather, it will remain an elusive process in European-American relations that influences the whole fabric of the alliance.

For decades East-West relations have displayed some combination of antagonism and cooperation. How these two intrinsically related elements combine varies with circumstances and prevailing policies. In the West this perennially requires us not only to reconcile two kinds of policies that at times tend to become incompatible, but also to establish a minimum consensus between two respective constituencies. Divergencies over how to cope with the Soviet Union are built into domestic settings, and time and again they spill over into the alliance at large.

While joint, consistent, U.S.-western European policies toward the Soviet Union are more the exception than the rule, emphasis on antagonism or cooperation in policies toward the Soviet Union tends to oscillate according to changing domestic and intra-alliance conditions rather than to opportunities and challenges on the other side. Managing relations with the Soviet Union and eastern Europe thus is a dual task. It concerns both the structure of these relations and the consensus within Western countries. This dual task is exacerbated by the fact that Soviet Westpolitik can be pursued in a more consistent and coherent manner: Because the pursuit of Soviet Westpolitik is more intrinsically related to the stability of the Soviet system, it *is* part of the internal management. The Soviet Union thus has opportunities to influence what appears to be a cyclical development of Western policies toward the Soviet Union. This asymmetry in how either side can influence the other complicates the dual task of Western efforts to manage relations with the Soviet Union and eastern Europe. Thus, building a consensus in the pursuit of policies toward the East relies on the following elements: the generation of appropriate concepts, the balancing of domestic and intra-alliance forces in order to have sufficient freedom to maneuver, and the existence of a machinery for policymaking that enables the bringing in line of opportunities, challenges, and restraints.

Today, the implementation of a mixed Western strategy toward the East demands the strengthening of both the competitive and the cooperative components of this strategy and the assurance of an optimum of complementarity and coordination of those two components.[1] In this perspective, this chapter considers the needs for and the limitations of innovative processes in the West (and particularly in U.S.-German relations) to improve the given set of procedural and institutional infrastructures. It does not intend to deliver ready-made solutions; rather, it investigates the scope of adaptation that Western political management has to undergo to cope successfully with the challenges of East-West relations.

Competitive Policies and the Scope for Institutional Innovation in the Alliance

Western Military Strength and Reform of NATO

Building a consensus in the alliance today is oriented, first of all, toward the adoption of a mixed strategy toward the USSR and eastern Europe. An indispensable part of this endeavor is the strengthening of Western deterrence. Although this is basically a genuine and traditional task for NATO, it seems that it will not be enough to do business as usual. NATO is confronted with a military challenge, which is perceived to be growing continuously in almost all respects, while the West is faced with an internal process of uncertainty characterized by a wide-ranging shortage of resources and a far-reaching debate over the effectiveness of the current military policy. The agenda includes many profound questions, the answers to which will determine the viability of NATO's doctrines, force structure, and perhaps even the strength of its political foundation for many years to come.[2]

Alliance consultations and the machinery of NATO will have to manage a reconsideration stimulated by the current debate concerning the role of nuclear weapons in NATO's strategy. This reconsideration has already led to a widespread belief that NATO should improve its conventional forces to avoid being faced with a choice between defeat or the early use of nuclear weapons in the case of a Warsaw Pact attack. Even if a substantial conventional reinforcement program were to succeed, planning for NATO's *nuclear* deterrent in the 1980s and 1990s will still be necessary in the future deliberations within the alliance.[3] As NATO is now constituted, European suspicion of American intentions is so active as to subvert the will to resist Soviet pressure. The question being posed indirectly but constantly is: Who is using whom? As an example, many Europeans are convinced that the United States would prefer to see a nuclear war confined to western Europe and that the American commitment to "go the last mile" in nuclear warfare is open to doubt. This is not an unreasonable doubt based on a sensible reading of the American national interest. And it is an ineradicable suspicion given the present structure and strategy of NATO.

Meanwhile, the U.S. Congress, by putting a cap on U.S. force levels in Europe in the fiscal 1983 defense appropriation bill, has already signaled that it is not prepared to expand the commitment of U.S. ground forces to European defense. Great Britain, given its expensive presence in the Falklands, would be fortunate if it succeeded in maintaining the British Army of the Rhine at current levels and capabilities while at the same time modernizing British strategic nuclear forces. French strategy now contemplates the early participation of French forces in response to a Warsaw Pact attack, but Socialist President Mitterrand's government has projected reductions in French conventional forces to permit modernization and expansion of its strategic nuclear forces. Bonn, while clinging to NATO's forward defense, is running into crucial demographic problems that will seriously affect the manpower of the Bundeswehr in the second half of the 1980s. Most of the other European allies are faced with a widening set of difficulties when it comes to holding or increasing their contribution to strengthen NATO's deterrence.

Against this background it will be difficult to manage the introduction of emerging technologies. On the one hand new defense technologies promise to help NATO move away from excessive reliance on nuclear weapons. On the other hand it is largely unclear how public debate should be controlled and who will pay for these systems, which, according to most analysts, are likely to be more expensive than the nuclear weapons they are intended to replace. General Bernard Rogers, NATO's supreme allied commander, has suggested that the allies need to plan 4 percent real growth in defense spending over the next decade to implement a new, less nuclear-reliant strategy. Given the Federal Republic's geographic position and its leading role in providing NATO's conventional forces, whatever strategy NATO may be able to endorse and implement may well depend on what the defense consensus in West Germany will support. Present developments in this respect do not warrant much optimism. There is a growing cleavage between the center-right and the center-left parties combined with some harsh realities of the German economy.

Given these challenges the strengthening of the deterrent function of NATO is likely to become an extremely complicated and difficult task for allied governments. Obviously, to lead the required strategic debate, to work out a reliable conceptual consensus, and to handle the implementation of any slight shift in strategic policy demand a new quality of intra-alliance management. Existing consultative bodies will have to be used more effectively and new coordination devices might be required. Moreover, unlike earlier periods of NATO history, the reestablishment of a broader strategic consensus (on the multilateral as well as on the national level) demands a certain amount of influencing of each other's domestic political processes. This, in turn, is likely to create problems of its own. Yet, these problems may have to be accepted to move NATO in an innovative direction.

Some observers claim that there is almost no hope to save the moribund Atlantic alliance. In fact, in their view the public disillusionment on both sides of the Atlantic is such that a radical reconstruction may be the only way to keep NATO from disintegrating entirely.[4] Henry Kissinger has made far-reaching suggestions: (a) a more important role of Europe within NATO, (b) a reform of NATO's organization, and (c) a consideration of U.S. military forces in Europe.[5]

Nevertheless, NATO does not seem to be that inadequate and closed to evolutionary reform. In recent years important military programs have been implemented, and the NATO apparatus has responded constructively. Short of an arms reduction treaty with the Soviets the deployment of medium-range nuclear weapons in western European countries is, after all, important evidence of the allies' ability to modernize their nuclear arsenal despite a tremendous Soviet propaganda effort to prevent such modernization. A number of other programs have also been introduced to strengthen NATO's military power, examples being the U.S.-

German agreement on wartime host nation support; NATO's infrastructural program; the modernization of NATO's air defense; and the long-term defense program (including the 3 percent pledge). Of course, there are areas and expectations in which NATO should have done better, but this is not to say that the institution itself has worked ineffectively. Rather, it demonstrates that the member governments have failed or were unwilling to either support it or to provide for institutional compensation.

In this respect the Europeans have a regressive record. In the 1950s and 1960s, when Europe had its doubts about the effectiveness of NATO and the credibility of the U.S. guarantee, the obvious reaction was the quest for a European substitute either by developing an independent nuclear capability or by broadening European defense cooperation.[6] Today the French seem to have run out of new models, while the Germans (together with the Italians) are trying solemnly to declare the "European voice in NATO" to be a major step in the European and transatlantic security system. The extent to which the Genscher/Colombo project of a "European Act" was watered down until it was signed in Stuttgart in June 1983, shows the narrowness of these attempts.[7]

However, American initiatives will hardly reach far either. Washington's expectations of a reoriented NATO conceived as a "real alliance," in which the allies would not only contribute more to their own defense, but also take part in a global strategy of containing the Soviets, appear largely unacceptable to today's Europe. In fact, the Reagan administration's visions, with their nostalgic overtones, have practically been rejected by the way Europeans reacted to recent Soviet challenges. There is even a danger of further alienating the Europeans if Washington insists on reinstrumentalizing NATO for all conceivable kinds of security threats.

Yet marginal, albeit significant, institutional changes have taken place and will also be possible in the future. Some changes were introduced when either the Europeans or the Americans wanted them. This was the case with the creation of the Nuclear Planning Group in 1967. It was true also with the establishment a decade later of NATO's High Level and Special Consultative Groups. Moreover, West German foreign minister Genscher's initiative to hold "Gymnich type" meetings of the NATO foreign ministers, which was put into practice in September 1982 with a gathering at La Sapinière, near Ottawa, may also be mentioned to characterize the type of reform the NATO structure allows.[8] In this context the old idea of having NATO foreign ministers meet together with their colleagues from finance, economics, and technology would be an interesting enterprise to try.

Still the overall situation will not change much along with these alterations at the margin. Fundamental questions will continue to arise: What should be the precise mix of defense and détente in East-West relations? Can the doctrine of "flexible response" last? How much East-West economic transaction should there be? How should third world conflicts be handled? The particular challenge of strengthening the West's deterrence capabilities is intrinsically intertwined with the answers to all of these questions and the dilemma seems to be inescapable: NATO, in its current state, is not likely to provide structural solutions and thus may become less relevant. Ways have to be found to break this dilemma, or at least to manage it. Neither the marginal change nor the total rearrangement approach will be an appropriate remedy for NATO's troubles. Required are specific answers to specific deficiencies. Some suggestions for coping with some of these deficiencies are the following:

1. *Rejoin political and military reality.* To guide the political and military activity on the amelioration of NATO's strategic doctrine, the organization needs more joint staffing and ministerial sessions with both foreign and defense ministries involved. The discussion and planning of the technical military aspects, arms control implications, and domestic politics have to be kept abreast. A body like the Nuclear Planning Group, as a defense ministers' group, does not suffice to make decisions on sensitive political issues. Likewise, foreign ministry equivalents like the Special Consultative Group have had problems in synchronizing the technical and political processes.

While amending the doctrine of "flexible response," the alliance has to avoid centrifugal evolutions of the kind that accompanied the transformation of U.S. nuclear doctrine and led to France's dissociation from the military structure of NATO. The experience of the multilateral force (MLF) proposal and the enhanced radiation weapons (ERW) program[9] suggests that the link of technical analysis to political reality should be more thoroughly organized.[10]

2. *Enhance European self-assertiveness.* Despite obvious obstacles the Europeans should make a special effort in order to strengthen NATO's military power. The Eurogroup's report on its members' contribution to the alliance (published in May 1983) was relatively impressive and was recognized as such by the U.S. Defense Department. Meanwhile, the European NATO countries decided to develop the Eurogroup to become an important forum to secure European defense interests. However, there is still a long way from declaration to substance. More political claims have been made in the European public recently with regard to a European Defense Community, a European Arms Procurement Agency, a vitalization of the West European Union (WEU), and an instrumentalization of the Independent European Program Group (IEPG). Most of these initiatives create a large amount of political irritation while remaining modest as to their practical use to strengthen the West's military potential. There is a danger of blurring the real situation and of mistaking wishes for results already achieved. This relates particularly to the plans of strengthening the "second pillar of the alliance" by way of the WEU, an initiative that was launched in October 1984 by a joint meeting of the seven member states' foreign and defense ministers.

On the bilateral level the Franco-German decision to enhance military cooperation is a more constructive although limited attempt to cope with specific challenges in the European theater. Although this initiative of Helmut Kohl and François Mitterrand relies on a hitherto unapplied clause in the Franco-German Friendship Treaty of 1963, a wide range of new management problems will have to be solved. Particularly sensitive are two adaptations: the operational link of the upcoming Force d'Action Rapide with existing NATO infrastructure in peacetime, and the political link between the new Franco-German activities and the wider alliance circle.[11]

3. *Link European and American decision-making processes.* Existing arrangements provided Europeans and Americans with a reasonable guarantee that their mutual interests would be taken into account. Upcoming major decisions on policies to counter Soviet military challenges will demand a closer coordination of Western decision-making processes and a more independent assessment capability on the NATO level. An assessment body could be attached to the secretary general. It might consist of military and nonmilitary senior experts and would be designed to make European NATO members feel less dependent on U.S. assessment, especially in nuclear matters.

The alliance should also allow for further involvement of the Europeans in decision making on nuclear policy in ways that reflect their increasing stakes but do not strain their domestic politics. One proposal is to revitalize the pre-1966 NATO Standing Group in Washington for this purpose.[12] The group would consist of the representatives of the military chiefs of staff of the major NATO countries and would make sure that crucial nuclear decision processes would be "multilateralized" as early as possible.

One of the most striking deficiencies of NATO is the fact that since its foundation "no system of collective decision-making that would stand the test of a major world or European crisis" has been developed,[13] although it has been obvious that the Soviet Union would prefer to create and exploit crises rather than wage war. To cope with this weakness a "Crisis and Defense Cabinet" has been suggested "which assembles in Washington as soon as one of its members feels that European influence on the course of a crisis is waning and that the North Atlantic Council cannot keep pace with accelerating politico-military developments."[14] This cabinet should be composed of national representatives (vice prime ministers) of Great Britain, Germany, France, and Italy, and all other NATO nations would be represented by the secretary general of NATO. As in the case of the Western Economic Summits, in which the president of the Commission of the European Community (EC) is "representing" the nonparticipating members, this arrangement will certainly meet some of the criticism that other suggestions of the kind have received in the past.[15] Moreover, the proposition to establish this body in Washington would enable participants to have more immediate access to the U.S. political-military headquarters and decision-making processes.

These suggestions for institutional innovation are aimed neither at a replacement nor at a circumvention of NATO. They should ameliorate and complement its traditional function. The goal is the amelioration of NATO's traditional role of deterring Soviet military power. However, given Moscow's increasing ability for worldwide power projection, institutional reform in the Western alliance will have to go beyond the immediate NATO structure and take other networks of Western security management into consideration.

The "Principal Nations" Approach to Geostrategic Challenges

How to interpret and deal with threats to Western security arising outside of NATO's boundaries has been one of the most difficult issues for the alliance in recent years. It is not only the U.S.-European divergencies over how to contain the Soviets globally that cause major management problems among the allies, but also the objective difficulty in areas of common understanding to provide for the required capability and to balance Soviet geostrategic gains. Thus the challenge of the years ahead will be to improve projection capabilities on both sides of the Atlantic and to pool these in a more efficient way than in the past.

In the history of the alliance no serious attempts have been made to design and implement a Western containment policy, or even to coordinate (other than on an ad hoc basis) the military, diplomatic, and economic instruments of individual nations. While Washington and, to a certain extent, Paris and London, have repeatedly shown their geostrategic flags, the Federal Republic has not been at the forefront of recognizing this part of the global power balance. Bonn was not excluded but has been reluctant and tried to compensate in other ways. This reluctance to get involved in military action and global strategic deterrence is basically caused by historic and psychological reasons. The Federal Republic has become used to living under a number of constraints that legally and politically limit more deliberate activity. Given the extended challenge of Soviet global power and the increasing German as well as overall Western interests at stake, it may well be necessary for future governments in Bonn to reconsider some of these constraints.[16]

Considerations on strengthening NATO's geostrategic outlook and performance have been made periodically: in the Three Wise Men's Report of 1956, in the Harmel Report on Future Tasks of 1967, in the Ottawa Declaration on Atlantic Relations of 1974, in the Report on East-West Relations of 1978, and in a great many more recent statements. All of these demonstrate that in the given state NATO will not be able to counter threats from outside the treaty area on the basis of common plans or even joint operations.[17] Nevertheless, efforts have been made to enhance the potential role of major allies in out-of-area contingencies.

Certainly, consultations can take place in Brussels or in any of the allied capitals about any given threat. The Atlantic Policy Advisory Group (APAG) has been active in the late 1970s. Experts in NATO have met twice a year since the early 1960s to examine all the regions of the world. The North Atlantic Council and the Defense Planning Committee (DPC) have discussed and analyzed requirements and events on a global scale. Assessments of this kind are important but inadequate. Decisive is the quality of consultations that include (a) exchange of information, (b) consultation about national action, (c) consultation with a view to parallel national actions, and (d) consultations with a view to collective action.[18] NATO has practiced much of (a) and (b) but needs to proceed to stage (c) as long as (d) remains unachievable or unadvisable.[19]

A second approach worth considering is a closer coordination of U.S. and western European policies outside the NATO institutions. In this respect the European Political Cooperation (EPC) should be used more actively as a co-actor to Washington's geostrategic policies. EPC has no military arm but is coordinating a growing part of those nonmilitary instruments that the Europeans can provide to strengthen the geostrategic position of the West. The imposition of embargos connected with the conflicts in Iran, the Falklands, and Poland have been monitored through cooperation among the ten member states of the EC, interconnected with and accompanied by measures of the EC proper. It is a routine by now that EPC will back up or accompany action of some of its members during conflicts in regions of the third world, prominent examples being the support of Great Britain's answer to the Argentinian invasion of the Falklands, the encouragement for the four European participants in the Sinai and Lebanon peace-keeping forces, and the backing for the European members in the Namibia Contact Group. In sum, the Europeans are in a process to develop a certain capacity of their own to manage third world security.

These activities are an important element of a wider U.S.-European security consensus. It seems, however, that neither Washington nor the Europeans have yet addressed the central implications of this process. One of the crucial questions both sides will have to answer is whether this particular type of consultations will continue to grow, and if so, whether this growth will contribute to existing divergencies in the alliance or rather help to overcome them and open a new field of transatlantic understanding. The Gymnich agreement of June 1974, which suggested a pragmatic concertation between U.S. diplomacy and EPC, will have to be taken a step further toward a more structured liaison of the two decision-making settings.

A third approach to Western management of geostrategic response does not engage NATO or the EC/EPC as such, but those allies who are interested and able to contribute. This circle of "principal nations" should be organized on the assumption that the participating countries are ready to take over specific responsibilities.[20] It would be a standing group for as long as a specific challenge exists. Examples are the four-power working group on Berlin, the Multilateral Force and Observers (MFO) in the Lebanon conflict, and the Namibia Contact Group, which have quite a mixed record, but they demonstrate the particular concern and the converging interest of some of the Western allies. These types of key-country operations should be extended in a reasonable way. Although the countries concerned would continue to operate independently, they would not exclude links to the wider European or Atlantic settings.

None of the three approaches presented is totally new. The experience in recent years with these models leads to the recommendation to favor the "principal nations" approach as the main mechanism to assure a better Western performance on the geostrategic level. NATO does not become obsolete in this regard, but changes its function. It will be more of a backup than a central actor. The same is true for the diplomatic transatlantic "axis." It will have to assure the wider intergovernmental consultations. This still leaves many questions open, one of them being the problem as to how to bring about public support for a relatively loosely constructed system of Western geostrategy.

To strengthen the competitive instruments of the West vis-à-vis the Soviet Union demands both innovation within NATO to keep a convincing level of military deterrence and improvement of the capabilities for the geostrategic and regional challenges. The first task requires adaptation of a traditional apparatus to new challenges, and the second asks for the transformation of a diverse set of procedures into a more reliable cooperative system. Both adaptations are linked to each other.

Cooperative Policies and the Requirement of German-American Policy Coordination

EPC and East-West Cooperation

To make a mixed strategy work, the West has not only to strengthen its military power and its geostrategic position, but also to coordinate its cooperative policies toward the USSR and eastern Europe. Since mid-1960 various instruments (political dialogue, arms control, and selective accommodation) have tried to shape the political contact with the East, and trade has been used to build up cooperative relationships. However, the West has had major difficulties implementing consistent policies, let alone achieving its objectives and bringing about change.

The rules and the machinery for coordinated Western action, although fairly well developed, do not seem to form a coherent set of policymaking. Contrary to the field of military deterrence, in which the allies started off with a treaty and an organization, cooperative policy was planted into the existing NATO texture or had to develop its procedural and institutional setup along with ad hoc challenges. The cooperative side of the mixed strategy was and still is not fully integrated into the management of alliance policy toward the East. This may become a heavy burden given the complexity and uncertainty of a cooperation policy and the particular diversities among the allies in this regard.[21]

Since the 1970s institutional innovation has been more dynamic in Europe than in the Atlantic setting. This process has obvious limits but is likely to continue gradually for a while.[22] As a major example, political cooperation among the member states of the EC has become a vital element in the formation of European foreign and, in some respects, security policies. Progress toward greater monetary and economic integration in western Europe has been slowed down by the current recession, but EPC has continued to develop. The consultations among the Ten now interfere in the national decision-making process on a regular and routine basis, sometimes having an important influence. Even in cases in which there is not a common European policy on the record, there is increasingly a pool of parallel national policies that provide the potential for common positions when the occasion arises.[23]

The Federal Republic was among those European states that tried to make EPC a more efficient tool for pooling and pursuing common foreign policies. Bonn and London pushed EPC to become a crisis management instrument. Bonn and Rome showed particular interest in including political and economic aspects of security into the EPC process. But it was the demand from third world countries that stimulated EPC to embark on regular political consultations with a number of important countries, including Turkey and Norway, Japan and the ASEAN group, and

China. The consultations are not supposed to deal with military security issues. In reality EPC has gradually moved further into the gray area between foreign and security policy, including a large part of East-West relations, albeit limited by the nonparticipation of defense ministers.

Although this evolution is basically a good thing, there is a dangerous distortion in these developments that stems from an overemphasis on cooperative policies and a quasi-exclusion of competitive policies. EPC has a decisive share in running the European side of the Conference on Security and Cooperation (CSCE) process. It is fascinating to see how much the institutional development of EPC and the conduct of détente and arms control policies are intertwined and how much they mutually support one another. (The EC, too, has an inclination to favor cooperative policies.) Thus, as western Europe is particularly dealing with the cooperative side of the mixed relationship with the USSR and developing its identity there while referring the hard-core military deterrence to NATO, any Western mixed strategy will be influenced by this institutional cleavage.[24] EPC is not creating an alternative to NATO, but it is undoubtedly the central catalyst for a gradual transformation of NATO[25] and for a rearrangement of European-American relations. But is this the kind of Europeanization of the Atlantic alliance one should encourage?[26]

The Europeans have developed or preserved institutional autonomy in areas that are not fully integrated into the collective security system of NATO: out-of-area geostrategic competition, political dialogue, and trade with the USSR and eastern Europe. Although this may be a natural evolution, it has led to a compartmentalization of Western policymaking processes that has to be recognized as a crucial structural deficiency. The task, therefore, is to develop the appropriate link between the NATO structure and the other institutional bodies that emerged around it.

Shaping Economic East-West Relations: COCOM as a Test

Although trade with the USSR and eastern European countries has always contained an element of controversy among Western allies, the years 1980 to 1982 saw specifically serious intra-alliance divergencies and the spillover of these divergencies into Western security issues. Measures intended to have an impact on Soviet behavior turned out to do more political and economic damage to the West than harm to the East.[27] This kind of experience is just too costly to be repeated, especially at times of major economic recession and of shaky strategic consensus among the allies. Rather, one should consider ways and means to hamper the escalation of such controversy in the future and to conceive of a damage-limiting procedure.

Elements of such an approach were displayed after the controversies and misunderstandings during the summer of 1982. A group of major Western allies initiated a number of studies on questions of East-West trade in general and the Yamal pipeline deal in particular and asked various Western institutions, including the Organization for Economic Cooperation and Development (OECD), IEA, Coordinating Committee for Export to Communist Areas (COCOM), and NATO, to produce factual data and joint assessment. Moreover, at the Williamsburg summit, Western leaders took the issue of East-West trade out of the spotlight and thus contributed to bringing the controversy down to a manageable level.[28] Washington and Bonn are particularly interested and uniquely suited to develop such escalation control procedures further and to add an early-warning system. The mechanism is to make sure that issues of East-West trade do not produce a psychological overload among the allies and upset Western priorities.

A damage-limiting device is, by definition, unable to overcome underlying structural problems. Today most of the recent problems seem to be shelved rather than solved.[29] This is true for the following two issues, which need to be treated more attentively in the future.

1. *Conflict between economics and security.* Because the experts of trade and defense matters normally remain in their realm, the alliance has to conceive of ways to bring an adequate security awareness to economic institutions like OECD and the appropriate economic assessment to NATO. The question is, how and where to integrate the two issue areas more efficiently

in order to deal with their overlap. This overlap occurs primarily in two ways. The first is in the context of an economic denial strategy of the West, which attempts to restrain Western countries from helping the USSR to facilitate its military buildup The second is part of the cooperation strategy of Western countries, which uses economic exchange as a means for building up relationships with the Soviet Union and eastern Europe. Because both strategies 'are, to a certain extent, mutually exclusive and differently favored by the United States and most of its western European allies, there is a major management problem to be solved.

2. *Unilateralism versus multilateralism.* Unlike defense policy, trade with Eastern state economies has basically been a bilateral affair. Historic reasons and economic rationale seemed to exclude institutionalization beyond selective gentlemen's agreements among the allies. Recent experience, however, demands a reconsideration. Given the strategic importance of economic transfers to the Soviet Union and the divergent views on this matter among the allies, one has to ask whether and to what extent the West can continue to afford such economic individualism, and whether a more comprehensive cartel is indispensable to effectively shape security-related trade relations with the Soviet Union and eastern Europe. This question must be of interest to protagonists of both major persuasions, i.e., those who favor a denial strategy *and* those who are stressing cooperative policies. In either case a certain amount of Western commonality is needed to reach the political goal behind the economic strategy. And more important, in both cases a high level of economic East-West exchange has to be achieved before it can be instrumentalized, as a carrot or as a stick.

These management problems are fundamental. They will remain on the agenda until innovation brings about the necessary changes within the alliance and its institutional machinery. A number of adaptations are under way, but the obstacles are many and deeply rooted.

To organize foreign trade collectively is running counter to the philosophy of liberal economies, even if they belong to a collective security system. The case is different with the EC, whose member countries are endeavoring to achieve gradual political integration. These and other reflections have induced some defense analysts to propose bringing NATO and the EC closer together and finally merge their functions and responsibilities.[30] But in contrast to NATO, neither the EC nor the OECD has ever had its central focus specifically on the Soviet Union or on security threats in general. Rather, EC and OECD have tried to organize and support economic exchanges among the small but, in terms of economic power, strong groups of countries in the West and to develop their relations with the large number of third world countries. Thus these organizations have contributed mainly to the well-being of Western industrialized economies. They may in this sense be seen as among the most efficient multilateral devices to strengthen the West's position in what may be termed the "indirect competition" with the Soviet Union. Although it is not an easy task to evaluate their implicit contribution to Western assets in the East-West rivalry, this side of their record should not be underrated.

But beyond that the EC has had a certain role in Western consensus building for East-West trade. Although it is one of the areas that is the least "Europeanized," the Ten have built up some potential for coordination. Thus it was a political decision of this grouping not to establish mutual EC-Comecon relations between the two organizations, but to develop special trade and financial relations with individual eastern European countries on a contractual basis. The EC is certainly one of the Western instruments to reach these countries, especially if initiatives are combined with approaches on the wider Western level. The successful coordination of Western positions during the CSCE process (especially concerning the subjects of Basket II) provides an interesting model of alliance consensus building by combining EC and NATO experts. This model should be developed and applied more widely, also beyond the specific CSCE context.

To a certain extent OECD has been instrumentalized already for backing up Western security interests, examples being a certain tradition to regulate credit conditions vis-à-vis Eastern countries on the basis of a gentlemen's agreement, and the establishment of the International Energy Agency (IEA) in the mid-1970s to provide the West with an energy safety net. It is not likely that in the field of energy security the IEA members will be able in the next few years to elaborate substantially the existing emergency mechanisms. The IEA is used effectively in two directions: (1) to encourage a better prospecting and exploitation of energy resources as an alternative to Soviet energy supply, and (2) to make better use of its apparatus in collecting information that would lead to more transparency concerning the question of "dependence" on Soviet resources. Despite the present relative oil and energy glut, it is important to keep up this activity and to get Western governments more used to taking into account the results of the agency.

Energy supply was at the heart of many of the intra-alliance quarrels in recent years. Technology transfer is probably going to become the next subject of controversy. In this respect OECD could be the best place to "institutionalize" Western study and discussion of East-West economics. It is NATO's duty, however, to set guidelines as to what kind of trade policy with the Soviet Union and eastern Europe would be most compatible with alliance security. Most U.S. allies (including France) have no difficulty in elaborating common studies, but they clearly want to make policy individually. There is no enthusiasm among the allies for those plans in Washington that intend to develop a broad common doctrine on East-West transactions and to use NATO as the permanent place for coordination of security-related economic policies. Likewise, an alliance policy, or even enforcement mechanism, on export subsidies and the level and conditions of credit has a slim chance of succeeding given the divergence of national practices and interests.

The only other forum in which things might really move is COCOM, although it remains unclear with what speed and in what direction. None of the allied countries ever disputed the necessity to deny to the Soviet Union and its clients such products as have direct military implications. That is why there have not been cases of disregard of COCOM norms, although there is no official agreement and no parliamentary control that would strengthen the common rules. The main problem, however, arises for other technology transfers of strategic importance.

Washington has always had tighter procedures concerning these technologies than other participants of COCOM. The Europeans, for practical economic and political reasons, have difficulty accepting Washington's "critical technology" approach, which the United States introduced into COCOM. This notion refers to dual use and to "future technology," which tend to cover a wide range of products.

Here again the underlying conceptual differences between U.S. and western European positions are structuring the debate. The Reagan administration, for a while, seemed to be interested in a transfer policy that came close to a trade war. However, there were substantial differences between the various departments involved: Commerce, Defense, State.[31] An additional problem is the fact that there is no central agency in the U.S. government to coordinate policies for "strategic" trade. Maybe the revision of the Export Administration Act, which was due in September 1984, will lend more clarification to the issue.

The Europeans, while accepting that the embargo lists of COCOM have to be adapted to changed conditions, have expressed their interest in continuing and developing economic exchanges with the Eastern countries. They need a legitimated area of trade that guarantees continuity. The Federal Republic, therefore, is interested in a clear separation of "critical" and "noncritical" technologies.[32] In Bonn, too, interadministrative divergencies are relevant. It was probably not the best solution to have the COCOM responsibility—in the German case— centered in the Ministry of Economics. Moreover, the recent (1983) establishment of a special desk for COCOM questions within this ministry seems almost like a preemption of any initiative that might have shifted the responsibility for technology transfer to either the foreign affairs or the defense ministry. An interministerial committee would probably be the most adequate solution.

Given the different starting points and objectives for East-West trade and the obvious need for more institutional clarification, the United States and its allies have to look for solutions that—as compared with the "Suppliers Club"—combine practicability with reconciliation of interests. A "Technology Transfer Club" will almost certainly be overloaded with wider political implications of its increasingly technical work. Both the growing strategic importance as well as the confidential and sensitive character of most of the modern technology items demand more sophisticated procedures to handle them adequately. However, bureaucratic deficiencies and political divergencies are most likely to hamper a quick institutional reform of COCOM. The domestic lobbies—businessmen as well as trade unionists—are part of this predicament. Thus the reform of COCOM may well be a test of the reform of the Atlantic alliance at large.[33] It seems that policymakers in Washington are more aware of this than their European counterparts. The Europeans should shape up and contribute to a joint Western solution of a common problem.

Implementing Comprehensive Strategy

Although considerable but different efforts are necessary to strengthen the West's cooperative as well as competitive policies, it will be even more difficult to combine the two in order to realize a comprehensive mixed strategy. Since the Nixon-Kissinger concept of a "strategy for peace" the attempts to cope with the USSR in a complex manner have gradually declined and the consensus on a joint Western strategy, which was lost during the Carter and early Reagan years, has not yet been regained. "In the winter of 1983–84, there is no such strategy."[34]

James Thomson has displayed the scope of commonality as well as of diversity that exists among Western allies and particularly between the United States and the Federal Republic of Germany.[35] After years of experience and debate it is time to sit down and develop the elements of a comprehensive strategy that combines and orchestrates the employment of possibly all the instruments available to the West in its relations with the East. An intellectual task force like those in 1956 and 1967 could help with this enterprise.[36]

The strategy of mixing both competitive and cooperative elements was estabished in principle in the Harmel report and continues to be valid. What is needed at this juncture is a dual evolution of this concept. First, it should be adapted to the current strategic circumstances in order to incorporate new areas and challenges of East-West relations. Second, it should give some guidance as to how various components and actors of Western policy would have to be reconciled in a coordinated or common approach. A new doctrine is not required, but rather a conceptual platform that the allies can draw on to shape their future policy toward the East.

Such a platform should also address the most pressing structural and organizational questions that need to be answered in order to assure the implementation of a reconsidered strategy. Among the structural problems the inability of the Atlantic allies to accomplish an effective strategy over a protracted period is particularly severe. Most of the preservation and change goals, let alone the objective of stability in East-West relations, can be approached only by a steady and coherent policy. Such a policy is hard to achieve given the kind and the frequency of change in government in Western democracies. The rhythm and sequence of campaigning, presidential elections, midterm elections, and preparation for yet the next campaign lead to a kind of built-in oscillation in U.S. foreign policy. This certainly does affect the possibility of U.S.-German coordination in East-West relations.

Moreover, there is a strong pressure for short-term management on the U.S. side, whereas German governments tend to stress the importance of long-term solutions, the predictability of attitudes, and the reliability of negotiations and contracts as stabilizing elements in East-West relations. While a new American administration tries to convince Bonn and its other allies as quickly as it can of the benefit of any new foreign policy course, the allies mostly stress continuity and want to wait until a U.S. president has gradually left the heights of campaign rhetoric to come down to the lower ground of practical policy.

Anyway, these cyclical moves have to be studied carefully when it comes to the design of a longer-term strategy vis-à-vis the Soviets. Reflections in the United States should be oriented toward the development of more bipartisan backing for foreign policy. Other considerations should focus on those multilateral Western bodies that deal with East-West relations. These bodies would have to be strengthened, as they seem to have a built-in tendency for less radical shifts given their more permanent staff and their mixture of various national stands.

The second structural problem to address is the compatibility of competitive and cooperative policies. Although successful policy does not exclude dialectic approaches, major problems will normally arise if policies are running against one another. Such conflicts have to be dealt with more extensively in order to develop better damage-limitation devices and to defuse underlying discrepancies. In some cases it may be necessary to agree to disagree. However, this should not be made a rule among Western policymakers because it could become an easy way out and would reduce pressure to work on a compromise.

The organizational problems, too, would grow with a wider, more consistent Western strategy. They would emerge on the bilateral as well as on the multilateral level. In this regard significant changes are under way on both sides of the Atlantic. While the respective embassies, the German and central European desk at the State Department as well as the U.S. desk of the Auswärtiges Amt, continue to provide a substantial part of the day-to-day work of U.S.-German relations, there is a growing community of personalities, specialized bodies, and agencies on both sides that participate in shaping the bilateral contacts. Several ministries, especially defense, commerce, and treasury, claim a right of their own to deal with East-West relations. This tendency in both the U.S. and Federal Republic administrations mirrors the increased variety and complexity of jointly treated issues and the attempt to adapt the policymaking processes accordingly, but it leads also to a compartmentalization of complex issues.

In an ever more specific dialogue the positions and functions of the participants become more and more incongruent because the policymaking processes in Washington and Bonn are not structured along the same lines. The traditional, official consultation channels remain important. But new *informal* ways to communicate are on the rise: dispatch of personal advisers, special envoys, and personalities of confidence.[37] Although these "bypasses" of the classic power lines provide an alternative way to promote important and sensitive issues, they certainly enhance frustration among diplomats and desk officers. Decisions and communications, as a consequence, are likely to become characterized by bureaucratic infights.

The proliferation of actors and the broadening of U.S.-German communication meet, in principle, the organizational requirement of a complex policy toward the Soviet Union. These developments, however, have to be paralleled by an adequate measure of guidance and coordination. As the United States and the Federal Republic are crucial to the building of a Western consensus, so the cohesiveness and the scope of their dialogue is crucial for the implementation of a comprehensive strategy.

Although the U.S.-German "two-ism" is vital for the continuity as well as innovation of policy in the alliance and beyond, the tandem can achieve its goals only in a multilateral setting. For West Germans this has been a constant imperative no matter whether East-West relations were in a cold war period or in a phase of building relations with the East. Although NATO continues to be the central organization to cover Western security needs, other multilateral forums increasingly will have to complement it. This refers to OECD, COCOM, the principal-nations groups, and the various western European institutions. Within each of these organizations and among them policymaking should be organized in such a way as to enable a more effective coordination of competitive and cooperative policies.

Exactly how the various instruments and policies are to be combined depends on the specific choice of strategy. This choice, however, is limited to the extent that certain combinations of policies and instruments are either blocked or poorly organized: Skillful management of the heterogeneous and compartmentalized Western institutional setup would provide the West with a wider variety of options to deal with the East. At present, the Western summit is the only body to achieve such overall coordination of Western policies.

In this perspective the Summit of the Seven might enlarge its horizons to embrace a wider range of security questions. In fact, this enlargement has been evident from Venice, in 1980, to Williamsburg, in 1983. But a meeting of heads of state, by its very nature, cannot engage in the detailed short-term work that is required to render policy concepts operable. The summit group can only point in directions generally agreed on, with the detailed work to be done elsewhere.

The West would, however, overexert itself if it were to attempt to integrate all activities concerning the East in one common scheme. It would be useful, on the other hand, to reduce some of the most striking compartmentalizations: the division between NATO and EC/OECD, the insufficient link between EPC and U.S. diplomacy, and the almost complete absence of Japan in the central Western bodies that deal with East-West relations.[38] There has been only limited experience in connecting the Atlantic and the Pacific alliances. But this task will certainly become more pressing in the future. Redefinition of German-American or European-American policy toward the Soviet Union would produce parochial results if it disregarded this dimension.

Notes

1. See Chapter 11.

2. For a fuller treatment of this assessment see Chapter 8.

3. James A. Thomson, "Nuclear Weapons in Europe: Planning for NATO's Nuclear Deterrent in the 1980's and 1990's," *Survival* 25, no. 3 (May/June 1983): 98–109.

4. From the many voices that have expressed pessimism on the fate of the alliance, three may be mentioned: Irving Kristol, "What's Wrong with NATO?" *The New York Times Magazine* 26 (25 Sept. 1983): 64–71; Stanley Kober, "Can NATO Survive?" *International Affairs* 59:3 (Summer 1983): 339–363; Pierre Lellouche, "Does NATO Have a Future?" in *The Atlantic Alliance and Its Critics,* ed. Robert W. Tucker and Linda Wrigley (New York: Praeger, 1983), 129–154.

5. Henry Kissinger, "Plan to Reshape NATO," *Time,* 5 March 1984, 16.

6. See the French-German talks between 1958 and 1963 as well as the Fouchet plans.

7. The Preamble of the "European Act" mentions that "the security of Europe must also be guaranteed by joint action in the field of security policy which, at the same time, helps to maintain the common security of the partners in the Atlantic Alliance." Cited in Joseph H. H. Weiler, "The Genscher-Colombo Draft European Act: The Politics of Indecision," *Revue d'intégration européenne/Journal of European Integration* 6, nos. 2–3 (1983): 129–153.

8. Gymnich meetings are informal gatherings of either the heads of state or foreign ministers without their staffs. This is supposed to help with bringing about consensus in the official multilateral institutions. The European Community has made "Gymnichs" a habit since the mid-seventies. The name derives from Schloss Gymnich, near Bonn, where the first of this kind of meetings took place.

9. MLF was supposed to be a military solution to a political problem but was unconvincing on military as well as political grounds. The ERW (between 1974 and 1977) proceeded easily through the alliance negotiations at the technical level, but there was no special body in NATO that served to provide early warning of the possible political impact or pressed the issue on political leaders of allied governments.

10. Some recommendations along these lines are made by Gregory F. Treverton, "Managing NATO's Nuclear Dilemma," *International Security* 7, no. 4 (Spring 1983): 93–116.

11. Konrad Seitz, "Deutsch-französische sicherheitspolitische Zusammenarbeit," *Europa-Archiv* 37, no. 22 (Nov. 1982): 657–664.

12. Treverton, "Managing NATO's Nuclear Dilemma," 114.

13. This assessment of many years ago still holds for today. See Alastair Buchan, *Crisis Management—The New Diplomacy,* The Atlantic Paper NATO Series II (London, 1966), 46.

14. Gerd Schmückle, *Crisis Management in an Alliance of Sovereign States,* Woodrow Wilson Center, No. 63 (Washington, D.C., 1982).

15. For a discussion of alternative organization schemes to cope with third world security see Derek C. Arnould, "The Institutional Implications of NATO in a Global Milieu," in *The Future of European Alliance Systems,* ed. Arlene Idol Broadhurst (Boulder, Colo.: Westview Press, 1982), 121.

16. While NATO's basic strategic document recognizes the importance of out-of-area threats, West Germany was not only constrained by politics and history but by the defense requirements at NATO's central front. For the difficulties of such a reconsideration see Chapter 1 and Reinhardt Rummel and Wolfgang Wessels, "Federal Republic of

Germany: New Responsibilities, Old Constraints," in *National Foreign Policies and European Political Cooperation*, ed. Christopher Hill (Winchester, Mass.: Allen & Unwin, 1983), 34–55.

17. In the communiqué of the Rome ministerial meeting in April 1981, the foreign ministers of the NATO members discussed the problem at length again. Paragraph 7 of the communiqué is a departure in many ways from the traditional outlook of the allies, and its implications for the future are well worth examining. The main theme of this new language is the assertion that the individual NATO members are prepared not to allow membership in NATO to hamper their efforts to ensure their security interests in areas not covered by the treaty or their adherence to defense arrangements not envisaged in the treaty. This new philosophy leaves a wide range of political and organizational alternatives open.

18. Harlan Cleveland, *NATO: The Transatlantic Bargain* (New York: Harper & Row, 1970), 22.

19. Johan J. Holst, "NATO and the Wider World: Strategic Interests and Domestic Constraints" (Paper presented at the Conference on European Defense Perspectives, Sandia National Laboratories, Livermore, California, 16–19 May 1982), Norsk Utenrikspolitisk Institutt, Notat No. 252, Oslo, 1982.

20. Karl Kaiser, Winston Lord, Thierry de Montbrial, and David Watt, "Western Security: What Has Changed? What Should Be Done?" Report prepared jointly by the Forschungsinstitut der Deutschen Gesellschaft für Auswärtige Politik, the Council on Foreign Relations, the Institut Français des Relations Internationales, and the Royal Institute of International Affairs, 1981.

21. Werner Link, "Entspannungspolitik—Bewährungsprobe westlicher Zusammenarbeit," *Aus Politik und Zeitgeschichte* 37/79 (15 Sept. 1979): 3–18.

22. The German initiative is part of a broader approach that was launched by the European Parliament. Report drawn up by Niels Haagerup on behalf of the Political Affairs Committee on European Political Cooperation and European Security, Working Documents of the European Parliament, 3 Dec. 1982.

23. David Allen, Reinhardt Rummel, and Wolfgang Wessels, eds., *European Political Cooperation* (Guildford, UK: Butterworth, 1982).

24. S. I. P. van Campen, "NATO Political Consultation and European Political Cooperation," in Frans A. M. Alting von Geusau, *Allies in a Turbulent World* (Lexington, Mass.: Lexington Books, 1982), 63–74.

25. Pierre Lellouche, "The Transformation of NATO: Parallel European Cooperation," in *Future of European Alliance Systems,* 87.

26. Laurence Radway, "Towards the Europeanisation of NATO," *Atlantic Quarterly* 1, no. 2 (Summer 1983): 129–148.

27. For a wider treatment of these policies, their objectives, and consequences, see Abraham S. Becker's chapter in this volume (Chapter 7).

28. "East-West economic relations should be compatible with our security interests. We take note with approval of the work of the multilateral organizations which have in recent months analyzed and drawn conclusions regarding the key aspects of East-West economic relations. We encourage continuing work by these organizations as appropriate." (From the Williamsburg Economic Summit communiqué.)

29. Stephen Woolcock, "East-West Trade After Williamsburg: An Issue Shelved but not Solved," *The World Today* 39, nos. 7/8 (July/August 1983): 291.

30. Nils Orvik, "NATO and the European Community: Merging Functions and Responsibilities?" in *The European Community at the Crossroads,* ed. Nils Ørvik and Charles Pentland, Canada-Europe Series No. 1/83, Center for International Relations, Queen's University, Kingston, Ontario, 1983, 228.

31. In the fall of 1983 a dispute within the U.S. COCOM negotiating team broke into public warfare. It was a dispute between the hardliners, led by assistant Defense secretary Richard N. Perle and assistant Commerce secretary Lawrence J. Brady on the one hand, and the moderates, in this case led by William A. Root, director of the State Department's East-West trade office, on the other.

32. Moreover, the Germans, as well as their western European neighbors, will object to any attempt of the U.S. administration to introduce, through the rules of the Export Administration Act, a regime of restrictions that in fact goes beyond the CoCom arrangements.

33. "CoCom, a Test of the Health of the Atlantic Alliance," *National Journal,* 19 Nov. 1983, 2407.

34. William G. Hyland gave this assessment in the context of the December 1983 Conference on the Future of the Western Alliance held in Brussels under the auspices of the Center for Strategic and International Studies of Georgetown University. See the report on the conference by Joseph Godson, "The Year After: NATO's Post-Euromissile Strategy," *IHT,* 10 Jan. 1984, 4.

35. See Chapter 11 of this volume.

36. Such a "group of wise men" was proposed by Henry Kissinger and supported by Helmut Schmidt early in 1984.

37. These "bypasses" seem to be more typical for Washington's diplomacy than for Bonn's. Outstanding are the Bahr-Kissinger meetings on Ostpolitik in the early 1970s and Vice-President Bush's tour of Europe in quest for support of President Reagan's arms control and Central American policies.

38. Particularly underdeveloped are the relations between Japan and the western Europeans, while an increasingly strong case can be made for building up a strategic cooperation between them. See the plea of Masashi Nishihara, "Promoting Partnership: Japan and Europe." *The Washington Quarterly* 6, no. 1 (Winter 1983): 107.

Chapter 10

The Enduring Competition with the Soviet Union: Western Political Strategy Reconsidered

Uwe Nerlich

In the early 1980s the Atlantic alliance has gone through unprecedented political turmoil. The political impact of Suez in 1956 or of the Vietnam War may have been more lasting. However, the alliance has never before faced a situation in which polarization within and between most member countries has so jeopardized alliance cohesion. The most crucial relationship on which the political rationale for the Atlantic alliance has depended ever since the 1950s was the one to suffer most badly: that between the United States and West Germany.

Changing Patterns of U.S.-West German Divergencies

How to deal with the Soviet Union has undoubtedly been at the core of the controversy between the United States and West Germany. As in earlier instances this controversy was stirred by Soviet initiatives and the need for the West to respond. But the pattern was different. U.S. policies in response to Soviet action in Berlin and Cuba in the early 1960s induced profound West German concerns over superpower bilateralism at western Europe's expense and the risk of a "collapse of American support for practically all [the Federal Republic's] major premises on East-West agreements."[1] U.S. policies during the Vietnam War triggered in West Germany not only public outrage, but also sharp opposition to the diversion of American military forces from Europe, which reflected more profound policy changes and oddly reinforced superpower bilateralism.[2]

The most recent controversy, although increasingly fore-shadowed by events throughout the 1970s, broke into the open over two crises: how to deal with overt Soviet aggression in Afghanistan and how to cope with suppression in Poland. At this stage, however, the controversy arose over whether the western Europeans should support the instant and tough U.S. responses that were conceived in terms of U.S. global policy or whether the United States was endangering the political stability of what was understood to be a kind of islandized Europe.

In earlier crises the United States appeared to disregard European security diplomacy or NATO's strategic requirements; it had become fatigued with its entanglement in a stalemated European situation and frustrated over what it regarded as West German unwillingness to implement the emerging new military strategy of flexible response. In the early 1980s the United States was widely perceived as obstructing European diplomacy, despite the fact that a decoupling of the United States from European diplomacy would reduce whatever political leverage West Germany possessed. Conversely, in the United States, West German reluctance to join a renewed American containment effort was widely considered as either disinterest in self-defense or a presumption that the United States had no choice but to defend western Europe.

Almost as a rule, major frictions within the alliance have occurred as a result of East-West crises that resulted from Soviet actions. However, earlier cases displayed an increasing disentanglement of the United States from the narrow framework of European security diplomacy and the rise to a superpower status that forced an open-ended competition with the Soviet nuclear rival power. Moreover, each crisis was accompanied or followed by an American policy of accommodation with the USSR that was viewed with anxieties by western Europeans, particularly West Germans.

The recent crises are distinctly different. Given the widening context of the superpower competition, the United States must meet Soviet challenges with tougher responses under worsened circumstances. There are now fewer options than in the 1960s and early 1970s for constructive initiatives to improve relations with the Soviet Union. Then the military balance still seemed to allow for the disposition of military assets in order to achieve politically significant arms control agreements. Prospects for U.S.-western European-Japanese economic cooperation with the Soviet Union seemed to correspond with "the new direction of Soviet economic strategy."[3] Most important, political issues still existed in Europe—like in Berlin—that called for settlements within the confines of either side's basic concept of European order.

In all three regards, circumstances have changed. The European situation hardly allowed for further near-term structural improvements. It was seen to be in a long-term process of political change no matter whether West Germany wanted this or not. It was a process that could turn either way. In fact, the process, its desirable long-term goals, and the structural changes in European East-West relations that had already been achieved were considered vulnerable to inappropriate Western and, in particular, American policies toward the Soviet Union.

It was the shrinking range of options for reconstructing political relations with the Soviet Union in the near future and the causes for this decline that made the United States weary of their continued pursuit, while western Europeans—West Germans in particular—seemed all the more committed to protecting whatever options were left under the circumstances. This was a reversal of earlier U.S. and West German positions: from American policies of accommodation that were viewed as premature in West Germany to West German policies of accommodation that were considered overtaken by events in the United States. On the other hand, western Europeans, particularly West Germans, were profoundly worried over the potential impact of U.S. global policy in the pursuit of "extended containment."[4]

Worsening political and strategic conditions in the enduring competition with the Soviet Union have rendered the United States and West Germany ever more dependent on each other. However, the deterioration of circumstances also exacerbated the intrinsic divergencies of roles and interests. For the United

States, containing Soviet power and reducing Soviet influence on a global scale is bound to be the overriding objective whether American leadership likes it or not. In this effort western Europe and in particular West Germany, where the systemic competition is most obvious, are both the highest stake and the best trump irrespective of what modes of emphasis happen to prevail in Washington. The Soviet Union certainly has never lost sight of this basic fact, be it in terms of Soviet aspirations or anxieties over what might eventually endanger the Soviet empire.

For West Germany, on the other hand, a modus vivendi in Europe and increasing influence over how the long-term process of change in European East-West relations will develop are the dominant priorities. In this perspective, close relations with the United States have become what has been called West Germany's second Basic Law. Given the proximity of the Soviet military machinery on the continent, there was no possible substitute for American protection as a precondition for West Germany's endurance in the political competition with the Soviet Union over the political fate of Europe.

However, under conditions of diminishing strategic options to protect western Europe and reduced opportunities for the United States to shape political outcomes in Europe, the relationship with western Europe, and especially with West Germany, was bound to become more precarious and less instrumental. Conversely, the policy framework for West Germany's cooperation with the United States appeared increasingly confined to the one level where American policy options were less and less a matter of traditional statesmanship and where the Soviet Union could hope most to increase its political influence in West Germany—the level of nuclear deterrence. As a result it became ever more difficult to translate the intrinsic relationship with the United States into public opinion and even practical policy.

Neither the United States nor the Federal Republic have the chance to ever become ordinary countries: The United States cannot escape its role as a democracy with unprecedented responsibilities for the avoidance of a nuclear holocaust, nor can West Germany change its role as a democracy under unprecedented conditions of antagonistic political competition.[5] No other Western country has the option to unilaterally change the structure of European East-West relations—be it by folly or intent. The United States could eventually redefine its nuclear responsibility just as West Germany could redefine its role in the European long-term process of political change. Either way it would spell the end of the U.S.-German relationship and indeed the Atlantic alliance. But extended nuclear deterrence and the political division in central Europe are basic facts that are difficult to get accepted as elements of a durable European order if only because both will continue to be kept in the center of Soviet efforts in the competition with the West. Although there is no substitute for close cooperation between the United States and West Germany as a means to prevail in the political competition with the Soviet Union, this intrinsic relationship cannot be separated from either anomaly—extended nuclear deterrence or the political division in central Europe. However, American policy elites find it increasingly harder to understand the intricacies of the German division in terms of a perennial challenge, just as German policy elites have ever greater difficulty adapting to the enduring dynamics of extended deterrence. In fact, near-recognition of the political status quo in intra-German relations makes it hard even for West Germans to assess the situation, just as the secular loss of strategic superiority reduces American confidence that extended deterrence can remain a basis of U.S. foreign policy.

It is under Soviet shocks that divergencies among Western powers, and particularly between the United States and West Germany over how to cope with the Soviet challenge, evolve most strongly. With diminishing options for structural improvements of relations with the Soviet Union in Europe and increasingly precarious strategic options for the protection of western Europe, such shocks no longer simply induce policies of accommodation on the part of some Western nations that are resented by others. Rather, existing divergencies within the West come more fully into the open.

A few observations are in order. First, on the governmental level, divergencies surface in terms of specific and in fact rather narrow policy issues that become high policy matters only because "their source typically lies elsewhere."[6] Thus the precarious nature of extended deterrence under current circumstances became a high policy matter in the encapsulated form of the intermediate-range nuclear forces (INF) issue, which, if seen in retrospect, is a remnant of a comprehensive, although modest, theater nuclear forces (TNF) modernization program that NATO conceived in the mid-1970s and of which it was not nearly the most important element. Moreover, although this particular program could be seen as a correction of earlier American failures since the early 1960s that was eventually induced by West Germany, its implementation turned into a demonstration of West Germany's diminishing capacity to deliver decisions on matters of extended deterrence on which its political survival so crucially depends.

Similarly, the precarious nature of the political modus vivendi in central Europe and the protracted process of change in European East-West relations became the focus of allegations over potential strategic implications of trade with the Soviet Union, which, if seen in retrospect, was only a scarce remains of what has been expected to become an essential means to restructure political relations with the Soviet Union in the early 1970s. Restrictions to minimize strategic advantages to the Soviet Union from economic cooperation with the West had been necessitated, above all, by American trade practices, whereas the Coordinating Committee for Export to Communist Areas (COCOM) and other machineries displayed, above all, a lacking Western capacity to deliver policy decisions on trade with the Soviet Union in terms of its political and strategic instrumentality.[7]

Second, there is a kind of economy of alliance troubles at work. Underlying divergencies surface somehow. But except for unusual mismanagement, like in summer of 1982, things tend to get channeled so as to avoid cumulations of disasters. In this perspective the inescapable priority of the INF issue in 1983 helped to tone down disagreements over trade issues in East-West relations.

Third, divergencies over how to respond to actual Soviet challenges have always had detrimental effects within the West.

However, in the late 1970s and early 1980s they have affected relations between the United States and West Germany—and in varying degrees some other western European countries—in ways that did not even seem tolerable between France and the United States in the days of President de Gaulle. Disagreements over how to cope with Soviet challenges turned into processes that were minor in terms of the substantive issues concerned but became dominant through politicization within the West. In fact, countries with vital stakes in the alliance's viability put the alliance at stake over issues like the double-track decision, which, on substantive grounds, were of secondary importance.

It is too early to tell whether a new pattern has emerged or whether Western bodies politic will learn better how to avoid or minimize such policy conflicts. But the precedents are there for measures that were meant to induce more constructive behavior on the part of the Soviet Union, yet in effect hurt alliance states badly, reduce further the scope for coordinated responses to Soviet challenges, and indeed serve Soviet political interests in Europe better than any inducement the Soviets might have initiated on their own.

Two Crises in Retrospect: Extended Sanctions and INF

Two cases in particular illustrate this. One relates to attempted *denials* of advantages to the Soviet Union; the other, to attempted *agreements* with the Soviet superpower. The two prime examples are, of course, the extended pipeline sanctions of June 1982 and the INF issue.

In the pipeline case the United States wanted the western European countries involved to cancel the deal—something that would have required the abrogation of agreements—as a way to discontinue a political process in Europe that had become discredited in the United States under the heading of "détente." However, although the administration regarded this as a chance to assert a principle of what was considered a new foreign policy, it did so in a tactical context. It was meant to punish the Soviet Union for undoing the most dramatic political changes that have as yet occurred under Soviet rule in eastern Europe, although these changes in Poland would not have been conceivable without the context of détente during the 1970s, which the administration was so anxious to see discontinued.

Moreover, while sanctions were imposed without explicit political demands that might have provided a more specific measure for failure, the extended sanctions turned into a punishment of western European countries through the extraterritorial application of U.S. laws to American firms in western Europe. The United States thus not only got into an unprecedented conflict over the sovereignty of American allies rather than Warsaw Pact countries, but also invoked a major political crisis among the principal allies that was bound to minimize whatever Western leverage might have been left in Poland. This in turn opened up a whole new dimension of U.S.-western European divergence that the Soviet Union could hope to capitalize on. The repercussions on West Germany's relations with the United States were worse than elsewhere because they combined in particularly awkward ways with the nuclear issue.

In the meantime the extended sanction controversy has been diffused on the diplomatic plane. However, the language of the pending Export Administration Act of 1983 suggests that the issue has not been settled yet, and that in a subsequent crisis the administration could cause even bigger problems through even stronger legal provisions.[8]

By and large western Europeans, and West Germans in particular, tended to have a clearer notion of what the context was that had facilitated change in Poland and thus were felt to have greater stakes in the continuity of political relations with the East and indeed in inducing more forthcoming cooperativeness on the part of the Soviet Union than was the case on the U.S. side. Yet the pipeline deal was not simply a matter of continuity, nor was it rendered into a political incentive for the Soviet Union. It was defended as a means to assure political continuity in East-West relations under extreme circumstances, yet it was engineered as a commercial matter and in nearly total disregard of Soviet pressure on Poland, where the continuity of the process of European détente was undergoing its most important test yet.

Both sides—the United States and the major western European countries—have thus contributed to a situation in which economic deterrence and denial in trading with the Soviet Union were the issues. They did so with little negative impact in the East, whereas a new kind of serious cleavages within the West and between the United States and West Germany in particular became the outstanding result. However, it was the American side that deliberately chose to introduce punishment of allies into the arsenal for containing Soviet influence and expansion. The notorious INF issue tells the same story in reverse.

In the INF case western European governments, and the West German government in particular, had taken pains to persuade an American administration that was determined to review its arms control policies in the light of changing strategic circumstances and current events to enter into INF negotiations with the Soviet Union as early as possible and in fact to reach some kind of an agreement within a narrow time frame. In the past it had always been the West Germans who had insisted on the integration of such negotiations into the broader strategic arms negotiations. Now this pressure on the United States not to pursue INF negotiations as part of a reconsidered overall arms control policy, but to initiate them right away, was bound to decouple them from strategic arms control. One expectation was the earliest possible resumption of nuclear arms negotiations between the two superpowers as the most promising way to prevent a further worsening of U.S.-Soviet relations, which might have impeded further the continuity of European détente.

West Germany regarded the INF issue as a matter of principle—the continued avoidance of Soviet nuclear privileges on the continent codified through agreements with the West[9] and the demonstrated right of the alliance to deploy U.S. nuclear weapons as a means of extended deterrence on western European soil. But (like the United States in the pipeline case) the Federal Republic did so in a tactical context: American INF deployments, however regulated as the result of negotiating outcomes, were understood to reduce the advantages the Soviet Union has gained through the most dramatic strategic change in Europe as yet—above all, the SS-20 deployment—although the change clearly would have appeared easier to cope with if it had not occurred in the context of European détente, which West Germany was so anxious to see continued. In other words, as things turned out, the INF negotiations were used eventually as a means to mitigate the tensions between the continued Soviet military buildup—with the public almost entirely focused on the SS-20—and the West German demands for continuity in East-West relations in Europe.

The West German government thus induced the U.S. administration to table the zero option as the U.S. negotiating proposal. It embodied the principles West Germany wanted to see established through an INF agreement but was primarily meant to preempt internal pressures to forgo any U.S. deployments in exchange for some unspecified Soviet reduction of SS-20 levels in Europe. At this juncture a political constituency inside and outside the West German government grew that called for American rather than Soviet sincerity in Geneva, for lowering American negotiating demands in the face of Soviet intransigence, and for increasing allowances for the Soviets as a compensation for French and British strategic nuclear forces. As John Van Oudenaren has put it, "it is hard to recall an alliance in which the smaller members set a virtual precondition for participation that its largest member compensate its adversary for the military capabilities of these allies themselves."[10]

For the first time in two decades the United States had reluctantly come around to deploying medium-range nuclear weapons in western Europe, and these forces were deliberately undersized with regard to the newly deployed Soviet nuclear forces in Europe. However, instead of continued concerns in West Germany over how to negate Soviet strategic options, the United States became the target of hostile opposition in West Germany and was even blamed for intruding in West Germany's sovereignty by deploying the weapons the West German government had been the first to request.[11]

Again, one should add that the American administration had a clear notion of what the context was that had facilitated both the change of strategic relations and the diminishing political capacity in the West to conduct genuine arms negotiations, i.e., to attempt negotiated constraints on Soviet military power. There thus was genuine reluctance to fall again quickly into the traps of previous arms control negotiations. However, although there remained an important segment within the administration that engaged in arms control negotiations as a way to manage political relations, but opposed agreements almost as a matter of principle, the dominant new political posture soon was to become the old one—to pursue arms control as an end in itself, yet with little hope to actually constrain Soviet power.

Just as in the extended sanction case the U.S. administration itself finally diffused the issue, so did the West German government in the INF case—if only because of a change in government that reduced political pressures increasingly to the level of intra-opposition problems. However, in either case the damage is done. The U.S. administration that appropriately concentrated its efforts on correcting military imbalances failed to recognize in its handling of economic relations with the Soviet Union that "the more we retreat into an angry, cold war confrontation, the more we reduce the competition to those levels on which the Soviet Union is strongest . . . wielding raw power through military might."[12] Given the recent U.S. posture, which despite increasing U.S. exports to the Soviet Union pungently denounced the political instrumentality of economic cooperation with the Soviet Union, it will take years before the Soviet Union will consider engaging in large-scale economic cooperation with the United States, which in Moscow is understood only too well in its competitive dimension.

Similarly, West Germany, in trying to secure the continuity of what it still considered the "process" of détente, lost sight of the fact that the more cooperation with the Soviet Union is dominated by arms control negotiations or, in Soviet jargon, "military détente," the more the political competition is once again confined to the one level that is best suited for Soviet political strategy, i.e., the military level. An "obsessive interest in arms control and in the codification of certain forms of military parity between the two sides are also symptomatic of and in turn help to perpetuate a 'militarized' rivalry."[13] What is worse, internal political pressure to reach arms control agreements with the

Soviet Union or even to give up what little bargaining leverage the West has left (which in turn will lead to further unilateral constraints) puts the Soviet Union in the position of an innocent observer waiting for the outcomes of intra-Western bargains between those who want symbolic parity agreements and those who want to codify unilateral restraint through agreement with the adversary. Moreover, this did not deprive Soviet military power of any of its political or strategic instrumentalities, but in fact maximized both. Again, it will take years of sustained Western security policy in order to convince the Soviet Union of the need for restraining its military power display as a price for rewarding political cooperation with the West.

Both American obsession with curtailing western European economic cooperation with the Soviet Union and West German obsession with driving the United States into nuclear arms control thus have profoundly incapacitated the West in its pursuit of political strategy in the competition with the Soviet Union. Both have caused self-inflicted damage on an unprecedented scale. However, given the differential of constraints, it will be less difficult for the United States to undo the political disruption of economic cooperation with the Soviet Union than it will be for the Federal Republic to reduce domestic imperatives in its definition of strategic requirements.

Policy Toward the USSR in a Changing Domestic Context

Just how difficult it will be to avoid similar political disasters and eventually arrive at a more strategic political approach toward the Soviet Union depends in part on whether foreign and, in particular, security policy can be sufficiently disentangled from new types of political processes. Although frictions between governments over policy issues relating to the Soviet Union were bad enough, the dominant political fact in recent developments was that they were not confined to the governmental level. There had been a confluence of protest movements in the United States and West Germany during the Vietnam years. But the more recent situation saw governments out of pace with an increasing propensity to overreact and with exacerbating repercussions on the domestic scene on either side that tended to reinforce interactions between respective oppositions. This in turn pulled governments even further apart.

This concurrence of unprecedented societal interactions between opposition movements in the United States and West Germany and of unprecedented intergovernmental recriminations (with the former reinforcing the latter) left either side with few opportunities to restore constructive relations between the two core allies. On either side preemptive mechanisms tended to lock governments further into a situation that combined immobilism on policy with worsening repercussions on politics.

Already in the late 1970s any major policy initiative on either side instantly became part of the problem rather than the solution: Once the U.S. administration showed reluctance to take some initiative it got blamed in Bonn for lack of leadership, just as initiatives taken usually were received as deviations from common policies, if not impositions of unilateralist will. Conversely, once the West German government was dominated by constraints, the prevailing view in Washington was that this displayed fading partnership. On the other hand, West German initiatives were widely seen as confirming existing worries over West Germany's alleged propensity to alienate itself from the United States and to encourage some vaguely defined central European entity as the emerging framework for defining German interests.[14]

In the early 1980s the cleavage worsened. As a result, political tendencies surfaced on either side that eventually might have spelled the end of an alliance that has preserved peace in Europe for more than three decades: impatient unilateralism in the United States and stubborn West German efforts to transform the alliance into a framework for political change in Europe. Mutual misperception and indeed genuine concern was bound to follow on both sides.

The new American leadership that had come into power on a conservative wave saw a preoccupying need to respond to unfavorable changes in the military balance that had occurred throughout the era of détente. In West Germany there was a large constituency that viewed renewed military efforts in the

United States as a quest for military supremacy, even though West Germany would be among the first to feel the consequences of diminishing American protection. In fact, pledges for equidistance from the two superpowers and description of the United States as a threat to rather than as a guarantor of West Germany's political viability were not confined to political fringes.

Conversely, the West German Social Democratic party/Free Democratic party leadership was nervously responding to the unfolding effort to contain Soviet power in order to insulate political changes in Europe that had occurred in the early 1970s from the deterioration of East-West relations. Although this reflected genuine concerns, it also was clearly recognized as a precondition for extending further its stay in power. In so doing the West German government appeared to be posturing as a mediator between the two superpowers, thus evoking the nightmare of a vacillating Germany in the center of Europe that instantly haunted a Socialist French government and a conservative American administration alike. West Germany's endeavors to protect relations with eastern Europe and, in particular, with the German Democratic Republic—which had replaced the earlier nightmare of *quereles allemandes* in the midst of increasing East-West tensions—were widely perceived as a trend to drift apart. Moreover, the central role of the nuclear issue was bound to reinforce creeping anti-Americanism. West German "self-Finlandization" and "neutralism" tended to become high-level assessments in Washington of what was going on in West Germany, and many among the new unilateralists even regarded West Germany—and the Atlantic alliance at large—as a nuisance in the competition with the Soviet Union rather than as the crucial stake that it had been ever since the United States had engaged in this competition.

This could have led into a fatal crisis for the Atlantic alliance. Changing relations between the United States and West Germany always had been the primary objective of Soviet security diplomacy in Europe, and the unfolding situation seemed to open up opportunities for the Soviets to play on the keyboard of U.S.-West German societal interactions.[15] Soviet armament policy, diplomacy, and propaganda had created conditions in Europe to which bodies politic in western Europe and the United States had to respond somehow in ways that predictably were to have intricate domestic and intra-alliance implications.

However, the subsequent disarray within the alliance resulted, above all, from domestic circumstances on both sides of the Atlantic, noticeably in the United States and West Germany. Major elements within the two governments that tried to stick to a middle-of-the-road pragmatism had to integrate more radical wings within the ruling parties through policies and rhetorics that were bound to exacerbate cleavages between the key allies and provide welcome pretexts to oppositions on the other side to step up the controversies. This development reduced further the chances to preempt opposition at home through policies that so infuriated the partner on the other side of the Atlantic. Managing internal opposition thus spilled over into the ways governments and indeed domestic opposition movements on either side began to interact.

In 1983 most of the key issues relating to the Soviet Union were still on the agenda. However, there has been a determination on all sides not to escalate further controversies over how to deal with the Soviet Union. Political guidelines have been issued on the regulation of trade with the Soviet Union and eastern Europe that provide a framework for coordination. Consultations over arms control have never been more intimate. There have even been some unprecedented manifestations of common diplomacy. The most important was the Williamsburg declaration on security. Yet what all this means is essentially a less troubled, more persistent middle-of-the-road approach toward the Soviet Union: What is different from the preceding phase of profound irritation is *not* the *basic policies* toward the Soviet Union, but the *domestic context* within which they are being pursued.

In western Europe a trend back toward moderate conservatism had become dominant. The election outcome in West Germany on March 6, 1983, was its most important manifestation. In a campaign with unprecedented advocacy of Soviet positions,[16] the West German electorate clearly came out in favor of

centrism in an election that required unusual electoral sophisti-
cation. Despite the politicization of the INF issue, domestic concerns—above all, economics—turned out to be decisive.[17] None
of the German parties ever proposed a constructive long-term
policy toward the Soviet Union, yet the West German electorate
corrected the one thing that mattered most: the domestic setting
of West German policy toward the Soviet Union. As in virtually
all other Western countries, considerations of access to domestic power will continue to play an important role in West Germany's approach to the East. But for some time to come this
is unlikely to drive the approach to the USSR again with regard
to content, pace, pressures toward symbolic achievement, and
preemption of bipartisanship, as was the case in the preceding
phase.

This change has resulted mostly from self-regulating societal
mechanisms.[18] But the external environment did play some role.
Soviet heavy-handedness and reluctant American moderation
have been factors. Probably more important was the support for
the moderate conservatives from a Socialist French president—
following earlier and at times troubling endorsements for the
previous West German government by a conservative French
president. Similarly, the turn to moderate conservatism in the
Scandilux countries, especially in the Netherlands, which had
been the source of many irritations, reinforced the trend toward
centrism in West Germany. This in turn stabilized a middle-of-
the-road policy toward the Soviet Union and eastern Europe. As
a result, little had changed in the businesslike conduct of relations with the Soviet Union. However, despite basic continuity
of policies on the Soviet Union and eastern Europe, the change
of the domestic setting led to a gradual change of foreign policy
priorities away from a primacy of Eastern policies: Strengthening the political role of western Europe became the main focus.

Change occurred not only in West Germany and indeed most
of western Europe: U.S. policy on how to deal with the Soviet
Union also began to return to centrism. As in western Europe,
what was changing was the domestic setting of U.S. policy toward the Soviet Union. The scarce record of the Reagan admin-

istration's foreign policy achievements combined with the dominance of economic issues. As a result the administration's policies on relations with the Soviet Union were increasingly driven toward a middle-of-the-road pragmatism. Oscillations in American policies on relations with the Soviet Union were dampened by domestic politics—above all, economics.[19] This involved some changes in specific policies toward the Soviet Union. There may evolve a new political interest in the pursuit of arms control on a high policy level. Strains on defense budget increases, the need to prevent the Democrats from getting political mileage out of this issue, the relative absence of major foreign policy achievements, and the instrumentality of arms control in renewing U.S.-Soviet summitry tended to combine to restore a stronger political interest in arms control, albeit without making it again the prime framework for defense policy decisions.

The irony in all this is that on either side—in the United States and in West Germany—precisely those political forces that had been committed to profoundly changing policies toward the Soviet Union tended to become guarantors of continuity, whereas oppositions stood for major departures from established policies, with some prospect, however, for confluence and mutual reinforcement rather than divergence and mutual recrimination if they were to return to power. Indeed, calls for a more comprehensive policy or grand strategy toward the Soviet Union that became more frequent almost always come from policymakers who were in a position to review their own recent record—Helmut Schmidt and Lord Carrington in western Europe or Henry Kissinger and Zbigniew Brzezinski in the United States.[20] Typically, the European ex-leaders addressed the "muddle" they had not been able to avoid, whereas the American foreign-policy makers of the 1970s combined nostalgic retrospect with growing disbelief in America's capacity to avoid the characteristic oscillations in U.S. policy toward the Soviet Union and to conduct a comprehensive and long-term policy in relations with the rival superpower.

These changes could suggest a return to normalcy, and in a

number of ways this is precisely what it is. On both sides domestic settings are more conducive to the conduct of a centrist foreign policy. Interactions between opposition movements may continue, if only because of the multiplying roles some of the media are playing. But their impact on the political process is likely to have passed its peak. Direct Soviet political influence on western European bodies politic that not long ago looked like the most promising development the Soviet Union had going in its favor has instantly declined once political left-of-center forces in countries like West Germany have gotten into a position where they have to regain the center in order to return to power. The return to centrism with a more manifest pro-alliance orientation in all major Western countries also reduced the felt need to be clear about the West's political strategy toward the Soviet Union and predictably the need to agree on a common political strategy.

On the Disjunction of U.S. and German Interests

The West may enter into more demanding situations in which policies of reassurance that had sufficed to restabilize centrism among Western electorates may no longer provide sufficient answers. In the words of John Van Oudenaren, "there are fundamental and perhaps widening conflicts between the United States and West Germany. The basic conflict is between the American interest in managing a day-to-day rivalry with the Soviet Union, and the West German interest in encouraging long-term change in Europe."[21]

Differences in style, tradition, and political culture are part of what determines the framework for coordinating policies toward the Soviet Union. As Dean Acheson has observed, the United States tends to cope with the enduring Soviet challenge by placing "the strategic approach to practicable objectives, concretely and realistically conceived" in order to achieve "more limited and, it was hoped, transitory ends."[22] Through the decades there has thus existed an American propensity not to recognize the long-term nature of the competition, although U.S. policy has never been guided by expectations of fundamental change in relations with the Soviet Union either.

For West Germany, fundamental change in relations with the Soviet Union is in effect even a constitutional requirement. But it can only be left to the course of history. A West German proclivity has therefore developed not to foreclose unspecifiable long-term options by producing stalemates if allies move too fast or move in undesirable directions, or by inducing movement once West Germany tends to get locked into an undesirable status quo. Caught between a continuous need for Western multilateralism and a long-term commitment to change in Europe, West Germany has little room for major initiatives of its own, whereas it has always seen itself as vulnerable to policy changes within the alliance.[23] Conversely, West Germany's allies are time and again faced with incentives to reduce further West Germany's bargaining power: They attentively watch whatever moves the Federal Republic may undertake next in the East-West context.

This difference in decisional behavior between the two countries reflects national responsibilities as well as constraints—the need for the United States to manage the nuclear threat and the need for West Germany to mitigate the tension between its long-term commitment to change and short-term immobilism that has become both habitual and enforced by circumstances.[24] In neither case is there a conceivable solution for what is pursued in a continuous process—to create durable, i.e., politically effortless, stability of nuclear relations or to establish a durable, i.e., uncontested, political order in central Europe. Given the nature of a process in which both the United States and West Germany are bound to pursue unspecifiable long-term objectives, both also fail to be guided by an understanding of the long-term nature of the political competition with the Soviet Union.

Profound structural changes in strategic relations and in the political status quo in Europe already *have* occurred. On the other hand, the West will increasingly fail to control the process because it is running out of options on either level unless it manages to agree on both a common diplomacy and a collective security policy with common intermediate goals. But both tend to view changes and moves in rather abstract terms: Since the early 1960s the United States has been seeking a stable system, West Germany, a stable process. In the American case this means, above all, denial of Soviet options to disrupt the system; for West Germany the important thing is to keep the momentum by keeping options open. Despite American military restraint the United States had to discover that strategic relations have become increasingly unstable. To maintain the system of East-West relations the United States had to engage in a bargaining process to prevent its deterioration. Similarly, West Germany, its political sacrifices notwithstanding, faced a situation in which political process became rather stagnant and stabilizing the central European subsystem by insulating it from political deterioration elsewhere was widely seen as a national imperative.

Stability of the system in the American case and continuity of the process in the West German thus were not only susceptible to changes of criteria of strategic stability and political progress that reflected the shrinking range of options, but their very validity as overriding objectives was cast into doubt. Strategic stability was sought to be regained by mere increases without specific strategic options the United States was determined to generate. Similarly, the mere continuity first of arms control and then trade was seen to be imperative for West Germany in order to keep the momentum of the process in European East-West relations irrespective of delicate issues that posed themselves with regard to both arms control and Eastern trade policy. Increased American defense spending, which will not nearly make up for the decline during a long preceding period, serves as a substitute for strategic policy, just as defending trade with the Soviet Union that amounts to only 2 percent of West Germany's exports against imaginary charges serves as a substitute for political strategy vis-à-vis the Soviet Union.[25]

The Soviet Challenge Redefined

A divergence between an "American interest in managing a day-to-day rivalry with the Soviet Union and the West German interest in encouraging long-term change in Europe" has existed for decades. Why is it that it may turn into a basic conflict although the bodies politic within both countries have reinforced centrism and reduced both policy cleavages and the likelihood of damaging domestic repercussions? Ever since the early 1960s American nuclear policy had irreversibly eliminated the scope for a genuinely common military strategy, just as American détente policy in the Kennedy years had reduced the scope for a common European security diplomacy. At the same time there never was a viable substitute for American protection, nor a chance for European détente without American support. Conversely, the military role of West Germany was increasing because of growing regional preponderance of Soviet military power in all areas in which the United States was actively engaged outside the Western hemisphere, and because of a progressing neutralization of American strategic power in regional contingencies. Similarly, although less recognized, West Germany's political engagement in Europe was crucial for the pursuit of American political interest in Europe.

What is new in the emerging situation is that the Soviet Union has increased leverage over the two developments that are central to U.S. and West German preoccupations, respectively—the military East-West competition and European détente. However discouraging things may look from Moscow, the Soviet Union has locked the United States into a situation in which it is engaged in a continuous catch-up effort, which provides the Soviet Union with ideal political opportunities. It is difficult to see how the United States could regain military stability in the major areas of interest, although this has become the residual objective of U.S. global policy. Moreover, the United States will be unable to stay in the competition alone, yet increasing the military roles of allies will require a broader common political base, which is more and more difficult to establish, in all major regions concerned.

The dilemma is reinforced by the fact that the United States has to concentrate so much on the military level. This reduces the scope for broadened regional cooperation with allies. It is also the one level on which the Soviet Union can expect to compete successfully. The United States is ailing in a competition that lets it appear at times as preoccupied with military power simply because a major political effort is needed to sustain. Yet this strains relations with America's allies who are most dependent on U.S. military power and most vulnerable to political repercussions of U.S. catch-up efforts. This in turn means that increasing Soviet military preponderance in Europe, as well as in northeast Asia and southwest Asia, and increasing strains on American allies in the regions concerned will more and more turn Soviet military preponderance into political bargaining power.

Similarly, Soviet diplomacy has locked West Germany into a situation in which it is engaged in a continuous effort to maintain some momentum in the process of East-West cooperation in Europe, which again provides the Soviet Union with political opportunities that are incommensurate with Soviet fortunes elsewhere. It is difficult to see how West Germany could regain the initiative in a process the continuity of which has become the residual goal in its European security diplomacy. Neither arms control nor economic cooperation nor the residual political issues offer any option to regain the initiative and pursue intermediate political objectives in the course of this continuous process. In any case, not risking alienation from the United States and, indeed, an active American involvement are mandatory. This in turn tends to reduce the scope for closer strategic cooperation between the United States and West Germany. As a result the Soviet Union will have the best of both worlds. West Germany's commitment to continuity of East-West cooperation meets the Soviet interest in projecting the image of "irreversibility" of détente, whereas the continued American military effort and the growing need and shrinking political capacity for allied military cooperation will channel East-West cooperation to maximize the political bargaining power of Soviet military preponderance in Europe.

Its enormous weaknesses notwithstanding, the Soviet Union has thus increased leverage over two central processes. Moreover, the United States cannot opt out because it would reduce instantly the role of the United States as a global power, nor can

West Germany because it would mean mere acceptance of a political status quo that it had accepted with the expectation that this "helps to make it good."[26] If the United States were to forego its role as a global power, or if West Germany were to decide to be an ordinary country, this would make either the target of more direct pressure with much reduced chances for support from other Western nations and with almost no prospects left for coordinated political responses to Soviet moves. Although the Soviet Union continues to fail in most efforts to consolidate political influence within the West, there is continuous progress in Soviet efforts to change those political structures and priorities within the West that are prerequisites for the continued political viability of western Europe and eventually of the United States.

It is essential to get Western political strategy reoriented in a long-term perspective, and the essential objectives ought to be to reduce the political role of military power in East-West relations and to induce long-term change within the Soviet orbit, or at least in Soviet external behavior. However, this is a *two-sided* game in which Soviet and Western political strategies increasingly interact. The West's political viability and resourcefulness are likely to prevail except for increasing needs to cope with a growing military challenge, just as the Soviet system is likely to deteriorate except for eventual successful exploitation of military power. Ignoring the Soviet military challenge in the pursuit of long-term change is going to be as self-defeating as attempts to confine Western efforts to military responses. Either way it will play directly into Soviet hands.

Issues and Choices

Both the Soviet Union and the West have dual objectives: to preserve existing power structures within the respective orbit and to induce political change within the other system. In both cases preservation goals prevail over policies of induced change. Moreover, within the two multilateral systems policies of change are driven by perceived requirements for stability. At times and for some players on either side this can mean that proclaiming policies of change in the absence of actual policies is the best choice.

There is, however, a basic asymmetry between the two interacting policies of change: Although both may militate against the perceived requirements for political stability on the other side, Soviet policies of change in the West are defined in terms of an enduring antagonism between the two systems, and this is so precisely because of the way Soviet preservation goals are perceived by Soviet power elites. On the other hand, to the extent Western policies of change respond to prevailing moods of liberal societies rather than intermittent alarmist apprehensions, they tend to stress cooperation rather than antagonism: Possible intrusive political effects within the Soviet-controlled system notwithstanding, policies of change will be widely seen in the West as a way to mute antagonism and to drag the other side into a cooperation that is assumed to serve its true self-interests.

In other words, there is conceptual congruence on the Soviet side between its internal requirements for expanding political control and actual policies of change in the West, although this may eventually become a decisive obstacle in the way to both internal evolution and sustainable policies toward the West. Conversely, in the West there tends to be a disjunction of internal impulses for policies of change in the East and specific policy objectives, and if domestic impulses dominate, this turns into a disjunction between policies geared toward irenic cooperation that will stabilize regimes on the other side and policies aiming at political change. Even so, the former may have intrusive effects that would serve the latter, but internal feedbacks of general policies driven by internal considerations tend to restrain the scope for policies of deliberately induced change.

Given Western options, however, there may not be too much difference in how either approach affects developments on the Eastern side, although it does affect the domestic setting of Western policies of change, as it does affect the scope for Soviet influence. Although either approach may in fact be conducive to change within the Soviet orbit, neither can be oriented toward intermediate policy objectives. The political modus vivendi established in the early 1970s does not in itself require further significant regulation. Conditions for economic cooperation do not allow for major expansion in the foreseeable future within the East or the West. Arms control has become ever more part of the problem rather than the solution and certainly requires both prior military adjustments and conceptual reorientation.

As a result Western policies of change tend to be reduced to political well behavior in order not to disrupt the modus vivendi, to continuity of economic cooperation as a stabilizing condition for eventual political evolution, and to arms control that may generate political symbolism, yet is almost unrelated to the basic objective of military security under conditions of reduced political instrumentality of military power. However, the less political strategy toward the Soviet Union can be presented in the West as something pertaining to specific longer-term objectives, the more likely an incremental process or policies of incremental change tend to become dominated by internal interests. By the same token, efforts to get a more comprehensive political strategy accepted easily become divisive.

It is here that Soviet policies of change have distinct advantages. Although the Soviet Union, too, would find it hard to define negotiable intermediate objectives, Soviet policy has much better leverage to determine what issues will evolve on the East-West agenda.[27] The Soviets can play to Western audiences. Given the Soviet commitment to antagonism, Soviet initiatives or Soviet readiness to negotiate often seem like opportunities not to be missed. The West tends to see itself in a demandeur's role precisely because cooperation corresponds with Western liberal values and is assumed to be more demanding for the other side.

In this context two things combine: First, the Soviet Union can create needs for the West to seize the initiative on those levels of the competition where the Soviets have the best chances to control initiatives—the military competition and political détente in Europe. If the West were to accept Soviet military preponderance, or if West Germany were to accept the division as permanent, it would open up new opportunities for the Soviet Union. On the other hand, Western efforts in the military field will rarely regain strategic initiative, just like German initiatives on détente tend to endanger links with the West.[28] Second, the Soviet approach is guided by a political long-term strategy, and although it is hard to describe an eventual political order in Europe that reduces Soviet influence in eastern Europe or is not dominated by military power, changes in U.S.-western European relations and in fact inside western Europe that concur with Soviet long-term objectives are conceivable. This opens up another asymmetry: The Soviet Union does pursue explicable long-term objectives for change in Europe that provide political direction to processes in East-West relations.[29] Moreover, it guides Soviet policies toward the West without severe internal interference. However, at the same time Soviet policies of change require eventual success for reasons of internal stability.

The quintessential lesson for the West is this: It must not get locked into situations that seem to call for Western initiatives under conditions where (a) the Soviet Union virtually controls initiatives, (b) western Europeans and, in particular, West Germans are anxious not to foreclose long-term options, and (c) "an American propensity" comes into play "to perceive change as at hand and to believe that transitional periods can be both recognized and demarcated precisely."[30]

Within the European context this leaves the West with three broad approaches in order to avoid the mad momentum of a mere process unrelated to specifiable objectives: First, the existing European situation could be reinterpreted as a *conflict order*[31] that combines antagonism with both a lack of unilateral options to change the situation fundamentally and reciprocal interests in avoiding a breakdown of the system. In its *enduring* nature this conflict order is in a steady state. It could be susceptible to more positive political interpretations, but essentially it requires a continuous pursuit on either side of both preservation goals and cooperation.

Second, the European system could be seen in terms of an *evolution of political order* that will eventually be different from intermediate stages like the current one to be stable and durable. Given the discernible Soviet political strategy, this requires that Western policies be related to long-term objectives. Although it is possible and indeed challenging to reconstruct the history of East-West relations in Europe since the late 1940s in terms of an evolving political order, it is hard to extrapolate in view of both the political and military instabilities on either side. Western efforts to establish principles and to define conditions relevant to what can be described as a more developed and durable order— just as is implied in Soviet political strategy—would concern the very essence of the competition and thus tend to undermine the existing modus vivendi.

This leaves a third approach. One can assume that change will occur within the Soviet orbit in the longer run that would allow a reordering of East-West relations. The West will be better prepared for such a choice if East-West relations are stabilized as a steady state and if, in the absence of intermediate goals, the West steadily continues to cooperate with the other side in order to establish conditions favorable to change without either major disruptions or major initiatives. Along with low profile but steady cooperation, military security would be regarded as a *holding operation* (with unspecifiable objectives), denying political advantages from military power for an indefinite period, yet based on assumptions about change within the Soviet orbit that is considered unavoidable eventually.

The conflict order is endless; the evolutionary order requires defined long-term objectives. The third view combines the realities of the steady state with long-term expectations of change. The advantage of the third approach is that it is the easiest for Americans and western Europeans to agree on. It is the closest to current practice. It does not require a consensus on what European structure one eventually wants to see emerge. It does not need major initiatives that are beyond the reach of Western governments. It does, however, demand a broader understanding of how the process works in the conduct of East-West relations. It also requires that Western governments abstain from generating hopes for "change at hand." This in turn will afford to explain security policies in public as a continuous task, yet as something distinctly different from arms racing.

Although policies of military stability should be conducive to eventual political regulation, they should, above all, be oriented toward Western preservation goals. Denial of political advantages from military power is a preservation goal along with others, and there may be built-in tensions between various Western preservation goals. The essential point is that all preservation goals relate to the structure and stability of Western societies. In this sense, military security, if it is balanced against other preservation goals, is a Western priority in that it gives priority to Western cooperation over cooperation with the East. This is so, however, only in conjunction with the whole range of Western preservation goals. The priority in Western foreign and security policymaking should thus clearly rest with the *stabilization within the West* that does include the political neutralization of Soviet military power in Europe. In fact, this may be seen as the most promising way to compete with the Soviet Union.

Even within this context two major conceptual tensions remain in U.S.-western European and specifically in U.S.-German relations. The first concerns *Europe as a regional context* of East-West competition. In German perspective a stable pattern of low-profile cooperation with the other side is regarded as an important condition of stability, whereas in the absence of noticeable changes it may tend to get ignored in American approaches. To a degree it does not matter because some continuity of cooperation is likely to occur in any case, whereas the volume of cooperation may render U.S.-German agreement on the political interpretation of continuous cooperation with the Soviet Union and eastern Europe unnecessary. Some implicit understanding of the differential of roles and, if needed, an agreement to disagree as a way to manage divergencies of secondary importance may suffice. Except for situations in which corrective measures tend to dominate (which in the American political culture can easily turn into a temporary preoccupation), there is a basic agreement that some mixture of denial and cooperation is needed in Western approaches toward the Soviet Union and eastern Europe. Both elements are always present in any case, and in this sense the now-famous Harmel formula is a truism. The irony is, however, that American approaches tend to be status quo-oriented in Europe and thus do not see cooperation as part of the competitive process. The Germans, on the other side, are less prepared to view the state of East-West relations in Europe as permanent and are more aware of the competitive aspects of cooperation.

As a result an American propensity has developed to blame German emphasis on cooperation with the East simply because it is seen as a detraction from denial efforts. Moreover, Americans usually fail to recognize the political instrumentality of military denial policy in Europe both in the preservation of western Europe as the highest stake in the competition and in the long-term process of change. American understanding of the competition with the Soviet Union shifts in typical oscillations. At times cooperation dominates the American approach, which usually means that Europe is regarded a stable area and in any case as secondary to the needs of superpower détente. At times there is greater awareness of the competitive nature of the superpower relationship, but then again Europe tends to be regarded as a stable area and European policies easily get ostracized as detrimental to denial efforts. The American failure is not to see that under any variation of East-West policies, the East-West competition is most crucial in the European regional context and that American policies will continue to determine essential boundary conditions for antagonism in this regional context.

One should add, however, that western European interests in the European process of change are seldom offered to American administrations as a matter for joint consideration. Rather, emphasis on western European policies of change often goes along with a degree of considered alienation from the United States that is anticipated or regarded as tolerable and occasionally even seen as part of a trade-off in a long-term bargain over future East-West relations in Europe. If Americans thus are inclined to ignore that they eventually control Soviet political success in Europe more than any other Western nation—something Adenauer and de Gaulle jointly regarded as *the* major source of instability as early as 1958—western Europeans, and West Germans in particular, often reinforce those processes in American politics that are known to be most detrimental to European interests. At times it is even flatly disregarded that without a degree of synchronization between processes in European East-West relations and superpower relations, i.e., without a degree of American support, there is little hope for continued Western control of European processes, let alone favorable outcomes. For the Germans, or to a degree the western Europeans, to explain the relevance of antagonism in the European regional context to American global policy is as hard as it is for Americans to understand that the Soviet Union could gain political advantages in Europe that would hurt the United States devastatingly precisely in terms of the ongoing global competition with the Soviet Union. The important task ahead, therefore, is to base political strategy on a more common understanding in the West of how the global competition will get decided in regional contexts and what unique role the European context is playing in the American interest as well as in European self-interest.

This relates to the second conceptual tension. Just as neither Americans nor Germans have sufficient definitions of the kind of regionalism the West ought to pursue in Europe, so neither has considered definitions of what globalism should mean in Western perspective. The United States tends to call for European support for U.S. global policies usually if an administration faces a confluence of European and domestic concerns. Other than that there has been little effort at any stage to get American allies involved in issues outside their own region. At the same time, or so standard European criticism goes, American policies are not sufficiently responsive to political evolution in most or all regions and thus have to respond once a critical situation actually emerges. This then tends to turn regional conflict quickly into a part of the superpower competition, with increasing emphasis on military power.

At the same time it is true that an allegedly better European understanding of political evolution in other areas does not involve resources or commitments. In effect it leaves the United States alone. There are few exceptions to this. Occasional French intervention in Africa is one. What is crucial is that the East-West competition in the European context can get decided outside the region. Moreover, regional instabilities are distributed and intensified in ways that do require action rather than protected long-term change only. It would be neither prudent nor feasible to leave it to the United States alone to cope with regional instabilities and their increasing militarization. It is beyond doubt that this would overburden the United States and it would have myriads of direct and indirect repercussions in Europe, however strongly Europeans might try to insulate Europe from external change.

What Americans often request from Europeans is alien to a common political strategy. European opposition is bound to grow when U.S. conceptions of common strategy only conform to American interests. But Europeans have failed badly over the years by simply responding to clumsy American approaches in parochial ways. It is in the European interest to propose to the United States a framework for how to agree on assessments of regional conflicts and for how to develop more compatible, if not common, responses. Western Europe and, in particular, the major European countries have a global role to play. But just like competition in the European context will turn into failure without a degree of genuine American support, so Europeans will fail to influence outcomes outside Europe unless they de-unilateralize American policy. In either case there is a need for common political strategy that allows for different roles and, to a degree, even for different interpretations of conflicts, yet helps to reinforce Western efforts to cope with Soviet competitiveness.

It is with these two major tensions in mind that the West should emphasize Western priorities again rather than measure political success in terms of negotiated agreement with the other side. This is a tall order. Moreover, given the legacies of the 1970s it will require agonizing reappraisals both in the United States and in West Germany. It is over internal tensions that the alliance may break down or be disrupted. Renewed Western priorities are not in themselves a recipe for political success. In fact, they may produce new divisive issues. But without this reorientation both management of internal divergencies and dealings with the other side will time and again burden the alliance with major policy conflicts.

The essential need for the alliance is to rebuild a broader framework for European-American cooperation. One important consideration ought to be, however, that renewed Western priorities do not simply spell renewed Atlanticism. In fact, a gradual shift from détente to intensified western European cooperation would appear to be the most prudent course to take. It would not renounce continuity in the conduct of relations with the East, but would stress unsettled East-West business along with continuity. It would make this kind of continuity a routine matter of western European politics. Most important, it would aim at improving western European cooperation within a broader European-American framework.[32] This will be demanding for both American and western European, particularly West German, elites. For western Europeans it is crucial not to fall into the trap of anti-Americanism along with increasing emphasis on western European cooperation. For Americans it will provide what may be a last chance to take western European cooperation on matters of common interest as the most expedient way to deal with western Europe.

Notes

1. Charles R. Planck, *The Changing Status of German Reunification in Western Diplomacy* (Baltimore: Johns Hopkins University Press, 1967), 37.

2. While U.S. policy in the early 1960s led to serious U.S.-German cleavages over how to deal with the Soviet Union, at the same time they exacerbated divergencies between the United States and France in ways that deprived West Germany even further of a chance to pursue its basic foreign policy objectives within a multilateral framework. In effect this was the end of a *common diplomacy* toward the Soviet Union as seen from Bonn—with the 1971–73 interval as a subsequent happy coincidence between the United States and West Germany, however strongly disapproved by France. During the Vietnam War, when U.S. forces in Germany at times had been thinned out by 25 percent because of the American preoccupation with a peripheral crisis, West Germany discovered the limits of what had been regarded as a *common military strategy*—a lesson that was to be reinforced by the exit of France from NATO in 1966 and the resolution of NATO's nuclear control issues in terms of the U.S. consent to the nonproliferation treaty with the Soviet Union. Oddly, all this happened along with NATO's acceptance of MC 14/3, i.e., NATO's basic document on military strategy ever since.

3. Peter G. Peterson, *U.S.-Soviet Commercial Relationships in a New Era* (Washington, D.C.: Government Printing Office, August 1972), 8.

4. Charles Wolf, Jr., *Extended Containment: Countering Soviet Im-*

perialism and Applying Economic Realism, N-2000-FF (Santa Monica, Calif.: The Rand Corp., April 1983). See Chapter 3 in this volume.

5. West Germany is placed in the center of the enduring political competition between the Soviet Union and the West. However, West Germany, if seen from within, has also acquired more attributes of an ordinary state (see Chapter 1). For a variety of views on Germany as a country in search of an identity see Werner Weidenfeld, ed., *Die Identität der Deutschen,* Schriftenreihe der Bundeszentrale für politische Bildung, vol. 200 (Bonn, 1983).

6. See Wolf, *Extended Containment,* 1.

7. See John P. Hardt and Donna Gold, *East-West Commercial Issues: The Western Alliance Studies Issue,* brief no. IB 83086, Library of Congress Congressional Research Service, 19 May 1983.

8. Under section 8 of the new bill the president would be authorized "to prohibit offenders of the national security provisions of the EAA from importing goods or technology into the United States." On the legal position of extraterritorial U.S. firms in the extended sanctions case as seen from the United States see "Break of Contract," *Wall Street Journal,* 23 July 1982.

9. The so-called Andropov proposal on INF was the clearest expression yet on this level of authority of what principles the Soviet Union tries to get accepted by the West as part of its design for Europe.

10. See Chapter 3.

11. For the most outspoken pledge of this kind see Egon Bahr, *Was wird aus den Deutschen?* (Hamburg, 1982).

12. Richard Nixon, "Hard-headed Detente," *New York Times,* 18 August 1982.

13. John Van Oudenaren, *Potential Threats to U.S.-Soviet Deterrence: The Political Dimension,* P.-6826 (Santa Monica, Calif.: The Rand Corp., Nov. 1982), 10.

14. To a degree this reflected genuine conceptual differences, however vaguely defined. It also without doubt stemmed from ill-considered delays as well as initiatives on either side. Personal mismatches worsened things rather seriously (see Brzezinski's comments on Helmut Schmidt in *Power and Principle: Memoirs of the National Security Advisor 1977–1981* [New York: Farrar, Straus & Giroux, 1983]; Helmut Schmidt's forthcoming publications are expected to make similar points). But none of these shortcomings could have been nearly so disruptive if domestic developments on either side had not led to a deterioration of the political fabric of U.S.-German relations and either side's capacity to pursue a constructive foreign policy.

15. See Chapter 6.

16. Helmut Schmidt is reported to have expressed massive complaints about this in cabinet session on March 3, 1981 (see the published notes in *Der Spiegel,* no. 23 [6 June 1983], 21).

17. For a discussion of this surprisingly low attention see Hans Rattinger, "Public Opinion on National Security in Germany," Atlantic Institute, Paris, 1983 (unpublished manuscript), 51 ff.

18. See Chapter 1.

19. See Chapter 2.

20. For two recent western European calls for grand strategy see Helmut Schmidt, "Der Westen ist nicht schwach," *Die Zeit,* no. 19 (6 May 1983): 5; and Lord Carrington, "The 1983 Alastair Buchan Memorial Lecture," *Survival,* July/August 1983, 146–153. See also Zbigniew Brzezinski, "For a Broader Western Strategy," *Wall Street Journal,* 19 Feb. 1982, 28.

21. See Chapter 3.

22. Dean Acheson, *Present at the Creation* (London, 1970), 727.

23. For a recent perspective see Philip Windsor, *Germany and the Western Alliance: Lessons from the 1980 Crises,* Adelphi Papers, no. 170, The I.I.S.S. (London, 1981).

24. As a result, as Pierre Hassner has observed many years back, "Germany is in danger of having a national policy without national goals, a recipe for instability if ever there was one" (*Change and Security in Europe,* part 1, *The Background,* Adelphi Papers, no. 45, The I.I.S.S. [London, 1968], 13).

25. While the volume of West Germany's trade never was a serious target of American criticism, if only because the volume of American trade increased concurrently, American demands, especially with regard to strategically important trade, were not met constructively even though this concerned a negligible share of Eastern trade and could have reduced it even further through sharper criteria.

26. Helmut Schmidt, *The Balance of Power* (London, 1969), 33.

27. See Chapter 6.

28. In an American foreign policy elite survey Catherine McArdle Kelleher states that "almost everyone interviewed . . . mentioned any major change in the German question" as a reason to make the European situation "hotter ("America Looks at Europe: Change and Continuity in the 1980's," in *The Troubled Alliance,* ed. Laurence Freedman [London, 1984]).

29. See John Van Oudenaren's chapter, "The Soviet Conception of Europe," in *Soviet Power and Western Negotiating Policies,* ed. Uwe

Nerlich, vol. 1, *The Soviet Asset: Military Power in the Competition over Europe* (Cambridge, Mass.: Ballinger, 1983), 161–194.

30. Kelleher, "America Looks at Europe."

31. The term is Paul Seabury's. See his *The Rise and Decline of the Cold War* (New York/London, 1967), chap. 7.

32. See Chapter 9.

Chapter 11

Formulating Western Political Strategy Toward the USSR: The American-German Debate

James A. Thomson

The Western alliance ended 1983 on a note of self-congratulation. And no two countries had more reason to congratulate themselves than the United States and the Federal Republic. Compared with 1982, the year 1983 saw these two countries united in purpose and action. The deep strife of 1982 over economic policy toward the East, demonstrated most visibly by the pipeline debacle, was set aside as the two countries faced 1983—the year of the intermediate-range nuclear forces (INF) debate. In the face of domestic turmoil (especially in the Federal Republic) and increased Soviet political maneuvering and pressure tactics, the Western alliance nonetheless did what it had said for four years it would do—proceeded with the deployment of INF. This was a notable political achievement for which governments could be justifiably proud.

Yet, as Uwe Nerlich pointed out in Chapter 10, it was precisely because of the overwhelming political priority of the INF issue that the earlier disputes were set aside—but not resolved. The future policy agenda for the United States and the Federal Republic will likely continue to feature differences over various aspects of East-West policy. The year of INF will probably prove to have been only a temporary respite, not a fundamental turning point, in the structure of the American-German policy agenda.

　James A. Thomson

Nothing could underline this point more sharply than a highly publicized spat between Helmut Schmidt and James Schlesinger less than three weeks after the first INF missiles became operational. At a major conference on the future of the Western alliance, these two former officials, both regarded as planted in the political center of the security policy debate in their respective countries, provided two catalogs of complaints—Germany's about America and America's about Germany. These catalogs covered a far broader spectrum of issues than the subject matter of this volume and of this chapter—political strategy toward the East—but that subject is at the heart of the problem.

The repeated calls of former Western officials[1] for an alliance consensus on grand strategy toward the USSR emphasize this. The cause has now been taken up by such current officials as Belgian foreign minister Leo Tindemans, who successfully convinced his allied colleagues to authorize a new NATO study of East-West relations.

Although there is no shortage of pleas for a new (or renewed) consensus on a concept for dealing with the East, there is a shortage of specific proposals about the building blocks of a grand strategy—the strategic objectives to be pursued, the instruments to be used to pursue them, and, more important to the process of strategy making, a priority ranking of those objectives and instruments. To the extent that objectives are discussed, they are usually characterized in such broad terms (e.g., peace and freedom) as to be operationally meaningless. Real policy choice inevitably involves some sort of trade-off among objectives and instruments; yet when they are discussed, they are usually treated as though they were equally important in all circumstances. In the conceptual terms of grand strategy, the recent policy disputes between the United States and the Federal Republic reflect not so much a disagreement about what the objectives should be as one about the priority ranking of those objectives and of the instruments to be used in pursuing them—in short, about how strategy should be formulated and pursued.

Actual debates inside governments about proximate policy decisions, at least in the U.S. government, are rarely conducted in such terms, even though their outcomes reflect a strategy choice. Thus to be useful to day-to-day policy choices a debate over grand strategy must be carried to such a level of specificity that the implications for policy choices are clear to all participants. Otherwise, a consensus on grand strategy will not be a consensus at all.

This chapter seeks to analyze the current American-German policy agenda in the conceptual terms of grand strategy toward the East. Its purpose is to elucidate the differences in concepts between and within the two countries and then to examine the degree to which these conceptual differences matter on concrete policy issues.[2] To accomplish this the analysis draws heavily on recent American-European (or American-German) discussions and disputes on policy issues. For a debate on grand strategy is continually underway, even if it is not called that.

Objectives and Instruments

Strategy making is often obscured by terminology. But if a new consensus on grand strategy is to help avoid confusion and policy dispute, terms will have to be clear. This section sets up an analysis of the debate about grand strategy. The term "grand strategy," or "political strategy," if the adjective grand sounds too grand, is used to distinguish it from military strategy, which is but one component of grand strategy. Grand strategy combines and orchestrates the employment of all the instruments available to the West toward the USSR.

Broadly speaking, the West's strategic objectives against the USSR encompass two sets: the preservation of the Western political system against threats from the USSR and the induce-ment of political change in the Soviet orbit so as to reduce the Soviet threat to the West. The objectives in the first set are quite concrete, including such goals as physical security, absence of threats or pressure, low international tension and likelihood of war, and maintenance of human rights and the quality of life. The preservation goals tend to be oriented toward the status quo, except to the extent that preservation is at risk. The second set is more opaque because the nature of desired change in the Soviet system needs to be defined; this matter is discussed later in the chapter.

The instruments available to the West to pursue these objectives can be categorized as either competitive or cooperative. It is by now commonplace to describe Western political strategy in these terms. For the purpose of the analysis of this chapter, the strategic instruments can be categorized relatively straightforwardly as follows:

Competitive Instruments
  Military power
  Geostrategic position (e.g., coalition building, global presence)
  Political action (e.g., ideological competition)
Cooperative Instruments
  Political dialogue
  Arms control
  Selective accommodation (of outstanding disputes)
  Economic relations (trade)
  General accommodation

These instruments can be applied against either the preservation goals or the change goals. Exactly how they are combined depends on the choice of strategy. Thus for any strategic choice it is possible to set up a matrix of objectives and instruments, as shown in Figure 1. This sort of matrix is a useful aid for analyzing the Western strategic debate and therefore will be used throughout the chapter. As do almost all such mechanistic tools, it has obvious weaknesses; for example, division of goals into preservation and change obscures the old adage that the best defense is a good offense—or that the best way to preserve the West is to change the East; in addition, instruments such as arms control can be competitive as well as cooperative.

Western Objectives and Soviet Objectives

Both the Soviet Union and the West have dual sets of objectives: to preserve existing structures within the respective orbit and to induce favorable political change within the other system. In both cases, preservation goals usually prevail over change-inducing goals. Although there are similarities between the two

OBJECTIVES   INSTRUMENTS

	Competitive	Cooperative
Preservation		
Change		

FIGURE 1

interacting sets of objectives, there is a basic asymmetry: Soviet policies for change are defined in terms of an enduring antagonism between the two systems—the same terms used to define Soviet preservation policies. In the West, however, to the extent that policies for change respond to the moral codes of liberal societies rather than to alarmist apprehensions, they tend to stress cooperative rather than antagonistic policies as the best way to induce change.

The identification of cooperative policies with the Western change-inducing objectives (and "competitive" policies with the preservation objectives) sets up a tension in Western strategy making that the Soviets do not suffer from to anywhere near the same degree. In other words, there is a conceptual congruence between Soviet internal requirements for maintaining and expanding political control and Soviet requirements for inducing change in the West. Conversely, in the West, domestic impulses toward cooperation with the East may not always conform to the strategic objectives of change in the East, especially if cooperation helps to stabilize and shore up regimes on the other side.

A problem for the formulation of Western strategy is that cooperative policies serve the change goals of both sides, but that the Soviet approach toward cooperation is not always undertaken in the same "cooperative" spirit as in the West. To many observers this means that the West must approach cooper-

ation with a modicum of defensiveness and caution. The degree
to which this point is stressed is an important dividing line in the
debate over Western strategy toward the USSR.

Two Options for Western Political Strategy

Widely held perceptions in the United States of German policy
toward the East and in the Federal Republic of Germany of
American policy serve to demarcate the end points in the spectrum of strategy options that are at least theoretically available
to the West. Indeed, it is important to spell out these end points
precisely because they describe widely held perceptions and
therefore help to show why the perceived gap between American and German policy toward the East is wider than it really is.

The first strategy option would be solely offensively oriented.
It would be based on a view of the existing East-West relationship, especially in Europe, as one of permanent conflict and
mutual hostility. In this option, Western strategic objectives
would be dominated by the preservation goal—the means to
pursue that goal would be highly competitive—Western military
power, and an active policy to contain the USSR geostrategi-
cally. The strategy would also embrace the change goal; the
means to pursue that goal would be entirely consistent with the
means used to pursue the preservation goal. Thus the purposes
of military power and geostrategic competition would be offensive—oriented on building up pressure on the Soviet system,
potentially seizing offensive opportunities if offered. These instruments would be coupled with a heavy dose of political actions, such as an aggressive policy of ideological competition
and propaganda, designed to foment unrest and instability within
the Soviet orbit. As a consequence the goals-instruments matrix
would have no cooperative elements. (See Figure 2.) The strategy would eschew cooperation with the East in all its available
forms—economic, arms control, and political dialogue. Indeed,
this strategy option would include such strategic notions as economic denial (or economic warfare) designed to shut the Soviet
bloc off from economic contact with the West, leading hopefully
to economic collapse and thereby to political change in the East.

GOALS	INSTRUMENT	
	Competitive	Cooperative
Preservation	Military power Geostrategic position	
Change	Political action Military power Geostrategic position	

FIGURE 2

Even if such purely competitive strategies were desirable and analytically well founded, both of which are dubious propositions,[3] they would not be viable domestically in any Western country. As described in the previous section, Western domestic political impulses drive inevitably toward cooperative elements in Western strategy. Hence the issue is not whether there should be cooperative elements, but rather what the nature of those elements should be and what they are expected to accomplish.

Notwithstanding the fact that this strategy option is outside the realm of real policy choice, it is unfortunately not far away from the caricature of Reagan administration policy that is fashionable in many quarters in Europe. The Reagan administration's almost legendary antagonistic rhetoric toward the USSR has been widely interpreted in Europe as consistent with this strategy. Although the administration's actions have been far more muted than the rhetoric, especially since its first year, the image of a purely antagonistic strategy persists—a strategy conducted, moreover, recklessly.

If overblown perceptions of American strategy exist in Germany, the converse is also true. This is demonstrated by the strategy option at the other end of the spectrum.

The second strategy option would be the other side of the coin from the first. It would be consistent with a view of the Soviet Union—its objectives and instruments—far more benign than that presented in earlier chapters of this volume,[4] as well as with a view that political change is necessary and possible in the near term. Thus in this strategy option the change goal would be of overriding importance: The main purpose of the strategy would be to create a new political order in the center of Europe. This would be accomplished by a general political accommodation with the USSR, accompanied by a distancing of Europe, or perhaps only of the Federal Republic, from the West.

For this option the goals-instruments matrix would have no competitive elements, only cooperation. Of course, in more sophisticated views of this strategy it would be necessary to include some transitional competitive elements aimed at preserving the West (or at least western Europe), while simultaneously seeking to reach a general political accommodation with the USSR. Nevertheless, the emphasis is on the cooperative side of the chart. (See Figure 3.)

Like the first strategy option, this option is obviously a strawman. It has no chance of succeeding on terms that are acceptable to the West. It plays right into Soviet strategic aims. It is based on a view of the likelihood of near-term positive political change in the Soviet orbit that does not stand up to analysis.[5] And for these reasons it would not be viable domestically in any Western country.

INSTRUMENTS

Goals	Competitive	Cooperative
Preservation	(Military strength)	Arms control
Change		General accommodation Trade

FIGURE 3

Yet this is strategy that many American observers (and some in other Western countries) implicitly impute to West Germany—or at least to important elements of the West German political spectrum. In part, this is a consequence of German rhetoric, especially the use of such imprecise terms as "normalization" and "European peace order" to describe German aspirations toward the East. It also reflects the increasing tendency in Germany to speak of the "two superpowers" and of Germany being caught between them. This rhetoric serves to fuel suspicions in some quarters that Germans harbor secret ambitions to disconnect themselves from the West and accommodate with the East in order to establish a new "peace order" in central Europe, an order that includes German reunification on terms that would separate it from the West.[6]

Suspicions notwithstanding, there is little domestic support for strategies aimed at near-term fundamental political change in the center of Europe. Yet American suspicions persist and are strengthened by the use of imprecise or utopian terms to describe the aims of German Eastern policy, just as German suspicions about American strategy are increased by American anti-Soviet rhetoric.

The Reagan administration's activities with the USSR in the diplomatic arms control and trade areas demonstrate that the United States is not pursuing the first strategy option, but rather a strategy of mixed competitive and cooperative elements. Neither the Kohl nor the Schmidt government has pursued the second option, or anything remotely like it; they have also pursued a mixed strategy. Still the fact that these two strawmen have been getting some heavy pummeling lately indicates that they continue to play a role in the debate over grand strategy. As will become clear, the more subtle differences of emphasis that do exist between the United States and the Federal Republic on strategic direction contain tendencies that point toward these two options, although not approaching them by any means. That is why these perceptions persist, even if they are not consistent with the policies of either the United States or the Federal Republic.

The Mixed Strategy—The Harmel Doctrine

Once the theoretical strategies of pure competition or pure cooperation have been set aside, the realm of real strategy choice is
of strategies that mix elements of both. The most famous conception of such a mixed strategy is the so-called Harmel doctrine
of the NATO alliance[7]—the doctrine of "defense and détente,"
the "two-track" strategy, or, in the vernacular of this chapter, the
strategy of competition and cooperation. References to the Harmel doctrine have by now become ritualistic in the NATO alliance, and any perceived deviations from it are likely to be met
by a chorus of pleas to return to the alliance doctrine of Harmel.
This is precisely what happened during the early phases of the
Reagan administration.

Unfortunately, the Harmel doctrine is better suited as a de-
scriptor of the inevitable mixing of competitive and cooperative
instruments in Western strategy than it is as a grand strategy that
provides a precise guide to the choice of policy about the employment of these instruments. It is consistent with a wide variety of interpretations. This is hardly surprising in that the
Harmel document was conceived in different times and different
strategic circumstances and, in any case, represented an umbrella under which the NATO allies could agree on Ostpolitik
and various other Western initiatives toward the East.

Also unsurprisingly, Harmel is least precise in the area of
greatest contention—the nature of change goals and the means
by which the West hopes to achieve them. The Harmel doctrine
speaks of two complementary functions of the alliance. The purpose of the first function is more or less clear: A strong defense,
coupled with Western political solidarity, will protect us and also
help to shape Soviet perceptions of the external world to the
benefit of the West. Thus the first function of the alliance encompasses the competitive instruments of strategy and serves both
the preservation and, to a lesser extent, the change goals. But
the change goals do not figure heavily in the first function.

The objectives and instruments of the second function, a
"search for progress," are less clear. Although oriented toward
change ("a relaxation of tensions" is not a final goal), the Harmel

report swings from modest to far-reaching change goals—from "a more stable relationship" to fostering "a European settlement," "overcoming the division of Germany and creating a lasting peaceful order in Europe." Thus the second function encompasses the cooperative instruments of strategy and also serves both the preservation ("a relaxation of tensions") and the change ("a lasting peaceful order in Europe") goals.

If there has been an abandonment of the Harmel doctrine since the early 1970s, it has been in the area of the second function. The issue is not whether the second function should exist; it is about the feasibility of the far-reaching change goal and the priority with which that goal should be pursued.

On the one hand many in the West—not only in the United States—believe that a relaxation of East-West tensions and a more stable East-West relationship is about the most that can be expected from the second function. This is not to say that a European settlement is undesirable, but rather that it is, at best, a distant goal because it would require far-reaching changes in the Soviet system—changes that are neither likely in the near- to mid-term nor amenable to Western influence. According to this view it is fine to enunciate such far-reaching change goals as a European settlement (including German reunification), but these goals should have little relevance to today's strategy.

On the other hand others in the West are placing greater emphasis on the far-reaching change goals, holding that they do have relevance to today's policies because policies can either create or foreclose opportunities that could promote a long-term positive evolution in the Soviet system. Only through such an evolution can the West hope to achieve change in the East that will lead to "a lasting peaceful order in Europe."

Thus at the heart of the strategic debate within the confines of the Harmel doctrine are differing assessments about the likelihood of change within the Soviet system, both in the USSR and in eastern Europe, and about the ability of the West to influence those changes. These differing assessments cover a series of hypotheses about the likely course of change in the East. Many of these have been touched on in earlier chapters.

The first hypothesis is that reform within the Soviet system is likely. The most commonly cited evidence in support of this hypothesis is the economic reforms in eastern Europe, especially in Hungary. The most common retorts are that the Hungarian reforms are overrated, that Hungary is not the USSR, that current Soviet economic difficulties have not propelled far-reaching reform of the Soviet system, and that economic problems deep enough to cause a major reform in the USSR are unlikely.

The second hypothesis connects economic reform with gradual political reform within the Communist system—in a sense systematic change from above carried out by reformers inside the system. The skeptics suggest that discipline and crackdown are the more likely responses of the system to changes that seem to threaten it, and that this has been the norm in eastern Europe. They argue that systemic change, if it comes, is more likely to be tumultuous rather than evolutionary and to be forced from below, from societies. Western strategy should be prepared for that kind of change, not evolution, according to the skeptical view.

The third hypothesis connects internal systemic change with a change in Soviet external policy, because Soviet ideology shapes Soviet external policy. This is the old argument about whether we are threatened by the Communists or by the Russians. The retort to the third hypothesis, then, is that internal reform would not change the basic geostrategic outlook of the USSR, which is based at least as much on geography, culture, and power as on ideology.

The final hypothesis is that Western policy can affect the internal processes that lead to the changes just described, usually beginning with economic cooperation and economic reform. One retort to this hypothesis is that the link between cooperation and moderation of Soviet behavior was proven false during the period of détente in the early 1970s. (To which the counterreply is that the experiment of détente did not have enough time to prove or disprove the link.) Another is to point out that those real or market-oriented economic reforms that have been seen in eastern Europe have not occurred because of economic ties to market economics, but rather because of national trauma— Yugoslavia, 1948, and Hungary, 1956.

The point of describing these hypotheses and their counters is not to settle the arguments one way or another, but to describe the nature of the debate about strategy that can and is taking place within the broad confines of the Harmel doctrine. These arguments are more than academic, for they bear on the policy choices that must be made when the two functions of the alliance (to use Harmel's term) are not consistent with each other, that is, when they begin to interfere in a way such that a policy designed to be supportive of one function is destructive of the other. Harmel provides no guidance about such situations, seeing the two functions as "complementary"; yet such situations are the daily fare of Western policymakers.

The Instruments of a Mixed Strategy

Western strategy will inevitably contain competitive and cooperative instruments, and it will be aimed at both preservation and change goals. To this degree there is a consensus about Western political strategy, one that can be captured by the objectives-instruments matrix shown in Figure 4.

There are two important changes in the array of instruments on this chart compared with those associated with the two strawman strategy options. First, military power and geostrategic position are not listed next to the change goals, as they were under

INSTRUMENTS

Objectives	Competitive	Cooperative
Preservation	Military power Geostrategic position	Political dialogue Arms control Selective accommodation
Change	Political action	Trade Arms control Political dialogue Selective accommodation

FIGURE 4

the offensive options. This alteration indicates that the Western alliance views itself as a defense alliance in the military sense and therefore has denied itself the use of military power as an offensive instrument. This statement would not meet universal approval in the West, especially in the United States, for the sound strategic reason that the West's self-denial of offensive military strategies and doctrines creates an asymmetry when compared with the East's offensive orientation and thus places the West at a disadvantage. A debate on this issue is growing in the West.[8] Nevertheless, as the chart shows, there remains a solid consensus among allied governments about the militarily defensive orientation of the alliance, not to mention the fact that there is no significant offensive capability, especially in the ground forces, that would be the linchpin of an offensive strategy.

Second, the chart does not include the term "general accommodation." This term was included with the second strawman option to indicate a process of accommodation with the East designed to settle *all* outstanding East-West disputes, including, of course, the division of Europe. In the current environment, given our assessment of Soviet goals, strategies, and capabilities, such a process would inevitably include accommodation to Soviet power, accommodation on Soviet terms. This is why the second strawman is a political nonstarter and why it has not been included here. No Western government or—outside the political fringes—political actor is suggesting that such a process be opened. Those in the West who feel that it is important to emphasize the far-reaching change goals are *not* suggesting that a far-reaching process of accommodation be started. They *are* suggesting that our strategy should foster an evolutionary process of change in the East, leading to such a change in Soviet external policy that a general accommodation, on Western terms, is possible.

To reflect the lowered expectations of political accommodation, the chart now speaks of selective accommodation—the settlement of disputes on a case-by-case basis as opportunities arise. This process would not involve the central dispute between East and West over the division of Europe.

In addition to these comparisons with the earlier strawman

strategies, there are a few other general points. First, most cooperative instruments are seen as working toward both preservation and change goals. Cooperative policies are sometimes associated solely with the change goals, missing the point that carefully considered and reciprocal cooperation with the USSR can serve Western interests, regardless of change goals: It can reduce tensions, bound the competition, increase its predictability, and reduce its risks and costs.[9] Second, the only noncooperative instrument of change shown on this chart is political action, which is chiefly ideological competition and, in any case, responds as much to Western political values as to strategic calculation. This lack of Western instruments to enforce change in the East explains why a close conceptual link has grown between the cooperative instruments and the change goals.

Strategy making involves more than listing goals and matching instruments to them. It requires a careful balancing among them—the inevitable necessity to emphasize one at the expense of another, when two or more goals or instruments interfere with one another. It is in these policy choices that the consensus on strategy begins to break down. Some goals and instruments must have higher priority than others, and there are differences in view within the West about the nature of these priorities.

Two Models for a Mixed Strategy

To understand these differences and how they would affect actual policy choice, it may be useful to consider two basic models of strategic priority. These models grow out of the earlier discussion concerning differing views within the alliance on the importance of the change goals. The two models are competition first and cooperation first.

Believers in the first model—competition first—downplay the change goals, not necessarily on the grounds of desirability, but rather of feasibility, as already described. In addition, some take the view that the Soviet military buildup and global political and military activities have put the preservation goals at risk; thus these goals must be accorded a higher priority than the change goals. Hence the cooperative instruments are seen as a complement to the competitive instruments in pursuing the preservation goals. To the extent that the cooperative instruments hold open options for future change in the East, that is a benefit, but not a necessity and not something to be counted on. Because the competitive instruments—military and geopolitical—are the sine qua non of preservation, they must come first if cooperation appears to be getting in the way of competition. Thus adherents of the model would gladly advocate linkage (or accept its political inevitability). If Soviet behaviors warrant it, they would have no qualms about shutting down elements of cooperation, since they did not expect much from them anyway.

The first model does not rule out change in the East, specifically in eastern Europe, but expects that it will be forced from below (from societies)—either rapidly and tumultuously or as a result of regime accommodation to societal pressure. The model hopes for such a change and is prepared to try to increase its likelihood with both competitive and cooperative policies, while recognizing the dangers inherent in stimulating political unrest in eastern Europe.

The second model—cooperation first—sees the priorities differently. Believers of this model think it important, for a variety of reasons, to hold open options for fundamental systemic change in the East. These reasons are connected with the propositions concerning change in the East discussed in the last section, and with a belief that Western domestic constituencies will not support a strategy—represented by the first model—that seems status quo-oriented and does not take seriously public aspirations for an end to the East-West struggle.

Believers in the second model would be willing to take risks from time to time in cooperative policies, even recognizing that they might harm competitive efforts. A crucial issue, however, is the extent that they would be willing to move beyond this criterion—taking risks about cooperation's harm to competition—to become concerned about competition's effect on cooperation. If they did, then they would be worried that overly competitive processes either would cause the USSR to impose linkage, shutting down cooperative activities, or would create instabilities in the East that could set back the hoped-for process of evolutionary change.

Neither the first nor the second model would be offering the Soviets a choice between competition and cooperation, as President Carter once suggested. Of course, the Soviets always have such a choice. But the offer of a choice is not an available strategy option, merely a rhetorical flourish. The West would not really mean it because it is not prepared to conduct either a purely competitive or purely cooperative strategy. In any case it would probably be impossible to say whether and how the Soviets had chosen, even if they told us.

It is tempting to immediately label the first model the United States and the second model the Federal Republic. That would not be entirely correct for two reasons. First, the models are just that; they are designed for analysis and are not meant precisely to describe government policies, which are far more complex. Second, the models could find adherents in both countries, since both countries have an internal debate about strategy.

Still the models are not pure abstractions; they are designed to capture, to some degree, the differences between the weight of leadership opinion in the Federal Republic and the weight of leadership opinion in the United States. On the two issues that most separate the two models there are clear differences of emphasis between the United States and the Federal Republic. The United States stresses the overriding importance of the military buildup and other geostrategic efforts against the USSR on the grounds that the West has neglected these areas, has fallen behind, and desperately needs to catch up. And it is in Germany that the vernacular of political debate contains such words associated with the far-reaching change goals as normalization, European peace order, and German reunification. For these reasons the models have some validity in understanding the strategy debate between the two countries. This point is developed in the following review of the debate in terms of the individual strategy elements.

Issues in the Strategy Debate

The two models indicate in a crude way how two schools of thought might set strategic priorities—in objectives and in the instruments that are used to pursue them. These priorities can be imposed on actual policy choices concerning the employment of the instruments that collectively make up the West's political strategy toward the USSR—whether to seek 3 percent real growth in the national defense budget, whether to formulate a new proposal for arms control talks. Of course, such policy choices are guided by more than views about the appropriate political strategy toward the Soviet Union. This section seeks to describe the policy debate concerning the instruments of political strategy between the United States and the Federal Republic, using the two models to characterize the debate and separating differences that arise on the basis of different views on strategy toward the USSR from other differences.

Military Power

There is a broad consensus among allied governments, especially between the American and German governments, that Western military strength needs to be built up and that such an effort is the sine qua non to the competitive/cooperative Harmel strategy. Yet at the present time there are clearly some differences over how this should be accomplished. The defense planning agenda between the United States and the Federal Republic is always long, a result of the facts that the two nations field the largest forces in NATO and that 250,000 American troops are present on German soil. The issues cover a broad spectrum, ranging from INF and new conventional strategies, such as the AirLand battle concept, at one end to burden sharing and host nation support at the other. The very existence of such a large agenda is an indication of a close relationship between the United States and the Federal Republic on defense matters; and for that reason, differences are usually worked out satisfactorily to both sides.

Military power may be an instrument for which differences over the appropriate political strategy toward the USSR are dwarfed by other considerations. Chief among these is the appropriate role of nuclear weapons in deterrence: Historically, the United States has placed great stock in the need for greater conventional force strength, whereas Europeans, in particular the Germans, have preferred to rely more on nuclear deterrence. Although this long-standing philosophical difference appears to have narrowed recently, it remains in practical terms as a result of growing costs associated with modern conventional forces and current differences in public willingness to spend money on defense in the United States and the Federal Republic. Cost and domestic politics aside, however, there is general agreement that more should be done and about how it should be done. if cost and politics would permit.

However, when tensions between the competitive and co-operative policies arise, new problems creep into the defense planning agenda. Adherents to the cooperation-first model of strategy making might be concerned that certain elements of Western military policy seemed likely to provoke the Soviets and cause the Soviets themselves to invoke linkage, shutting down elements of cooperation, just as they did in late 1983. In this way opposition to INF deployments could be justified on the grounds that they would set back the détente process. Similar, albeit less dramatic, issues could loom in the future concerning, for example, the size and especially the shape of a conventional force modernization program that harnessed new technologies. Adherents to the competition-first model would worry far less than the cooperation-firsters whether such a program would be seen by the Soviets as offensive and hence provocative, or would create new obstacles to progress in arms control.

Geostrategic Position

That the West's security depends on the global containment of Soviet power is a commonplace, one that is not in dispute in the West. Still there are considerable problems in putting together a consensus on Western containment policy outside of NATO. The problem, to paraphrase Henry Kissinger, is that America is a global power and Germany is a regional power. Consequently, the United States is much more likely than the Federal Republic to cast extra-European issues in geostrategic and anti-Soviet terms, while the Federal Republic is likely to see these issues

more through other eyes—economic, ideological, and political—
and to judge them as of lesser significance to the Federal Republic than European issues. The result is a certain drifting apart
between the United States and the Federal Republic on global
strategic calculations. In the mid-1960s, Europe was the main
geostrategic preoccupation of the United States; the United
States and the Federal Republic thus had shared strategic tasks.
Now, although Europe remains the central strategic stake for the
United States, it is not America's sole strategic preoccupation.
The United States sees growing global threats and opportunities
in its competition with the USSR; Europe is not its only problem. The Federal Republic could not experience, and therefore
has not experienced, a similar shift in strategic preoccupations.
There is a built-in set of differences in the American-German
relationship as a consequence. Three areas of the world come to
mind:

1. In the Caribbean Basin the United States is concerned
about the growth of anti-American and pro-Soviet regimes in the
area, such as Nicaragua, and about the intrusion of military
threats, whether Soviet or Soviet proxy, into the region—an area
of important U.S. lines of communications for peacetime resources and wartime supply, especially for the defense of
NATO. There is a growing possibility of substantial diversion of
U.S. strategic attention and military capability into the area.
Although many West Germans share these concerns, on the
whole West Germany does not see the strategic problem that the
United States sees. The differences of view over the U.S. invasion of Grenada demonstrates this point. While the United
States concerned itself with the danger of Cuban military presence on the island and potential Soviet access to a long airstrip,
the West Germans were worried about violations of sovereignty
and international law. Unless the political situation in the Basin
turns around—a highly unlikely event—more numerous and
more serious differences are likely to arise.

2. In the Middle East and Persian Gulf the United States is
preoccupied with the Western alliance's dual strategic vulnerability—the West's dependence on Persian Gulf oil and the prox-

imity of the region to NATO's Southern Flank. Although U.S. policies toward the region are motivated by a desire to reduce the instabilities that might ignite a major conflict, they also have a strong component of geostrategic competition with the USSR—a motive of excluding or at least halting the further expansion of Soviet power into the region. This is especially true of policies aimed at the Persian Gulf, but it is also true of U.S. attitudes toward the Arab-Israeli peace process, and even toward Lebanon. Again, Europeans—especially Germans—see it differently. They naturally have a lesser strategic preoccupation and upgrade the importance of other issues—especially political and economic. They worry about a U.S. military overreaction upsetting political stability and harming the West's access to important trading partners.

3. East Asia is a third case in point. The United States sees a growing Soviet military buildup, especially naval, threatening Japan, Korea, and U.S. lines of communication in the area. The United States also sees China as an important strategic counterweight to Soviet power in the region. Again, it is not that Europe, and Germany, do not see these strategic interests—they do; they simply do not see them as important as the United States sees them, and they thus tend to put more stock in their economic relationships in the East. However, this relative difference in strategic perspectives does not hold the same potential for disagreement as the other two areas because East Asia is relatively quiescent. The issue of Soviet Asian-based SS-20s could prove problematic if Europe attempted to convince the United States that a limit on those forces did not need to be part of the Western position in INF arms control. However, this has not occurred and appears unlikely.

These built-in differences between the U.S. and the Federal Republic are compounded when the strategy is looked at as a whole. Here again, the matter is one of the possibility of Soviet-imposed linkage. The cooperation-first model concerns itself with an overly active U.S. policy of geostrategic competition, worrying that this could lead to a cooling down of East-West cooperation. This is related to a familiar theme—that détente in Europe should be insulated from U.S.-Soviet troubles that are external to Europe—a plea in this case aimed at the USSR, not the United States, since the concern is about Soviet-imposed linkage.

In sum, there are built-in differences between the United States and the Federal Republic concerning America's policies of geostrategic competition with the USSR, especially in the Caribbean Basin and the Middle East. (There are latent problems in East Asia, but these currently do not loom large.) These problems are sharpened substantially when the issue of interference between cooperation and competition arises. To the extent that elements of the German political spectrum lean toward the cooperation-first position in its more extreme form, they will oppose active U.S. anti-Soviet policies outside Europe on the grounds that they will prove harmful to détente in Europe.

Political Competition

This instrument refers to Western efforts to compete with the USSR on a political basis, to attempt through political (or diplomatic) means to orient Eastern governments or, more to the point, societies or elements of societies, toward the West. To the extent that it emphasizes political competition—human rights, etc.—it springs from the common moral roots that underpin Western society and that are especially emphasized in the United States and the Federal Republic. In addition, it can often be used passively; Eastern societies are exposed to Western ideas and ideals as a by-product of other activities, whether diplomatic or economic. This is especially so for eastern European countries, owing to the greater amount of East-West intercourse that occurs there compared with the USSR, and that in turn is a function of the pro-Western orientation of most of eastern Europe compared with the USSR. East Germany is the paramount example. The Federal Republic's intra-German policy has sought a variety of connections with East Germany—human, economic, political; and again, some of the most important gains can be obtained passively, as demonstrated by the effects on East Germany of its exposure to West German television. In order to increase opportunities for such interchanges the

West has sought, through the Conference on Security and Cooperation (CSCE) process, to increasingly open Eastern societies to the West, especially to Western media.

As long as the instrument is used passively or has no dramatic effect, there is a U.S.-Federal Republic consensus on this strategy element. Problems arise, however, over the use of political actions aimed at driving wedges between Eastern governments and their peoples. These differences spring in part from different views of the process of change in the East. Believers in the competition-first model tend to downplay the likelihood of slow, systemic change in the East and instead feel that, if change comes, it will probably be a consequence of political changes in society, potentially convulsive, not by Eastern governments, but in spite of them. Thus believers in the first model are prepared to stimulate this process, to the extent possible, through the use of media and other political means, especially in times of political crisis in the East (such as the Polish crisis of 1980–82). If their hand is stayed, it is because of concern that such actions could mislead Eastern political factions into believing that Western military aid would be available in the event of revolution (as occurred in Hungary in 1956), or that instability in eastern Europe could spark an East-West military confrontation.

The hand of believers in the cooperation-first model is stayed by more concerns. Because they see positive political change in the East resulting from an evolutionary, rather than revolutionary, process, they are loath to take steps that might lead to internal trouble in the East—whether these steps are political or something else (e.g., economic). Indeed, they are concerned that political instability will set back the process of evolutionary change, as the inevitable crackdown is followed by a stiffening of the attitudes of the Soviet and eastern European countries. Finally, they are also worried that an active policy of political competition will get in the way of cooperation by harming the political atmosphere for the conduct of economic relations, arms control negotiations, etc.

In sum, although the United States and the Federal Republic have a common foundation for the conduct of political competition with the Soviets, and broadly agree on the passive use of this instrument, e.g., through policies aimed at opening Eastern societies to Western ideas, differences arise when this instrument is used actively. In the future, as in the past, political actions aimed at widening the rifts between Eastern governments and their societies are likely to be a source of controversy in the West, including between the United States and the Federal Republic.

Political Dialogue

This cooperative instrument of strategy refers to the process of political contact between East and West—both formal and informal exchanges of views on issues that the two sides face. The agenda is not fixed and can range from strategic matters, such as Afghanistan, to the environment or fisheries. Of course, the process could serve other instruments, such as arms control agreements or selective accommodation, but in this context the instrument refers to the utility of the process itself. In addition, a strict categorization of political discourse as a cooperative instrument is somewhat misleading, since it can also serve as a venue for political competition. As described earlier, this may be more true for the Soviets than for the West. Nevertheless, a broad political dialogue can also be used to infuse Western ideas into Eastern societies.

When viewed as a cooperative instrument, political dialogue serves both the preservation and the change goals: Political interchanges help to avoid misunderstandings and reduce tensions that could lead to conflict—thus serving preservation goals—as well as help to hold open the option for long-term change in the East. Consequently, there are no serious differences in the West over the desirability of a broad political dialogue with the East.

Differences loom, however, when political dialogue is examined in the context of the construction of an overall strategy. The competition-first model would be far more willing to forego elements of political dialogue with the East than would the cooperation-first, for two reasons. First, the competition-first model stresses the preservation goals, not both preservation and change, and thus sees political dialogue as having more limited utility. Second, believers in the competition-first model are concerned about the effects of such dialogue on the domestic political support in the West for the conduct of competitive policies, such as the maintenance of adequate levels of defense spending.[10] They are wary that the channels of political dialogue serve as instruments of Soviet strategy to undermine the Western political base for competitive policies. Soviet efforts to manipulate Western public opinion through their behavior in the arms control process, such as the INF experience, represent the most noteworthy examples.

As a consequence the competition-first model sees fewer gains and higher risks in broad political dialogue than the cooperation-first and is far more willing to sacrifice elements of political dialogue, either by imposing linkage (reducing diplomatic contact, breaking off specific negotiations) or by accepting linkage's political inevitability, if Soviet behavior warrants it. The different American and West German attitudes following the Soviet invasion of Afghanistan are a classic example of how these differing views can be played out in policy choices. Americans tended to see the invasion in geostrategic terms, but since they had no geostrategic counters to the Soviet move, they reached for political counters in order to send the Soviets a signal of disapproval—cutting off a variety of political exchanges with the USSR. Not only did West Germans fail to see the invasion as a geostrategic threat of the same order as seen by Americans, but they also were far less willing to impose linkage—to sacrifice elements of détente in Europe to satisfy America's geostrategic concerns.

Arms Control

The comments made earlier concerning political dialogue in general also apply to the arms control process more specifically. However, in this context the arms control instrument refers to the achievement of arms control agreements between East and West.

Arms control agreements are oriented chiefly, if not exclusively, toward the preservation goals. Although they have been restated numerous times, the goals of arms control originally proposed by Thomas Schelling and Morton Halperin[11] have not been improved: (a) to reduce the costs of preparing for war, (b) to reduce the likelihood of war, (c) to reduce the destructiveness of war if it occurs, and (d) to dampen the momentum of armament accumulation. Most other proposed goals for arms control can be interpreted so as to fit under the original Schelling and Halperin goals. A notable exception is Johan Holst's suggestion that arms control should seek to reduce the political weight of military force in relations among states.[12]

These goals, even with the Holst amendment, are all related to the preservation goals. In recent years most observers have come to regard the second goal—to reduce the likelihood of war—as the most important and have sought to achieve it chiefly by reducing crisis instabilities in the East-West force balance. For example, the current U.S. position in the strategic arms reduction talks (START) is aimed at mitigating first-strike incentives by cutting each side's ability to mount successful missile attacks on the other side's ICBMs. This arms control goal, together with the Holst addition, is in many ways identical to the overall goals of the military power of the West—to reduce the political weight of the adversary's military power; thus both are preservation goals. Similarly, the first and fourth goals can be accomplished by bounding the arms competition and thereby making the future more predictable for defense planning (an attribute often ascribed to SALT II by its supporters); in this way arms control is the handmaiden of the principal instrument of preservation—military power.[13]

Hence only when arms control is viewed in terms of the contribution of the arms control *process* to the East-West political dialogue is it possible to see arms control as supportive of the change objectives as well. And it is precisely in this context of the process that differences can arise between the United States and the Federal Republic over arms control policy.

For the United States and the Federal Republic probably share a broad consensus about the goals of arms control agreements— they see them as complementary to defense efforts and they have but modest expectations of what can be accomplished, notwithstanding occasional political rhetoric on both sides of the Atlantic.[14] Differences arise over the value of the arms control process, in two senses. First, the Federal Republic tends to see more value in the process's contribution to the change goal than does the United States, as already discussed. Second, both countries increasingly rely on arms control as a means of managing public opinion, of building or maintaining public support for defense efforts. When the respective public opinions of the two countries are out of phase, sharp differences over arms control policy arise. Differences arising in this second sense probably overwhelm and thus obscure any differences that arise in the first sense.

This point was most firmly underlined during the first year of the Reagan administration, which responded to an electoral mandate that appeared highly skeptical of arms control's value by moving very slowly on opening arms control talks with the USSR. In the Federal Republic the pendulum was swinging the other way: As the 1983 INF deployment loomed closer, arms control—specifically INF arms control—seemed ever more vital to manage the domestic policies of INF, and the Schmidt government joined other allies in mounting considerable pressure on the Reagan administration to open INF talks.

These differences have been narrowed, although not eliminated, as the domestic policies of arms control have been transformed in the United States. U.S. arms control policy is now responsive to public opinion in both the United States and the Federal Republic, witness the Reagan administration's "flexible" stance in both START and INF. This is not to say that an arms control policy that responds to public opinion is necessarily welcome; if that were the sole or major criterion for setting policy, possibly severe harm could be done to other elements of the political strategy toward the USSR. Rather, the point is that German-American differences over arms control policy are more likely to be driven by differing perceptions of the need to shape arms control policy to respond to public concerns. Because the swings in public opinion in the United States and the

Federal Republic are not always in phase, differences are likely
to arise again.

Once arms control agreements are in place and performing
their modest and complementary-to-defense functions, the
United States and the Federal Republic would differ over the
issue of whether the agreements should be cancelled in certain
circumstances. Believers in the competition-first model would
not only be more inflexible in the positions they would advocate
in negotiations, but they would also be more willing to scrap
existing arms control agreements if these were perceived as hindering necessary defense efforts. The cooperation-firsters—because they saw more value to the agreements—might be more
cautious. Although this is so far a theoretical issue, an actual test
could arise over the ABM Treaty if the Reagan administration's
"Star Wars" proposal moves from concept toward military hardware. But again, the strong role played by public opinion in
shaping arms control policy could easily mask these sorts of
differences. For example, the Reagan administration continues
to adhere to the SALT I interim agreement and the unratified
SALT II treaty despite earlier criticisms of these agreements,
including the "fatal flaws" of the latter.

In summary, the United States and the Federal Republic share
a common framework about the role of arms control *agreements*
in overall strategy toward the USSR. To the extent that differences arise, they concern the role of the arms control *process.*
Although there can be different views about the role that the
process can play in overall strategy toward the USSR, which
was discussed in the previous section, the growing domestic
political role of arms control in both countries is often likely to
mask or render moot any such differences.

Selective Accommodation

As in the case of arms control, this instrument of strategy refers
to actual agreements, not to the negotiating process, which is
subsumed under political dialogue. These agreements settle
selected disputes between East and West but are not expected to
reach a general accommodation. In the past the West and the

East have made such selective accommodations as the Austrian State Treaty, the German Eastern Treaties, the Quadripartite Berlin Agreement, the Helsinki CSCE Final Act, and so forth.

It is tempting to say that the analysis of selective accommodation is identical to that of arms control above, but that would not be quite the case. In the first instance the goals of agreements on selective accommodation cannot be characterized generically, as they have been for arms control, for they depend on the specific issue in dispute. Consequently, agreements could have some orientation toward change—arguably, the intent of the German Eastern Treaties was to change the very nature of Germany's relationship to the East—as well as their clear preservation goals of reducing tensions and the chances for conflict.

In the second instance there is no nearly continuous "process" of selective accommodation as there is for arms control. The process is fitful, depending on the nature of outstanding issues. In the current East-West chill there is no process to speak of aside from sporadic attempts to negotiate a Soviet withdrawal from Afghanistan. The major exception is the continued inter-German dialogue and other West-East European talks.

Although the intrinsic value of both the process and specific agreements is not in serious dispute among Western governments, the problem of relative worth or priorities can emerge for this instrument as well. The competition-first model would not be anxious to open negotiations on specific issues because of concern that the process of negotiation could provide the Soviets avenues to pursue their own aims. For example, the United States was highly skeptical of European suggestions for negotiations with the Soviets over withdrawal from Afghanistan on the grounds, *inter alia,* that such negotiations would legitimate the Soviet presence there. The Helsinki agreement came under strong criticism in the United States. And it is no secret that the U.S. government was somewhat skeptical about Chancellor Brandt's openings to the East.[15]

Similarly, the competition-first model would be more willing than the cooperation-first to scrap existing agreements, whether for purposes of linkage or because the agreements seemed to stand in the way of competitive policies. For example, during the

Polish crisis of 1980–82 some in the United States advocated the renunciation of the Helsinki Final Act, a move that would have found little support in the Federal Republic.

In general, Germans see far greater value in the process of selective accommodation up to now than do Americans, insofar as that process has affected the European situation. They see the agreements reached under the rubric of Ostpolitik as positive steps that have changed for the better the nature of the East-West confrontation in the heart of Europe. Consequently, German officials repeatedly told American officials during the Afghanistan and Polish crises that Germany did not want to risk losing the fruits of détente in Europe that had already been achieved.

Trade

The role of the West's economic relations with the East provokes perhaps the greatest controversy in the debate about strategy toward the USSR.[16] It is the sole cooperative instrument of strategy oriented toward the change goal (aside from the domestic economic benefits of trade—discussed later—no one would argue that it is strongly oriented toward the preservation goals). And indeed the favored scenario for systemic change in the East is predicated on a hoped-for shift in domestic economic policy in the East that subsequently would have presumed political consequences. Thus a Western political strategy toward the East that had a strong emphasis on the change goals would call for a forthcoming Western attitude toward economic relations with the East.

The competition-first school of thought, because it does not value the change goals highly, sees trade in a different light. It is concerned that the West's trade with the East assists the Soviets with their military buildup and thus harms the pursuit of the preservation goals. This assistance takes a number of forms: Direct assistance can include Soviet acquisition of goods that can be immediately converted to military use, of goods or know-how that can assist in the production of military hardware, or of normally civilian goods or production know-how that can be converted to military use. Assistance can take more indirect forms. For example, trade subsidized by the West through credits or other means provides a flow of resources from West to East that can reduce the Soviets' domestic economic burdens and allow more resources to flow into the military sector Trade with eastern Europe could have a similar effect of relieving Soviet burdens. Taken to their limit, such arguments about indirect assistance would imply that the West should deny all trade to the East.[17]

But these arguments would not be taken to the limit by the competition-first school because of a recognition of the role of international trade in domestic economies—with economic consequences that for certain goods and services can be quite localized within Western countries. Consequently, trade with the East can play a politically important role in the West when looked at strictly from the point of view of Western economies. The realities of domestic policies have demonstrated that Western statesmen do not have a completely free hand in designing the trade component of their strategy toward the East. This tends to narrow the range of debate between the two models to the issue of what might be called "bad trade"—that trade which has the most obvious strategic value to the USSR. Both models would agree that such trade should be restricted but would still differ on the definitions.

- Competition-firsters would cast a wide "bad trade" net over technology or technological know-how. To make a concrete example, competition-firsters would not have permitted the early 1970s U.S. sale of the Kama River truck factory to the Soviets[18] on the grounds that the trucks could have military use; cooperation-firsters would have permitted the sale, counting on the long-term payoff for the change goal. Similar disagreements develop in other technology areas, information-processing capabilities being the most noteworthy example of dual use (civil-military) technology.
- Competition-firsters would be more inclined to fight the

natural tendency of businessmen (and nations) to offer credit subsidies as trade inducements. They would argue that such subsidies are tantamount to subsidizing the Soviet military machine. The cooperation-first school would be more relaxed about credit subsidies and inclined to let the marketplace set the terms, or even to promote state subsidies on domestic political grounds.

Clearly, the trade issue holds the potential for a major controversy about the conduct of political strategy toward the USSR. The 1982 pipeline fiasco surely showed us that. But the domestic political realities of localized constituencies that benefit from Eastern trade, such as American farmers, work to narrow the disputes to the appropriate definition of "bad trade." As Abraham Becker has suggested in Chapter 7, these disputes can probably be managed, especially if steps are taken to improve the intra-alliance study and consultation of trade and economic issues.

A critical question for the future is the likely extent of Western trade to the Soviet Union. To the extent that it remains relatively small or diminishes, disputes over trade policy ought to be easier to manage. Two trends point in this direction: The slowdown in Soviet economic growth may diminish the Soviet role as an importer; the declining availability of raw materials for export, especially oil, may affect the Soviets' export position as well. At the same time, however, a continued decline in European competitiveness in Western markets, as those markets become more oriented toward "hi-tech" industries and away from "smokestack" industries, may lead western Europe to search for expanded markets in the East. Such a development would reawaken the Western debate about Eastern trade and its role in Western strategy.

Conclusions

This chapter's purpose has been to analyze—from the perspective of the American-German debate over political strategy toward the USSR—the likely consequences and differences between the United States and the Federal Republic over future policy decisions.

Although governments rarely formulate their policy decisions in terms of grand strategy toward the Soviet Union, an examination of day-to-day policy decisions in the United States and Europe reveals that there is a substantial debate about grand strategy continuously underway in the West below the surface. The debate is not about the objectives and instruments of grand strategy, but about how those should be ranked in priority order.

It is important to note that despite all the problems that have arisen since the 1970s between the United States and Europe, and between the United States and the Federal Republic, there remains a basic consensus about what the alliance hopes to achieve by its strategy toward the USSR and how it hopes to achieve it. This consensus is still captured by the alliance's Harmel doctrine of defense and détente—a doctrine that involves a mixed strategy of competition with and cooperation toward the USSR. Notwithstanding occasional charges or suspicions that the United States or the Federal Republic is pursuing either a purely competitive or purely cooperative strategy toward the USSR, both nations are clearly pursuing a mixed strategy.

The Harmel doctrine fails, however, in precisely those areas that would likely prove to be the most difficult to resolve in any contemporary Western debate about grand strategy toward the USSR.

- Harmel articulates sweeping long-term goals for a European settlement, including the reunification of Germany. Yet Harmel was unable to state, except in the most vague way, how such goals would be accomplished. Again today, such goals are articulated—far more so in Germany than in the United States—yet no one is able to be any more precise about their achievement.
- Harmel sees the defense and détente functions (or competition and cooperation) as complementary. Yet the experience of the nearly two decades since the alliance agreed to the Harmel doctrine has taught us that the two functions often get in each other's way, that they interfere with each other.

It is precisely for this reason that a true consensus on grand strategy ought to contain some conception of strategic priority.

When the issue of priority is joined it becomes clear that the two failings of Harmel are closely linked—different views of priority spring from different views about the importance to contemporary strategy of the sweeping goals for change in Europe and about how they should be pursued. On this matter, differences are discernable between the approaches of the United States and the Federal Republic, with the Federal Republic tending to emphasize to a greater extent than the United States the change goals and the role of cooperative policies with the East in achieving them.

These differences can shape national positions on concrete policies: In the defense area an emphasis on the change goals and cooperative policies could lead to preferences for military strategies or programs that might appear to be less provocative toward the USSR than others. The same emphasis could result in a German desire to insulate European détente from the global geostrategic competition between the United States and the USSR and—if this appears impossible—to argue for a moderation in American anti-Soviet policies outside Europe. Conflicting views on the likely nature of political change in the East, if it were ever to come, can lead to some differences in policy choices toward eastern Europe. Those who downplay the importance of the change goal are far more likely to proceed with caution in political dialogue with the East and to be willing to impose linkage in the event of Soviet misbehavior by closing down channels of political dialogue, and even by scrapping arms control or other agreements with the Soviets. Similarly, those who downplay the change goal tend to favor strict restrictions on trade with the East, especially for dual-use (civil-military) technology and for credit subsidies.

Although tendencies toward policy differences exist throughout the spectrum of East-West policies, they are not new, and as described here, they are not deep, being more a matter of emphasis than of fundamental orientation. Thus as long as political actors on both sides of the Atlantic remain within the broad confines of the mixed strategy defined here, the differences can probably be politically managed, at least for a time. Increased sensitivity to each other's views, improved consultation mechanisms, and an understanding that it will occasionally be necessary to agree to disagree, could all contribute to maintaining the Western solidarity without which it would be impossible to conduct the policies toward the East that are vital to the preservation of the West.

If the differences will remain manageable, then it is worth asking whether it is necessary or wise to embark on a thoroughgoing review of Western grand strategy, as many Western ex-leaders seem to be suggesting. There are two possible outcomes: The review could result in a broad umbrella compromise, like Harmel but without addressing Harmel's failings (this is the most likely outcome): If this occurred, it would not be clear why the review was necessary in the first place. On the other hand the review could trigger a deep and divisive debate about the long-term aims of the United States and its European allies, especially the Federal Republic, concerning the future of Europe, including the realistic and acceptable terms of German reunification. Although many would argue that such a debate is already underway in the wake of the INF controversy, the West is not yet ready for it. For this reason the route of improved consultation is the better one.

Notes

1. Zbigniew Brzezinski, "For a Broader Western Strategy," *Wall Street Journal* 199: 28 (19 Feb. 1982); Lord Carrington, "Can We Deal with the Soviets?" *World Press Review,* Nov. 1983, 25–27; Lord Carrington, "The 1983 Alastair Buchan Memorial Lecture," *Survival,* July/ August 1983: 146–153; Henry Kissinger, "Strategy and the Atlantic Alliance," *Survival* 24 (Sept./Oct. 1982): 194–200; Helmut Schmidt, "A Policy for Reliable Partnership," *Foreign Affairs,* Spring 1981, 743–755.

2. It is reasonable to ask why it is necessary to examine concepts at all. Americans often tend to see conceptual debate as sterile (and academic in the worst sense of the word), preferring to seek agreement

on policy actions on a case-by-case basis without worrying whether the participants in the agreement have the same motivations. In this view, conceptual debate only adds another complication. But the various calls for grand strategy indicate that this pragmatic approach is unsatisfactory not only to Germans, but to Americans as well. It is symptomatic of the so-called management approach to the USSR (see Chapter 10) and leads sometimes to inexplicable swings in policy (and to German complaints about a lack of calculability to U.S. policy—see Chapter 1).

3. See Chapter 7 for a discussion of economic warfare.

4. See Chapters 4 and 6.

5. See Chapter 4.

6. The appearance in 1982 of an article entitled "Freedom for Europe, East and West," by an official in the German Press and Information office, Klaus Bloemer, highlights the existence of these American suspicions. In his article Bloemer called for a major reorientation in European policy toward both East and West—the creation of a neutral third force in the center of Europe. The article was widely read in the United States, almost certainly more widely than official German pronouncements on policy toward the East, and—to the chagrin of German officials and security analysts—began making its way into American analyses of German security policy (Klaus Bloemer, "Freedom for Europe, East and West," *Foreign Policy* 50 [Spring 1983]: 23–28).

7. "North Atlantic Treaty Organization: Facts and Figures," *NATO Information Service* (Brussels, 1981), 288–290.

8. Samuel Huntington, "Conventional Deterrence and Conventional Retaliation in Europe," *International Security* 8: 3 (Winter 1983–84), 32–56.

9. See Richard M. Nixon, "Hard-Headed Detente," *New York Times,* 19 Aug. 1982.

10. West German and American experiences differ on this point, thus leading to differences of view that transcend the issue of competition-cooperation. In the United States, periods of détente have been accompanied by declining political support for defense spending, and periods of tension have seen growing support for defenses, whereas West Germans point out that support for the Federal Republic's defense spending was strong during the heydey of détente in the early 1970s and has now declined during a period of increased East-West tensions.

11. Thomas Schelling and Morton Halperin, *Strategy and Arms Control* (New York: Twentieth Century Fund, 1961).

12. Johan Holst, "Confidence Building and Nuclear Weapons in Europe" (conference paper), Norwegian Institute of International Affairs, Oslo, 1983.

13. The third Schelling-Halperin goal—reducing the destructiveness of war if it occurs—has been all but abandoned as infeasible owing to the awesome power of nuclear weapons.

14. A looming problem not for discussion here is the growing gap between government's modest expectation of arms control and the public's appetite for arms control.

15. Henry Kissinger, *White House Years* (Boston: Little, Brown, 1979).

16. For a fuller treatment of this issue, see Chapter 7.

17. Although the resulting denial policy would be identical to the policy of the first strawman option, this argument for a denial policy is more limited. It focuses solely on the effect of trade on the Soviet military buildup, whereas the more extreme economic warfare arguments also hope for a dramatic effect on the Soviet economy and internal political structure—e.g., collapse.

18. For discussion of the Kama River truck factory, see Ted Agres, "The Dark Side of Technology Export: U.S. Builds Soviet War Machine," *Industrial Research and Development,* July 1980, 5_-54, 56; and M. Stanton Evans' article, *National Review,* 29 Nov. 1980, 462.

Index

413

Selected List of Rand Books

Becker, Abraham S. *Military Expenditure Limitation for Arms Control: Problems and Prospects, with a Documentary History of Recent Proposals.* Cambridge, Mass.: Ballinger Publishing Company, 1977.

Curry, Jane L. (trans. and ed.). *The Black Book of Polish Censorship.* New York: Random House, Inc., 1984.

Dinerstein, H. S. *War and the Soviet Union: Nuclear Weapons and the Revolution in Soviet Military and Political Thinking.* New York: Frederick A. Praeger, Inc., 1959. (Reprint Edition: Westport, Conn.: Greenwood Press, 1976.)

Goldhamer, Herbert. *The Adviser.* New York: Elsevier North-Holland, Inc., 1978.

Goldhamer, Herbert. *The Soviet Soldier: Soviet Military Management at the Troop Level.* New York: Crane, Russak & Company, Inc., 1975.

Hosmer, Stephen T., Konrad Kellen, and Brian M. Jenkins. *The Fall of South Vietnam: Statements by Vietnamese Military and Civilian Leaders.* New York: Crane, Russak & Company, Inc., 1980.

Hosmer, Stephen T., and Thomas Wolfe. *Soviet Policy and Practice Toward Third World Conflicts.* Lexington, Mass.: Lexington Books, 1983.

Hsieh, Alice Langley. *Communist China's Strategy in the Nuclear Era.* Englewood Cliffs, N.J.: Prentice-Hall, Inc., 1962. (Reprint Edition: Westport, Conn.: Greenwood Press, 1976.)

Janis, Irving L. *Air War and Emotional Stress: Psychological Studies of Bombing and Civilian Defense.* New York: McGraw-Hill Book Company, Inc., 1951. (Reprint Edition: Westport, Conn.: Greenwood Press, 1976.)

Johnson, A. Ross, Robert W. Dean, and Alexander Alexiev. *East European Military Establishments: The Warsaw Pact Northern Tier.* New York: Crane, Russak & Company, Inc., 1982.

Johnson, John J. (ed.). *The Role of the Military in Underdeveloped Countries.* Princeton, N.J.: Princeton University Press, 1962.

Kecskemeti, Paul. *Strategic Surrender: The Politics of Victory and Defeat.* Stanford, Calif.: Stanford University Press, 1958.

Leites, Nathan. *The Operational Code of the Politburo.* New York: McGraw-Hill Book Company, Inc., 1951. (Reprint Edition: Westport, Conn.: Greenwood Press, 1972.)

Leites, Nathan. *Soviet Style in Management.* New York: Crane, Russak & Company, Inc., 1985.

Leites, Nathan. *Soviet Style in War.* New York: Crane, Russak & Company, Inc., 1982.

Rush, Myron. *Political Succession in the USSR.* New York: Columbia University Press, 1965.

Solomon, Richard H. (ed.). *Asian Security in the 1980s: Problems and Policies for a Time of Transition.* Cambridge, Mass.: Oelgeschlager, Gunn & Hain, Publishers, Inc., 1980.

Stepan, Alfred C. *The Military in Politics: Changing Patterns in Brazil.* Princeton, N.J.: Princeton University Press, 1971.

Whiting, Allen S. *China Crosses the Yalu: The Decision to Enter the Korean War.* Stanford, Calif.: Stanford University Press, 1968.

Wolfe, Thomas W. *The SALT Experience.* Cambridge, Mass.: Ballinger Publishing Company, 1979.

Wolfe, Thomas W. *Soviet Power and Europe, 1945–1970.* Baltimore, Md.: The Johns Hopkins University Press, 1970.